Intellectual Change and Political Development in Early Modern Japan

Ono Azusa
COURTESY OF WASEDA UNIVERSITY LIBRARY

Intellectual Change and Political Development in Early Modern Japan

小野梓

Ono Azusa, A Case Study

Sandra T. W. Davis

Rutherford • Madison • Teaneck
Fairleigh Dickinson University Press
London and Toronto: Associated University Presses

Associated University Presses, Inc.
Cranbury, New Jersey 08512

Associated University Presses
Magdalen House
136–148 Tooley Street
London SE1 2TT, England

Associated University Presses
Toronto M5E 1A7, Canada

Library of Congress Cataloging in Publication Data

Davis, Sandra T. W.
Intellectual change and political development in early modern Japan.
Bibliography: p.
Includes index.

1. Ono, Azusa, 1852–1886. 2. Politicians—Japan—Biography.
3. Japan—Politics and government—1868–1912.
4. Japan—Intellectual life—1868–

DS884.045D38 952.03'1'0924 [B] 76–14762
ISBN 0–8386–1953–3

Printed in the United States of America

To Ed

Contents

Acknowledgments

The development of a historical work and a historian is the result of the collective efforts of many people over the course of years. For my studies in Japan and for assistance in the research and writing of this work, I am deeply indebted to Professor Itō Isao of the Faculty of Law of Sophia University, whose guidance and encouragement over the past decade have made this book possible and whose calligraphy adorns it. To Professor Hilary Conroy of the University of Pennsylvania, I owe a profound debt of gratitude for introducing me to Japanese history, for serving as my dissertation supervisor, adviser, and *sensei* over the years. My deepest and belated thanks go to the late Professor Takano Zen'ichi of Waseda University for his advice, generous loan of source materials, and assistance, and to Professor Honma Shirō of Aichi Gakuin University for his interest and help. My thanks go to Ms. Ōkura Setsuko, Ms. Sagane Setsuko, and Mr. Nakamura Yoshihide for their skillful assistance and patience in research and for years of friendship and encouragement, and to Mrs. Nakamura Yoshie for arranging our visit to Kōchi and Sukumo and the interviews with the

Ono family. I should like to express my appreciation to Waseda University Library for the picture of Ono Azusa; to Fuzanbō, publisher of *Ono Azusa zenshū* and *Ono Azusa den,* for permission to quote extensively from these works; to Nihon Hyōronsha, publisher of *Meiji bunka zenshū,* for permission to quote from my article in volume 28: "Ono Azusa, Meiji no chishikijin"; and to *Monumenta Nipponica* for permission to quote from my article in volume 25: "Ono Azusa and the Political Change of 1881." To Mr. Ikuo Kyoichi, our friend and host during several summers of research in Tokyo, I offer thanks for his generosity and patience. Words can not express my gratitude to my parents for their understanding, encouragement, and assistance over the years. Most of all, my thanks go to my husband, Ed, for sharing this experience with me and for typing the manuscript so many times.

For the errors and shortcomings in this work, I alone am responsible.

Charlotte, N.C. S.T.W.D.

Intellectual Change and Political Development in Early Modern Japan

ABBREVIATIONS USED IN THE NOTES

Chūō kōron	*CK*
Hōgaku shimpō	*HS*
Hokkaidō Gakugei Daigaku kiyō	*HGDK*
Japan Weekly Mail	*JWM*
Jōchi hōgaku ronshū	*JHR*
Kōza Nihon kindai hō hattatsu shi	*KNKHHS*
Law in Japan	*LIJ*
Meiji bunka shi	*MBS*
Meiji bunka zenshū	*MBZ*
Meiji shi	*MS*
Monumenta Nipponica	*MN*
Nihon rekishi ronkyū	*NRR*
Ono monjo	*OM*
Shichō	*SC*
Waseda Daigaku shi kiyō	*WDSK*
Zinbun gakuhō	*ZG*

1
The Mind of the Meiji Intellectual

The dominant concept propelling intellectual and political developments in the early Meiji period was the dramatic realization that Japan was unable to resist Western incursions and demands and that drastic changes were necessary if the country was to survive as an independent state.[1] Following a period of intense anti-foreign feeling, which lasted from the Treaty of Kanagawa (1854) to the Restoration (1868),[2] there developed in the first three decades of Meiji a determined and rational effort for self-improvement and national development. Progress through determined effort and in the form of orderly change became the keynote of the period. Progress, however, was considered to be not merely for the good of the individual; it was fused with the concept of progress for the welfare and safety of the nation.[3] Concomitant with this idea was the goal of developing a strong and prosperous country capable of ridding itself of the humiliation imposed by the unequal treaties and of taking its place as an equal with the Western powers. Progress in the form of modernization was the official policy of the government and the watchword of the political and intellectual leaders. Nonetheless, both within and without the bureaucracy, opinions differed on the extent to which change was needed and on the means of implementing reform.

The ideas and activities of a new generation of Western-educated intellectuals played a major role in the introduction and organization of programs designed to promote reform. Born and reared in the declining years of the Tokugawa period, educated in both the traditional Japanese system and abroad, these men acted as a bridge between the feudal and modern eras. They served as advisers and strategists to the new government as well as to its opponents and as the critics and mentors of the time. Some sought to institute change from within the administration. Inoue Kowashi is the outstanding example of the student of Western legal systems who became the leading government adviser on constitutional and political matters. Others returned from their studies abroad to criticize the government and to become the brain trusters of the developing political parties. Thus, Nakae Chōmin used his knowledge of French political theory to support Itagaki Taisuke and became one of the intellectual leaders of the Jiyūtō (Liberal Party).[4] Fukuzawa Yukichi, the intellectual pioneer of the Restoration era,[5] remained outside the bureaucratic and party structure, contributing to the modernization process through his writing and through the establishment of the Keiō Gijuku, the forerunner of Keiō University.[6] Fukuzawa served as the example for his student and disciple Baba Tatsui, who also stayed outside the government although he was active for a brief period in the party movement.[7] In contrast, Yano Fumio and Ono Azusa, who were students of British law and government, accepted official appointments; but after brief careers in the bureaucracy, they resigned and entered the popular rights movement as the chief advisers of the statesman Ōkuma Shigenobu.

As the group most aware of the world beyond Japan and of the needs of their own society in a period of crisis and rapid change, these men were the advocates and critics of modernization. Yet, at the same time, they represented a continuity of tradition, albeit a tradition that they rejected in words but unconsciously retained in their thought patterns and life styles. Ono Azusa is one of the outstanding examples of the new Meiji intellectual. A member of the rural *shōya* (village headman)-*gōshi* (rural samurai)-merchant group of Tosa, he was part of the rural elite that in the last century of Tokugawa rule became increasingly dissatisfied with its declining status and with the economic changes brought about by the development of *han* (clan) monopolies. The education that this group received in the private acadamies found throughout Tosa in the nineteenth century was an education in loyalty to the imperial house, a loyalism being propagated by the *kokugaku,* the School of National Learning. The *bakumatsu* period saw the *shōya-gōshi* loyalists as the most dynamic element in Tosa and responsible for clan participation in the imperial restoration. Yet, despite this new outlook, they tended to see issues in terms of universal principles, a characteristic inculcated by training in the official "ideology" of Shushi-gaku, the Neo-Confucian school based on the commentaries of Chu Hsi, which was used to justify the system of feudal relationships and to stress loyalty to one's lord and clan. The growing hostility between the castle town of Kōchi and the "countryside" contributed to the emergence of loyalism over loyalty.[8] This was forcefully demonstrated in 1869 when Ono and his fellow clansmen, retainers of a minor vassal of the daimyō of Tosa, refused to join Tosa *han* on the abolition of their clan.[9] The versatility of the rural elite can be seen in the ablity of those members who responded to the demands of a new era and became the leaders of the Restoration, the reformers of the Meiji era, and the outstanding figures of the movement for popular rights and parliamentary government.[10]

The repeated crises brought about by the arrival of Perry, the opening of the country, the vacillation and weakness of the shogunate in the face of foreign demands and gunboats, and the movement to overthrow the *bakufu* produced an atmosphere conducive to change. The confusion and conflict of the times permitted greater freedom of debate on government policies on all levels of society and contributed to a sense of psychological disorientation among the samurai and rural elite. Loyalty, that traditional value used by the shogunate to legitimize its power, became reoriented from lord to clan and now moved toward the emperor. The imperial institution became a transcendental symbol of temporal continuity of culture, people, and nation. It enabled personal, that is feudal, loyalty to lord and home area, to be transferred to the abstract ideal of the state[11] by means of a human symbol. Loyalism expressed in terms of devotion to the throne transcended the person of the emperor and became nationalism. Thus, the *shishi,* the patriots of the *bakumatsu* era, became the national leaders of the new centralized government, which spoke in the name of the emperor but for the state.

The Meiji mind was one of continuity and change. The Meiji intellectuals saw themselves as living in a momentous period of change. They were committed to change and to progress, a commitment that often led them to disregard the continuity of tradition expressed in their words and actions. Their initial lack of knowledge of the world led them to exaggerate the threat of a direct foreign take-over of the country. The immediacy of events led, at times, to a lack of perspective, an exaggerated sense of upheaval, an unfounded fear of violent revolution, and a frequent disregard of the past and tradition as irrelevant to the time. While denouncing their heritage of Chinese learning, they sought a new, encompassing philosophic outlook of ethics, social relationships, and political institutions based on "reason" and scientific criteria. The advocates of "civilization and enlightenment" of the 1870s and 1880s turned to positivism, natural rights, and utilitarianism[12] as a foundation for the new order they were building. Utilitarianism, in particular, offered a modern, rational justification for political and social change. Utilitarian criteria justified the overthrow of the Tokugawa regime in favor of "enlightened government" and reforms which, though not regarded as radical by their initiators, were revolutionary in long-range effect.

The mind of the Meiji intellectual fluctuated between a heritage to which he was emotionally committed by birth, upbringing, and early education and a new era and wider outlook to which he was intellectually and psychologically bound by foreign travel and training, Western influence, and hope for the future—for himself and for Japan. The Meiji intellectual was offered a series of alternatives in occupation, training, life style, and philosophic outlook. Depending on his education, intellect, ambition, and connections, he had new opportunities for social advancement beyond that imagined by his parents' generation. Nonetheless, he maintained the same commitment to duty and service; he saw himself as a *shishi,* bound to work for the nation while, if fortunate, serving his own interests. For the young intellectual trained in the West, particularly for those from the Satchō Dohi clans that led the Restoration movement, there was in the early Meiji era an opportunity to move rapidly up the bureaucratic ladder of social position and financial success. The dominant figures in the government had use for the ideas and technical skills of those trained abroad, and the young intellectuals became the brain trusters of the new Meiji leaders and were responsible for the formulation of government policy and reforms for which their elders took the credit.

Ono Azusa was a key figure in the Meiji drama and one of the outstanding examples of the new intellectual. In a career that saw him in the role of scholar, bureaucrat, politician, educator, and pioneer in the movement for a constitution and parliamentary government, he was directly responsible for many of the events leading to the political change of 1881 and for the rise of political parties in modern Japan. His writings and activities span the crucial decades of the 1870s and 1880s and offer important insights into major developments of the Meiji period and into the mind of a Meiji intellectual.

NOTES

1. Marius B. Jansen, *Sakamoto Ryōma and the Meiji Restoration* (Princeton, N.J.: Princeton University Press, 1961), pp. 3, 347.

2. Kōsaka Masaaki, ed., *Japanese Thought in the Meiji Era,* trans. David Abosch (Tokyo: Pan-Pacific Press, 1958), pp. 20–48; Fujii Jintarō, ed. *Outline of Japanese History in the Meiji Era,* trans. Hattie

K. Colton and Kenneth E. Colton (Tokyo: Ōbunsha, 1958), p. 20.

3. Marius B. Jansen, ed. *Changing Japanese Attitudes Toward Modernization* (Princeton, N.J.: Princeton University Press, 1965), pp. 65–67.

4. Joseph Pittau, *Political Thought in Early Meiji Japan 1868–1889* (Cambridge, Mass.: Harvard University Press, 1967), pp. 65–67.

5. Itō Isao, "Fukuzawa Yukichi's Idea of Natural Rights," *Jōchi hōgaku ronshū* 8, no. 1 (1964): 178.

6. Kōsaka, *Japanese Thought*, pp. 71–88.

7. Hagihara Nobutoshi, "Baba Tatsui," *Chūō Kōron* 81. nos. 944 (June 1966): 43; 946 (August 1966): 393–94; 948 (October 1966): 389–95, 410–16; 950 (December 1966): 320. For a comparison of Inoue Kowashi, Baba Tatsui, and Ono Azusa, cf. Hagihara Nobutoshi, Sandra T. W. Davis, and Peter Ch'en, "Young Intellectuals and the 'Establishment' in Meiji Japan," a panel presented at the 1971 meeting of the Association of Asian Studies.

8. Marius B. Jansen, "Tosa During the Last Century of Tokugawa Rule," in *Studies in the Institutional History of Early Modern Japan*, ed. John W. Hall and Marius B. Jansen (Princeton, N.J.: Princeton University Press, 1970), pp. 331–42.

9. Takemura Teruma, *Sukumo shi shi no gairyaku* (unpublished manuscript by Professor Takemura of Sukumo city, Kōchi prefecture, April 1967; in the author's possession), p. 3.

10. E. S. Crawcour, "Changes in Japanese Commerce in the Tokugawa Period," in *Studies in the Institutional History of Early Modern Japan,* p. 91, discusses the importance of the merchant class in the Meiji era. For a discussion of the careers of some of Ono's fellow clansmen, cf. pp. 21–22.

11. Fujita Shōzō, "The Spirit of the Meiji Revolution," *The Japan Interpreter* 6, 1 (Spring 1970): 78–88. Jansen, "Tosa During the Last Century of Tokugawa Rule," p. 346.

12. Thomas R. H. Havens, *Nishi Amane and Modern Japanese Thought* (Princeton, N.J.: Princeton University Press, 1970), pp. 3–8.

2
The Formative Years

Ono Azusa was born in Sukumo, an isolated fishing village and port on the southwest end of Shikoku, which was part of Tosa *han,* in 1852, one year before the appearance of Commodore Perry's fleet in Tokyo Bay.[1] Tosa, now Kōchi prefecture, in the mid-nineteenth century was under the rule of the *daimyō* Yamauchi Yōdō (Toyoshige),[2] who used the crisis precipitated by the arrival of the Black Ships to institute reforms in *han* administration, finance, and military organization. Western-style arms and cannon were introduced, a small army on the Western model was established, and the *han* school was replaced in 1862 by one that emphasized letters and military science. Until the conclusion of the treaties of 1854 and 1855, Yamauchi had originally been an advocate of the union of court and shogunate (*kōbu gattai*), of military preparation, and of maintaining the policy of seclusion.

The *bakufu's* request for court approval of the treaties transferred attention to Kyoto as the center of national politics and awakened the court nobility to its political potential. Discontent with social and economic conditions in Tosa was accentuated by Yamauchi's reforms. The inability of the government to resist foreign demands for trade and diplomatic relations revealed the weakness of the *bakufu* and led to anti-Tokugawa activities by the opponents of the shogunate at Kyoto. Fear of Western military power and economic penetration and political maneuvers centering on the imperial court led to increased interest in the writings of the School of National Learning and heightened loyalist feelings in the *han*. In August 1861, Takechi Zuizan (Hanpeita) organized the Tosa Loyalist Party to drive out the foreigners and restore the Japanese spirit. However, the shelling of the Satsuma and Chōshū *han* capitals in retaliation for the anti-foreign activities of their retainers resulted in a realization of Japanese military unpreparedness. With the development of the anti-*bakufu* alliance between Satsuma and Chōshū, Tosa support for the shogunate was no longer unquestioned. In 1866, as Tosa began to gravitate toward the Satchō alliance, Nakaoka Shintarō introduced Fukuzawa Yukichi's *Seiyō jijō (Conditions in the West)* into the *han* and began to urge sweeping changes, spiritual unity, and the use of foreign technical and military science to attain national independence and equality.[3]

The winds of change were not long in reaching Sukumo, an impoverished coastal village ruled by the Iga clan. To enhance its position among the five major retainers of the daimyō of Tosa and its circumstances, the Iga clan encouraged education among its retainers. In 1831, the magistrate of Tosa *han* established in Sukumo a school called Kōjunkan and appointed a commoner as the teacher. Renamed the Sukumo Bunkan in 1863 and Nisshinkan in 1867, it served about two hundred students of both upper and lower samurai families, who attended free of charge. In 1867 the curriculum included the Four Books and Five Classics of Confucianism, history, mathematics, composition, and the military arts. The headmaster at the time was Iwamura Michitoshi and the faculty included Ono Gishin and Nakamura Shigetō. Some of the students were sent to study with scholars of Dutch learning (*rangaku*) in

Uwajima, a village eighty kilometers away. In 1865 Sakai Nanrei (Mitsuji), a samurai who had studied in Osaka and Kyoto and who had taught at the *han* school, established a private school of Chinese learning (*kangaku*) called Bōbiro. Nanrei was devoted to the imperial family and had great influence on his contemporaries and his students, including Iwamura Michitoshi, Takeuchi Tsuna, Hayashi Yūzō, Ōe Taku, and Ono Azusa, all of whom participated in the military campaigns leading to the Restoration and in the political activities of the early Meiji era.[4]

In the summer of 1866, as political power began to center in Kyoto and as Satsuma and Chōshū concluded plans for war with the *bakufu,* Ono Setsukichi, the father of Ono Azusa, was sent to Kyoto to observe the situation and to promote Sukumo trade and products.[5] In December, Iwamura Takatoshi and Ōe Taku were sent to the imperial capital to study. While there, they participated in the riot of Kōya-san. Following the announcement of the restoration of imperial rule in January 1868 and the battle of Toba-Fushimi on January 27, Hayashi Yūzō and Ōe Taku requested permission from Yamauchi Yōdō to send Sukumo troops to join the Tosa detachment. This request was refused, and not until July 14 did a company leave Sukumo for the Battle of the Hokuetsu. Following the return of the fiefs to the court and the reform of *han* policies, in 1869, Sukumo *han* was declared abolished and became part of Tosa *han;* but many Sukumo samurai did not want to serve Tosa and seceded.

Iwamura Michitoshi left to become magistrate of the Hokkaido Reclamation Bureau while his brother, Takatoshi, became examiner of the Military Affairs Bureau. Takeuchi Tsuna was appointed governor of Osaka prefecture, and Ono Gishin was made superintendent of railways in charge of constructing the Osaka Seikyo railway. Ōe Taku became assistant judge of Kobe, and Hayashi Yūzō remained for a brief period as assistant teacher of the Kōchi *han* battalion before being sent to Europe in 1870 to study military tactics during the Franco-Prussian war. On his return to Japan, he became the first governor of Kōchi prefecture. Ōe and Hayashi soon moved from the bureaucracy to the developing movement for freedom and popular rights (*jiyū minken undō*); and during the Satsuma rebellion, the two planned an attack on Osaka castle and the assassination of officials while the government was preoccupied with events in the Southwest. For their efforts, they were sentenced to ten years' imprisonment. Following their release, they continued their political activities as leaders of the Jiyūtō (Liberal Party) and served in the House of Representatives after the establishment of the National Assembly. Ōe led the attack in the first Diet to reduce the budget and Hayashi was elected eight times to the Lower House and twice held cabinet posts.[6] Both remained in contact with their fellow clansman, Ono Azusa, who soon left Sukumo to begin the journey that would ultimately lead him into the movement for parliamentary government.[7]

ONO AZUSA: THE EARLY YEARS

Ono Azusa was born on February 20, 1852, into a house of wealth, status, and historic loyalty to the throne. His family traced its origins to Nitta Yoshisada (1301–1338), one of the principal supporters of the Emperor Go-Daigo during the Kemmu Restoration (1334–1336) and the commander of the imperial forces that opposed Ashikaga Takauji.[8] His descendant Ono Kyūemon Yoshitoshi (born 1618) moved to Ōshimaura, Sukumo, during the Kan'ei era (1624–1628). In 1647 he was appointed headman of Ōshimaura by Yamauchi Kō, Lord of Sukumo, a position to which his descendants succeeded. The family originally served as shipping agents but gradually, through marriages with powerful families of rich merchants and exchange brokers, expanded its activities. Due to the poverty of the area, those with sufficient money were allowed to take family names following an earthquake in 1854. In return for a gift of silver to the Lord of Sukumo, one member of the family was permitted to use a surname and sword and was appointed the headman of Sukumo. Another purchased the rank of *gōshi*. By the nineteenth century, the family consisted of wealthy merchants, shipowners, and storekeepers. Ono's grandfather, Ryōji, was a merchant of the highest rank. His father, Setsukichi, who was in the sake brewing and wholesale drug business, was appointed ***bussankata*** (production officer in the office handling the production and sale of clan monopolies), a position of lower samurai status, in 1856.

Ono Setsukichi was an educated and wealthy man whose business ability was recognized by the local magistrate, Takeuchi Tsuna.[9] In 1866, when Azusa was fourteen, Setsukichi was sent on official business to Kyoto.[10] Nishimura Shinji claims that while in Kyoto Setsukichi met the Tosa loyalist Takechi Zuizan, but this meeting is not documented in Ono's autobiography. Setsukichi is said to have been saddened by the weakness of the imperial house, which had issued an edict excluding foreigners from the country, and at the contemptuous attitude of the *bakufu* toward the court. He advocated respect for the emperor and the overthrow of the shogunate and, along with his three cousins, Iwamura Michitoshi, Ono Gishin, and Nakamura Shigetō, decided to devote himself to public affairs. His dedication was short-lived; for following his return from Kyoto, Setsukichi was stricken with a hemorrhage of the lungs.[11] Before his death on December 29, 1866, he urged his son to "try to be a really great man," to never hesitate in carrying out what he believed to be right, and to write "an immortal book" to benefit posterity. Knowledge, he declared, was useless unless put into action. On his deathbed he recalled his descent from Nitta Yoshisada and told his children that it was a great honor for a man to sacrifice himself for his country.[12] Setsukichi's words were never forgotten by his son, and scholarship and loyalty to the throne became the dominant themes in Ono's life and activities. His death provided the model for a brief melodrama on loyalty entitled *Aiai zōshi* (*Tale of Love and Affection*), which Ono wrote in November 1884. The title, based on the *Aiai monogatari* (*Tale of Love and Affection*), is a reflection of the son's feeling for his departed father. The play itself is the story of a man who sets an example for his son by his willingness to die to help restore the emperor to power.[13] Setsukichi had pointed out the path Ono was to walk, and Ono acknowledged this in his two major works—the organization of the second political party in Japan, the Rikken Kaishintō

(Constitutional Progressive Party), and in his plan for constitutional government in Japan, *Kokken hanron* (*Outline of the National Constitution*). Following the organization of the party, Ono wrote to his brother: "All that I have done is due to our late father's will. . . ." [14] In the memorial presenting his book to the throne in 1883, Ono wrote that he would "serve the emperor and work for the state not only to succeed to Nitta Yoshisada's service but also to obey my father, Setsukichi's will. . . . I have a great duty to the emperor and state." [15]

Ono Azusa was the second child born to Setsukichi and his wife, Sukeno. As a child he was weak and often ill because his health had been affected by injuries received in an earthquake in 1854. His education began at the age of five when he was taught to write, but he showed neither ability nor interest in learning. At nine he was enrolled in a private school of Chinese studies run by Sakai Nanrei, a student of the loyalist Rai Sanyō; but here he was lazy and often slept during class. When Nanrei left for Kyoto to continue his studies, Ono entered the *han* school, the Sukumo Bunkan, where he soon became ashamed of his low grades. His father, taking advantage of his repentance, lectured him severely, saying that even if there was only one child prodigy in Sukumo to whom his son was inferior, there were many prodigies in the wide world with whom he could not compete. As a result of his father's admonition, Ono began to concentrate on his studies. Under Setsukichi's tutelage he progressed to the point where he wanted to leave Sukumo; and Setsukichi agreed with his intentions. When Ono was fourteen, Sakai Nanrei returned, and Ono studied for a year at Bōbiro concentrating on the *Analects, Mencius,* and Chinese composition.[16] Encouraged by his teacher whose memory he was to honor two decades later,[17] he entered the enlarged *han* school, now renamed Nisshinkan, and so distinguished himself that his seat was moved to a position in front of the children of the *kiba* (upper samurai class). This was an unusual honor for a boy of his status and was followed by a gift of money from the Iga clan. After his father's death, Ono acceded to Setsukichi's position which, as a result of the abolition in 1869 of both *han* and feudal titles, made him a member of the *shizoku* (former samurai class). He was encouraged to continue his studies by his cousins, Nakamura Shigetō, Ono Gishin, and Iwamura Michitoshi, the last his legal guardian, who told him that he needed to study in Europe and America.[18]

In the spring of 1867, as warfare between the *bakufu* and its opponents in the Southwest seemed evident, Tosa *han* adopted English military tactics. The Iga clan followed suit, and Ono as a student at the official *han* school began to study gunnery and to participate in military exercises. The resignation of the shōgun in November 1867 and the attempt of Tokugawa forces to enter Kyoto in late January 1868 saw the beginning of a brief civil war between the supporters of the court and the shogunate. Prior to the outbreak of hostilities, arrangements were made to send the one hundred eleven men in the Sukumo *kiseitai* (militia) to join the Tosa *han* forces. Ono requested permission to go with them and was recommended by Nakamura Shigetō. Although initially rejected because of his youth, he was finally allowed to accompany the troops. This was Ono's first venture away from Sukumo, and he traveled with the *kiseitai* to Osaka and Kyoto and participated in the fighting at Toba-Fushimi in January 1868 and at Aizu, now Fukushima prefecture. After the surrender of the Tokugawa supporters in Aizu and Shōnai, now Tsuruoka in Yamagata prefecture, the Tosa troops returned in triumph and Ono went home to Sukumo.

Following the abolition of Sukumo *han*, Iwamura Michitoshi decided to leave; and knowing of Ono's desire to study in the Kansai or Kantō area, he told his ward he would take him to Tokyo. With his mother's permission, Ono joined Iwamura on the boat to Osaka, a thirty-day trip, where they stayed with Gishin and discussed the youth's future. After a visit to Kyoto, the two travelled to Tokyo, where Ono lived with his guardian and studied Chinese literature. Ono regarded Iwamura as his benefactor because of his continual concern. However, their relationship deteriorated after Iwamura, in a drunken fit, struck the boy with his fan and told him he was very inferior to his father, Setsukichi, words that Ono found "so piercing and so regrettable." Shortly thereafter Iwamura received a judicial appointment in Hokkaido, which was the beginning of his bureaucratic career.[19] Although he and Ono remained in contact,[20] Ono no longer regarded him in the same way. Ono now decided to remain in Tokyo and to attend the Shōheikō, the former *bakufu* school for Dutch studies. Ono wanted to remain in the capital in order to associate with people from other clans and "to know the current of the world." However, Tosa had established a school in the clan residence and ordered all clan members studying in Tokyo to return and attend it. The idea of an institution limited only to Toshū men did not appeal to Ono, but although he was the only youth of low rank from Tosa admitted to the Shōheikō, the Iga clan objected to his decision to attend a school not affiliated with the *han*.

In November 1869 the clan ordered him to return home. Angered "at being treated like a criminal" and knowing the clan disliked his behavior, he decided to leave the clan. His decision was strengthened when, to his fury, he learned on his arrival in Kōchi that there was no work awaiting him. He now believed that he had been restrained by the clan merely because of his status and it would be best to free himself of his rank and to become a commoner. After discussions with his mother and brother and after the Iga clan refused his petition to become a commoner, he achieved his goal by having his father's older brother, Ono Zenpei, adopt him. Despite criticisms of his short temper and hurried decision, Ono's determination was based on his observation that "it is easy for a commoner to do anything," especially to travel abroad.

At the age of eighteen Ono left Sukumo for the last time and went to join Gishin in Osaka. Gishin appreciated Ono's desire to return to his studies and his daring at becoming a commoner, and he promised to look after his future. According to Ono, Gishin did more for him than did his parents and made him "a man of independence." Ono now began to study English but was subject to distractions thought up by less ambitious friends. While living with Gishin, he was taken by one of his "bad" companions to drink at a bar in Horie, the worst red-light district of Osaka. When Gishin heard of this, he and Nakamura Shigetō admonished Ono, saying: "Even if you did not buy a prostitute, how could a youth with great ambition go to such a place?" Ono repented his action deeply and asked their forgiveness, saying he would never go to such a place again, a promise he prided himself on keeping.

Ono's main desire was to study abroad, and after he had spoken of this to Gishin, his benefactor told him to go to Shanghai, promising to handle the cost of the trip. In July 1870 Ono left for China under the name of Tōtō Kōji, a pseudonym meaning "One who will work to improve the eastern island (Japan)." Four months of travel[21] did not satisfy Ono's desire, and he wrote to Gishin: "In a dream I suddenly felt I could find no peace. . . ."[22] In November the two met in Shanghai and, after talking over many things, Ono decided to return to Japan at once and then to go to the United States or Europe to study.[23] Ono's first essay on government and his earliest extant work was written in Shanghai and reflects his reaction to the situation in China in 1870. Entitled *Kyūmin ron* (*On the Salvation of the People*), it began with the observation:

> The world has, thus, grown smaller than before. Furthermore, we now have international law on which every nation bases its association with others in an apparently consistent structure, a phenomenon which does not exist in reality. . . .
>
> That Heaven nurtures the living is universal and no different in different lands. Heaven has taught us the way to nourish one another and to live together and has provided us with the right to self government and freedom so we can maintain life and enjoy wealth and good fortune. . . . It was not until the time when men multiplied and customs altered that the vice of the strong mistreating the weak arose. . . . It is because of this that wise men rose up and developed government to punish the strong and to save the weak, making all equal. . . . They recognized the right of self-government and freedom. Each person was sufficiently provided for and lived peacefully without discontent. Thus, government was organized.
>
> What a pity that in later generations the sly and tricky men of the world gained hold of the government and used it as an instrument to achieve their desire. They killed and abused their power, ignoring public opinion. . . .
>
> Now for the sake of people who live in all countries, there is no better plan than to establish a republican government

> and nominate the most respected sages from all over the world to be the leaders. A large legislature should be established and talented people from every land should be made officials, decide on public laws, and deliberate the affairs of the world. Those in power who govern well should be so praised and those who govern poorly punished. Education for the common people should be encouraged. Thus, we may say we have served the people, enabled them to live together, and nourished self-government and freedom. . . .
>
> It is the various governments that are responsible for implementing this. I hope the governments of every land will understand the will of Heaven, cast aside egotism, and work on this program. If you think the people are already peaceful and do not try to achieve this policy, you are against the will of Heaven and ignorant of the fact there is no difference among people.[24]

Kyūmin ron was the beginning of Ono's search for a different world order to which he and his contemporaries could relate, and its mixture of Neo-Confucian and Western policial theory reflects his traditional education and his awareness of the new intellectual currents then prevalent in Japan. The idea that Heaven does not differentiate between men, the need for government by the most wise and able, and the duty of the state to encourage education are a reflection of Ono's studies of the *Analects* of Confucius and of the writings of Mencius and Chu Hsi.[25] His thoughts on the origin of the state, his description of republican government, and to a degree his ideas on education are similar to those found in Fukuzawa Yukichi's *Seiyō jijō*, first published in 1868.[26] Since this work was widely circulated, it appears that Ono either read it or at least knew of Fukuzawa's ideas. As Carmen Blacker has shown, the moral pattern assumed in the school of natural law of Grotius and Wheaton[27] and in the writings of Francis Wayland, which so influenced Fukuzawa,[28] was not incompatible with Neo-Confucian doctrine. The logical extension of such a natural law-moral world order was a form of incipient world government by a sage-ruler, and this is what Ono contemplated in *Kyūmin ron*. Ono's vision remained private; for although the essay was written in *kambun* (Chinese composition), the Chinese press was not interested in publishing it and Ono's English was, at the time, too poor to ask the foreign language press to translate and print it.[29]

Ono returned to Osaka with Gishin, and in the Spring the two moved to Tokyo. About this time, Ono married Gishin's sister, Rie.[30] Ono's family life was uneventful, for he was faithful to his wife and devoted to their five children. Neither his diary nor his poetry contains many references to Rie; his poetic outbursts are addressed to the emperor, the promised constitution and national assembly, and to nature, not to his wife. Politics and writing absorbed his energies, books were his passion, Gishin was his main source of income. Rie was not well educated and neither assisted nor influenced her husband. Her relationship with him may not have been very harmonious, for as Ono became increasingly ill with tuberculosis she did not want to care for him. During the last ten years of his life his sister stayed in Tokyo to nurse him. Rie remarried after his death, and of their five children, only two daughters survived.[31] Ono was an affectionate father; his diary contains numerous references to his children, his care of them when they were ill, and a brief statement on June 6, 1882. "My son died today." His frequent mention of visits to their graves are equally terse,[32] for Ono expressed his emotions only in poetry, which was usually political and rarely personal.[33] His lifelong friend and confident was Gishin, who now sought to prepare his brother-in-law for a successful future by sending him abroad to study.

Ono prepared for the trip by taking English lessons in Yokohama with an American missionary, Samuel R. Brown. In February 1871, at the age of nineteen and without his new bride, Ono left by ship for the United States. From San Francisco, Ono traveled by train to New York and finally settled in Brooklyn, eager to begin to learn law. He felt that, unlike government-supported students, he could not waste time and, instead of enrolling in school, hired a tutor, a Dr. Johnson, and "studied with him night and day." He soon conceived of the idea of "specializing in the principles of law," not in studying contemporary American law, which he now felt could not be adopted directly for use in Japan. He decided to concentrate on the Constitution of the United States and on administrative law. Although told his method was irregular, he did not change his mind, and, after returning to Japan, he wrote that his method profited him more than conventional programs. In 1872 he was instructed by the Ministry of Finance to go to Great Britain to investigate banking and economics as a government-financed student. Since he suffered from a stomach ailment at the time and the doctor had recommended a change of climate, he was pleased with the order and proceeded to London. There he concentrated on banking organization and finance in the day and continued on "the principles of law at night" with a tutor. Even more important was his observation of the political movements in England, which included the fall of the Gladstone cabinet in 1874 and the resulting election that brought Disraeli to power.

Ono also tried to associate with people of social standing to whom he was introduced by his friends. In March 1873 he was invited to a party by a wealthy Englishman and "the guests that evening were all society people." Because it was a rarity for a Japanese to be present on such an occasion, many of the guests came to Ono and questioned him about Japan. Toward the end of the party, one guest asked Ono whether Japan was a vassal state of China. Ono smiled and informed him that Japan was an independent state. The man then asked if the Japanese lived in houses. Ono felt that he implied that the Japanese did not have permanent residences but "lived in tents like the Arabs or Mongols." Although Ono regarded the man as impolite and narrow-minded, at the same time he realized how little foreigners knew of his homeland. He therefore replied: "The Japanese do not live in the same type of house as you, but we build railroads and telegraphs and have a civilization which makes it possible for us to make use of these facilities." The guests who overheard the exchange applauded Ono's response, and his host came to his aid, stating that Japan had made great progress in the twenty years since seclusion had ended. Later that evening the inquisitive guest called at Ono's room to apologize for his behavior and thus began a brief friendship between a British military officer and the young Japanese student.

Ono also kept in contact with other Japanese students in London through the Nihon gakusei kai (Japan Students Association),[34] which had been organized by Baba Tatsui, a student from Tosa, to break down the clan enmity and suspicion that divided the Japanese abroad. The Nihon gakusei kai was established in September 1873 and had as its object friendship and mutual aid for Japanese students in London. Baba served as chairman of the meetings and taught English to the members. The group was the predecessor of the Kyōzon dōshū (Coexistence Association), an important Meiji intellectual society.[35] Membership in the Nihon gakusei kai, however, was not sufficient to keep Ono from feeling homesick at times, although he regarded himself as "still loyal and faithful" to his orders.[36]

England was conducive not only to Ono's intellectual development but also to a bad attack of rheumatism, which forced him to leave London in early 1874 for the Continent. While there, he traveled through France, Germany, and Italy,[37] and European history, especially its numerous conflicts, now became alive to him. Europe now became part of the search for a new world order and furnished the theme for a poem that stated:[38]

> The unification of the world is not a time-wasting matter.
> Europe is the center of the world.
> Ye gods! Europe, the leader of the world. . . .
> Once Europe is at peace, the world will find peace.[39]

On his return to England the rheumatism recurred, and his physician strongly recommended that he go home. At the same time, Ono was ordered by the Ministry of Finance to leave for Japan. With money that was to have been used for a second trip to Europe, he purchased books on economics, law, and other topics. He decided to return by way of Suez in order to view the historic ruins of ancient Egypt. Seeing "the monuments of ancient kings . . . recalled ancient times"; but it was contemporary Alexandria, Cairo, and Port Said, where his ship stopped, that furnished important examples of political ineptitude leading to loss of independence for his later writings. On May 22 the *Vancouver* arrived in Yokohama;[40] Ono had returned after twenty-seven months in the West.

The journey that began at Sukumo had led to China and across the Pacific to the United States, Great Britain, Europe, and Egypt; and the years 1871 to 1874 were crucial in determining the path that Ono Azusa would follow in his efforts to carry out his father's will and in the formation of his ideas and political philosophy. For over two years Ono had lived under constitutional and parliamentary governments, studied Anglo-American law and constitutions, and observed representative government in action. He had become an admirer of the dramatic career of Gladstone and of the spirit of the parliamentary system in England, and he later found in Ōkuma Shigenobu a Japanese statesman and politician fit to equate with the British prime minister and in the movement for freedom and popular rights, a means to instill the spirit of representative government into Japan. Having seen in England the results of political reforms that greatly increased the electorate, he was henceforth a follower of British political thought and a strong advocate of the establishment of a national assembly in Japan. In this period Ono became sufficiently well versed in English to read political and legal theory. He came under the influence of the ideas of Bentham, the greatest of the English utilitarians. Volumes 2 and 4 of the *Complete Works of Jeremy Bentham,* edited by Thomas Bowring, which belonged to Ono, are now in the Waseda University Library, but the notes they contain belong to generations of Waseda students. Ono became aware of the ideas of James Mill, John Stuart Mill, and other writers in this period. Unfortunately, because Ono's still extant diary and papers do not mention the works he read while abroad, it is difficult to judge how much Western political theory he really understood at this time. Not until the summer of 1881 does material become available on his scholarly interests. Notations from his diary show that he had purchased and read Woolsey's *Politics,* Francis Lieber's *Self-Government* and *Theory of Autonomy,* and the biographies of Gladstone and Arai Hakuseki. In 1882 he read Herbert Spencer's *Representative Government* and began to study economic policy and fiscal problems in India. In 1883 and 1884 he read on economic policy, European commercial regulations, the American Civil War, and Japanese-Burmese relations.[41] As is seen from one of Ono's papers now in the National Diet Library in Tokyo, Ono was aware of other Western writers and politicians such as John Charles Sismonde, Mirabeau, Stern, Turgot, Richard Price, Alphonse de Lamartine, Palmerston, John Russell, Macauley, William L. Melbourne, Robert Peel, James Kent, J. S. Mill, James Hill, Benjamin Franklin, and John Adams.[42] His travels had widened his intellectual horizons, given him some fluency in English, and introduced him to new concepts of political, legal, and economic organization and theory.

These new ideas had to be integrated in some way with those learned in the environment and education of his youth, for the philosophic and political systems that Ono attempted to create were to be a composite of the best aspects of East and West. As a child of late feudal and early modern Japan, Ono had been reared in the traditional culture of the Tokugawa era and educated in *kangaku.* He was a student of Chinese literature and philosophy who in his spare time read the classics, for "nothing excells Mencius and Chuang-tzu in good Chinese literature," and was also an accomplished writer of Chinese poetry.[43] He was a member of the Jōdo shinshū sect of Buddhism and on close terms with Shin priests in Tokyo.[44] Immediately following his return to Japan, he was active in a Buddhist intellectual society and study group known as Byakurensha (White Lotus Society), which was established by his close friend Shimaji Mokurai, of the Tokyo Nishi Honganji in the summer of 1876. Organized to discuss ways of expanding the spirit and doctrines of Buddhism in the contemporary world, its members included young scholars like Ono, who often brought friends such as Baba Tatsui to meetings, and well-known officials such as Yamagata Aritomo. Among the Buddhist clergy he was closest to Ōuchi Seiran, the tutor to the Chief Abbot of the Shin sect, and to Shimaji, who left Nishi Honganji and in 1884 established a reformist study group of Nishi and Higashi Honganji members in Tokyo called Reichikai to apply Western theories and ideas to Japan. In early 1872 Ōuchi was invited by the French government to come to Europe as an instructor of Buddhism, and Ono recommended that he go for several reasons. Ono felt that the invitation was important, for Ōuchi could "show the reality of

Oriental literature to the Occident and this can be a beginning in blowing away Western contempt for the East, a contempt caused by ignorance. Second, Ōuchi was the first Japanese to be invited by a foreign country as an instructor. Third, it was the first chance to dispel false charges against Buddhism. Hiramatsu Rie, one of the founders of Reichikai, wrote that Ono believed that the development of Japan depended on the prosperity and advance of Buddhism and that the propagation of Buddhism eventually would increase the national well-being and happiness of the people. Ono's friend Yamada Ichirō believed that Ono's views on Buddhism were that "each sect should keep its doctrine inside and priests outside and show its real value by the dignity and virtue of its own doctrine. It should not rely on the skill of its priests." Ono's conversations with Ōuchi reveal his attitude toward life as completely temporal and materialistic, since his standard of value was based upon utilitarianism. Yet, in the late 1870s, he felt that the Shin sect had much to offer, and when the question of reform led to division among the priests of the main school of Shinshū, Ono joined other believers in presenting a letter to the Shin master Myōnyo Shōnin asking him to institute reform and not to extinguish the "brightness of the sacred light." When the issue of change led Shimaji to establish Reichikai as an instrument of reform, Ono joined, along with Hiramatsu Rie, Akamatsu Renjō, and others.[45] Yet, by 1884 Ono no longer believed that Buddhism was a vital force in society, and on April 15, he wrote an essay entitled "Religion will Perish." In February 1885 he told several Buddhist priests who called on him: "Religion will be destroyed. Christianity can not compete against physics. Islam faces self-destruction because of internal differences. Buddhism is dying because priests have no knowledge; and thus, it has lost its main support."[46] The clergy had not met the challenge of the new era, and Ono no longer saw Buddhism as a guidepost on the road to the new order he sought.

The principal marker on Japan's path to the future came from the nation's most ancient institution: loyalty to the imperial family. Loyalty to the throne was not an abstract political concept but a vital force justifying civil war, political upheaval, and change. Loyalty was advocated not merely by the *kokuga-*

kusha (scholars of National Learning) but by Ono's teacher, Sakai Nanrei, his father, and his clansmen who had fought in the civil war that led to the fall of the *bakufu*. Loyalty was a living force in Ono's life and the motivation for his political activities and writings. A poem written during his European tour begins with the sentence: "To die in glory rather than to live in disgrace, solemnly and touchingly these words run through the ages."[47] The place to seek such glory was Japan, for: "Yet now there is no need to ask the way to refuge . . . the holy and prudent emperor now administers a broad-minded policy."[48] His total devotion to the throne was expressed in a poem written on October 25, 1881, when, following his dismissal from office, he was warned by Gishin that he was being watched:

> My soul is yours, and my body.
> I would contribute my soul if you should need it.
> I would contribute my body if you should need it.
> Make use of my soul and my body if you should
> need them to accomplish your work of unifying
> Japan under your rule.[49]

The most explicit statement of his loyalty came at the height of Ono's political career when, in a speech given on June 5, 1883, he reiterated Rikken Kaishintō (Constitutional Progressive Party) policy statements as a form of personal devotion to the emperor. *Kinnō ron* begins with a brief explanation of the service of the Ono family to the throne and then continues:

> There are many ways to devote [oneself] to the emperor, but the most important way is to strive for the prosperity of the royal family and the happiness of the people. . . . There must be some explanation, however, when I say that the happiness of the people is the way to serve the emperor. What kind of imperial family do we have? In regard to the royal families of other nations, don't we know that they deprive and oppress the people? The king regards the people as an enemy, and the people regard the king as an enemy. If one wants to serve the king, one must oppose the happiness of the people in such countries. Is our imperial family like them? . . . our imperial family has never deprived nor oppressed the people. Since the beginning of our empire and for three thousand years, the real intention of the

> emperor has been to work for the happiness of the people. The people also . . . have never regarded the emperor as an enemy.
>
> The emperor and the people are one and united . . . all emperors desire this. The present emperor promulgated the Charter Oath and the Imperial Rescript on the Constitution. Such an admired and revered emperor can not be compared with foreign kings. So if we are to be devoted to the emperor, we should not only serve the emperor, but we should [also] work for the happiness of the people. It is my deepest wish to achieve the everlasting welfare of the emperor and the perpetual happiness of the people.

Following a summary of the historic forces dividing the emperor and the people, Ono concludes:

> I strive for the prosperity of the imperial family and the happiness of the people. I am not content with any temporary vanity and happiness [for such temporary solutions] insult the emperor and people. I firmly declare that those [advocating such temporary solutions and ignoring eternal prosperity and happiness] are my political enemies.[50]

By 1883 Ono had come to identify complete self-sacrifice for the welfare of the throne with service to the nation. The emperor's concern was for the people; what benefited the people and made them happy *ipso facto* was the welfare and happiness of the imperial family. Emperor and nation were united, and service and devotion to one meant service and devotion to both. Those who opposed this concept were the enemies of Ono and of the nation. Loyalty to the throne, therefore, was to Ono the equivalent of nationalism, for emperor and people were part of a unified, historic, and harmonious whole.

Loyalty to the emperor had to be interpreted in such a way as to benefit both the ruling family and the people, and the standard of measurement was found in the concept of utility as defined by Jeremy Bentham in *An Introduction to the Principles of Morals and Legislation.* Utilitarianism as measured by the greatest good of the greatest number became the next guidepost in Ono's search for a new order and the second major tenet of his philosophic and political outlook. In 1879 he introduced Bentham's theory of utility to Japan in his *Rigaku nyūmon*

(*Introduction to Utilitarianism*). Although the preface states that Ono drafted the theory in 1878, he appears to have been engaged in studies of utilitarianism as early as the winter of 1874–75. At this time he was having trouble translating the word *utility* into Japanese, for he felt that *ri* (benefit, profit) did not convey Bentham's meaning. However, Ōuchi Seiran suggested the use of *ri* in the sense of the Buddhist phrases *shinjitsu no ri* (true benevolence) or *mujō tairi* (ultimate benefit), which differed from the meaning of *ri* as used by Mencius. Ono, therefore, used the term *rigaku* to translate "utility" in the Benthamite sense and, thereafter, decided to write *Rigaku nyūmon.* Ōuchi believes that Ono was the first to use *rigaku* to mean "utilitarianism."[51] Nishi Amane had translated Mill's *Utilitarianism* into Japanese in 1877 under the title *Rigaku;* but because Nishi emphasized Mill's inductive method,[52] *ri* here meant "reason." Since Mutsu Munemitsu's translation of Bentham's *Introduction to the Principles of Morals and Legislation* was done between 1878 and 1881, while Mutsu was in prison, and published as *Rigaku shōshū* in 1883,[53] Ono, therefore, was the first writer to explain Bentham's principle of utility in Japan and to use *rigaku* to mean "utility."

In *Rigaku nyūmon,* Ono states: "It is natural human sentiment for men to love those who benefit them and hate those who harm them. The foundation of true utility is based on this sentiment." Pain and pleasure are the "milestones which lead us to the right path," and to understand them one must investigate their causes:

> What is pain on earth? Poverty, hardship, sorrow, fear, and anger are all called pain. Then what is pleasure? Joy, ease, tranquility, and agreement are all called pleasure. In other words, pleasure is everything that does not trouble us. In my opinion, very few scholars in the East have argued on the problem of pleasure and pain and have understood little about it. The Buddha expounded the eight pains, but he did not try to explain them in detail. The pleasures of plain food which Confucius advocated and the three pleasures of a man of noble character which Mencius advocated are rougher and less detailed.
>
> ... When we look at European scholars, we see there have been many unsatisfactory explanations. Among them, only

> Bentham's explanation seems to succeed in analysis; and even in his case, the explanation does not touch the heart of the matter. He said: "There are four sources of pleasure and pain, i.e., the law of nature, the customs of society, government, and religion."
>
> Later he said: "The causes of pain and pleasure are not only these." Thus I will divide the four into two categories, those dealing with human beings and those dealing with religion, and subdivide these into six divisions: the law of nature, rewards, love and pity, hatred, reputation, and government.

Ono explained Bentham's idea by the following chart:

Sources of pain and pleasure	human	law of nature, rewards, love and pity, hatred, reputation, government
	religious	Christianity

Ono looked for the causes of hedonism more so than Bentham. He said that, since there is no other source of pleasure and pain than the senses, it was necessary to seek the physical causes of pleasure and pain in the laws of the universe, that is, in the physical laws of nature, and in "action." He explained this idea in the following way:

Causes of pleasure and pain: The Law of Nature	1. Physical Science	1. gravity 2. chemical combination and interaction 3. light and heat 4. electricity 5. "harmony" [metabolic processes governing body functions] 6. vital phenomena [laws governing growth, change, and disappearance of matter]

Causes of pleasure and pain: The Law of Nature	2. Action	1. "active" or that which we do ourselves 2. chemical combination and or done to us by others a. government, reputation, punishment, reward, manners and customs, evil intentions, and indifference

The "active" principle, or what we do by ourselves, causes most of man's pleasures and pains. "If we enlighten ourselves in regard to this illusion, we can become wise." Hence, by understanding that pain is unpleasant and undesirable and pleasures are enjoyable and desirable, one can control oneself and govern a nation. The true scholar can estimate the degree of pain and pleasure, making clear virtue and vice, for the greatest good of the greatest number.[54] Bentham's principle of utility states that mankind is governed by pain and pleasure and the utility or value of any thing, system, or action is judged by the extent to which it produces benefit, advantage, pleasure, good, or happiness, or prevents mischief, pain, evil, or unhappiness. Pain and pleasure have four sources, i.e., the physical, the political, the moral, and the religious. Pain and pleasure are the result of one's physical condition, sensory perceptions, mental, moral, and psychological outlook, sex, age, rank, education, climate, lineage, government, and religious profession. Taking these factors into consideration, a government act may be said to conform to the principle of utility insofar as it augments the happiness of the community. The first, third, fifth, sixth, and seventh chapters of *An Introduction to the Principles of Morals and Legislation*[55] are the source of Ono's interpretation of utility. Ono's emphasis on the physical causes of sensuality is the product of the more scientific age in which he lived and of his own vague knowledge of modern science. His division into "active" and "passive" principles is more from the Chinese school of *yin* and *yang* than from Bentham. His statement that by understanding the "active" principle man can attain enlightenment and thereby govern himself and others shows that utilitarianism was being interpreted through his own background in Buddhism and Neo-Confucianism. This is perhaps most easily seen in the terminology used by Ono. The phonetic equivalent of Nishi Amane's *Rigaku* was therefore interpreted using *ri* from the Buddhist term *riyaku* (divine favor). *Utility* as such was translated as *shinri* (true benefit). Utility, however, was used from the viewpoint of Mahayana Buddhism to mean to work in the interest of others. The opposite of utility or *shinri* was self-indulgence or Bentham's principles of mortification and antipathy. These principles were translated as *gedō* (a heretical doctrine).[56] Thus, *Rigaku nyūmon* represents a merger of Japanese tradition and utilitarianism, a combination that characterized Ono's outlook and his writings.

Ono saw himself as a *shishi*,[57] a man of high purpose, devoted to his sovereign and nation. Confident of his own ability, he once declared: "Azusa was born for Japan and will not easily die. I am immortal. My spirit is so great that even illness shall not dare approach me." He was an ambitious man who desired to accomplish great works on the model of Arai Hakuseki, but his ambition came from confidence in his own ability. His confidence even led him to recommend to the government in September 1881 that he be appointed vice-minister of finance,[58] an offer that was not accepted. Duty and ambition led him to ignore his own ill health, although by the winter of 1881 it was becoming obvious that he, like his father, had tuberculosis. Ono viewed his physical condition with bitter humor and wrote in April 1882: "I have been sick for half a month. . . . However, Japan is a sick country, and it is advantageous to serve a sick country with a sick body." Yet he also wrote: "The spirit is the master of the body, and even the devil of illness is afraid of it."[59] True to his words, and though bedridden during much of the spring and summer of 1882, Ono in his sickroom held meetings on party organization; and that year saw the establishment of the Rikken Kaishintō and Tokyo Senmon Gakkō (Tokyo Professional School), the forerunner of Waseda University. Fear of death increased his motivation, for as his illness progressed, his writings grew in number. However, by October 1885 his condition was critical and he no longer had the strength to keep his diary. He died January 11, 1886, at the age of thirty-three.[60]

In 1874 the future was uncertain; but Ono's outlook was optimistic as he moved into the ranks of these calling for "civilization and enlightenment" (*bunmei kaika*). The road that led from Sukumo to Tokyo was now to become a search for a new philosophy of social organization, new political forms, and a new order for Japan. The foundation of this lay in the imperial institution and in the writings of Jeremy Bentham, and its structure would be modeled upon that of Great Britain. Ono had returned to Japan, and a new stage of his journey was about to begin.

NOTES

1. Nishimura Shinji, *Ono Azusa den* (Tokyo: Fuzanbō, 1935), p. 6; Nagata Shinnosuke, *Ono Azusa* (Tokyo: Fuzanbō, 1897), pp. 3, 5.

2. In Kōchi the name is pronounced as "Yamauchi." The standard Tokyo pronunciation is "Yamanouchi."

3. Marius B. Jansen, *Sakamoto Ryōma and the Meiji Restoration*, pp. 59, 60, 68, 70, 72, 75, 76, 105, 108, 243–52; Kyoto Daigaku Bungaku Kokushi Kenkyūshitsu, ed., *Nihon shi jiten* (Tokyo: Sōgensha, 1961), p. 317; Kodama Yukita and Kitajima Masamoto, eds., *Monogatari han shi*, 8 vols. (Tokyo: Jinbutsu Ōraisha, 1964–1965), 7: 242–45; Ikeda Yoshimasa, *Sakamoto Ryōma* (Tokyo: Chūō Kōronsha 1968), pp. 43–48; Kazamaki Gen'ichi, *Sakamoto Ryōma—sono hito to shōgai* (Tokyo: Kin-ensha, 1970), pp. 43–49.

The Tosa Loyalist Party arose over the issue of *kōbu-gattai* (union of the court and *bakufu*) as symbolized in the marriage of the younger sister of Emperor Kōmei, Princess Chikako (popularly known as Kazunomiya) to the Shōgun Iemochi. Takechi Zuizan established the party at a meeting held in a detached residence of the Tosa clan in Edo in August 1861 in order to uphold imperial rule and expel the foreigners from Japan. There were approximately two hundred members, including Sakamoto Ryōma and Nakaoka Shintarō.

4. Takemura Teruma, *Sukumo shi shi no gairyaku*, pp. 3–14. From interviews with Takemura Teruma, a historian and resident of Sukumo who is writing a book on Sukumo history, and Matsuzawa Takurō in Sukumo city on March 24, 25, 1967. Both men are professional historians and were interviewed by the author on the history of Sukumo and Kōchi.

5. Yamada Ichirō, *Tōyō Ono Azusa kun den,* 2 vols. (Tokyo: Dōkōkai, 1866), 1: 7–8. Publication no. 48 in the Ono monjo (Ono Documents), Constitutional Documents Collection, National Diet Library, Tokyo.

6. Takemura, *Sukumo shi,* pp. 6, 7, 14.

7. Ono Azusa, "Ryūkakusai nikki," *Ono Azusa zenshū,* 2 vols., ed. Nishimura Shinji (Tokyo: Fuzanbō, 1936), 2: 488, 505. Hayashi Yūzō secretly wrote to Ono while in prison and told Ono that now he should be the pipeline between Tokyo and Sukumo and should act to bring new ideas to their home village. The letter is dated only "October" and is in the possession of the Hayashi family in Sukumo City, Kōchi prefecture. In his diary Ono noted on March 7, 1884, that he had received a letter from Hayashi expressing appreciation for copies of Ono's works that had been sent to him and for Ono's condolences on the death of their teacher, Nakamura Shigetō. On August 21 Ono noted that he visited Hayashi at Iwamura Michitoshi's home (the two were cousins) to congratulate him on his release from prison. On August 30 Ono again visited Hayashi, and the next day Ōe Taku called on Ono.

8. Nishimura, *Ono Azusa den,* p. 16; Yamada, *Ono Azusa kun den,* 1: 9; Nagata, *Ono Azusa,* p. 5.

9. Takemura, *Sukumo shi,* p. 13; Takemura-Matsuzawa interview. According to Takeuchi Tsuna, Ono Setsukichi (posthumous name Yoshioki) was known by the personal name of "Kinsui" or "Zuiso." He was proficient in prose and poetry and a good calligrapher (Nishimura Shinji, "Takeuchi Tsuna kaikyūdan," *Waseda gakuhō,* No. 157, March 1908, 24). Nagata states that Azusa's father was a gentle and sincere man who was full of spirit, deeply concerned over the future of the nation, and determined to help save the country (Nagata, *Ono Azusa,* p. 5).

10. Yamada, *Ono Azusa kun den,* 1, 7–8.

11. Nishimura, *Ono Azusa den,* pp. 17–18, Ono Setsukichi, Ono Gishin, Iwamura Michitoshi, and Nakamura Shigetō were cousins. The family relationship was explained to the author by Ono Fukashi, the great-nephew of Ono Azusa, during interviews in Sukumo on March 24 and 25, 1967. Yamada, *Ono Azusa kun den,* 1: 8; Nagata, *Ono Azusa,* p. 5.

12. Nishimura, *Ono Azusa den,* p. 19; Yamada, *Ono Azusa kun den,* 1: 8, 9; Nagata, *Ono Azusa,* pp. 13, 14.

13. Ono Azusa, "Aiai zōshi," *Ono Azusa zenshū,* 2: 226–53; idem, "Ryūkakusai nikki," pp. 511–12.

14. Ono Azusa, "Ono Shigematsu ate shokan," *Ono Azusa zenshū,* 2: 110–11.

15. Ono Azusa, *Jicho Kokken hanron o tatematsuru no hyō,* trans. Mrs. Itō Isao and Ōkura Setsuko. An unpublished copy of the memorial to the emperor, dated January 7, 1883, and signed "Ono

Azusa," is now in the possession of Gotō Norio of Sukumo city, Kōchi prefecture, Japan. It differs slightly from the version published in Nishimura, *Ono Azusa zenshū,* 2: 143–44. Cf. Nagata, *Ono Azusa,* pp. 233–34. On the presentation, cf. Ono, "Ryūkakusai nikki," pp. 427, 430.

16. Yamada, *Ono Azusa kun den,* 1: 3–6; Nishimura, *Ono Azusa den,* pp. 6, 8, 21–23, 325; Nagata, *Ono Azusa,* p. 6.

17. Ono, "Ryūkakusai nikki," pp. 362, 378, 379, 494, 496, 497. Ono Azusa, Ono Gishin, Iwamura Michitoshi, Nakamura Shigetō, and Takeuchi Tsuna wrote the epitaph for Sakai Nanrei's tomb.

18. Yamada, *Ono Azusa kun den,* 1: 7, 9, 10; Takemura-Matsuzawa interview.

From interviews with Kitamura Kiku, the niece of Ono Azusa, in Sukumo city on March 24, 25, 1967. Mrs. Kitamura, who was eighty-five at the time of the interview, is the eldest daughter of Ono's sister, Ren, who cared for Ono during the last ten years of his life. She discussed Ono's personal life and the history of the Ono family with the author.

19. Jansen, *Sakamoto Ryōma,* pp. 334, 381; Yamada, *Ono Azusa kun den,* 1: 10–13; Nishimura, *Ono Azusa den,* pp. 26, 27, 30, 31; Nagata, *Ono Azusa,* p. 22.

20. Three unpublished letters written by Ono Azusa to Iwamura Michitoshi show that Ono requested money from his former guardian on January 13 (no year given), suggested a tutor and his fees for Iwamura's son on May 15 (no year), and thanked Iwamura for a visit while he was ill and promised to send him a copy of *Minpō no hone* since it was due for publication in a few days (December 24, [1884?]). Letters in the possession of Iwamura Hitoki, the youngest son of Iwamura Michitoshi, Ogikubo, Tokyo.

21. Yamada, *Ono Azusa kun den,* 1: 13–16; Nagata, *Ono Azusa,* pp. 23–30; Nishimura, *Ono Azusa den,* pp. 6, 30–34, 325; Takemura-Matsuzawa interview.

22. Ono Azusa, "Tōyō shibun," *Ono Azusa zenshū,* 2: 127.

23. Yamada, *Ono Azusa kun den,* p. 16; Nishimura, *Ono Azusa den,* p. 34.

24. Ono Azusa, "Kyūmin ron," *Ono Azusa zenshū,* 2: 139–40; Tokoyama Tsunesaburō, "Ono Azusa no udaigasshū seifu ron," *Asahi shimbun* 12, no. 29297 (July 21, 1967): 9. This essay portrays "Kyūmin ron" as a Meiji work on world federalism; however, this interpretation does not fit the context of Ono's ideas nor of the time in which he wrote.

25. See Wm. Theodore de Bary, ed., *Sources of Chinese Tradition* (New York: Columbia University Press, 1960), pp. 35, 107, 108, 539–40; Arthur Waley, trans. and ed., *The Analects of Confucius* (London: George Allen & Unwin, Ltd., 1956), pp. 163–66; 13: 1, 2, 9, pp. 171–72.

26. Itō Isao, "Fukuzawa Yukichi's Idea of Natural Rights," *JHR* 8, no. 1 (1964): 178; Keiō Gijuku, ed. *Fukuzawa Yukichi zenshū,* 21 vols. (Tokyo: Iwanami Shoten, 1958), 1: 289, 290, 291, 416.

27. Carmen Blacker, *The Japanese Enlightenment. A Study of the Writings of Fukuzawa Yukichi* (Cambridge: Cambridge University Press, 1964), pp. 126–27.

28. Itō, "Fukuzawa Yukichi," p. 157.

29. Nagata Shinnosuke, *Ono Azusa* (Tokyo: Fuzanbō, 1897), p. 33.

30. Yamada, *Ono Azusa kun den,* 1: 16; Nishimura, *Ono Azusa den,* p. 107. The date of Ono's marriage is uncertain. While in China, Ono addressed Gishin as his "elder brother" in a letter, but this may have been out of politeness or affection. Cf. Ono, "Tōyō shibun," p. 127.

31. Kitamura interview; Nishimura, *Ono Azusa den,* pp. 321, 330, 331. Ono's two surviving daughters were Sumiko and Yasuko, who became a medical doctor. Sumiko married Matsumura Senzo and her son was adopted by Yasuko, who remained single, to continue the Ono family line.

32. Ono, "Ryūkakusai nikki," pp. 351, 362, 363, 368, 375–78, 395, 396, 462, 474, 484, 489, 492, 505, 529–31.

33. See Ono Azusa, "Tōyō shibun," *Ono Azusa zenshū,* 2: 127–38.

34. Nishimura, *Ono Azusa den,* pp. 34–36, 45, 50; Nagata, *Ono Azusa,* pp. 37–38, 40–49; Yamada, *Ono Azusa kun den,* pp. 16–20; Katakozawa Chiyomatsu, "Shimada Saburō," *Sandai genron jinshu,* ed. Jijitsūshinsha, 8 vols. (Tokyo: Jijitsūshinsha, 1963), 4: 255.

Samuel Rollins Brown, D.D. (1810–1890) was a missionary of the Reformed Dutch Church in America who served in China as a teacher for the Morrison Education Society from 1838 to 1846 and in Japan from 1859 to 1879 as teacher and pastor of the First Reformed Protestant Church in Japan. See Otis Cary, *A History of Christianity in Japan: Protestant Missions* (New York: Fleming H. Revell Company, 1909), pp. 46–55.

35. Meiji Bunka Kenkyū Kai, ed. *Jiyū minken hen* in *Meiji bunka zenshū,* 16 vols. rev. ed. (Tokyo: Nihon Hyōronshinsha, 1955–59), 14: 340.

36. Ono Azusa, "London Nihon gakusei kaiin bō no kikoku o okuru," *Ono Azusa zenshū,* 2: 129.

37. Yamada, *Ono Azusa kun den,* 1: 20.

38. Nishimura, *Ono Azusa,* p. 38.

39. Ono Azusa, "Chōya gin," *Ono Azusa zenshū,* 2: 129.

40. Yamada, *Ono Azusa kun den,* pp. 20, 21; Watanabe Ikujirō, *Monjo yori mitaru Ōkuma Shigenobu kō* (Tokyo: Nisshin Insatsu Kabushiki Kaisha, 1932), p. 445; Nishimura, *Ono Azusa den,* pp. 38–39.

41. Ono, "Ryūkakusai nikki," pp. 359, 361–63, 367–71, 373, 377, 378, 380, 384, 475, 476, 479, 487–89, 495, 498, 505, 512–14, 520; Nishimura, *Ono Azusa den,* p. 308.

42. Ono Azusa, *Ono monjo,* no. 20. An unpublished, undated document containing the names, occupations, and major ideas of several American, British, and European political writers; the document appears to be a series of notations from a basic text in political science and is in Ono's handwriting.

43. Ono, "Ryūkakusai nikki," p. 372; idem, "Tōyō shibun," pp. 127–38.

44. Enomoto Morie, "Meiji shonen no kōrishugi–Ono Azusa 'Rigaku nyūmon' no kōsatsu," *Shichō* 8, no. 1 (1962): 5; Nishimura, *Ono Azusa den,* pp. 95–97.

45. Nishimura, *Ono Azusa den,* pp. 94–101; Ono, "Ryūkakusai nikki," pp. 317–28, 338, 492, 504; Yamada, *Ono Azusa kun den,* 2: 1–2.

The name *Byakurensha* was used to symbolize purity of spirit and had no relation to the Chinese White Lotus Society. Ōuchi Seiron edited the *Meihyō shinshi,* a magazine published by the society. Nishimura has incorrectly called the Society *Byakurenkai*; however, the correct title is *Byakurensha.* The members of Reichikai included Ozu Tetsunen, Akamatsu Renjō, Hiramatsu Riei, Yoshitani Kakuji, Atsumi Kaien, and Ono Azusa. From information supplied by Tsunemitsu Konen, chief editor of the *Bukkyo taimusu,* Tokyo, during an interview on March 28, 1968, in Tokyo.

Ōuchi Seiran (1845–1918) was a religious social worker and scholar of Zen Buddhism who contributed to reforms in Buddhist circles. He organized the *Akebono shimbun, Kōkō shimbun,* and *Meikyō zasshi* to promote social reform.

46. Ono, "Ryūkakusai nikki," pp. 492, 528.

47. Ono Azusa, "Shiei kō," *Ono Azusa zenshū,* 2: 131.

48. Ono Azusa, "Tōgen no zu ni daisu," *Ono Azusa zenshū,* 2: 135.

49. Nishimura, *Ono Azusa den,* p. 138.

50. Ono Azusa, "Kinnō ron," *Ono Azusa zenshū,* 1: 257–82.

51. Ono Azusa, "Rigaku nyūmon," *Ono Azusa zenshū,* 2: 149; Nishimura, *Ono Azusa den,* pp. 119, 280, 281, 299; Enomoto, "Meiji shonen," *SC,* p. 5. Cf. Jeremy Bentham, *A Fragment on Government and an Introduction to the Principles of Morals and Legislation,* ed. Wilfred Harrison (Oxford: Basil Blackwell and Mott, Ltd., 1960), pp. 125–63.

52. Kōsaka, *Japanese Thought,* p. 105.

53. Nagata, *Ono Azusa,* p. 89; cf. Mutsu Munemitsu, *Rigaku shōshu,* 2 vols. (Tokyo: Bararōshi, 1883, 1: preface.

54. Ono, "Rigaku nyūmon," pp. 161–64.

55. Bentham, *Introduction,* pp. 125–31, 147–50, 155–99.

56. Enomoto, "Meiji shonen," *SC,* pp. 3–6.

57. Ono, "Ryūkakusai nikki," p. 372.
58. Nishimura, *Ono Azusa den,* pp. 338, 339.
59. Ono, "Ryūkakusai nikki," pp. 534, 538.
60. Ibid., pp. 360–63, 371–76, 379, 531, 533, 538, 540; Nishimura, *Ono Azusa den,* pp. 15, 135, 138, 194, 272, 316; Nagata, *Ono Azusa,* p. 6.

3
The Public Years Begin

The first few years after the Meiji Restoration were regarded by the Japanese public as a period of restoration, of return to the ancient past as symbolized by the government reorganization under the Seitaisho (Organic Act) in 1868 and the elevation of Shintō to the position of a national cult in January 1870. The opening of the country, however, had stimulated the trend toward modernization. After the return of the Iwakura mission to the West in 1873, increased awareness of foreign military power, of the disadvantages of the unequal treaties, and of the world outside Japan led the government to promulgate legislation that instituted basic changes in society. By 1873 the period could no longer be characterized as one of restoration but rather as an age of civilization and enlightenment, and its spokesmen were a new self-conscious intelligentsia, who called for progress and reforms in every aspect of life.

As early as 1868 the government had begun to legislate fundamental changes in the social structure when the monopoly rights of guilds and merchant associations were rescinded and a free market was sanctioned. The following year commoners were prohibited from wearing swords, a regulation applied to samurai in 1875, and given the right to take a surname. Five years later the use of surnames was made obligatory. Legal discrimination against the *eta* (outcast class) and *hinin* (pariahs) was removed, and the samurai lost the right of *kirisute* (to cut down an offending commoner). Restrictions on dress were ended, and society was reorganized into three classes: peers, *shizoku* (former samurai and their descendants), and commoners. National conscription was decreed in 1872, and freedom of occupation was granted to all classes. Property rights were recognized, and the sale of land permitted. The Land Tax Regulations of 1873 guaranteed the state a permanent source of revenue. Administrative reforms between 1871 and 1877 brought control of the government under the Dajōkan, a centralized Council of State, and laid the basis for a modern bureaucracy.[1] Reform of the legal and judicial systems was a prerequisite for new social relationships, for commercial life, and for treaty revision. Beginning in 1870 the government sponsored the translation of the *Code Napoléon* as preliminary to the compilation of the new civil code and employed two French lawyers, Georges Hilaire du Bousquet and Gustave Emile Boissonade, as advisers on legal reform.[2]

The issue of civilization and enlightenment was the keynote of discussions in a number of learned societies sponsored by the new intellectuals. Of these groups, the first and best known was the Meirokusha (Society of the Sixth Year of Meiji), organized in 1873 by Mori Arinori, former *chargé d'affaires* in the United States, and the writer and moralist Nishimura Shigeki. It called for the advancement of learning and the establishment of new norms of morality and published the *Meiroku zasshi* (*Meiroku Magazine*), which carried articles ranging from women's rights to politics. In 1874 the publication initiated the debate on popular assemblies, and it had, for the time, a large circulation of three thousand. Through the encouragement of Fukuzawa Yukichi, the Meirokusha introduced Western-style speech making, and its public speaking society attracted great attention. The society was active until November 1875, when the government began to restrict freedom of speech and the press. The promulgation of the Law Prohibiting Libel and Slander, which prohibited defamation of character, and the Press Law, which made articles advocating changes in the form of government and violence a crime, forced the *Meiroku zasshi* to cease publication. The Meirokusha represented a transitional phase between the era of civilization and enlightenment and the movement for popular rights, and its members served as a bridge between feudal and modern Japan.

By 1874 the political concepts introduced by the new intellectuals had begun to take root in the fertile soil offered by the division within the ruling oligarchy over the issue of domestic development as opposed to adventurism abroad. The result was the emergence of political associations such as the Kōfuku anzensha (Society for Happiness and Security) in 1973 and the Aikokukōtō (Patriotic Public Party) in 1874, calling for an elected national assembly and the formation of political rights. The Aikokukōtō petition for the establishment of an elected assembly began a debate in the press on freedom, human rights, and sovereignty, and laid a theoretical basis for the party movement.[3]

THE KYŌZON DŌSHŪ

The Japan to which Ono returned in 1874 was quite different from the country he had left in 1871. While surprised at the changes in the cities and the general atmosphere in the country as a whole and at the many aspects of Western culture that had been introduced, he was also concerned with the political disorder of the time.[4] Since the government, which had recalled him, did not offer a position at this time and, because he felt that returned students had a poor reputation due to a lack of achievement, he decided not to attract attention to himself. Instead, he concentrated on activities that at first reflected the Meiji concern with the question of civilization and enlightenment and then the developing popular rights movement. Following the example of the Meirokusha, Ono and some former members of the Nihon gakusei kai decided to establish a learned society to adapt European ideas on art and science to Japan. This would "blow away the ignorance caused by the isolation of three thousand years."

The Kyōzon dōshū was organized on September 20, 1874, as a club formed by young intellectuals who had been abroad. Initially it attracted little attention; and of the fifty persons Ono invited to the inaugural dinner, only six of his friends appeared.[5] These included Akamatsu Renjō, Ozaki Mitsuyoshi, Iwasaki Kojirō, Miyoshi Taizō, Hirose Shin'ichi, and Matsudaira Nobumasa. They were later joined by Kaneko Kentarō, Shimada Saburō, Hatoyama Kazuo, Masujima Rokuichirō, Kikuchi Dairoku, Koezuka Ryū, Taguchi Ukichi, Baba Tatsui, Shimaji Mokurai, Marikōji Michifusa, and Ōuchi Seiran. Ono, Iwasaki, Miyoshi, Kikuchi, and Baba had studied in England, Kaneko had been an official clan student in the United States, and Shimaji[6] and Akamatsu had traveled extensively in Europe.[7] Those who had been abroad subsequently played the leading roles in the society. In 1874 the average age of the members of the Kyōzon dōshū was about twenty-six. Most of the members at the time were neither in government service nor otherwise well known. They favored accelerating the tempo of political development and the establishment of a national assembly. Their youth and lack of achievement contrasted sharply with the members of the Meirokusha, whose average age was forty-three, who were well-known scholars and officials, and who believed it was too early to establish a parliament.[8] With the dissolution of the Meirokusha, Kyōzon dōshū membership increased, since it appealed to young men who wanted to introduce new ideas, improve themselves, or learn more about the West. Within four years it had fifty members, including *shizoku* and commoners, from all prefectures. Representing business, industry, agriculture, newspaper editors, bank presidents, the head of a steamship company, clergy, university graduates, bureaucrats, and scholars of *kangaku* and Western studies, they sought to fulfill the title of *coexistence* among all sectors of Japanese life.

The Kyōzon dōshū was regarded by its founders as a continuation of the Nihon gakusei kai, and its name implied a society where men of similar views could work together regardless of clan or social status.[9] Ono drafted its regulations and defined its purpose:

> The people of our country have long been used to suppression and still preserve the evil influence of feudalism. The upper and lower classes are divided or troubled by one another, and people of different prefectures are separated as if by a fence between them. . . . We now are forming a small group which we name the "Kyōzon dōshū." We shall try to promote friendship and increase our knowledge, discuss what should be discussed concerning the coexistence of human beings, and save what must be saved. Thus, we shall clarify the views of the people and encourage them in their duties, thereby adding to their future betterment.[10]

These aims were pursued through lectures and public meetings, the *Kyōzon zasshi* (*Kyōzon magazine*), and the opening of a modern public library. Meetings were held on the second and fourth Saturdays of each month, with the members breaking into four smaller groups to discuss topics on law, education, economics, and sanitation. In addition, on Wednesdays speeches were given by members on topics of current interest such as treaty revision, constitutional government, the modernization and reconstruction of Japanese society, and the enlightenment of the people. For example, on January 22, 1879, at a seminar on "coexistence among people" (literally *kyōzon*) and again on February 12 Ono spoke on the subject of utilitarianism. On the morning of January 15 he discussed his views on policy toward the Ryūkyūs. On July 9 Baba Tatsui lectured on *Rōma ritsuyō* (*Roman Law*), Taguchi Ukichi on *Reiki no shurui* (*Varieties of Awe*), and Shimaji Mokurai on *Mojisetsu* (*Theory of Letters*). In 1881, since the issue of the constitution and national assembly attracted increased attention, Ono spoke on the first part of his book *Kokken hanron*.[11] The speeches dealt with the major topics and problems of the day and were so popular that Prince Arisugawa, president of the Genrō-in (Senate) attended as an official visitor accompanied by the vice-president of the Genrō-in, Kōno Togama.[12] As a result, the membership list gradually increased until it included several hundred names.[13]

According to the *Kyōzon dōshū jōrei* (*Regulations for the Kyōzon dōshū*), drafted by Ono on December 11, 1874, the society was open to all applicants upon submission of a written request countersigned by one member and agreed upon by two-thirds of the group. Discussions were to include "all things relating to the coexistence of mankind," and meetings were open to all members and their guests, including women if agreed upon in advance. However, there is no record of a woman ever attending a meeting. All proposals and the chairman for each meeting were voted upon by ballot, and expenses were met from initiation and membership fees.[14] As this source was insufficient, Ono, who served as secretary, Miyoshi Taizō, and Iwasaki Kojirō decided to propose a fund-raising campaign.[15] Despite limited membership and financial difficulties, in 1877 the Kyōzon dōshū was able to construct a meeting hall, the Kyōzon shūkan, in the Kyōbashi ward of Tokyo. Two years later in 1879, following a proposal made by Ono on July 16, a library called the Kyōzon bunko was organized with borrowed funds and contributions, including fifty yen from Ono Gishin. Ono Azusa regarded establishment of the library as one of his most important projects and even thought of opening a branch of the Kyōzon dōshū in Osaka and a bookstore. His plans for the library first were discussed with Iwasaki, Ōuchi, and others, and he drafted the regulations for its use by members and the public. He regarded the Kyōzon bunko as a means of expanding education and contributing to the development of Japanese civilization.

The Kyōzon dōshū used as its theme the phrase *Ningen kyōzon no michi* ("The path of human coexistence") [16] and advocated social and political change. Its activities were divided into three categories: political reform, academic independence, and the broad circulation of good books. By lectures and discussions, the establishment of the Kyōzon bunko, and the publication of the *Kyōzon zasshi,* it sought to enlighten public opinion. The *Kyōzon zasshi* was published monthly from January 1875 until August 1876 (nos. 1–13) and, after a brief interlude, weekly from March 29, 1877, until May 1880 (nos. 14–77). In style, it owed much to the *Meiroku zasshi;* and between the summer of 1875 and 1876, it attained a circulation of 2,520. Ono was responsible for publication arrangements and served as chief editor of twenty-nine issues between 1879 and 1880; he contributed a total of thirty-nine articles.[17]

The activities and purpose of the Kyōzon dōshū are mirrored in Ono's articles. In the first issue of the *Kyōzon zasshi* (January 1875), Ono opposed Nishi Amane's idea of replacing *kanji* (Chinese characters) by a Western alphabet in the Japanese language. Ono advocated the use of the Japanese syllabary (*hiragana* and *katakana*) as the medium for both higher learning and mass education.[18] In 1878 he advised his colleagues who were new in the art of public speaking that "when a man opens his lips, his words are irrevocable. He must be careful when he speaks, not only of his words but also to elevate the spirit [of the audience]."[19] In the issue of February 12, 1880, possibly worried about the Law Prohibiting Libel and Slander, he warned against shaming one's opponent in debate and suggested the use of reason to show erroneous opinions.[20] Public lectures were only one means of enlightening the public, for the purpose of all Kyōzon dōshū activities was to promote the spirit of national unity. Ono attacked this problem in the third issue of the *Kyōzon zasshi* in March 1875.

Kokumin nanzo kore o omowazaru (*Why do the People Think this Way?*) begins by pointing out that feudal practices and customs still continue. The word *han* has been replaced by *prefecture,* but feudal practices remain unchanged. The people of a prefecture still take pride in the grandeur of their former *han,* and some will not respect people unless they are clansmen or from samurai families. Because of this, the establishment of the prefectures was merely a change of name; and in reality the *han* have not been abolished. This attitude prevents coexistence, that is, national unity. Love of one's native place has resulted in the loss of patriotism, which was defined as: "A feeling of joy and sorrow about the success and failure of our nation with the country as the objective." Since people love their birthplace more than the nation, anti-government activities threaten domestic peace and order and national security is neglected. Japan has concluded treaties with various European countries, and the English and French troops are to be recalled. Yet, although international law is said to be the only true means of protection, strong countries violate it and make their own law. Thus Japan is surrounded by countries that can be regarded as potential enemies. Since Japan is neither prosperous nor powerful, the great powers desire contacts that have no sanction in international law. The nation is now in a crucial period, and if public spirit and patriotism are not elevated above personal feelings and localism, civil war will erupt and the nation will return to feudalism. "The white bear [Russia] will take advantage of an unguarded moment and seek a bloated prize. If this happens. . . , the sun in the Japanese flag will set. Should not we Japanese be concerned over this situation?"[21]

Four years later in the May 14, 1879, issue of the *Kyōzon zasshi,* Ono again repeated his call for a unified state that would be strong enough to maintain its independence. *Tada Nihon ari* (*There is Only Japan*) begins with: "Japan belongs to the Japanese people, but consider the situation realistically. There are, ironically, two kinds of illusions prevalent in Japan today. One is the thinking of those who regard Japan as a European Japan. The other comes from treating Japan as the private property of a given area [i.e., of a particular clan] and not as the country of all the Japanese." Those who seek to introduce European machinery, technology, and law to benefit the country are true loyalists. A man who "walks proudly down the street, a derby on his head, a cigarette in his mouth, and [with] creaking leather shoes . . . cannot be satisfied with things Japanese. . . . He wants to change too many things to enumerate. Still we can try to be patient with him." However, there are men so intoxicated with everything European that they want to import European laws, manners, and customs without evaluating them. They forget that foreign invasion is not accomplished by arms alone and thoughtlessly abandon Japanese things. They do not intend to benefit the country but seek to create a Europeanized Japan. "Those who are too cowardly to insist on their rights against the dishonesty of foreigners" out of fear of European power impair national dignity and independence. They, too, seek to make Japan similar to European countries. Those who have lost the spirit of nationalism because of their love for certain clans have forgotten Japan as a whole. "They regard the Japanese Empire as the private property of a particular *han*. . . . Japan is not the country of all Japanese. . . . Thus, we have lost our vitality and our independence. Thus, we have lost the unity [needed] for progress, and we remain at the starting line. . . . Fellow Japanese! Japan does not belong to one clan alone. . . . Japan is Japan alone. Foreign countries are foreign countries. Do not confuse the two. They are not our country."[22]

Ono's concern over the lack of national unity is also apparent in his private papers. In an unpublished manuscript entitled *Minshin ron* (*Essay on Popular Feelings*) and dated November 1875, he wrote:

> There are two reasons for losing popular support. One is to oppress the people, and the other is government inefficiency and poor administration. Although the Meiji government does not have popular support at this time, it is not due to these reasons. It is because of its policy of continued interference [in the people's lives and livelihood]. Though its intentions are not bad and it gives incentives to the people, it annoys them. Another reason is the improper behavior of officials. This damages the new government's image and causes it to lose popular support. I think this is very regrettable for the Meiji government.[23]

In 1875 Ono entered the debate on liberty and natural rights in an article entitled *Kenri no zoku (A Discussion on Rights)*. It begins with an attack on the misuse of the terms *rights* and *liberties* by "once youthful but shallow-minded students, . . . those who harbor personal enmity . . . and use popular rights for their own purposes . . . and those who want fame and honor." The more popular rights are discussed, the more common the terms become until it becomes necessary to clarify the meaning of the words. There are two kinds of liberty: natural and civil. Natural liberty means the fundamental, uncontrolled state that Heaven has bestowed on man. If not restricted in temper or disposition, man does not think of others and there is conflict. Natural liberty is, therefore, destructive; it is best replaced by popular rights, which can maintain physical well-being and protect honor and property. The rights or liberty that men want to attain are rights based on common reason or justice. Such rights protect the people's happiness, increase pleasure, and alleviate pain. The government has promulgated unfair laws, which restrict popular rights and harm the people. These laws have shown that the government is neglecting the common good and popular rights. It is the people's right to resist the government and end this evil. Americans did this when they fought for independence from England; the British did this when they made King John sign the Magna Carta. The government has imprisoned persons of doubtful guilt, shown discrimination in taxation, prohibited freedom of publication, and has not established parliamentary government. It is our right as Japanese to blame the government and by so doing to correct the situation. However, only those engaged in agriculture, industry, and commerce have the right to do this. The peers and samurai have long neglected the common welfare and do not stand on their own feet financially. Therefore they gave up the rights they had. If we study and explain liberty and rights to the common people, they will come to realize the meaning of such concepts. "I hope that we Japanese, thirty-five million in all, will move forward and that the people will work together to promote the common good, and all will insist on the extension of popular rights. Liberty must be explained so that there will be justice for all, or the people will betray liberty."[24]

The first four months of 1876 saw Ono "intent on unifying the Kyōzon dōshū" and translating into Japanese R. de Tracy's English version of *A Treatise on the Roman Law and Upon Its Connection with Modern Legislation* by J. E. Goudsmit of the University of Leiden. Ono had been sent the book by his former tutor in London, and he translated it because at that time people studied only the letter of the law in order to explain law. Few people searched for the principle of the law.[25] Furthermore:

> Western law has its origin in Roman Law and in the *Code Napoléon* and the *Code Frederick,* which arose from Roman law. Therefore, in Europe and America, every scholar of law makes it a rule first to study Roman law. One cannot understand the structure or the strengths and weaknesses of law if you do not know its origin. When I, a translator, began to study law during my stay in Europe, I first studied the institutions of Gaius and Justinian for this reason. Now our emperor and people are studying Western law, trying to understand it, and adapting it to our system. Therefore, I hope that this

translation of Roman law will serve as reading and reference for our emperor.

Rōma ritsuyō brought Ono to the attention of the government. On the recommendation of one of the original members of the Kyōzon dōshū, Hirose Shin'ichi, who worked in the Bureau of Legislation, Ono was appointed vice-chief of the Civil Law Section of the Ministry of Justice on August 15, 1876, at the age of twenty-four.[26]

From his new vantage point within the bureaucracy, Ono began to criticize the official establishment. *Rippōkan no ichidai kotsuryaku* (*Major Blunders of Legislators*) appeared in the June 18, 1879, issue of *Kyōzon zasshi*. The great mistake of legislators was not in issuing laws but in their failure to make the laws known and understood by people. To overcome this lack of communication, Ono suggested a seven-point program:

1. Laws must first be compiled and published.
2. The meaning of laws must be made clear to the people.
3. Major articles of the law should be compiled into a textbook for students to memorize.
4. Laws must be posted in all public places.
5. Laws must be written in *kana* because few below the middle classes understand *kanji*.
6. Laws must be translated into the languages of those countries with which Japan has foreign relations; if extraterritoriality is to be abolished, foreigners must understand Japanese law.
7. Outlines of the laws on contract and securities should be published.[27]

In *Hōshi no nikyū* (*Two Points That Should be Improved Immediately in the Administration of Justice*), published on August 27, Ono criticized the judiciary because the courts worked a total of only 73.5 days a year. This caused delays in the handling of cases and increased expenditures, and Ono favored having the courts in session every day of the year from 8 A.M. to 6 P.M. Because judges are subject to human error, he favored a form of "quasi-appeal," appeal to another court by the accused if he was not satisfied with the verdict. This process would, he claimed, encourage correct judgments, end delays, save expenditures, and keep the prosecutors vigorous.[28]

The *Kyōzon zasshi* was the forum through which Ono criticized existing conditions and proposed programs that would promote national unity and modernization and that could be judged by utilitarian criteria. Taking the greatest good of the greatest number as his standard of value, he opposed the movement led by Motoda Nagazane (Eifu) and Sasaki Takayuki to check the autocracy of the ruling oligarchy by direct imperial rule and to improve the position of the imperial household by making Shintō the state religion.[29] In *Kokkyō teichi no hei o ronzu* (*Essay On the Evil of Establishing a State Religion*), which appeared January 14, 1880, Ono firmly stated his opposition to the use of religion as a means of government. "National policies should be concerned with the public affairs of men and should not deal with their hearts. Religion is different. It has to do with the heart of man . . . and should not enter into temporal affairs. This is what is called the separation of religion and politics. . . . If people are compelled to believe in an established state religion . . . it will cause the nation's treasury to be spent wastefully. It will also cause immorality because people will not believe in the state religion." Bentham once said that government funds should be expended only for rewards and punishments. If public funds are spent for a state religion, it will be necessary to raise taxes and to punish those who will not accept the established faith. The people will be alienated from the government and the country will be weakened. If the state expends money for rewards and for administrative purposes unwisely, the nation's wealth will be wasted. Therefore, a state religion will cost more than any benefits it can bring. Buddhism, Christianity, Islam, and Hinduism have no great difference in basic doctrine, and it is useless to select one as the national religion that people are to believe. Faith means surrendering oneself completely to a religion. This is the way of moral people. It is very important that people should feel free to decide what religion to follow. Compulsion by the state to believe in one or another religion will force people to deceive others and themselves and will cause great evil.[30]

These ideas were later repeated in the *Minpō no hone* (*Essence of Civil Law*),[31] as well as an interview with Foreign Minister Inoue Kaoru in 1884, where Ono stated his approval of the end of ban on Christianity.[32]

The generation gap also occupied Ono's attention, and in *Fubo no kokoro e chigai* (*Mistakes of Parents*), published November 12, 1879, he criticized parental dependence on children as a social evil that needed reform. Thus: "Filial piety is fine. It is the highest level of human morality." However, the traditional view of parents that their children are a form of social security that will enable them to retire at fifty is against true utility. Even at this age, people still have much energy to expend in their occupations. When children have to support their parents and their own family simultaneously, they are always hard pressed to make a living, do not want to undertake any great enterprise, and will be content with only a minimum of success. Such a situation is detrimental to the economic development of the nation.[33]

In addition to these articles, Ono's contribution to the *Kyōzon zasshi* included the following works:

Kyōzon dōshū jōrei (*Regulations for the Kyōzon dōshū*), January 1875, Appendix to no. 1.

Zanshoritsu o oku no gi (*Opinion on the Establishment of the Libel Law*), March 1875, no. 3.

Tenpu no riyō (*Use of Natural Resources*), April 1875, no. 5.

Dokusho yoron (*My Theory on the Imperial Edict*), May, June, September 1875, nos. 6, 8, 9.

Minkei nihō jitsuri (*Practical Use of Civil and Criminal Law*), March 1877, no. 11.

Tsūhō no teichi o ronzu (*On the Two Necessities for the Encouragement of Learning*), May 1877, no. 12.

Kokken ronkō (*Study of the National Constitution*), March, April, June 1879; January, March, April 1880, nos. 14, 16, 17, 24, 55, 61, 63.

Rigaku nyūmon (*Introduction to Utilitarianism*), June, August, September, October 1879, nos. 27, 32, 34, 38, 40, 41.

Nihon yunyū zei ron (*Discourse on the Import Tax in Japan*), September, October, November, December 1879; March, April 1880, nos. 36, 42, 44, 48, 62, 65.

Minkan hyaku hei no ichi (*One of the Hundred Bad Practices in Civil Life*), November 1879, no. 45.

Kyōhaku kyōiku (*Compulsory Education*) December 1879, no. 50.

Nani o ka kore seifu no honmu to iu (*What is the Duty of Government?*), January 1880, no. 52.

Dare ka kokkai no kaisetsu wa shōsō nari to iu ya (*Who Says It is Too Early to Establish a National Assembly?*), March 1880, no. 60.[34]

Ono's writings reflected the wide range of topics covered in the *Kyōzon zasshi* as well as his views on the major issues of the time. They reflected his concern with the question of loyalty to the throne as expressed by nationalism and patriotism, the conflict between Japanese tradition and Western influence, and the need for a new standard by which social values and institutions could be judged, namely, the principle of utility of Jeremy Bentham. His articles also show a gradual progression from the ideas characteristic of the age of civilization and enlightenment to those of the era of popular rights. In 1875 Ono's concern was with education, national unity, and the explanation and expansion of the rights and liberty of the people. However, between 1872 and 1879, as a result of his direct contact with administrative problems and the rising debate on the need for a national assembly, Ono began to concentrate on issues relating to the structure and processes of government, particularly constitutional theory. His essays now became critical of the monopolization of power by the ruling oligarchs. By March 1880 the transition was complete; after four years in the bureaucracy, Ono had formulated his basic political philosophy and added his voice to those calling for the immediate establishment of a national assembly.

Ono and his fellow members in the Kyōzon dōshū were advocates of liberty and popular rights, but they were aware of the dangers arising from the abuse of such rights and of Western efforts to curb illegal excesses. The first instance of libel in Japan came from newspaper statements about a peer, Akizuki Taneki, in the Sakata case. The Kyōzon dōshū asserted that malicious statements that defamed an individual's reputation had to be controlled and proposed that the government establish laws on libel and slander based upon Western models.[35] The recommendation, drafted by Iwasaki Kojirō with advice from Ono,[36] appeared in the March 1875 issue of the *Kyōzon zasshi* as *Zanshoritsu o oku no gi* (*Opinion on the Establishment of the Libel Law*):

> Honor is a vessel which enables us to enjoy and maintain life, and without honor man cannot achieve fulfillment in society. If others violate one's honor, the damage is greater than death. . . . In Europe and America libel laws are respected and placed upon the law books as are laws against murder and injury to others. One way to accuse is by speech and the other is by writing. The latter is called "libel," and this offense is more serious. This is because writing is made public and is transmitted to posterity. In England, freedom of the press is highly valued, and anyone may publish his opinion on current issues and on the good and evil of government without hesitation. Thus, the people are enlightened; and the foundation of the state is strengthened. Those who accuse others or defame their character without facts are fined or penalized. A man's right to his reputation should be protected by strict laws.[37]

In addition to the proposal that appeared in the *Kyōzon zasshi*, the Kyōzon dōshū submitted a draft law entitled *Zanshoritsu* (Law to Control Libel) to the government. Although the exact contents of the law are not known, it was written by Ono.[38] Three months later, the Dajōkan promulgated two laws, the *Shinbunshi jōrei* (Press Law) and *Zanbōritsu* (Law Prohibiting Libel and Slander), which were said to be written by Ozaki Mitsuyoshi and Inoue Kowashi. These laws were more severe than those envisioned by the Kyōzon dōshū. The Libel Law placed the responsibility for defamation of private individuals and public officials on the editors and writers of publications. Although it owed much to the draft prepared by the Kyōzon dōshū, the original intent was subverted and the law was used to suppress political opponents of the government.[39]

Underlying the issues of national unity, modernization, and legal reform was the problem of revision of the unequal treaties, which were regarded as a threat to national independence. Foreign objections to Japanese legal and criminal procedures and lack of knowledge of international law had forced the Tokugawa shogunate to recognize the right of extraterritoriality. This led to the establishment of consular courts and jurisdiction not only in the treaty ports but throughout Japan in cases involving foreign nationals. The Meiji government, as heir to the treaties signed by the *bakufu,* was unable to apply its administrative regulations to foreigners unless such regulations were first promulgated by the ambassadors representing the treaty powers. This resulted in discriminatory treatment in law between foreign nationals and Japanese citizens, and the fact that the foreign community was not subject to police or administrative regulations was regarded as a major weakness in the foundation of national power. The end of seclusion had linked Japan to the world market and Western nations saw Japan as a market for manufactured goods and a source of agricultural products. They demanded a policy of free trade and low tariffs with the rate of duty set by treaty. To the Japanese, national independence would not be attained until extraterritoriality was ended and tariff autonomy was essential to protect domestic industries from foreign competition and to secure needed revenue for the national government.[40] Treaty revision occupied the attention of the Ministry of Foreign Affairs and the press; and on May 21, 1879, at Ono's suggestion, the Kyōzon dōshū decided to send a letter to the treaty powers to promote revision and to establish the friendship of the members and "the whole Japanese nation" toward the West. Ono believed that even if the letter had no direct effect, changes in the treaties would be a product of future diplomacy.[41] Ono wrote in his diary that he had taken notes of his proposals concerning the promotion of treaty revision between Japan and the foreign powers and that these treaties must be revised for the sake of future Japanese foreign policy.[42]

Ono's ideas were incorporated into a letter that he and fourteen other members wrote and published in September. Translated into English and French and distributed in the United States and Europe to provide understanding for the Japanese position on treaty revision, the letter was addressed to the "public of Europe and America concerning the necessity of treaty revision."[43] Its contents were as follows:

We believe that the citizens of the world respect justice and equality. We are sending this letter so that you can understand our situation and assist us in restoring to the Japanese Empire the sovereign rights of the nation.

Our situation at the time of the conclusion of the treaties was: for three hundred years Japan was under feudal rule; freedom was restricted, intercourse with foreign powers was strictly prohibited; these years were peaceful but the development of the Japanese state was greatly retarded. When Japan finally opened its door to the West, it had no idea about the situation in the West, the rules of diplomacy, or the character and procedure of treaty negotiations. Therefore, in treaty negotiations, Japan had no choice but to let the foreign powers take the initiative and to accept whatever treaties were made. The result was the unequal treaties.

After the Meiji Restoration, social institutions were reformed . . . but matters concerning politics and national policy were kept as strict secrets from the public. Thus, the Japanese people had no way of knowing the various injustices and inequalities in the new treaties. . . . But now, upon realization of what the treaties really are and of their disadvantages in economic and political matters, we can no longer remain silent while the unequal treaties exist.

A treaty is a contract between nations. A contract made taking advantage of the ignorance of one side should be regarded as invalid from the principle of law.

Concerning the tariff:

There are two ways for a nation to secure national revenues, one by collecting direct taxes and the other by collecting indirect taxes. Before the Meiji Restoration, when there was still no intercourse with foreign countries, the national expenditure was small. After the Restoration, as the government started to have diplomatic and social relations with foreign countries, national expenditures increased over tenfold compared with the preMeiji period. Domestic improvements and the maintenance of diplomatic and social ties with the foreign powers are the causes of this great increase. . . ; but the treaties contain provisions that tariff revision is a matter for consultation and decision with the treaty powers. In brief, they forbid Japan from enjoying tariff autonomy and prevent independent tariff assessments. Goods are imported into Japan with very low or no duties; and, thus, the sum the government secures from the tariff is approximately one-thirtieth of the national expenditures. Moreover, as the government tries to make up for this loss by levying taxes on domestic products, the production of goods in Japan has deteriorated greatly, thereby hindering the economic independence and prosperity of Japan.

We wish to restore the right of tariff autonomy on both imported and exported goods so that Japan can earn a reasonable amount of money from the tariff. When this is achieved, the Japanese will no longer have to suffer from unreasonably high direct taxes and Japan will, moreover, enjoy the benefits of normal productivity.

Concerning extraterritoriality:

Autonomy, independence, and equal rights are the three great rights indispensable if Japan is to exist as a nation. It is a rule of international law that anyone living in a foreign country is subject to the laws of that country regardless of his nationality. . . . But Europeans and Americans in Japan have immunity from these laws; instead they were given extraterritorial rights by the treaties, and, thus, they do not have to respect Japanese laws. Moreover, they are not subject to trial according to Japanese law even if they should commit a crime in Japan. We are extremely dissatisfied with the extraterritorial rights given to foreigners. We regard these rights as violations of Japanese sovereignty and, moreover, as a betrayal of the principle of equality upon which all laws are based. Thus, we, the Japanese people, are eager to revise the treaties so that this practice will no longer be applicable to foreigners, that the three great fundamental rights will again revert to Japan, and that Japan can begin to associate with other nations on the basis of equality. . . . Thus, Japan can maintain its position as an independent empire.

. . . we suggest that the Edo treaties concluded in 1858 be revised so that the agreements concerning diplomatic relations and trade be dealt with as two separate treaties and that the nations concerned conclude separate treaties with Japan. Moreover, we demand that the Revised Covenant on Tariffs concluded in 1866 be abolished and that Japan, hereafter, be allowed to levy tariffs on imported goods independently. . . . We can guarantee that our government will carefully study the tariff rates executed abroad and assess tariffs fairly and justly in accordance with the rates in foreign countries.

. . . we believe that if you once come to understand Japan and if you once ask yourselves what justice is, you will naturally agree to the revision of the treaties. If foreigners residing in Japan violently oppose revision and take some steps to prevent it, we would have to regard such as the result of your influence and orders. . . . We would have to conclude that people in the West are the type who do not care what justice is and this will be derogatory to your fame and reputation. . . . There is no reason or logic to oppose revision of the treaties, but if you still continue to oppose revision . . . then we can no longer guarantee the continuance of our relations in the future. . . . Thus, we eagerly hope that you would agree to revision of the treaties for our mutual benefit.

We, the Kyōzon dōshū, are a group of people who respect your civilization. . . . In order to develop a high civilization in Japan, some of us have visited your countries and studied about your civilization. Together, we hope to establish a high and progressive culture in Japan. . . . Thus, we have come to write this letter asking for your cooperation for the best solution of the matters concerning treaty revision.[44]

By appealing to logic, international law, and economics, the letter sought to explain why the Edo treaties were invalid, illegal, and injurious to Japan and to future Japanese-Western relations. Beginning with the legal thesis that a contract is invalid if one of the parties is ignorant of the conditions, the Kyōzon dōshū emphasized that the lack of tariff autonomy was injurious to the state, public, and commercial development. It stated that failure to recognize Japan as an equal, independent state and to end extraterritoriality was a violation of international law. Separate treaties of amity and commerce should be concluded; and if the rules of international relations could not be applied to Japan, it might be preferable to end foreign contacts. The letter was denounced by the *Yokohama Herald*, which spoke for the foreign community. However, it received a favorable response from the *Boston Advertiser* and from Professor Horseford of Harvard University, who wrote to Kaneko Kentarō, a former Harvard student, promising assistance in the matter.[45] Appeals to conscience, reason, and international law were to no avail, and in 1884 Ono and his contemporaries were still using the same arguments to justify the call for revision.[46]

Even more important than the issue of treaty revision was the question of the ultimate form of government. In 1878, as public interest in, and agitation for, some form of constitutional government increased, the Genrō-in, which was the legislative organ of the government, was instructed to draw up a constitution, "taking into account the constitutions of leading countries of the world,"[47] but "modified to suit the customs and usages of this country." By late May 1879 the press carried reports of a draft said to begin: "The emperor being sacred, his orders cannot be transgressed by the people; and the rights of the people are likewise inviolable."[48] Rumors of official studies on a constitution combined with the rising debate over the issue of popular rights, which had been initiated in 1874 when Gotō Shōjirō, Itagaki Taisuke, and others petitioned for the establishment of a popularly elected assembly,[49] stimulated political associations, the press, and private individuals to draw up draft constitutions.

The Kyōzon dōshū followed the trend of the times, and in 1881 Ono Azusa, Miyoshi Taizō, and Iwasaki Taizō produced a sample constitution entitled *Shigi kempō iken* (*Private Opinion on the Constitution*) for the association. This document showed a strong tendency toward a bicameral legislative system with ministerial responsibility in the lower house.[50] The first three chapters were concerned with the problems of imperial succession, marriage, regencies, and rights. The emperor was declared sacred and without political responsibility. He presided over the government, convened and dismissed the national assembly, and approved and revised bills that he presented to the legislature. However, he could not present bills on taxation or the budget nor could he interfere with the enforcement of laws. He had the right to appoint and dismiss ministers, vice-ministers, prefectural governors, military officers, and judges but not permanent officials except in accordance with the law. He presided over the army and navy, declared war and peace, appointed and dismissed ambassadors and envoys, and made treaties which, if national finances were to be expended or changes required in the constitution, would become effective only on approval of the legislature. The emperor issued currency and awarded peerages, decorations, and pensions. He could revoke the decisions of criminal courts and order retrials; he could mitigate punishments and grant amnesties. The arrest, prosecution, and punishment of criminals were to be performed in his name.

Shigi kempō iken states that the national assembly is the legislative organ and consists of three divisions, the emperor and the upper and lower houses. It is to be convened annually, and hearings are to be public, except in special cases or on the request of more than ten Diet members. Bills rejected by one of the houses cannot be resubmitted to the same assembly, and the emperor cannot stop or prohibit debates on bills in either house. Each house has the right to establish its own regulations in regard to legislative matters. The lower house is composed of elected representatives from electoral districts, which shall be regulated by law. Each electoral district must have more than one representative in the lower house. Tenure of office for representatives shall be three years with reelection permitted. Japanese males who are citizens and over twenty-five years of age, and who meet the property requirements specified in the election laws, are eligible for election to the lower house. Representatives, however, represent all the people and not just their constituents. The lower house has the following privileges: 1) to originate bills concerning national finances; 2) to impeach officials for improper political behavior; 3) to call upon public officials and people in regard to important matters; 4) to establish qualifications for its members and handle suits concerning elections; 5) to select its chairman and vice-chairman from among the members subject to imperial consent. Representatives have judicial immunity for speeches made in the lower house, from civil suits, and from arrest, except for flagrant offences, for a period of twenty days before and after the legislative session. The chairman of the lower house has the right to appoint and dismiss officers of the house. The assembly may convene itself upon the death of the emperor, if not in regular session, and will continue to assemble until ordered dismissed by the crown prince. Such a session requires a quorum of over half the membership of each house.

The upper house is composed of members of the imperial family, peers, and persons appointed by the emperor who have served the country meritoriously. Members must be Japanese citizens over thirty-five years of age. Other prerequisites for membership may be established by law. Members serve a ten-year term with half the upper house subject to dismissal every five years. Members are eligible for reappointment, and the emperor appoints the chairman and vice-chairman from among the members. Members are immune from arrest without the consent of the upper house, except in case of flagrant offenses. The upper house has the right to try persons impeached by the lower house and reports the results of such cases to the throne.

The assembly has the right to levy taxes, float public loans both within Japan and abroad, establish administrative districts and boundaries, and institute legislation designed to carry out the rights accorded by the constitution. However, it cannot legislate ex post facto, and contracts concluded before new laws are established shall retain their validity.

Shigi kempō iken then proceeds to discuss the problem of constitutional amendment in detail. Amendment proceedings are initiated by a special meeting approved by the emperor and two-thirds of the members of both houses. Simultaneous with the convocation of this special meeting, the lower house is dismissed temporarily. Representatives to the meeting include members of the upper house and those specially elected according to the same regulations and procedures used for electing members of the Diet. Amendments require the approval of two-thirds of the membership at the special session and the upper house and the emperor. Upon completion of its duties, the special meeting is dissolved and the former Diet resumes its regular duties. All other legislation requires approval by one-half of the members present of both houses of the Diet.

Shigi kempō iken contains ten articles on the rights of the people. These articles maintain that all citizens are equal under law, and only Japanese citizens can enjoy political rights in Japan. Citizens can hold civil and military office, cannot be arrested without due process of law, have the right to petition the emperor and executive branches of government, the right to freedom of worship, and to receive the protection provided by the law in criminal cases, and will not have the privacy of their homes invaded at night except as provided by law. Private property can not be taken for public use without just compensation; and freedom of assembly, association, speech, and the press will be enjoyed by all citizens, who are responsible for their actions under the law.

The final section of the draft constitution deals with the structure of the executive or administrative branch. The emperor presides over the administration, which consists of the prime minister and cabinet, formed of the chiefs of the Ministeries of Internal Affairs, Foreign Affairs, Jurisprudence, Army, Navy, Industry, Imperial Household, and Development. The prime minister will also hold the portfolio of Finance. All members of the administration execute their duties on the order of the emperor and will be responsible to the lower house. A minister who does not have the confidence of the lower house must resign from office. Ministers have the right to originate bills, including those concerning the national budget, and submit them to the lower house. Administrative expenses must be reported to the lower house. Members of the administration can serve as members of either house concurrently. All administrative orders will be signed by the prime minister and countersigned by the heads of the respective ministries.[51]

The authors of *Shigi kempō iken,* Ono, Miyoshi, and Iwasaki, had all studied in England; Ono had also spent one year in the United States. As a result, the document reflected the British and American political systems. Sections of the draft constitution show similarities to Alpheus Todd's *Parliamentary Government in England.* First published in 1866,[52] Todd's work had been brought to Japan in 1876 and had been given to the Genrō-in for reference in drafting its constitution.[53] Whether or not Ono and his colleagues had copies of the book in their possession is impossible to say, but this text or a similar one appears to have provided the model for the Kyōzon dōshū draft. In addition, there are striking similarities between the *Constitution of the United States* and *Shigi kempō iken.*

The final section of *Shigi kempō iken* deals with the administrative or executive branch and appears based on the British cabinet system as described by Todd. Ministerial responsibility to both houses of the assembly, the right to initiate legislation and annual budgets, and to serve concurrently as members of either house followed contemporary English practices. The cabinet acts on orders from the throne, but the emperor is not responsible for the business of government. The British example of the sovereign's reigning but not ruling is implied in the relationship between the monarch and his chief ministers.[54] By placing finance in the hands of the prime minister, the position of the chief minister was strengthened. *Shigi kempō iken* was a blueprint for the establishment of a bicameral parliamentary system with power vested in a strong prime minister and cabinet responsible to both houses and with fiscal power residing in the elected representatives of the people. Ono, Iwasaki, and Miyoshi had learned the "principles" of Anglo-American law and political theory and now were ready to apply them to Japan.

In addition to the sample constitution, the Kyōzon dōshū drew up a proposal entitled *Gijō kōteisho* (*Presentation of a Strong Argument on the Necessity for Opening a Parliament*). This was prepared with the assistance of Ono and Baba Tatsui and was presented to the government in the name of Iwasaki Kojirō.[55] Unfortunately, the document is no longer extant, and its exact contents are unknown.

By the end of the 1870s the "enlightening" activities of the Meiji learned societies had become increasingly political. The public lectures and publications of the Kyōzon dōshū, Meirokusha, and similar associations and political groups were becoming very popular; the speakers included many public officials who were extremely critical of the government. In an attempt to curb opposition to its policies and practices and to prevent public reaction to such criticism, the government on May 9, 1879, informed all ministerial secretaries that officials were neither "to meet with the common people nor give lectures which are beyond the province of their offices." [56] The following day *Yūbin hōchi shimbun* reported that the "authorities, having found it inconvenient that officials should make speeches in public, the *Daijo Kwan* issued an order to the heads of various departments to take measures accordingly." [57] The *Chōya shimbun* objected to the measure in an editorial, which the *Tokio Times* reprinted on May 17:

> we find no cause to uphold the proposition that the officials of the government should not, during their leisure hours, in-

> dulge in a practice of itself neither inconsistent nor illegal. Speeches tend to improve the minds of the people and develop interest in public affairs. . . .
>
> . . . when the government orders that its officials shall not make speeches on matters which do not concern their duties, then such persons as Messrs. Kono, Egi and Ono, officials of the Gen Ro In, cannot in the future talk upon law, which has no connection with their functions but only with those of the judicial department. . . . We are not only sorry for the officials who lose their right of freedom of speech but lament the fact that institutions which tend to promote the civilization of the country must disappear.[58]

Ono, who had been scheduled to lecture on "The Theory of the Three Nonpolitical Powers," was now forced to cancel his speech. He was extremely upset by the situation and wrote in his diary on May 11: "The government took immediate, strong measures to prevent us from acquiring influence in society. If the government has such ideas, I cannot serve it any longer. I shall go to the office and make this clear; and according to the circumstances, I shall resign." Ono was then serving in the Accounting Inspection Institute, and by May 15 he had begun to discuss his resignation with friends, who advised against it. Not wanting to reject their advice, he decided to remain in office until his work on government accounting regulations had been completed; but he noted in his diary, "in this climate, I will have to resign in the near future."[59]

On April 18, 1880, the Regulations on Public Meetings were issued. These required that the content of speeches and names of all speakers be reported in advance; police were to be present at public meetings with the right to disband those deemed detrimental to public peace; and teachers, students, apprentices, the military, reservists, and policemen were prohibited from attending such meetings. Outdoor political speeches were also forbidden, and violators were subject to fines and imprisonment. Two months later these restrictions were supplemented by prohibitions against "radical" speeches in specified areas for given periods of time. The measure preventing government officials from giving public speeches dealt a major blow to the Kyōzon dōshū, for by 1879, with the exception of Baba Tatsui, most of the members were government officials.[60] In an attempt to circumvent the regulations, the Kyōzon dōshū decided to hold its monthly meetings in English "to prevent several of the members who had visited England and America from losing the knowledge of the English language they have acquired." [61] As only one mention of this decision appears in the contemporary press, the measure was apparently not successful. The 1879 decree deprived the society of its most reputable members, while the act of 1880 ended its public meetings and closed its doors to the most receptive elements in society. Bereft of both speakers and audience, the Kyōzon dōshū was dissolved on May 19, 1880, one month after the second regulation had been issued.[62] Thereafter, occasional lecture meetings were sponsored by an organization called the Kyōzon dōshū, with Baba as the lone speaker on academic themes,[63] but this was only a titular remnant of the former association.

Ono had served as founder, secretary, and central figure of the Kyōzon dōshu from its inception to its dissolution, and his writings and activities reflected his deep commitment to the process of civilization and enlightenment. His feelings about the society were expressed in a Chinese poem written in his diary on February 7, 1879:

> I am not a doll made of mud nor a man
> with a mind stiff as a stone,
> so I am always affected by every event of the day.
> Because of Kyōzon dōshū, I can discuss
> anything freely to my heart's content,
> and even such a fool as I can join the meetings.[64]

Government restrictions on freedom of speech and on participation by officials in political and intellectual societies was one factor in Ono's developing opposition to the ruling oligarchy and in his gradual emergence as a leader of the political party movement.

Despite its small membership and subscription list, the activities of the Kyōzon dōshū served as a catalytic force in a period of intellectual and political ferment. As an organization of Western-educated intellectuals, it was part of a movement to introduce new concepts and to urge reforms in all areas of Japanese life. Its meetings and publications attracted the educated elite as well as men important in government, business, and education, who sought answers to the problems of the time. It was therefore one of the many forces contributing to the movement for civilization and enlightenment. With the suppression of freedom of speech and the press, the members of the Kyōzon dōshū felt that purely academic activities were insufficient to produce rapid change, particularly in the government. Therefore they moved into the political arena as proponents of the popular rights movement.

The Kyōzon dōshū was not the only organization in which Ono participated during this period. In September 1879 Fukuzawa Yukichi organized the Kōjunsha (Society to Promote Social Contacts), composed of former Keiō Gijuku alumni and modeled after the clubs in England. Intended to enable people of various professions and viewpoints to exchange knowledge, it was inaugurated on January 25, 1880, with a membership of nearly six hundred; Fukuzawa, Ono, Baba, Kikuchi Dairoku, Yano Fumio, and Iwasaki Kojirō appeared on the twenty-four member standing committee. The Kōjunsha membership overlapped the Kyōzon dōshū, but it was more of a social club and, following Fukuzawa's leadership, was nonpolitical.[65] Yet, its members also produced a draft constitution modeled upon the British parliamentary system, with the emperor supervising a division of power among an administration led by the prime minister, the legislature, and the judiciary as represented by the supreme court. In August 1881 *Yūbin hōchi shimbun,* edited by Yano, produced a similar draft,[66] and both documents had much in common with the memorial on constitutional government that Yano and Ono wrote for Ōkuma Shigenobu later in the year. By October 1881 it had 1,750 members, who included 371 government officials, 365 scholars, 281 businessmen, 123 farmers, 12 industrialists, 21 peers, and 15 prefectural representatives. Following the political change of 1881, the proportion of public officers decreased, and gradually the group took on the character of a businessmen's club. It held lectures in Tokyo and in other areas and published a journal entitled the *Kōjun zasshi* three times a month.[67]

Thus, in the age of "civilization and enlightenment," Ono sought to contribute to the process of modernization by promoting ideas of nationalism, loyalty to the throne, and change through participation in various learned and intellectual societies. However, because freedom of speech and press were suppressed and because groups such as the Meirokusha and Kyōzon dōshū were silenced or dissolved, Ono increasingly became disaffected with the government and began to favor direct action against the ruling oligarchy. His experience in the bureaucracy had stimulated his interest in politics and allowed him to make valuable contacts with men of influence and national reputation. In 1879 he was ready to resign his position due to dissatisfaction with the prohibition on speeches by public officials. By 1881 his disaffection had become open rebellion as he came to believe that only the elimination of *hanbatsu* (clan government) rule would promote national unity and national strength. Ono's political maturity was the result of his personal experience as a government official, and it is during these years that he completed the transition from the new Western-educated intellectual to the new politician.

NOTES

1. Ishii Ryōsuke, ed., *Japanese Legislation in the Meiji Era,* trans. William J. Chambliss (Tokyo: Pan-Pacific Press, 1958), pp. 100–115.

2. Robert Epp, "The Challenge from Tradition: Attempts to Compile a Civil Code in Japan, 1866—1878," *Monumenta Nipponica* 22, nos. 1–2 (1967): 23–29, 37–38.

3. Kōsaka, *Japanese Thought,* pp. 61–63, 127, 128, 130, 136–59; Kōsaka Masaaki, vol. 4 ed. *Shisō genron hen* in *Meiji bunka shi,* ed. Kaikoku Hyakunen Kinen Bunka Jigyō Kai, 14 vols. (Tokyo: Yōyōsha, 1957), 4: 70–72, 92–138; Epp, "The Challenge," *MN,* p. 40.

4. Nishimura, *Ono Azusa den,* p. 34.

5. Ono Azusa, "Kyōzon dōshū jōrei," *Ono Azusa zenshū hoi,* comp. and ed. Takano Zen'ichi (unpublished materials in the library of Waesda University, Tokyo), pp. 167, 174. Notes compiled by Prof.

Takano will be cited as Takano, *Ono Azusa zenshū hoi;* Yamada, *Ono Azusa kun den,* 2: 2–4.

6. Nishimura, *Ono Azusa den,* p. 46; Miyoshi Taizō, "Saimontekiroku," in preface of Nagata Shinnosuke, *Ono Azusa* (Tokyo: Fuzanbō, 1897), p. 9; Takano, *Ono Azusa zenshū hoi,* p. 174; Ishizuki Minoru, "Meiji no jishikijin—'Kyōzon dōshū' to Ono Azusa," *Zinbun gakuhū* 24 (March 1967): 66–67; Fujii Shin'ichi, *Teikoku kempō to Kaneko haku* (Tokyo: Dai Nihon Yūbenkai Kōdansha, 1942), p. 42.

7. Rengo Press, *Japan Biographical Encyclopedia and Who's Who,* 2d. ed. (Tokyo: Rengo Press, 1961), p. 496.

8. Ishizuki, "Meiji no jishikinjin," *ZG,* pp. 66, 67.

9. Nishimura, *Ono Azusa den,* p. 46.

10. Enomoto Morie, "Ono Azusa no hanbatsu seitōron," *Hokkaidō Gakugei Daigaku kiyō,* 4, no. 1 (July 1953): 76.

11. Nishimura, *Ono Azusa den,* pp. 49, 70; Ono, "Ryūkakusai nikki," pp. 318, 319, 321, 337; Yamada, *Ono Azusa kun den,* 2: 4, 5.

12. Fujii, *Teikoku kempō to Kaneko haku,* pp. 43, 44.

13. Miyoshi, "Saimontekiroku," p. 9; Nagata, *Ono Azusa,* p. 55; Nishimura, *Ono Azusa den,* p. 46.

14. Ono, "Kyōzon dō shū jōrei," p. 167.

15. Ono, "Ryūkakusai nikki," pp. 317, 318, 325, 330; Nishimura, *Ono Azusa den,* pp. 53, 54, 81. Nishimura Shinji states that the Kyōzon shūkan was located at 7 Hiyoshi-chō, Kyōbashi-ku, Tokyo. The Kyōzon bunko was located at 4–5 Hiyoshi-chō (*Ibid.,* pp. 46, 59). The buildings are no longer extant, and the site is now 8 chome, Chūō-ku, Nishi-Ginza. Yamada Ichirō in *Tōyō Ono Azusa kun den* (p. 4), writes the Kyōzon shūkan was located at 7 Hiyoshi-chō, Shimbashi-ku.

16. Nishimura, *Ono Azusa,* p. 103.

17. Takano, *Ono Azusa zenshū hoi,* p. 73; Nishimura, *Ono Azusa den,* pp. 70, 93; Takano Zen'ichi, ed. *Takada, Ichishima seitan hyakunen kinen no tame ni.* From a copy of Ichishima Kenkichi's diary prepared by Prof. Takano Zen'ichi of Waseda University (unpublished materials in Waseda University Library), n.p.

18. Ono Azusa, "Tsūjō no kyōyō o ronzu," *Ono Azusa zenshū,* 2: 5–12.

19. Ono Azusa, "Dōshūin no gen ni mukuiru," *Ono Azusa zenshū,* 2: 21; Nagata, *Ono Azusa,* pp. 61–64

20. Ono Azusa, "Ben wa nao hei no gotoshi," *Ono Azusa zenshū,* 2: 55–60.

21. Ono Azusa, "Kokumin nanzo kore o omowazaru," *Ono Azusa zenshū,* 2: 13–16; Nagata, *Ono Azusa,* pp. 75–79.

22. Ono Azusa, "Tada Nihon ari," *Ono Azusa zenshū,* 2: 27–31.

23. Ono Azusa, *Minshin ron* (unpublished manuscript dated November 1875, in the Ono *monjo,* National Diet Library, Tokyo, n.p.).

24. Ono Azusa, "Kenri no zoku," *Ono Azusa zenshū,* 2: 17–20. Because copies of the *Kyōzon zasshi* prior to no. 13 are no longer extant, Nishimura Shinji is uncertain whether or not *Kenri no zoku* was published in the *Kyōzon zasshi.*

25. Nishimura, *Ono Azusa den,* pp. 40–41; Nagata, *Ono Azusa,* pp. 67–79.

26. Nagata, *Ono Azusa,* pp. 67–69.

27. Ono Azusa, "Rippōkan no ichidai kotsuryaku," *Ono Azusa zenshū,* 2: 32–34.

28. Ono Azusa, "Hōshi no nikyū," *Ono Azusa zenshū,* 2: 40–42.

29. Enomoto Morie, "Ono Azusa no seiji *ronri—Kokken hanron* seiritsu o chūshin ni," *Nihon rekishi ronkyū* (1963), p. 548.

30. Ono Azusa, "Kokkyō teichi no hei o ronzu," *Ono Azusa zenshū,* 2: 49–53.

31. Ono Azusa, "Minpō no hone," *Ono Azusa zenshū,* 1: 56, 57.

32. Ono, "Ryūkakusai nikki," p. 503.

33. Ono Azusa, "Fubo no kokoro e chigai," *Ono Azusa zenshū,* 2: 35–39.

34. Takano, *Ono Azusa zenshū hoi,* pp. 70, 71.

35. Enomoto Morie, "Ono Azusa," p. 77.

36. Nishimura, *Ono Azusa den,* p. 83.

37. Ono Azusa, "Zanshoritsu o oku no gi," *Ono Azusa zenshū hoi,* compl. and ed. Takano Zen'ichi, pp. 36–38.

38. Nishimura, *Ono Azusa den,* pp. 82–83; Miyoshi, "Saimontekiroku," pp. 9–12.

39. Takano, *Ono Azusa zenshū hoi,* p. 41; Kohayagawa Kingo, *Meiji hōsei shi ron,* 2 vols. (Tokyo: Ganshōdō Shoten, 1944), 2: 777; Ishii, *Japanese Legislation,* pp. 261, 262.

40. Ukai Nobushige, ed. *Kōza Nihon kindai hō hattatsu shi,* 14 vols. (Tokyo: Keisō Shōbō, 1958–1962), 2: 180–81, 185–87, 193, 194–97.

41. Yamada, *Ono Azusa kun den,* 2: 6.

42. Ono, "Ryūkakusai nikki," p. 328.

43. Nishimura, *Ono Azusa den,* p. 83; Miyoshi, "Saimontekiroku," p. 11; Yamada, *Ono Azusa kun den,* 2: 6.

44. Nishimura, *Ono Azusa den,* pp. 84–92.

45. *Ibid.,* p. 92; Miyoshi, "Saimontekiroku," p. 11; Kaneko Kentarō (1853–1942), one of the members of the Kyōzon dōshū, had studied law and economics at Harvard University in 1871.

46. Cf. Ono Azusa, "Jōyaku kaisei ron," *Ono Azusa zenshū,* 1: 137–208.

47. Fujii Shin'ichi, *The Constitution of Japan* (Tokyo: Hokuseidō Press, 1965), pp. 87, 88, 103–12.

48. *Tokio Times,* 5, no. 22 (May 31, 1879): 304. Trans. from *Kinji hioron.*

49. Kosaka, *Japanese Thought,* p. 136.

50. Fujii, *Constitution of Japan,* p. 107.

51. Yoshino Sakuzō, ed., *Seishi hen,* in *MBZ,* trans. Nakamura Yoshihide, 24 vols. (Tokyo: Nihon Hyōronsha, 1927–30), 3: 411–16.

52. Alpheus Todd, *Parliamentary Government in England,* rev. and ed. Spencer Walpole, 2 vols. (London: Sampson Low, Marston *& Co.,* 1892), 1: iii.

53. Fujii, *Constitution of Japan,* pp. 258, 259.

54. Yoshino, *Seishi hen, MBZ,* 3: 415, 416; Todd, *Parliamentary Government,* 1: 76–87; 2: 25–51, 60–85, 109–37.

55. Miyoshi, "Saimontekiroku," pp. 9–12.

56. Meiji Bunka Kenkyū Kai, ed., *Jiyū minken hen,* in *MBZ,* 16 vols. (Tokyo: Nihon Hyōronshinsha, 1955–1959), 14: 344.

57. *Tokio Times,* 5, no. 20 (May 17, 1879): 277. Quoted from *Yūbin hōchi shimbun,* May 10, 1879.

58. *Tokio Times,* 5, no. 20 (May 17, 1879): 277. Quoted from the *Chōya shimbun.*

59. Yamada, *Ono Azusa kun den,* 2: 6, 7; Ono, "Ryūkakusai nikki," pp. 326–27.

60. *Jiyū minken hen, MBZ,* 14: 344; Ishii, *Japanese Legislation,* pp. 262, 263.

61. *Japan Weekly Mail,* 3, no. 51 (December 20, 1879): 1695.

62. *Jiyū minken hen, MBZ,* 14: 344.

63. Hagihara, "Baba Tatsui," *Chūō kōron* 81, no. 947 (September 1966): 403.

64. Ono, "Ryūkakusai nikki," p. 321.

65. Hagihara, "Baba Tatsui," *CK* 81, no. 947 (September 1966): 398–401; Asakura Eijirō and Nishida Chōju. *Amano Tameyuki* (Tokyo: Jitsugyō no Nihonsha, 1950), p. 274.

66. Osatake Takeki, *Nihon kensei shi taikō,* 2 vols. (Tokyo: Nihon Hyōronsha, 1938–1939), 2: 541–545; Shimomura, *Nihon zenshi,* 9: 116–17.

67. Hagihara, "Baba Tatsui," *CK* 81, no. 947 (September 1966): 400–401.

4
In Public Office

The age of civilization and enlightenment had as its purpose the development of a unified, modern state able to rid itself of the humiliation of the unequal treaties and to maintain national independence. During the thirty-one year search for diplomatic equality, the treaties exerted great pressure on all aspects of Japanese society and stimulated the drive for modernization. Although revision was not fully attained until 1899, the process of negotiation led to debate between the Meiji government and the Western powers and among the Japanese, especially over the issues of consular jurisdiction, political reform, and economic ideology.[1] Western objections to Japanese law and legal procedure were stated in the strongest terms by foreigners in the treaty ports[2] and by the treaty powers.

If the Meiji government was to meet these objections, complete the process of national unification, avoid the threat of colonization by the Western powers, and attain control over foreign residents and commerce within its borders, modernization of the court and legal system was essential. Revision of the legal structure was not only a requirement for orderly interpersonal relationships and business transactions but also for peaceful international contacts and foreign trade. Legal reform was the key to treaty revision and to consolidation of domestic conditions, particularly in new commercial activities where there was no customary law on which to rely. Therefore, the adoption of Western principles was an inevitable aspect in the drafting of new codes of law. The government, by sponsoring compilation of a new civil code, attempted both to meet foreign demands and to establish modern legal relationships that would correspond to contemporary economic and social institutions. The process of compilation inaugurated a period of tension between conservative defenders of Japanese custom and tradition and the administration.[3] In order to strengthen its position and to facilitate the process of modernization, the government called into its service many of the young Western-trained advocates of change and invited foreign lawyers to Japan to serve as advisers and teachers. In 1869 it established in the Dajōkan the Seidō kyoku (Bureau of Institutions), later renamed the Hōsei kyoku (Bureau of Legislation) to translate Western legal codes, principally the Code Napoléon, and to compile the new legal codes.[4]

ONO AZUSA: THE PUBLIC OFFICIAL

Ono returned to Japan on May 22, 1874, shortly after the Saga rebellion and Taiwan expedition focused attention on the need for national unity and knowledge of international law. Although recalled by the Ministry of Finance, he was not offered a position and decided to concentrate on his own efforts at promoting national unity and reform, namely, the Kyōzon dōshū and translation of Goudsmit's *A Treatise on the Roman Law*.[5] Ono began to write *Rōma ritsuyō* sometime between 1874 and 1876, and it was this work that brought him to the attention of "some important people." Kōno Togama, vice-chairman of the Genrō-in and the senior representative from Tosa, was at this time appointed vice-chairman of the Hōsei kyoku, and he recommended Ono for the position of *hōseikan* (legislative official).[6] As a result in March or April 1876, Ono was informally advised to serve in the Hōsei kyoku. Because he had not yet completed *Rōma ritsuyō*, he did not accept the offer. However, after three months, he was admonished by the Ministry of Justice and told to take a position editing the civil code. On the advice of his brother-in-law, Gishin, and his friends, he agreed to work for the government.

On the recommendations of Kōno Togama and Hirose Shin'ichi, one of the original members of the Kyōzon dōshū, who was then employed in the Hōsei kyoku, Ono was appointed assistant director of justice and vice-chief of the civil law section of the Ministry of Justice on August 15. In the latter capacity he served on the civil code compilation committee, but after only ten days he felt that he "could not help but resign" from the committee. Ono was a student of Anglo-American law and his views differed from those of Mitsukuri Rinshō, the chief translator, and Gustave Emile Boissonade, the French legal adviser, who were advocates of the French school. On October 12 Ono was made an official of the sixth rank, but, because the position of bureau director was abolished in line with the government's policy of tax reduction and retrenchment of expenditures, he was dismissed from this post on January 11, 1877. Two days later he was named secretary to the Ministry of Justice and continued as vice-chief of the civil law section. On February 1 he was appointed secretary of the Dajōkan concurrently and ordered to work in the Hōsei kyoku.[7] The *Kan'in meikan* (*Directory of Names of Officials*) for 1877, however, lists Ono as secretary of the Ministry of Justice.[8] With a powerful sponsor, Kōno, who soon became Minister of Internal Affairs, and his own innate ability and Western education, Ono became well known and rose rapidly in the bureaucracy.[9] Nonetheless, he was dissatisfied with the political situation and "resolved to write *Kokken hanron* in sorrow at home . . . to show it to important people and make them recognize the proper time to establish the constitution." Unfortunately, his writing and career were interrupted by an attack of cholera that almost took his life in late November and kept him home for the rest of the year. In the beginning of 1878 he was transferred to the investigation section of the Ministry of Justice, which was studying local customs for the committee compiling the civil code; but he requested that he be allowed to resign from it. On April 27 he was named secretary of the Genrō-in. Eight months later he was again transferred and reappointed secretary of the Dajōkan and ordered to work in the Hōsei kyoku,[10] a position he held until March 1880.

Ono's work in 1879 and 1880 was primarily concerned with the drafting of legislation. His legal training and knowledge of foreign law now brought him into direct contact with the uppermost levels of the bureaucracy. As a specialist on Western law, Ono attended meetings of the Dajōkan and Genrō-in. He worked with Kōno Togama, Inoue Kaoru, Iwakura Tomomi, and Itō Hirobumi on problems relating to government regulations and laws. For example, on February 21, 1879, he participated in a meeting at which Inoue reported on the completion of the civil code. At this time, Ono suggested that it would be best for Japan to refer to the laws of various European countries for examples of civil law.[11] He became a member of a cabinet committee editing civil law, attended meetings of the Genrō-in, and there surprised many eloquent speakers by a most "splendid speech on the abolition of torture." [12] In this speech, which was delivered in June 1879, Ono appealed for the total repeal of the laws permitting torture from the criminal code. Torture, he stated, was one of the major obstacles to treaty revision and shamed Japan before the world. Judges should be permitted to try by evidence as well as by confession, and those instances of torture allowed by the Revised Law of 1876 should be repealed "to show that this country has taken another step toward improvement." [13] As a member of the Hōsei kyoku, he worked with Boissonade, and in his diary on August 27, 1881, he wrote that he had received various opinions on a matter that he was going to send to the French adviser.[14]

Ono was secretary to the Genrō-in at the time of the second prefectural governors' conference of 1878. He attended the conference as an official of the imperial household, a special appointment made for the occasion. The conference was presided over by Itō Hirobumi and examined the draft laws on rural government organization, prefectural assemblies, and local taxation. Ono's notes and comments on the discussions were incorporated into *Gian hihyō* (*Criticism on the Bill*), an essay written in April 1878 but not published until 1936. The bill to which the title refers was the Three (Great) New Laws, consisting of the Law Governing the Organization of Rural Divisions, City Wards, Towns and Villages; the Prefectural Assembly Regulations; and the Local Tax Regulations of 1878, which laid the foundation for local government in Japan.[15] Ono was again appointed an official of the imperial household for the 1880 prefectural governor's conference, but although he engaged in extensive preparations for this meeting, he was unable to attend due to illness.[16]

Gian hihyō is a detailed explanation and criticism of the 1878 laws. In discussing the first bill regulating local administration, Ono stated his opposition to those advocating a return to the former *gun* (county or district) system that was neither convenient for administrative nor communicative purposes. However, since smaller units could be governed more easily, the inconveniences of the new system could be lessened if the country were divided into approximately fifty-five prefectures and the administrative boundaries of municipal areas were drawn according to given population size. Furthermore, the distinction made by the law between the officials and people was unnecessary, for "if there were freedom in every corner, it would not be necessary to use such terms. This proves that freedom is not understood in Japan and that the government is uncertain on the amount of official control needed."

The Prefectural Assembly Regulations are similarly described and commented upon:

> The present prefectural government does not need any advice to emphasize its importance. The government should understand the viewpoints of the people and make useful bills which would further the welfare of the people and place the administration of the bills in the hands of district officials. This is one of the main tasks of the Meiji era. [According to the law,] the prefectural governor can decide when bills should be put into effect according to the condition of the people and the time. Such a decision depends mainly on the views of the prefectural governor, and I feel

> uneasy about this. If the people understand there is no great difficulty in establishing representative government in the prefectures, they will establish [this form of] government in every part of the country and provide for administrative decisions which are not made by the prefectural governor alone. I strongly urge the national government to establish [representative] prefectural government in every part of the country.

Ono opposed limiting the number of representatives to the prefectural assembly from each subdivision to two and advocated proportional representation according to population size. He did not favor having the governor approve the assembly chairman and vice-chairman because this reduced the importance of legislative decisions. He was critical of the failure to provide assembly members with a salary, for "in our country, there is a tendency for those with good ability not to be well blessed in financial matters." In addition, the legislative secretary should be appointed by the assembly and should also receive a salary. Voters and candidates for the prefectural government should not be limited to only those paying a ten yen prefectural tax. Instead, age, social status, and length of residency should determine eligibility for office. Payment of prefectural taxes of less than ten yen or property requirements for voters should be established so that two-thirds of the male population over twenty years of age would be enfranchised. Voting should be by secret ballot with the ballots counted in the prefectural capital. The voter should be asked to select five candidates in order of preference, with those receiving a given number of votes elected. Candidates at large should be allowed in areas lacking suitable persons to stand for office. Ono agreed with the provision for a three-year term for representatives and the use of staggered elections, similar to what he had advocated for the upper house in *Shigi kempō iken.* However, he felt that a thirty-day legislative session was too short to examine bills and favored an unlimited session to be brought to a close by the decision of the members themselves. The power of the Home Minister to suspend or dissolve the assembly for "disturbances" was regarded as a vaguely worded provision for proroguing and controlling the legislature. The right of the Home Minister to disqualify members of a dissolved assembly from reelection would produce instability and "great changes in the political world." The Home Minister's power to approve taxes requested by the governor but refused by the assembly was antithetical to the rights of the prefectural government. Therefore about half of the second bill required revision, and Ono produced a draft bill that incorporated his suggestions.

Ono believed the third bill, Local Tax Regulations, was the best written of the three and that the new land, commerce, and household taxes were preferable to those formerly levied. He felt that the new tax rates were equitable but that no final limit should be set on the land tax in case additional revenues were needed in the future. He opposed allowing the national government to set limits on prefectural business and miscellaneous taxes. This was contrary to the idea of local control, for it was the duty of the governor and assembly to determine the rate of prefectural taxes according to need. He favored using only prefectural revenues to meet prefectural needs such as local government, education, public works, sanitation, public health, and the distribution of vital information. Such expenditures should not be met from the national treasury because the prefectural assembly had no right to deal with matters involving national tax revenues and could only allocate funds acquired in the prefecture. Although public schools were included in the list of suitable areas for the expenditure of local tax revenues, Ono personally opposed using prefectural tax monies for education because this would produce financial difficulties for the local government. "Since the Japanese would never neglect the education of their children, the establishment and maintenance of primary schools should be left to towns and villages to manage as their own common property." Only after the governor has presented the prefectural budget to the legislature for approval can it be regarded as accepted. Ono also spoke out against any government interference in or aid to business, even in the form of public loans. Government funds should be used to expedite the exchange of information and to encourage industry and commerce.[17]

Gian hihyō represents a study in the continuing development of Ono's viewpoint and is the precedent for ideas that were developed in later writings and in *Kokken hanron.* As a student of British and American political institutions, Ono was quick to recognize that Meiji leaders did not intend to institute fully representative institutions on the prefectural and local levels but would retain control over the prefectural assemblies and local officials. In calling for proportional representation for the prefectural legislature, he was advocating a system similar to that used to elect members to the American House of Representatives. In opposing the dominance of the governor and Home Minister over the prefectural assembly and budget, he was seeking to promote parliamentary government and to strengthen the position of elected representatives. In calling for "useful bills" to promote the happiness of the people, Ono was repeating a utilitarian theme.[18] In advocating no permanent ceiling on the land tax, he was saying that the government should not cut itself off from future tax revenues. In proposing an unlimited session, he wanted to give the legislature time to deal with all matters and later mentioned this in *Kokken hanron.* In favoring complete laissez-faire, he proved that he had learned the surface ideas of contemporary economic theory, but he did not show how industrial development would proceed without government aid and financing. Finally, in opposing the use of prefectural tax revenues for education, he was suggesting a return to the Tokugawa system of local education financed by individual contributions and fees as in the *terakoya* (temple schools).[19] Although a follower of utilitarianism, he apparently did not know that Bentham's ideas and writings had laid the foundation for the modern British educational system and that Bentham believed education was a major function of the state.[20] By the time Ono had studied in New York, the system of tax-supported public education was well established in many Northern states.[21] The Meiji government and leading educators such as Fukuzawa Yukichi believed that it was the duty of the state to establish schools and develop the talents of its citizens.[22] As government tax revenues had increased while the land tax had decreased since 1868,[23] Ono's fear of additional tax burdens on the people due to publicly financed education was not borne out. Furthermore, he did not show how a decentralized educational system based on local, and thereby limited, finances could contribute to promoting national unity and modernization. This aspect of his criticism was inconsistent with his espousal of the greatest good of the greatest number. It was founded more on his fear of government control of education and on his growing concern with *hanbatsu* dominance than on facts or logic.

ONO AND BENTHAM: *RIGAKU NYŪMON*

In 1878 and 1879 Ono not only held important positions for his age in the bureaucracy but also began to formulate his own philosophy and theory of government. The basis of his political theory was the principle of utility as expounded by Jeremy Bentham. Ono sought to explain his concept of utility in *Rigaku nyūmon,* and the key to his political thought and action can be found in this essay:

> It can be said that pain and pleasure are tools to be used to control [people]. True politicians understand this as do those who respect moral training. If we do not teach that pain is undesirable and pleasure desirable to human beings, teaching does not deserve to be called "teaching." If we interpret this basic fact incorrectly and use it to restrict autonomy, we will be unable to lead men in the right direction.
>
> Furthermore, if politics is not directed toward the removal of pain and the giving of pleasure, it can not be called "politics." In general, the purpose of politics is to remove pain and to protect pleasure; and if it goes against these purposes, it will be unable to maintain order in the nation.
>
> We should keep in mind that pain is unpleasant and undesirable to human beings and pleasure is always enjoyable. With this, one can lead one's life and can control a nation. . . . A true scholar estimates the degree of pain and pleasure, making clear the relationship between virtue and vice, in order to control himself and the country. His primary objective is to analyze the elements of pleasure. Truth is sanction and reason and means the greatest good of the greatest number. In general, where there is good, there is no evil; and where there is no pain, there is pleasure. Therefore, perfect and harmonious welfare is truth.
>
> If we try to decrease pain and to increase pleasure, we can

say we are following the line of truth. Gautama's theory of self-interest and altruism is almost similar to this. The same can be said of the policies of a country. If . . . devoted to decreasing political pain and to increasing the people's happiness, we can say they are in line with truth. We can say the Magna Carta signed by King John of England and the United States Federal Constitution are forms of truth.

A true scholar preaches pain and pleasure as a means to control himself and a nation through "nature." When we serve man with perfect virtue, we should not say as do the Confucians that since man has innate goodness in his heart and mind, the meaning of perfect virtue can be expanded. One should say perfect virtue provides pleasure and does not give pain.

Rigaku nyūmon then goes into a discussion of those evils which prevent man from attaining righteousness:

> Truth is the path of righteousness. Pain and pleasure lead us in the right direction by serving as our outriders and preventing us from going into the wrong direction. If we do not follow the path of righteousness, we will be unable to reach our goal. There are two kinds of incorrect paths. One is self-righteousness and the other is self-indulgence.[24]

Those who care only for themselves and not about others are self-righteous. Those who are self-centered and seek to seclude themselves from the affairs of the world are self-righteous. Those who fear divine punishment, refuse common pleasures, and pray for happiness in another world are self-indulgent. The self-righteous man is arrogant, and the self-indulgent man is a fool. It is natural for man to live in human society and to care for the affairs of the world. "Those who set their minds at rest, understand the laws of nature, and share their pleasures with others are men under the control of [the principle of] pleasure and are noble in their deeds." The disciples of Lao-tzu, Chuang-tzu, Confucius, and Buddha are self-righteous and proud. Although Gautama and Confucius lived by benevolence and charity and advocated altruistic works in word and deed, their disciples worked for their own benefit and, though pure and innocent in deed, sinned against the teachings of their masters. It is said that Christ gave his life to save people. Those words show self-righteousness. The main point of Christianity is that unless one is pure and good one is unable to save others. Self-righteous and proud people say: "Don't seek pleasures or you will become evil." There are many kinds of pleasures, both of the senses and of the heart and mind. Should those of the spirit and intellect be thrown away? One who advocates the pleasures of the mind and knowledge should not ask for happiness in another life, for these belong to this world. In so far as man discards pleasure, he makes light of "nature's independence." Teaching that disregards "nature" is not righteous and is evil. Those who call things that are congenial to their tastes "righteous" and things contrary to their tastes "wrong" are self-indulgent. They do as they will, changing their attitudes as their tastes change. Such natures are evil, and poor administration or rule is due to this.

A second category of evil is dogmatism. A man who sets up his own views as the standard of righteousness and morality is a dogmatist. "We utilitarians criticize the *Spring and Autumn Annals* of Confucius very much." The basic idea of this work is: " 'I, Confucius, will decide the criterion of justice!' . . . what an extreme dogmatist Confucius was! Reward and punishment should be the supreme power of the state. Therefore, only those who have governmental power can grant rewards and punishment to the people. Nevertheless, Confucius at his own discretion rewarded and punished others and said: 'The law of Heaven is in me. I will do whatever I will.' " Mencius is also guilty of dogmatism. His theory of the innate goodness of man and the four beginnings of man are nothing but dogmatism. Feelings of shame, respect, right, and wrong vary according to position, circumstances, manners, and customs. Thus, man's innate nature differs according to the situation. If man expands his "beginnings" without knowing what they really are, he can not be on the right path. Lao-tzu's doctrine of *wu-wei* (nonaction) is another example of self-righteousness. The *tao* (way) one should follow shows his extreme dogmatism. Confucius, Mencius, and Lao-tzu attributed their doctrine to the law of nature while placing themselves above it. Thus, they tried to cover up their dogmatism.

Gautama preached *shinnyo* or "absolute reality," which

means the reality of all things in the universe. He said that there was a way to salvation from deep-rooted delusion and that the vicissitudes of life follow the law of cause and effect. Therefore, Gautama did not follow the wrong path of dogmatism. "Utilitarians have nothing to criticize in Mahayana Buddhism."

Christ and Mohammed "called themselves the 'Son of God' or the 'Servant of God.' They preached, 'God has sent me to save the world. . . .' What excess!" Even scholars such as Hume, Nietzsche, and Price are also guilty of dogmatism.

Dogmatism is also found in the legendary sage-kings of the Chinese classics. Thus, although Yao, Shun, Yu, T'ang, Wen, and Wu Wang were benevolent rulers, they were dogmatists because they believed that they were acting according to the will of Heaven. Those who overthrow a ruler, even if he is a tyrant, and say it is the "will of Heaven" are guilty of self-righteousness and dogmatism. Legalists such as Han Fei-tzu are not popular; but from a utilitarian point of view, his advice to govern according to the will of the people and by reward and punishment according to the law is more logical than using the phrase *will of Heaven.* Those who speak of acting according to the will of Heaven and the universe neither understand nor justify their words and deeds. They do whatever they want by saying it is the will of Heaven. "Though there are some dogmatists who truly benefit the people, they are still not on the right path; for the right path is the way without any kind of uncertainty." *Rigaku nyūmon* concludes:

> It is not above all human sentiment for men to love those who benefit them and hate those who harm them. The foundation of true utility is based on this sentiment. It is, in a sense, not too different from dogma. In this case, men adjust their feelings of love and hate on the basis of true utility. . . . Dogma is incorrect doctrine. If [men] try, they will be able to succeed and to set themselves on the right path. Utilitarians can not wholly ignore dogma.[25]

In *Rigaku nyūmon,* Ono sets forth the thesis that the principle of utility is the standard by which all the policies of the state and its leaders are to be judged. Those who find in natural law, the will of Heaven, God, or their own wisdom the ultimate justification for their actions are guilty of self-righteousness, egoism, or dogmatism, even if their intentions or actions are beneficial. The principle of utility is based on the fact that man is hedonistic and is motivated by self-interest. Bentham, however, raised utility beyond mere justification of individual concern with pain and pleasure. He said that the measurement of any action is not only the elimination of pain for the individual but for the greatest good of the greatest number. Ono reinterpreted Bentham's idea from the viewpoint of Mahayana Buddhism. In chapter 2 he states: "According to the *Bonmō bosatu kaikyo* (*Prayer to Become a Bodhisattva*) of Gautama, the bodhisattva should always have mercy for the people and be obedient to the purpose of relieving their [pain and suffering]. Thus, concern for the welfare or interest of others existed in utilitarian theory and in the philosophy of the Tendai sect." It is this concern for the welfare of others that Ono called *shinri* or "true benefit" as measured by the indicators of pain and pleasure. *Rigaku nyūmon,* therefore, was not a mere translation of Bentham but an original work that had its origin in utilitarian theory as interpreted through the eyes of the Meiji intellectual. The first chapters were published in the *Myōkyō shinshi,* which was edited by Ōuchi Seiran. The historian Enomoto Morie believes that Ono's article was intended to repay Ōuchi for his kindness and to cope with the ideas introduced by Nishi Amane's translation of Mill's *Utilitarianism.*

Ono's attack on the works of Confucius and Mencius, neither of whom are referred to by the honorific *shi* (Master), reflects his opposition to the theory of natural law, which he felt was disguised in Confucian robes. His criticism of Christianity and Islam similarly denounces adherence to a standard of judgment beyond that of man and the physical universe. Man's actions are to be judged by their quantitative results and not by their motives. Thus, the legendary Chinese sage-kings are presented in a favorable light for their contributions to society. Yao and Shun are shown as having governed well because they listened to the people's opinions and ruled accordingly. Yü Hsung's writing on government is quoted to show that "the people is the norm for choosing the officials." Thus, examples from Chinese history and philosophy are used to show precedents for a concept of government based on the welfare of the people. The wise rulers of the past are those concerned with the happiness of the people and who selected officials according to the judgment of the people. Self-interest is a natural human concern, but self-interest must be satisfied in relation to the welfare of society as a whole. Hence, the greatest good of the greatest number is the ultimate standard of judgement. Utilitarianism, in this way, is united with Mahayana Buddhism and justified by examples from Chinese history to produce a political philosophy that includes both self-interest and public welfare, making the latter the ultimate criterion for judgment. The theory of utility now becomes the justification for representative government. Those rulers who heed public opinion and who select officials according to the judgment of the people follow the principle of the greatest good of the greatest number. The legendary sage-kings of Chinese history furnish examples from antiquity; the Meiji Emperor can be the "wise ruler" of the present.

Ono's views were founded on neither religion nor resignation. Utilitarian criteria did not imply unchanging values or natural law and offered the opportunity for active self-emancipation. Nonetheless, Ono's interpretation of utility was through Buddhist precepts. The opening paragraph of *Kokken hanron* shows this when he states: "Everything in the universe happens in good season. . . . This is unavoidable. . . . Is there anything which happens unnecessarily? Everything has its own necessity for existence." Thus there were a natural order and logical necessity to life. *Shinnyo* to him represented this order which was reality. It was an order that could be understood contemplatively, which made it possible to anticipate the empirical laws of natural science and the humanities according to reason. Thus the time had come for the establishment of the national assembly, the promulgation of the constitution, and the reform of the legal code. In conforming to the natural order and proceeding to implement these things, one acted correctly, promoting his own self-interest and that of others.[26]

As recognized first by Rōyama Masamichi and later by Enomoto Morie and Takano Zen'ichi, Ono's theories of politics and law were permeated with Bentham's utilitarianism. However, Rōyama states that Bentham founded not a doctrine but a method, which was in his hands a powerful instrument of immediate practical interest. "In the case of Ono, it is doubtful if he understood Bentham's logical method. This is the reason why his positivism lacks logic though it was very utilitarian and why his thoughts lacked a remarkable clarity and did not contribute precise characteristics to the party movement. . . . He insisted on the necessity of new, clear measures for principles similar to Bentham's criticism of English legislation and his direction for reform. . . . Ono's utilitarianism was weaker [than Bentham's]. He was not a philosophic radical. Like most free thinkers in Japan at that time, he was a loyalist and nationalist."[27] Ono had taken Bentham for his mentor, but he did not fully comprehend Bentham's ideas or logical method. However, in seeking a rational base for his political and legal philosophy, Ono was attracted to Bentham's system, which documented in detail the rationale and means to institute major changes in political, legal, and social life. Bentham's voluminous writings contained a sample constitution and a model civil and criminal code. During his visit to England, Ono had witnessed the culmination of utilitarian-advocated reforms. He saw Bentham's works as a means of countering the introduction of French political and legal theories. The greatest good of the greatest number was an altruistic concept, which had parallels in the Chinese classics and history and in Mahayana doctrine. These similarities made utilitarianism intellectually and psychologically palatable. They enabled Ono to bridge the gap between his early classical education and Buddhist heritage and the ideas and systems he had studied abroad. Ono attempted to unite utilitarianism with Mahayana concepts and Chinese history and philosophy. In other writings he tried to combine the principle of utility with loyalty to the throne and nationalism. As a result, his political philosophy contains logical inconsistencies that are the culmination of his attempts to merge completely alien ideas and systems. In striking out at the intellectual domination of Confucianism but not at his Buddhist heritage, in seeking a rational basis for fundamental changes in society, he merged tradition and utilitarianism to bridge the mental gap within his own mind and within the minds of his contemporaries. If at times the scope and purpose of his ideas and writings are not clear, it is a reflection of the confusion within a society seeking to implement immediate change in all areas of national life and to merge tradition with foreign concepts and ways. This union of tradition, particularly loyalty to the throne, and utilitarianism contributed "precise characteristics to the party movement," as will be shown later in the discussion on the Kaishintō.

Rigaku nyūmon was a utilitarian statement that sought to establish a rational basis for a political system dedicated to the welfare of the people. These ideas were further developed by Ono in *Nani o ka kore seifu no honmu to iu* (*What Is the Duty of Government?*). Appearing in the January 7, 1880, issue of the *Kyōzon zasshi,* the article was a direct application of utilitarian principles to the problems of government. Beginning with the thesis that the duties of government change with time, Ono stated that functions such as the equal distribution of farmland and the regulation of social status, wages, and prices are no longer regarded as areas subject to state control. Instead, the state now is entrusted with the establishment of laws on education, public hygiene and health, food control, encouraging industry and commerce, and poor relief. The relationship between the people and the state has, therefore, changed:

> In my opinion, man's true utility consists of the four elements of subsistence, [i.e., necessities], abundance [i.e., wealth], security, and equality. Therefore, it is man's desire to raise [these] four elements to the highest level possible. As government is said to have as its objective the greatest happiness of the greatest number, I think its real duty should be to help [attain] these four purposes. However, we can imagine that government can not interfere directly in the subsistence and abundance of the people. We also understand mistakes such as the equal distribution of farmland. We understand that equality is wonderful, but we can try to achieve it only in cases where it does not violate the rights of others. Cases involving prices, equal [distribution of] property, and so forth, similarly are to be carried out without too much government interference.

> We would not need government if we could attain these three, i.e., subsistence, abundance, and equality, without obstruction: but unfortunately, we can not. One [man's] profit is another's loss. Thus, our society depends on reciprocity. Therefore, in order to attain these three for society, it is necessary to exert self-control and to give up some of our desires. This is how and why government was established for the first time in human history. People wanted to protect themselves against violence and interference and, thus, created government. If people can obtain peace and social stability, they will be absorbed in the struggle for existence, live in peace, own property, and maintain equality among themselves. Therefore, the responsibility of government is to keep the public peace and not go beyond this limit. If government goes beyond this, it abuses its power and is harmful to the interests of society. [It becomes the] public enemy. Government protection should remain within the limit of arresting violators of the peace and should not go beyond this.[28]

Nani o ka kore seifu no honmu to iu is not only a statement of utilitarian political theory but also an indicator of the direct influence of the ideas of the leading utilitarian writer, Jeremy Bentham, on Ono. The essay is a summarization of the main ideas found in chapters 2 to 5, 7, and 14 of Bentham's "Principles of the Civil Code" in *The Theory of Legislation*. Thus, chapter 2 begins:

> In the distribution of rights and obligations, the legislator . . . should have for his end the happiness of society. Investigating more distinctly in what that happiness consists, we shall find four subordinate ends:
>
> Subsistence.
> Abundance.
> Equality.
> Security.
>
> The more perfect enjoyment is in all these respects the greater is the sum of social happiness: and especially in that happiness which depends upon the laws.[29]

In chapters 4 and 5, Bentham further states that the law should do nothing directly to provide subsistence and abundance, but by punishments and rewards create motivation. In regard to equality: "We can not arrive at the greatest good, except by the sacrifice of some subordinate good. . . . Equality ought not to be favored except in cases in which it does not interfere with security; . . . if all property were equally divided at fixed periods, the sure and certain consequence would be, that presently there would be no property to divide."[30] Ono's statement on the rationale for government is borrowed from chapter 1, entitled "Formation of Government," in Bentham's *A Fragment on Government*.[31] His statement that the duty of the state is to preserve public peace and to go beyond this is an abuse of power is based upon chapter 8, entitled "Of Security," and chapter 14, Section I, entitled "Indigence" of "Principles of the Civil Code."[32] These ideas were to be expanded later in the first volume of *Kokken hanron*. Therefore, by 1880 Ono's political theories had begun to crystallize and he had started to pattern them directly after Bentham's major works. During the stage of his career when he was directly concerned with work on the civil code and various legislative acts, Ono was actively engaged in the study of Bentham's *Theory of Legislation*, particularly the "Principles of Legislation" and "Principles of the Civil Code." He later translated parts of these works into Japanese in *Kokken hanron*. During his public years, Ono had become a disciple of Bentham; but at the same time, he had been an employee of the Hōsei kyoku, which was translating French law and using French advisers who were advocates of the theory of natural law. Ono had become committed to utilitarianism, which was opposed to the doctrine of natural law and natural rights. This commitment and his training in Anglo-American law had led him to resign from the civil code compilation committee in 1876 and was a factor in his gradual disenchantment with the Meiji government.

ONO AND ŌKUMA: THE PARTNERSHIP BEGINS

As Ono became increasingly critical of government policy, he began to gravitate toward Ōkuma Shigenobu, the Minister of Finance from 1873 to February 1880, and a member of the

Dajōkan.[33] Following the split in the ruling oligarchy over the issue of Korea, Ōkuma, a native of Hizen, was the only non-Satchō member left in the uppermost levels of the hierarchy. In this period, he was one of the most powerful members of the government.[34] Ono met Ōkuma through his brother-in-law, Gishin, who was employed in the Finance Ministry. Exactly when they were first introduced is uncertain, but it was after Ono had returned to Japan and before 1878.[35] Ōkuma described the meeting and their later relationship:

> One day Gishin told me he had a brother-in-law named Ono Azusa who was studying in England. Gishin said that Azusa was coming back from England soon and that he was quite a brilliant person despite his youth. Gishin asked me to meet Azusa sometime and to see if I would like to accept him to work under my command. I met Azusa as soon as he came back to Japan. I found him to be a small, thin person without any heroic or gallant appearance; but from his face, I could see right away that he had some extraordinary qualities. As most government officials at the time were men wrapped in traditional, conservative thought, I rejoiced to find Azusa who was filled with new knowledge and new ideas. Thus, he began to work under my direction. As I came to know him better, I came to be increasingly astonished by his extraordinary ability. He was not only profound in academic knowledge but was also gifted with managerial talent. He became one of the most important members of my staff. Sometimes he worked as a secretary, sometimes as my assistant. Whenever I had an idea or policy to accomplish a certain thing, he promptly added flesh to the framework I had presented and skillfully organized the ideas so they could be put into actual practice. The plans and ideas he formed and organized were far better than my own.[36]

Ōkuma also wrote:

> Ono Azusa was one of my best friends. He was younger than I, but from the academic point of view I learned not a little from him because he was a hard worker with distinguished intelligence and new knowledge of Europe and America.[37]

Despite Ōkuma's laudatory statements, Ono did not begin to work under Ōkuma's direction until February 1880. The relationship that developed between Ōkuma, a senior member of the ruling oligarchy, and the young cabinet secretary was of an informal nature, and the two did not become close until 1880 or later. Nevertheless, as seen by a letter sent to Ōkuma on December 17, 1878, Ono had already met Ōkuma several times and had begun to send his writings to him. Sufficient letters had been exchanged so that Ono could state: "I know you will understand what I wrote," and could ask for instructions on how to act "if there is something which I must know at once."[38]

The friendship that developed between Ōkuma and Ono was, despite the difference in years, the result of similarities in outlook. From his youth, Ōkuma had been basically iconoclastic and anti-feudal, willing to subordinate *han* loyalties to the national interest.[39] Unlike his more cautious contemporary and rival, Itō Hirobumi, Ōkuma had "a natural gift to take risks and render very distinguished services; but when he prepares [for these services], he sometimes has a tendency to make omissions. It is on this point that he is inferior to Itō. When it comes to carrying out unusual matters and rendering unusual services, there is no one like Marquis Ōkuma for boldness and ability. As he decisively carries out what he believes, he has the potential to perform great services and make great mistakes at the same time. Marquis Ōkuma is not a man of defensive [nature], but he is a man of great pioneering [spirit]."[40] His refusal to support the Saga rebellion of 1874 had led to estrangement from his clan, and he had risen to prominence in the bureaucracy because of his economic and diplomatic abilities. Ōkuma had entered the government in 1868 and at first had served as a technical expert on foreign and financial affairs. Under the sponsorship of Kido Takayoshi (Kōin) and Inoue Kaoru, he gradually emerged as a major figure in the oligarchy; and in October 1873 he was appointed Minister of Finance. Under his supervision the ministry prepared plans to commute samurai pensions into long-term interest-bearing bonds, for long-range industrial development, the first national budget, a system of national banks, financed the campaign to suppress the Satsuma rebellion by loans and currency inflation and suggested that an office be established to encourage industry and agriculture.[41] Ōkuma's financial measures were highly controversial, particularly his use of domestic and foreign loans to promote modernization and enable pension commutation. In 1879 the Ministry announced plans to redeem the current national debt by 1905 and to stabilize the currency by withdrawing from circulation the special notes issued to pay for the 1877 rebellion. These policies contributed to the development of a centralized and stable financial structure; and despite later criticism from his political opponents, the contemporary press believed that they would free the nation from debt and enable it to maintain complete financial independence.[42] Ōkuma also advocated the adoption of a legal code based on Western principles as an indispensable measure that would lead to the development of centralized authority and treaty revision.[43]

As Minister of Finance, Ōkuma's influence permeated every department of government. His power as well as his financial reforms, budget, and policies were regarded as inflationary and radical by some of the oligarchs and led to several attempts between 1871 and 1880 to dismiss him from the government. After the deaths of Saigō Takamori, Kido Takayoshi, and Ōkubo Toshimichi in 1877 and 1878, Ōkuma rose to the position of chief councilor in the Dajōkan, with Itō Hirobumi as his major rival. As early as 1869 Ōkuma had faced opposition from conservative members of the oligarchy and Satsuma supporters, who prevented his appointment as councilor without portfolio. After 1878 the division within the bureaucracy widened. Of the nine councilors, only Ōkuma and Ōki Takatō were from Hizen. Kuroda Kiyotaka, Saigō Tsugumichi (Jūdō), Terashima Munenori, and Kawamura Sumiyoshi were from Satsuma. Itō, Yamada Akiyoshi, and Yamagata were from Chōshū. Prime Minister Sanjō Sanetomi and the Ministers of the Left and Right, Arisugawa no Miya Taruhito and Iwakura Tomomi, supported the Satchō group.[44] Thus Ōkuma's position as the dominant figure in the Dajōkan, his non-Satchō origin, and his views were major factors that attracted Ono.

After the failure of the Saga and Satsuma rebellions, the opponents of the government, led by the former councilor Itagaki

Taisuke, accelerated their activities and agitation for a national assembly. The increased number of memorials and draft constitutions, including the Genrō-in draft entitled *Nihon kokken an (Draft Constitution of Japan)* led Iwakura to conclude that the throne had to take the leadership in drawing up a constitution. Therefore, in 1879 he petitioned the emperor to order the junior councilors to present their views on the constitution. Those ideas deemed suitable were to be used in compiling a constitution.[45] As a result, in December 1879 the members of the Dajōkan were invited to submit their opinions on the subject of the constitution to the throne.[46] That month, Ono presented the following letter to Ōkuma:

> It is the destiny of nature that those who govern according to the tendency of the times will succeed and those who govern against it will go to ruin. . . . The present trend toward self-government by the people is getting stronger and those who want to participate in the national administration are increasing day by day. I have doubts that the proper policy is being used to cope with this situation. Although it is said that we now have government by the people, public participation is only nominal. We can say that we have government by the Dajōkan. In truth, the ministers in each office do as they like. They govern selfishly without principle. Consequently, people have begun to scorn them saying: "The orders of the morning change in the evening." At the same time, people have begun to lose confidence in the government.

Ono then stated that there was nothing to prevent wrongdoing by public servants who betrayed the people and benefited only themselves while neglecting reform. The government's measures went against the trend of the times so that:

> Now, among the people, those who are overly enthusiastic about "freedom" are getting excited and radical. Some of them might want to obtain political power. If the trend continues . . . , in several years, the government will strengthen its views and the people will seek after freedom even more. Thus, the conflict between them will become furious, and it will at least bring about the misery of the Paris revolution to Japan. If this occurs, the people will kill civil servants; and, at the worst,

> they will harm the imperial family. . . . I conclude that the government should carry out the emperor's message and establish the national assembly. Although the structure of the government has been reformed, we can see that its order is wrong and its attitude toward the people is not proper. Thus, I propose that the government decide on 1881 as the year in which to open the Diet and make all arrangements for this within the next two years.

The present governmental organization was such that if the administration were to meet the Diet, it would be overthrown. Therefore:

> the government should reform the present political system, appoint five councilors and allow them to participate in domestic policy formation. It should unify all political power in the cabinet to restrain ministers who govern as they please. It also should unify the sources of cabinet orders to develop a unified ministry and self-government by the people. Although [by such reforms], it unites [the powers of] the cabinet ministers, some of them will not obey cabinet orders. Therefore, it should establish a bureau of administrative justice in the cabinet to supervise the ministers and appoint an official to subject the bureaucrary to direct ministerial control. It should also permit the people to appeal against the illegal actions of administrative officials. It should reduce false charges and keep official positions free from corruption.[47]

Ono expressed similar ideas in *Dare ka kokkai no kaisetsu wa shōsō nari to iu ya* (*Who Says It is Too Early to Establish the National Assembly?*) in the *Kyōzon zasshi* (no. 60) on March 3, 1880. Although it was written in the early summer of 1876, Ono explained that he "decided to publish it now because of the tendency of the times." In this essay Ono refuted the arguments that the Japanese were not yet able, ready, or desirous of representative government. Those who declared the people did not want self-government assumed they were ignorant. If the political level of the people was still immature, it was the responsibility of scholars and public-spirited men to develop it further. The prefectural assemblies had shown the willingness and ability of the public to perform its duties as an electorate without compulsion. To assume that the representative system was too heavy a responsibility for the people to bear was to assume that they were content with feudal servility. This argument also had been refuted by the prefectural legislatures. "It is one of the exigencies of the times to give voting rights to people and to enlighten them."[48]

Dare ka kokkai no kaisetsu wa shōsō nari to iu ya and a later work, *Kinsei jūgi* (*Ten Important Problems for Contemporary Government*), were written in response to Aikokusha and Satchō criticism of Ōkuma's financial policy of floating loans both in Japan and abroad to finance the Satsuma campaign and developmental projects. Both works contained suggestions for the readjustment of financial difficulties resulting from the overissuance of paper currency and foreign loans.[49] *Kinsei jūgi* was written between February 27 and March 17, 1881, and submitted to Ōkuma on March 18[50] with the following poem:

> Because I am again concerned for the country,
> I wrote this essay of ten chapters.
> Although there are many people in the cabinet,
> Only you will listen to my point of view.

The ten points elaborated upon were as follows:

1. The organization of the cabinet must be changed.
   Because the cabinet members represent different groups, they have different opinions on various matters and there is no one minister able to exercise control over the entire cabinet. Therefore, Japan should adopt the European system in which the prime minister selects his cabinet from among the members of his party and, thereby, controls the direction of the administration.
2. The direction of the administration must be decided upon.
   The cabinet is not unified and the ministers are self-centered; hence, the direction of administrative policy is uncertain.
3. The flotation of foreign loans must be decided upon.
   Fluctuations in the value of paper money make it necessary to issue government gold bonds and to reduce the budget. Since it has been difficult to float loans in Japan, it is necessary to issue bonds equal to one-third the value of paper money in circulation for sale abroad.
4. The burning of paper money should be stopped.

Merely burning the excess paper money in circulation will not cure inflation, which is due to untimely issuance and inconvertibility of currency.

5. Advantage must be taken of the weak points of foreign countries.

   Since public opinion in foreign countries influences government policy, in order to revise the treaties, the government must first arouse public opinion in Japan. This will be reflected in the public opinion of foreign countries, that is, their fear of public opinion can be used to advantage.

6. Enforcement of the two laws must be postponed.

   Due to the financial costs involved, the enforcement of the new criminal law and law of criminal procedure should be postponed. Without necessary preparations including the expenditure of over one-half million yen and the revision of many laws, these two new laws which were promulgated to hasten revision of the treaties will cause great inconveniences.

7. The date for compiling the fiscal year must be changed.

   As the major source of revenue is the land tax, the date for compiling the fiscal year should correspond to the date for payment of the land tax.

8. The situation of the gold reserve must be corrected.

   As that part of the treasury reserves used for the conversion of paper money has declined in value, bonds must be sold abroad to correct the situation.

9. The responsibilities of public officials must be clarified.

   Laws must be promulgated to establish the responsibilities of, supervise, and discipline officials.

10. The Colonization Commission must be abolished.

    Due to incompetence, expense, and inefficiency, the Commission should be abolished and Hokkaido divided into three or four separate prefectures.[51]

Ono discussed these ten points with Ōkuma on March 20 and, thereafter, wrote in his diary: "He [Ōkuma] agreed on my point that the government should establish [certain] policies. . . . What really worries me is the administration of policies and the future of Councilor Ōkuma."[52] This concern was reflected in a letter written two days later but not submitted to Ōkuma until June 13. *Sangi Ōkuma kō ni teishi shiji no hōkō o sairon suru no sho* (*A Letter to Councilor Marquis Ōkuma on the General Policies of Administration*) begins with an expression of thanks to Ōkuma who "gave me the feeling that I had been living in [a momentous] period and participating in national politics. He [Ōkuma] also showed me how urgent it was to settle the direction of administration and congratulated me on opinions with which the Councilor himself agreed. I feel greatly honored." It then criticizes the senior members of the administration who are concerned with self-enrichment and have allowed the "administration to lose direction and the discipline of the imperial court to become confused." The government has not settled the direction of its policies and does not follow the course set by the Charter Oath. It is afraid of public opinion and easily pressured to change its policies. To "maintain the original intention of the restoration of imperial rule, magnify it, and advance. . . , the leaders of the cabinet must administer a national policy in which they believe and should not be influenced by the tide of public opinion." After calling on the government to devote itself to the welfare of the imperial family and Japanese people, the essay points out the strong hold of clan feelings to the detriment of the nation:

> The government seems to be occupied by those from Satsuma or Chōshū, and it is only those from Kōchi prefecture who can proclaim popular rights. . . . A man can be chosen prime minister, even if not talented enough to engage in politics, just because he is from Satsuma or Chōshū or for the same reason be appointed minister or vice-minister.

In view of the objective of national unification:

> This is unbearable. This country belongs only to the Japanese people and is no longer the private property of the imperial family nor of the people of Tosa, Hizen, Satsuma, or Chōshū. The affairs of state are the affairs of the Japanese people and are not subject to the arbitrary [control] of the emperor or the old clans. However, the leaders of the Dajōkan still cherish the honors of the post and behave as if this country, under the reign of our emperor, belonged to only a few chosen clans. Considered either from the sentiment of those who serve the throne or from the ideas of those faithful to Japan, their arrogance and rudeness are unforgivable. Certainly, their arbitrary and selfish behavior in seizing oppor-

> tunities and their lack of discipline results in disorder among the people. I have long deplored this.
>
> This is why I have taken every opportunity to speak or write to the government and to the imperial court on the situation. I am delighted to know that my humble opinion has something in common with that of the Councilor. Today the representatives from Satsuma and Chōshū together monopolize the affairs of state and the imperial court. I know with what efforts and difficulties you deal with matters between [the oligarchs and court]. You alone are in the position between the court and government to handle national affairs. This is the reason why I am writing letters and speaking to you.

Following an account of his father's devotion to the throne and of his own loyalty, Ono concludes:

> The people are now angry at the arbitrary rule of Satsuma and Chōshū and want the councilors to correct it. If you deal with them according to the will of the public and take away their power, [the people's will] will not be hard to achieve. Whatever the Councilor does is for the sake of the country. The Councilor has appointed himself for this task, and I know he will devote himself to it.[53]

Opposition to the continuation of feudal clan feelings detrimental to national unity, as personified in the Satchō domination of the leading positions in the hierarchy, and to government policies drew Ono to Ōkuma. The Councilor's willingness to listen to Ono's views on the need to implement representative government, clarify national objectives, and to institute fiscal reforms further cemented the ties. The fact that Ono's brother-in-law and sponsor, Gishin, was serving under Ōkuma also strengthened their relationship. However, Ono's continual criticism and outspoken views irritated his superiors other than Ōkuma, and he was often in danger of losing his job. He soon concluded that the best way to conduct himself and to prove his "purity" was to resign; but through the intercession of Ōkuma and others who appreciated his ability, his resignation was not accepted. Ōkuma arranged for Ono to keep his position, and Ono was so impressed by this that he decided not to leave office but rather to work to repay the Councilor for his kindness.[54] In 1880 Ono was transferred to the Board of Audit, where he worked directly under the supervision of Ōkuma.[55] As his disenchantment with the government increased and as his ability to express criticism publicly was limited by the various laws and restrictions on public speeches and publications, Ono began to favor more direct political action and moved towards the Satchō faction's main opponent, Ōkuma Shigenobu. Although the relationship was not close until after Ono began to serve in the Board of Audit, Ōkuma was well aware of Ono's ability even before this time and had begun to listen to the younger official's ideas. "From 1881 on, Ono was to occupy an important place in Ōkuma's ideas and to act as his disciple . . . and to dedicate his political life to Ōkuma."[56] This dedication came from Ono's belief that Ōkuma was indeed the "Gladstone of the East," able to lead Japan into a new era of national unity and political reform.

ONO AZUSA: THE AUDITOR

As division within the oligarchy on the subject of a future constitution increased and as the number of petitions and memorials to the Genrō-in on the projected constitution and other problems rose in number, the government in February 1880 instituted a major administrative reform,[57] which ended the situation whereby department ministers served concurrently as junior councilors. The measure was in accordance with the views of Itō Hirobumi and was intended to curb the power of Ōkuma, who as Minister of Finance had a voice in the affairs of every department. As soon as Ōkuma and his followers left the administration in October 1881, the earlier department arrangement was reinstituted. Ōkuma opposed the reform and recommended his friend Sano Tsunetami as his replacement. However, he was succeeded by Matsukata Masayoshi, who in October began the sale of government properties to curb expenses. The new system vested legislative power in the councilors and gave department ministers purely executive functions. Six ministries were created within the Dajōkan under the jurisdiction of ten councilors, and Ōkuma was placed in charge of accounting, foreign affairs, and commerce. To defend his position against the increased power of the Satchō group, which had now invaded the Finance Department, Ōkuma had the Board of Audit established on March 5.[58] Ōkuma's proposal to establish the new board was based on one of Ono's suggestions:

> Ono used to tell me that the clan government, the military government of the time, was the very thing preventing the prosperity and advance of Japan. He insisted at that time that the only way to break down the arbitrary use of power by the government and to unite the disintegrating national structure was to establish constitutional government on the model of Western civilized nations. My opinion on this matter coincided exactly with his. He suggested that the first step toward such a goal was to establish a Board of Audit and to give it full power to check on and examine finances and accounts strictly. This would be the way to manage a political organization. He thought that by doing this, the arbitrary use of power could be restrained and the squandering of national expenditure could be prevented.

Ono also emphasized these views in a letter written to the president of the Board of Audit in which he pointed out the harmful effects resulting from the "egoism" of officials who did not care about national finances and who acted arbitrarily on fiscal matters.[59]

The Board of Audit, established in April 1881, was under the supervision of the Privy Council and replaced the earlier Audit Bureau. Its functions included the examination and supervision of all aspects of state finance and the issuance of yearly reports on the budget. It also was to supervise the system for control of state properties and was to submit to the Dajōkan reports and memoranda on fiscal matters and official offenses and errors relating to financial regulations.[60] The Board was under the jurisdiction of three councilors, Itō, Ōkuma, and Terashima.[61]

Ono's open criticism of the government and "cabinet suspicions of his association with the noted commoner, [Ōkuma]," placed his job in jeopardy. Ōkuma's support enabled him to remain in the bureaucracy, but in February 1880 the Hōsei kyoku was abolished. The following month, Ono was relieved of his position as secretary to the Dajōkan. On April 3 he was transferred to the Board of Audit as an auditor of the third grade, and he remained as an employee of the Ministry of Finance until his resignation in October 1881. In addition, he served Ōkuma as secretary in charge of the administrative section. Ono's abilities and work in these positions earned him, in his own words, "a good reputation," and he rapidly rose to auditor, second and then first class, by August 1881. In July he was appointed investigator of the Government-owned Properties Supervision Law, as temporary investigator of the Board of Audit, and as the chairman of the group studying accounting law. On September 9 he was awarded the Fifth Order of Merit. As auditor first class, Ono wrote in an undated document now at the National Diet Library in Tokyo, he was ordered to draft a bill to control government property; and once he learned of the sale of the government-owned properties in Hokkaido, he censured its error.[62]

Following the administrative reform of 1880 and the establishment of the Board of Audit, Fukuzawa's followers who had remained outside the *hanbatsu* clique now joined Ōkuma and strengthened his position.[63] Yano Fumio (Ryūkei, 1850–1931), a graduate of Fukuzawa's Keiō Gijuku who had served under Ōkuma in the Ministry of Finance, was appointed secretary both to the Bureau of Statistics and the Dajōkan. Ono and Yano, who were Ōkuma's supporters, now occupied key positions in those bureaus concerned with investigating government accounts and became increasingly close to the Councilor as the year progressed.[64]

Ono's studies on banking and finance in England now were put to use and, along with his former training and experience in the Hōsei kyoku, led to his concentration on budgetary investigations and studies and the drafting of accounting regulations. The most important aspect of his tenure at the Board of Audit was his investigation into the management of government property, which began on June 28, 1881. On July 1 he visited the commissioner who had investigated the management of government property, and on July 21 he was appointed a member of the temporary investigating committee. On August 5 Ono visited President Yamaguchi of the Board of Audit to discuss the Hokkaido Colonization Commission. On August 22, despite an illness that kept him from the office, Ono began to draft regulations for the control of government-owned property with the aid of two fellow auditors, Fukai Kurisato and Mizutani Kinsen, at his home. Ono continued to work on the regulations during August, and his conclusions and the regulations for the disposal of government-owned land were discussed at the Dajōkan on September 5 and 6. The following day Ono held an official farewell party for traveling auditors who were going to Hokkaido. Though seriously ill and bedridden during much of September and October, Ono continued to work at home on the problem of the disposal of the government properties in Hokkaido, using materials, statements of accounts, and budget reports provided by the Board. All the materials that he requested were sent by his co-workers to his home, and discussions on the matter were done primarily by letter. On September 12 Ono finished writing the draft law on government-owned property, and two days later he discussed both the rules and matters concerning the traveling inspectors who would look into the Colonization Commission with President Yamaguchi. Four days later Ono wrote to Yamaguchi to request a rough estimate of the commission's revenues and expenditures for 1881.[65]

On June 28, 1881, Ono was ordered to investigate the Government-owned Properties Supervision Law. These instructions were the result of discussions in the Dajōkan on the sale of government properties in Hokkaido to the Kansai Bōeki Shōkai (Kansai Trading Company). In an attempt to develop the resources of the northernmost island and to attract colonists, the government from 1869 to 1880 had invested a total of fourteen million yen in developmental projects. However, fiscal difficulties[66] and the retrenchment policy of the new Minister of Finance, Matsukata Masayoshi,[67] led to a decision to discontinue the government undertaking. Ōkuma concurred with this view. As a result, Yasuda Sadanori, chief secretary of the Colonization Commission, Godai Tomoatsu, a former Satsuma clansman and now a leading

Osaka merchant, Nakano Goichi, the former governor of Yamaguchi prefecture and a native of Chōshū, and others organized a company to purchase the state properties, valued at thirty million yen, for ¥387,082 with interest-free payments spread over a thirty-year period. Godai was senior to his fellow clansmen, Councilors Kuroda Kiyotaka and Saigō Tsugumichi, and Nakano was a friend of Itō Hirobumi, Inoue Kaoru, and Yamagata Aritomo. The company, furthermore, had bribed Yasuda Sadanori, the chief secretary of the Land Development Office, in regard to its application.[68] It petitioned Kuroda to support its plan to purchase all government properties and to take charge of the purchase of Hokkaido rice and salt and the transportation and sale of taxed articles on a commission basis. Despite the opposition of Ōkuma and his friend, Treasury Director Sano Tsunetami, the Dajōkan accepted the company's petition on July 21, 1881. The incident concerning the disposal of the government-owned property in Hokkaido was to become a major political issue involving Ōkuma.[69] Ono opposed the method of disposition and favored a fair and impartial public sale to prevent the Satchō oligarchs from taking advantage of the situation.[70] He also feared that if the sale was carried out, it would turn the people against the government and the imperial household. "As one of the officials who examine the methods of controlling government-owned finances, I can not hold my tongue on this occasion."[71] As the most informed person in the bureaucracy in regard to information on government properties and the proposed sale, Ono had no intention of remaining silent, and he became the key figure in arousing Satchō opponents to the issues involved. At this time he was in the crucial position in the bureacracy in regard to information on the project and sale.

Other auditors similarly expressed concern over the disposal of the Hokkaido properties. On September 21, Ono, who again was bedridden, received a letter from his co-worker Fukai stating that the auditors had discussed the question of remonstrating with the government on the issue. The next day Ono requested his fellow auditors to forward a copy of their decision to him. In response, two of the auditors visited him to discuss the problem, and one "showed a strong desire to change the unfair [method of] sale and disposal." Ono promised to draft a memorial on the topic and began to write it immediately. He continued to speak on the problem and to work on the draft with five other auditors. However, on the thirtieth, the auditor Yasukawa wrote him that the other members of the Bureau had lost their courage on the matter. The following day Ono was informed of the poor morale of the auditors, who were waiting to hear the decision of the Dajōkan before acting on their own initiative. Despite Ono's letters and encouragement, the auditors' fear was greater than their indignation and Ono's memorial was never presented to the Dajōkan. In anger and disgust he wrote *Moshi ware mizukara ataraba* (*If I Were to Take it Upon Myself*), which he sent to Ōkuma.[72]

The memorial, which was never signed nor submitted, is entitled *Naikaku daijin ni teishi, kaitakushi shozoku kan'yūbutsu haraisage tō shobun no hi o gisuru no sho* (*Memorial Presented to the Cabinet Ministers on the Unfair Sale of Government Property Belonging to the Colonization Commission*). It began with the following introduction:

> I [Ono] began to write this letter on September 22, 1881, and finished it the next day. On the same day, I called all the auditors to the house of the president of the Board of Audit to decide to send this. Though at first they decided to send it, they hesitated. I, Ono, often called on the president to urge him [to send it]; but at last while the auditors hesitated, the sale of the government property ceased to be an issue of debate.

The memorial then discussed the development and value of the Hokkaido Development Bureau factories, ships, and other establishments and the terms of the proposed sale:

> The property is really worth more than thirty million yen. In addition the firm will be given a monopoly on the shipment of all products from Hokkaido by the government. This will be done not through prescribed formalities but by special order of the Dajōkan.

Ono then discussed the composition of the Kansai Bōeki Shōkai and the fact that the director of the bureau, Kuroda Kiyotaka, "is a meritorious retainer of the state and the officials of the bureau are his men." However, the "property belonging to the bureau was built by the sweat and blood of the emperor's children." The abolition of the bureau and the end of official control "is only natural," but "the ministers are benevolent to particular officials and not to the rest of the thirty-five million people. This is obviously not the will of the emperor. . . ." Ono then compared the proposed monopoly as similar to that formerly held by the East India Company in India and as detrimental to the prosperity of the northern island. The method by which the Dajōkan agreed to the sale was a violation of its own instructions:

> According to instructions issued on August 2, 1875, in case of the sale of any government property, the officials of the bureau concerned are not permitted to participate in public bidding. In addition, according to the regulations on the sale of factories belonging to the Hokkaido Development Bureau issued in November of the same year, any limited partnership or any person who had sufficient funds for the purchase must publicize it, ascertain if there are other interested parties, and then petition the prime minister to state that he wants to buy the factories. After that, the prime minister must organize a special committee to discuss the problem. Only after the petition is approved by the committee shall the government permit the petitioner to pay the working capital. Therefore, the government should handle this matter according to these regulations. But we have not heard that they did so yet. Is the government breaking the regulations which it established? Even if there were reasons for the sale, we would still be against the government disposal [of the property], for the method is illegal.

The memorial then attacked Kuroda and called on the government to follow the law and "set him right." It declared: "The government should follow public opinion and handle him according to justice." It concluded:

> If the cabinet does not follow public opinion, it will lose the support of the people, and its dignity will be injured. If

the laws are violated, how can the ministers rule our country? Therefore, we earnestly desire that you now call forth the spirit of equality and faithfulness, help our sagacious emperor, stop debate on this matter, and follow public opinion with impartial and fair measures according to the regulations. We . . . happen to have the honor of being court officials and bear the responsibility of being auditors. How can we keep quiet? . . . we do this from the spirit of loyalty and patriotism.[73]

As a result of his experience at the Board of Audit, Ono decided to recommend himself as vice-minister of finance. His reasons were neither egotistical nor opportunistic, but, as he explained in his diary on September 3, 1881:

At this time financial matters are in difficulty. The life and death of the government depends on finance. If they can not be settled, the government will cease to exist. In no more than three years, we Japanese will not have any desire to serve the government. I want to tackle this difficult problem not for my own sake but for the sake of the country. I hope the emperor will appoint me as vice-minister of finance, but I do not know whether or not it is possible.

On September 9 Ono discussed with Gishin the advantages and disadvantages of recommending himself for the position, and between September 19 and 21 he wrote a letter of self-recommendation for the position. Whether the letter was sent is not known, for there is no further mention of it in his diary. Ono believed that he could solve the economic problems facing the country and, therefore, that it was his duty to recommend himself for the position.[74]

ONO AZUSA: RESIGNATION FROM OFFICE

The memorial on the sale of the Hokkaido properties represented the culmination of Ono's disillusionment with the government. The resignation of Ōkuma from the government on October 12, 1881, which will be described in detail later, led to Ono's retirement from official life. Once before, in May 1879, Ono had planned to resign from the government. Following the prohibition on public speeches by officials, an action he regarded as dictated by fear and designed to limit "our growing influence and power," he had stated that he would resign. However, at the request of Kōno Togama and Miyoshi Taizō in particular, he had agreed to remain in office.[75] Because he came to regard the government as the "terrible, detestable, and hateful *hanbatsu*" and to believe that to oppose it was the "loyal attitude of the entire nation of Japan," [76] he decided to resign in March 1881. However, once again his sponsors, Kōno, Ōkuma, and Hirose Shin'ichi, persuaded him to change his mind.[77] He agreed "to remain in government if only to attain my purpose, but I don't know if it is possible." Following the political change of October 12, Ono resolved to resign, and in his diary he made the following notation on October 13:

> Last night, imperial decrees were issued announcing the national assembly will be opened in 1890 and the resolution on the sale and disposal of the government-owned property [in Hokkaido] will be cancelled. The same day Junior Councilor Ōkuma was discharged from his position. At last the matter has come to a conclusion. I knew that it would affect me. I made up my mind to leave public office. On my way home, I called at Mr. Ōkuma's residence and told him of my firm resolve to give up my position. Ōkuma said to me: "It is not good for you to give up your position at once; instead, you should fight against injustice within the administration. Afterwards, it won't be too late [to resign]. Then it will be better for you to leave your position. . . ." I answered: "Yes, but at this time, if someone won't stand up, who will deal with this problem and fight against this injustice? We should not overlook this. I understand there is a lesson that as a *shishi* one's course of action must be decided upon with deliberation. But I won't change my mind. I am going to resign from my position." I returned home and explained my firm resolve to Tōsai [Gishin] who was as opposed to my resignation as Ōkuma. The truth [of the situation] as described by Tōsai was reasonable. He hopes I will reconsider my resignation. I thought of the Board of Audit and many things which yet remain incomplete. It will take several days to settle matters. Even if I resign voluntarily, I can not neglect unsettled business. During the next few days, I am going to consider my course of action. Ogawa [Tamejirō] came to my home and discussed the matter. He encouraged me to leave my position, and then he left.

Ono therefore continued as an auditor for several more days in order to complete his work on the regulations for government-owned property and for the disposal of reclaimed land. By October 20 he could write in his diary: "No matters remain incomplete." In the meantime he discussed his resignation with Miyoshi Taizō, Gishin, and other close friends and prepared his letter of resignation. In this he stated that he was giving up his position because the administration was run for private considerations. On October 20 he presented the letter to Prime Minister Sanjō Sanetomi and Minister of the Left Arisugawa no Miya. The next day he submitted letters of resignation to three other ministers and informed his fellow auditors of his action by mail. In response, he received a letter from the cabinet secretary urging him to tender his resignation, and he did so at once. After further discussions with Ogawa Tamejirō, Kōno Togama, and Gishin, he wrote that he regarded the cabinet order as fortunate.[78] His decision to resign appears to have been purely voluntary, and his diary shows no external pressure forcing the matter to a conclusion.[79] Since he was encouraged to remain in office by Ōkuma and others who were aware of the situation and since he continued to work at the Board of Audit for eight days after Ōkuma's dismissal, there appears to have been no immediate effort to force Ono out of the government before he submitted his letters of resignation.

While waiting for the notice of dismissal, Ono wrote poetry and philosophized on his brief career: "As long as one earns his bread without contributing to the country, he can not avoid being laughed at. Because I feel touched by the kindness of the sea and Heaven, I can not bear my feelings at leaving office in spite of being [only] a lowly servant." Gishin warned him: "The government doubts you, and you had better take care of yourself." Ono replied: "I am loyal to the throne and a patriot and have never been two-faced. Why does the government insult me [in this way]? From my point of view, it is impolite for the government to send a letter to urge me to resign. Furthermore, are they going to arrest me? If the government arrests me, it is the government that is to blame. I have my own views. I am not wrong, my brother, so please relax." Ono then wrote the following poem:

In my mind, there is only the emperor,
I want to devote my five *shaku* of body to the emperor.
If devoting myself to the emperor is advantageous to the country,
I would act as before.

He then prepared a letter to submit to the throne explaining the reasons for his resignation. Following the receipt of his dismissal notice from the government on October 26,[80] he informed his brother, Shigematsu, and mother in Sukumo of his resignation.[81] His own view of his dismissal was:

> by the political change of 1881, I was fired from my position by strict order of the Cabinet.[82]
>
> When Ōkuma left [the government], I proposed to the ministers the necessity of reorganization of the Cabinet. They did not accept my opinion and I was discharged.[83]

Because the first statement is from a political speech, the second explanation from Ono's private papers is a more correct estimate of the cause of his resignation.

Ono saw himself as a loyal subject of the emperor who

With my heart's desire to repay the country for its favor,
I submitted a good plan to the prime minister and urged him to adopt it without hesitation.
But more or less, civil servants will not listen to my ideas.[84]

Following the completion of his work, neither Ōkuma, whom he was shortly to join in political opposition to the government, nor Gishin, who was hereafter to be his sole means of financial support, opposed his retirement. Gishin had served under Ōkuma in the Finance Ministry and later entered business as an adviser to Iwasaki Yatarō. Because Ono had not other way of supporting his family and lived in a house located in his brother-in-law's garden,[85] Gishin's agreement was crucial in his decision to leave the bureaucracy.

Ono briefly envisioned a peaceful retirement whereby

> I'll happily retire from public life and return to the country to write.

In the country there are few who will visit me.
And I'll have much time during the day.
I'll read books I otherwise would not.

Following his dismissal, he received congratulations from many of his friends who approved of his action.[86] However, his retirement from the public eye and the political scene was to be only momentary. Having been denied by the government first the platform and voice of the Kyōzon dōshū and, second, the opportunity to influence state policy, Ono now joined Ōkuma and other opponents of the *hanbatsu* in the party movement. With the political change of 1881, the transition from the era of civilization and enlightenment to the era of popular rights had been completed.

NOTES

1. Ukai Nobushige, ed. *Kōza Nihon kindai hō hattatsu shi,* 14 vols. (Tokyo: Keisō Shobō, 1958–1962), 2: 179.

2. *Japan Weekly Mail* (Yokohama) 5, no. 2 (January 14, 1882): 46–48. Quoted from *Nichi nichi shimbun.*

3. Epp, "The Challenge," *MN, pp.* 15, 16, 25; Mukai Ken and Toshitani Nobuyoshi, "The Progress and Problems of Compiling the Civil Code in the Early Meiji Era," *Law in Japan* 1 (1967): 30–34.

4. Hoshino Tōru, *Meiji minpō hensan shi kenkyū* (Tokyo: Daiyamondosha, 1943), pp. 9–11.

5. Yamada, *Ono Azusa kun den,* 2: 21, 22. Nishimura states that Ono returned to Japan together with Baba Tatsui. This is incorrect, for Ono returned aboard the *Vancouver* of the China-Pacific Sailing Company and Baba returned in 1874 aboard the *Lyeee-Moon.*

6. There is confusion as to exactly when Ono began to work on *Rōma ritsuyō.* Nagata gives two dates, 1874 and 1876 (*Ono Azusa,* pp. 4, 66). Nishimura states that Ono began the work in 1876 (*Ono Azusa den,* p. 11). Yamada writes that Ono began to prepare a work on Roman law on March 22, 1874 (*Ono Azusa kun den,* 2: 21, 22).

Ono Azusa, unpublished, undated manuscript in the *Ono monjo,* Document No. 18, National Diet Library, Tokyo, n.p.; Nishimura, *Ono Azusa den,* p. 107.

7. Nagata, *Ono Azusa,* pp. 67–69; Nishimura, *Ono Azusa den,* pp. 11, 42; Yamada, *Ono Azusa kun den,* 1: 22.

8. *Kan'in meikan [Directory of Names of Officials].* Pamphlet dated June 1877 and kept in the Constitutional Documents Collection, National Diet Library, Tokyo, p. 15.

9. Nishimura, *Ono Azusa den,* pp. 107, 108.

10. Yamada, *Ono Azusa kun den,* 1: 22.

11. Nishimura, *Ono Azusa den,* p. 12; Ono, "Ryūkakusai nikki," pp. 318–29.

12. Ono, *OM,* no. 18.

13. Ono Azusa, "Gōjin haishi no enkaku," *Ono Azusa zenshū,* 2: 255–63.

14. Ono, "Ryūkakusai nikki," p. 351.

15. Nishimura, *Ono Azusa den,* p. 104; Ishii, *Japanese Legislation,* pp. 213–30.

16. Ono, "Ryūkakusai nikki," p. 332; Nishimura, *Ono Azusa den,* p. 12.

17. Ono Azusa, "Gian hihyō," *Ono Azusa zenshū,* 2: 169–208. According to the law, each rural division and city ward was given one head official; small rural divisions were grouped together under one official. Cf. Ishii, *Japanese Legislation,* p. 216.

18. Bentham, *Introduction,* pp. 126–27.

19. E. P. Dore, *Education in Tokugawa Japan* (London: Kegan Paul, 1965), pp. 260–64.

20. W. L. Davidson, *Political Thought in England* (London: Oxford University Press, 1957), pp. 55–59.

21. Ellwood P. Cubberly, "History of Education," *Encyclopaedia Britannica,* 24 vols. (Chicago: Encyclopaedia Britannica, Inc., 1955), 7:983.

22. Itō, "Fukuzawa Yukichi," *JHR,* p. 170; Kada Tetsuji, *Shisōka toshite no Fukuzawa Yukichi* (Tokyo: Keiō Tsūshin, 1958), p. 67.

23. Ōkuma Shigenobu, "A General View of Financial Policy During Thirteen Years," *JWM* 5, no. 13 (April 2, 1881): 367, 368.

24. Ono, "Rigaku nyūmon," pp. 147–151. Cf. Bentham, *Introduction,* pp. 125–31.

25. Ono, "Rigaku nyūmon," pp. 151–62. Ono is particularly critical of statements in the *Analects* where Confucius says he knew the will of Heaven [2:4], he was known by Heaven [14:37], and Heaven was within him [7:22] (de Bary, *Chinese Tradition,* pp. 23, 24. Waley, *Analects,* p. 127). The "Four Beginnings" of Mencius are subject to interpretation similar to that found in chaper 6, "Of Circumstances Influencing Sensibility," in Bentham, *Introduction,* pp. 164–66.

26. Enomoto, "Meiji shonen," *SC,* pp. 4–11. I am indebted to Father Aloysis Chang, S.J., Professor of Chinese at Sophia University, Tokyo, for his translation and explanation of the statement on Yü Hsung in *Rigaku nyūmon.*

27. Rōyama Masamichi, *Nihon ni okeru kindai seijigaku no hattatsu* (Tokyo: Jitsugyō no Nihonsha, 1949), pp. 50–53.

28. Ono Azusa, "Nani o ka kore seifu no honmu to iu," *Ono Azusa zenshū,* 2: 45–48.

29. Jeremy Bentham, *The Theory of Legislation* (London: Routledge and Kegan Paul Ltd., 1950), pp. 96–102. Takano Zen'ichi has shown that similar ideas used in *Kokken hanron* came from Jeremy Bentham's *Leading Principles of a Constitutional Code for any State.* However, *Nani o ka kore seifu no honmu to iu* is closer to the "Principles of the Civil Code" in ideas and wording, and Ono does not appear to have used the *Constitutional Code* for this essay. *Cf.* Takano Zen'ichi, "Bensamu to Ono Azusa," *Waseda Daigaku shi kiyō* 1, no. 2 (1966): 1–18.

30. Bentham, *Theory of Legislation,* pp. 98–101.

31. Bentham, *Fragment,* pp. 34–35.

32. Bentham, *Theory of Legislation,* pp. 109–11, 127–33.

33. Junesay Iddittie, *The Life of Marquis Shigenobu Ōkuma* (Tokyo: Hokuseidō Press, 1956), p. 147.

34. Robert A. Scalapino, *Democracy and the Party Movement in Prewar Japan* (Berkeley: University of California Press, 1962), pp. 44, 55.

35. Watanabe, *Monjo yori mitaru Ōkuma,* pp. 156, 445.

36. Nishimura, *Ono Azusa den,* p. 106.

37. Ōkuma Shigenobu, "Junkyōsha to shite no Ono Azusa kun," *Ono Azusa,* ed. Waseda Daigaku Bukkyō Seinen Kai (Tokyo: Fuzanbō, 1926), p. 121.

38. Ono Azusa, "Ōkuma Shigenobu ate shokan," *Ono Azusa zenshū,* 2: 101, 102.

39. Joyce Chapman Lebra, *Japan's First Modern Popular Statesman, A Study of the Political Career of Ōkuma Shigenobu* (1838–1922), Ph.D. dissertation, Radcliffe College, 1958, p. 17.

40. Oguri Mataichi, *Ryūkei Yano Fumio kun den* (Tokyo: Shunyōdō, 1936), p. 30.

41. Lebra, *Ōkuma Shigenobu,* pp. 51–55, 60–62, 258–61.

42. *Tokio Times,* 6, no. 5 (August 2, 1879): 57–59.

43. Kōsaka, *Japanese Thought,* p. 367.

44. Lebra, *Ōkuma Shigenobu,* pp. 55, 367; Itō Isao, "The Struggle for Power in the Meiji Oligarchy," *JHR* 6, no. 2 (1962): 55.

45. Pittau, *Political Thought,* pp. 77, 91.

46. Iddittie, *Shigenobu Ōkuma,* p. 202.

47. Ono Azusa, "Bō daijin ni teisuru no sho," in Nagata, *Ono Azusa,* pp. 101–4.

48. Ono Azusa, "Dare ka kokkai no kaisetsu wa shōsō nari to iu ya," *Ono Azusa zenshū,* 2: 61–63.

49. Enomoto, "Ono Azusa no seiji ronri," *NRR,* pp. 547–50.

50. Ono, "Ryūkakusai nikki," pp. 337–39.

51. Ono Azusa, "Kinsei jūgi," *Ono Azusa zenshū,* 2: 264–75.

52. Ono, "Ryūkakusai nikki," p. 339.

53. Ono Azusa, "Sangi Ōkuma kō ni teishi shiji no hōkō o sairon suru no sho," *Ono Azusa zenshū,* 2: 276–80.

54. Yamada, *Ono Azusa kun den,* 2: 7.

55. Watanabe, *Monjo yori mitaru Ōkuma,* p. 446.

56. Meiji Shiryō Kenkyū Renrakukai, ed. *Meiji seiken no kakuritsu katei* (Tokyo: Ochanomizu Shobō, 1957), p. 115.

57. Fujii, *Constitution,* p. 101.

58. Lebra, *Ōkuma Shigenobu,* pp. 57, 59, 63; Waseda Daigaku Toshokan, ed. *Shunjō hachijūnen no oboegaki* (Tokyo: Waseda Daigaku Toshokan, 1960), p. 702; *JWM,* 5, no. 18 (May 7, 1881), 511; *Ishii, Japanese Legislation,* pp. 131, 132; Shimomura Fujio, *Nihon zenshi* (Tokyo: Tokyo Daigaku Shuppan Kai, 1958–1968), 2: 76. Shimomura states that Ōkuma opposed the administrative reform while Lebra writes that Ōkuma did not oppose the change because he believed it would curb Satchō power. (Lebra, *Ōkuma Shigenobu,* p. 59). In view of the fact that the change was designed to curb Ōkuma's power by ending his control of the Ministry of Finance, it seems doubtful that he would have favored such a measure.

59. Nishimura, *Ono Azusa den,* pp. 84, 109.

60. *JWM,* 5, no. 18 (May 7, 1881): 511, 512.

61. Takemura, *Sukumo shi,* p. 9; Lebra, *Ōkuma Shigenobu,* p. 57; Ono Azusa, "Ryūkakusai nikki," p. 345.

62. Ono, *OM,* no. 18; Nishimura, *Ono Azusa den*, pp. 12, 13, 109, 111.

63. Shimomura, *Nihon zenshi,* 2: 76.

64. Itō Isao, "The Constitutional Reform Party and Ōkuma Shigenobu," *JHR* 7, nos. 1, 2 (October 1963): 17; Lebra, *Ōkuma Shigenobu,* p. 102; Nishimura, *Ono Azusa den,* p. 109.

65. Ono, "Ryūkakusai nikki," pp. 333, 334, 341, 343, 345–48, 350, 351, 359, 360–62, 367.

66. Nishimura, *Ono Azusa den,* p. 120.

67. Hugh Borton, *Japan's Modern Century* (New York: The Ronald Press, 1955), p. 119.

68. Itō, "Struggle for Power," *JHR,* pp. 51–53.

69. Nishimura, *Ono Azusa den,* pp. 120–22; Itō, "Struggle for Power," *JHR,* p. 50.

70. Ishizuki, "Meiji no jishikijin," *ZG,* p. 84.

71. Yamada, *Ono Azusa kun den,* 2: 10.

72. Ono, "Ryūkakusai nikki," pp. 362–66.

73. Ono Azusa, "Naikaku daijin ni teishi, kaitakushi shozuku kan'yūbutsu haraisage tō shobun no hi o gisuru no sho," *Ono Azusa zenshū,* 2: 70–73. Although the published work mentions three million yen, the government expenditure was over fourteen million yen. This appears to be a misprint and should read thirty million yen.

74. Ono, "Ryūkakusai nikki," pp. 359–62.

75. Ibid., pp. 326–27; Nishimura, *Ono Azusa den,* p. 75.

76. Ono, *OM,* no. 18.

77. Ono Azusa, "Hirose Shin'ichi ate shokan," *Ono Azusa zenshū,* 2: 104.

78. Ono, "Ryūkakusai nikki," pp. 366–67. Tōsai was Ono Gishin's pen name as a *haiku* poet.

79. Watanabe, *Monjo yori mitaru Ōkuma,* pp. 454, 455.

80. Ono, "Ryūkakusai nikki," pp. 367–68.

81. Ono Azusa, "Ono Shigematsu ate shokan," *Ono Azusa zenshū,* 2: 107, 108.

82. Ono Azusa, "Meiji kaidō enzetsu sōkō," *Ono Azusa zenshū,* 2: 305.

83. Ono, *OM,* no. 18.

84. Ono, "Ryūkakusai nikki," p. 369.

85. From information given in a letter to the author from Ono Gishin's son, Ono Jugorō; Takemura, *Sukumo shi,* p. 15.

86. Ono, "Ryūkakusai nikki," pp. 369, 370.

5
The Turning Point

Even before the issue of the disposal of the properties belonging to the Colonization Commission arose, the government found itself increasingly drawn into the debate over the promulgation of a constitution and the establishment of a national assembly. The idea of a legislative body and written fundamental law increasingly appealed to Japanese intellectuals and officials as a means of attaining national unity and strength and as the symbol of a modern nation-state. Before the fall of the shogunate, Nishi Amane had drawn up a draft constitution for Tokugawa Yoshinobu (Keiki),[1] which divided power among the court, *bakufu,* and *han.*[2] Shortly after the Restoration, in the spring of 1869, Ichiki Shirō, Akamatsu Noriyoshi, and others discussed enlarging the Shūgi-in, which was then the lower house of the Dajōkan, because it was "incomplete." Akamatsu looked up ideas on the form of national assemblies in Western books and, following the abolition of the clans and establishment of prefectures, the group concluded it was necessary for the people to participate in government. They expressed their ideas to Saigō Takamori, Kido Takayoshi, and Ōkubo Toshimichi; but their efforts ended in failure for the time was not yet ripe for such ideas.[3]

With the successful development of a centralized administration and with increased understanding of Western political institutions, public and official opinion began to diverge over the future organization of the government. In 1871 Miyajima Seiichirō, a junior official in the Sa-in (the legislative branch of the Dajōkan) memorialized the chamber on the need to establish a constitution to temper "absolute autocracy . . . with a set of laws for sovereign and subjects alike" and to "clarify the rights and duties of both the government and people." He recommended a unicameral assembly composed of officials and prefectural representatives but faced opposition from Etō Shimpei, the vice-president of the Sa-in. Etō, who three years later was to be one of the co-signers of the petition for a national assembly, insisted at the time that legal reform was the most urgent problem before the government. In 1872 the two deliberative organs of the Dajōkan took up the issue of the constitution. The Sa-in sent a memorial to the Sei-in on the need for a deliberative assembly with elected representatives in order to prevent popular unrest and implement the Charter Oath. The memorial was adopted by the Dajōkan, and the Sa-in was instructed to investigate the problem of representative government and to draft a set of rules to govern a house of representatives. By July 1872, eighteen months before Itagaki, Gotō, Etō, and Soejima Taneomi presented their memorial calling for a popularly elected assembly, drafts of an election law and regulations relating to assembly procedures were completed. Two members of the Sa-in and Miyajima were appointed to inquire into the constitutions of leading countries of the world.[4]

During the Iwakura mission, both Ōkubo Toshimichi and Kido Takayoshi, senior members of the oligarchy, concluded it was necessary to institute a fundamental law to clarify the rights and duties of the state and people. Ōkubo ordered Itō Hirobumi to translate into Japanese the Fundamental Law of the German Empire and drafted a trial reorganization of the Dajōkan based on the principles of constitutional monarchy. Kido, on his return, memorialized the government on the need to check the arbitrary attitude of the ruling class and also wrote a sample constitution. As a result, Itō, Terajima Munenori, and two members of the Sa-in were appointed to draft a constitution taking into account the opinions of Ōkubo and Kido. Following the split within the bureaucracy over the issue of policy toward Korea, the dissident former councilors presented a memorial to the Sa-in on January 17, 1874. This called for the speedy establishment of a national assembly to remedy arbitrary rule, solidify the foundation of the state, and create a body to seek fair and impartial public opinion through freedom of speech. The memorial aroused public opinion and inaugurated a heated debate in the press on the issues of a constitution, popular rights, and a national assembly. It forced the government to seriously consider the problem of drafting a constitution. As opponents of the oligarchs organized the Aikokukōtō and Risshisha, the government moved toward more uniform administration and convened a trial conference of prefectural governors in 1873. Itagaki had resigned from the government in 1873 in protest against the cancellation of the Korean campaign, and Kido had resigned in 1874 in opposition to the Taiwan expedition. In an attempt to persuade them to rejoin the administration, a meeting was held at Osaka in 1875. Following the proposal of the two dissident ministers, the Genrō-in was established as the legislative body and the judiciary was given more independence. The Osaka conference neither ended "arbitrary rule" nor reestablished the former unity of the oligarchy. Itagaki and Kido soon resigned, and Itagaki returned to the leadership of the movement for popular rights and representative government.

In 1876 Prince Arisugawa received permission from the emperor to begin drafting a constitution based on "national polity, and taking into account the constitutions of leading countries of the world." He was given a copy of Todd's *Parliamentary Government in England* to assist him in his work. Four secretaries of the Genrō-in were appointed as the Constitutional Investigation Bureau. The resulting work, the *Nippon kokken-an,* was completed in May 1878 and provided for a division of power between a "sacred and inviolable" emperor who held administrative power and the deliberative assembly, which consisted of an appointed Genrō-in or legislative body and an elected lower house. The rights and duties of the people were described in some detail and were to be determined by law. Iwakura strongly opposed the draft, and Sanjō felt it inadvisable to present it to the throne and ordered the Genrō-in to continue its studies. Itō also criticized the work as a mere adoption of foreign constitutions unsuited to Japan. The government, prodded by both its followers and opponents, had by now moved into the controversy over the national assembly and constitution, and its actions, as well as the activities of the advocates of popular rights, stimulated the writing and publication of numerous sample constitutions.[5]

The Meiji leadership recognized the need for a constitution and led in the movement to study the question of the type of document best suited to Japan. Although the oligarchs themselves favored having a written fundamental law, they were divided over the nature of the future Japanese state and the organization of the power structure; this division soon came to be related to factionalism within the ruling hierarchy. Factionalism, which had originally been based on sectional interest and policy differences, now became identified with the popular rights movement. The change in the relationship among the leading oligarchs were initiated by a memorial presented by Iwakura to the throne in 1879. This requested that the junior councilors be asked to state their views on the constitution. With the exception of Ōki Takatō, the most conservative of the councilors, and Kuroda Kiyotaka, all the junior councilors advocated the establishment of a national assembly and the promulgation of a constitution. They maintained that the emperor should continue to be the repository of power. However, there were differences of opinion over the date when the assembly should be convened, over its composition, and on the structure of the administration.[6]

Until 1882 those leaders of public opinion who were not in the upper levels of the bureaucracy thought that the normal form of constitutional politics was that of England. They stated that the British system of party cabinets should be adopted in a constitutional state. They did not pay much attention to the American presidential system and ignored the German system. For example, Fukuchi Gen'ichirō of the pro-government *Nichi nichi shimbun* insisted that it was "natural" to adopt the English cabinet system. However, under the influence of Hermann Roessler, bureaucrats such as Inoue Kowashi came to believe that the Prussian system was best suited to Japan because it did not permit the legislature to control the executive.[7] According to the *Nichi nichi shimbun,* public interest in a parliament had been so aroused that thirty of the ninety-eight petitions presented to the Genrō-in between January and June 1880 were on the subject of the national assembly. Twenty-three of these were forwarded to the cabinet for consideration.[8]

Those concerned with the question of popular rights and representative government constituted a minute portion of the population in 1880. The liberal *Chōya shimbun,* while editorializing that "it is incontrovertible that every nation should have a National Assembly, and that the people should participate in the settlement of the affairs of their country," lamented that "the general body of the people maintain the most profound apathy in the matter."[9] Such apathy enabled the government to pay "no attention to the representations of the agitators." Yet, the debate that was progressing in the bureaucracy and among the intelligentsia had reached such proportions by late January 1880 that the *Akebono shimbun* warned:

> Will the Government, confident in their power, refuse the wish of the people for a National Assembly? Nothing can be said against the reasonableness of the demand, and if the Government oppose the scheme, we cannot say if the force of public opinion may not prove like a mighty river in flood, sweeping away all obstacles in its course and carrying destruction even [to] the adjacent land.[10]

In February, the *Chōya shimbun* noted that:

> It is necessary to curb the authorities with an iron bit, in order to prevent them from following a course of action which results in such a disaster as the sacrifice of a whole people for the advancement of a few powerful individuals. Therefore it

is of the utmost importance for every country to possess a constitution.

There are three things which constitute the backbone of a constitutional government and the very pulse of freedom. These are, 1st, that no monarch can levy taxes without the consent of the national assembly; 2ndly, all laws must be consented to by the assembly before they can be enforced; and 3rdly, no person can be arrested or imprisoned unless a warrant be first issued specifying his name and alleged offence. Every constitution contains many important laws, but the three we have mentioned are the most important of all, and if these three be once firmly secured, the freedom of the people is an assured fact, although the subordinate legislation may not be perfect.

. . . modern English history is the only history which affords us examples of how the monarchs attempted to transgress these three laws, and yet the people maintained their rights inviolate.

A demand for a national assembly has now grown up in Japan as strong as a fierce conflagration. The reason of this is that the people of the country are now alive to the fact that they cannot secure their freedom and welfare unless by the establishment of constitutional government. How this should be effected is a matter upon which we have many ideas, but as regards a constitution we would place no dependence in any measure of the kind, which did not contain the three great fundamental laws we have mentioned, as a protection to the people against the actions of unworthy rulers.[11]

Similar ideas were contained in a memorial presented to the Dajō-daijin (Prime Minister) Sanjō by the Miyagi prefectural assembly. As reported in *Mainichi shimbun,* it stated:

We respectfully submit that, until legislative powers are lodged in the hands of the people through their representatives, the judicature cannot be placed on a thoroughly satisfactory footing; and if this be the case with the judicature with how much more force does it apply to the executive? When the people are properly represented in the government, and the judicature and executive are in a satisfactory condition, then the wealth and prosperity of a nation increases. Every nation in Europe enjoys the advantages which are termed "constitutional government."

Furthermore, since the emperor had issued an edict that "constitutional government shall be gradually introduced" and as the people have organized "societies and leagues . . . in order to secure the boom," who, therefore, can say "the people are indifferent, or that they cannot be entrusted with participation in legislative functions? . . . if those members of political societies who are desirous for a national assembly should find their hopes frustrated, it is to be feared that they will rise in insurrection and refuse to be pacified."[12] In June *Akebono* attacked Satchō domination of the government:

> We cannot say that to allow the Satsuma and the Choshiu [*sic*] men alone to have the exercise of political rights without submitting it to the people is "in accordance with the general principles" spoken of. If the Emperor wishes to please the people, he has to yield to their will and not to oppose it. Now, our compatriots all desire to have a constitution granted, and a National Assembly established, so that they themselves may have a share in legislation; therefore, if the Emperor desires to please them, he will comply with their wish and take measures for the production of the required end. However, though they have forwarded memorials and petitions one after another to the government, the authorities have taken no notice of them. . . . if any one says that the Satsuma and the Choshiu [*sic*] men heartily yearn for the pleasures of power, and are careless about acting contrary to the will of the Emperor, we cannot combat his opinion.[13]

Participants in the movement for representative government believed that the constitution should be the law of the people and therefore that the draft should be discussed by government and the people. Therefore the most urgent problem was to establish the national assembly in order to begin deliberations on the constitution. The Diet had to precede the constitution, and political activists believed that they should tell the oligarchs how the legislature should be organized and when it should be convened. The logical conclusion of the idea of a constitution for all the people was a constituent assembly, and by the winter of 1880–81, it was recognized that the constitution would of necessity determine the ultimate composition of the legislature. The Risshisha and various other political societies were primarily concerned with getting the Diet established and had not yet clarified their ideas on the fundamental law. The *Tōyō Dai Nihonkoku kokken an,* written by Ueki Emori of the Risshisha, defined only the structure of the assembly, which was seen as a representative though not republican body. It represented the "progressive national assembly consciousness," which constituted the mainstream of the popular rights movement. Osatake Takeki questioned whether political organizations drafting private constitutions fully understood both the basic principles of constitutionalism and the consequences that would be the result of drafts such as they produced. While their influence on the general public was insignificant,[14] the government reacted strongly to the pressure they exerted.

In September 1880 the scholar-bureaucrat Nishi Amane declared that the "clamor" for a national assembly and the extension of popular rights was premature and that the Japanese were not yet ready "from an intellectual point of view" to offer men capable of the responsibilities of representation.[15] Inoue Kowashi also spoke for the government. In an essay written under Iwakura's name, he criticized the Kōjunsha draft constitution and branded the *Tōyō dai Nihonkoku kokken an* as a "radical" work. Official malaise over the popular rights movement[16] forced the oligarchs to attempt to reach some agreement on the constitution and the procedure by which it should be realized.

ŌKUMA'S MEMORIAL ON CONSTITUTIONAL GOVERNMENT

In December 1880, when Itō submitted his memorial on the constitution to the throne, he and Inoue Kaoru asked Fukuzawa Yukichi to publish a newspaper that would influence the public in favor of the establishment of a constitution. Inoue persuaded Fukuzawa that they had resolved to convene the Diet soon and to realize constitutional government but faced opposition from obstinate Satsuma councilors. He stated that when the majority of the members approve of government policy, the government could promote its policy, but when a majority opposed its policy, the government should resign and transfer power to the majority party. Ōkuma and Itō agreed with Inoue's ideas, and Fukuzawa asked Minoura Katsundo to come to Tokyo to establish a newspaper to stimulate public opinion, since Ōkuma and Itō were unable to carry out a progressive policy due to the powerful military party in the cabinet.

In order to formulate their policy on the constitution, Itō, Ōkuma, and Inoue met at Atami in January 1881. Ōkuma, accompanied by his wife and Yano Fumio, met daily with the other councilors. Although the three councilors reached a consensus on the necessity to establish a national assembly, Itō declared the Genrō-in had to be reformed before the assembly could be convened. In contrast, Inoue favored opening the Diet in three years, and Ōkuma suggested that the assembly be inaugurated before autumn.[17] No agreement was reached on the opening date or the structure of the Diet, but Ōkuma agreed not to submit a radical opinion on the constitution to the emperor without notifying Itō.[18] Both Ōkuma and Inoue later informed Fukuzawa of their views.[19]

With the exception of Terajima Munenori and Saigō Tsugumichi, who stated they had no opinions on the constitution, Ōkuma was the only councilor who did not submit his opinion on the matter as requested. As a result, the emperor urged Arisugawa to make Ōkuma present his views. Ōkuma stated that his thoughts were difficult to convey accurately in writing and he was afraid that they would be leaked to the public. The emperor therefore ordered Arisugawa to write down Ōkuma's ideas correctly, and in March Ōkuma submitted a letter containing his opinion with the requirement that Arisugawa not show it to anyone.[20] The main points of Ōkuma's 1881 memorial were as follows:

1. "The date for the establishment of a parliament should be promulgated."
2. High officials should be appointed on the basis of popular support according to "the will of the people." Thus, the leader of the majority party in parliament should place members of his party in important positions and have the power to control the administration. This will eliminate

friction between the executive and legislature and result in governmental unity. When a party loses power in parliament or has lost a vote of confidence, the emperor should "consider the will of the people and appoint to paramount positions persons from the party that has attained new strength." If the "party in power refuses to resign. . . , the emperor will dismiss it"; or the party may dissolve parliament and call for a new election. This is based on the model of England. In addition, three non-party chief ministers will serve as advisers to the emperor.

3. Distinction should be made between political party officials and permanent officials. The former should resign with the party and the latter should hold life tenure and have no official ties. Officials below the level of vice-minister should be neutral, permanent officials.
4. With imperial approval, a constitution, which states clearly where power is vested and the rights of the people, should be established.
5. Representatives should be elected by the end of 1882 and parliament convened at the beginning of 1883.
6. The principles of administration should be decided upon in order to win the support of the people. "Party struggles are struggles between principles of administration."
7. "Constitutional government is party government, and the struggles between parties are the struggles of principles. When its principles are supported by more than half of the people, a party wins control of the government. When the opposite is true, it loses control." [21]

Ōkuma's memorial, therefore, reiterated the view expressed at the Atami Conference that parliament should be established at an early date. In addition, it contained an outline for the establishment of parliamentary government under the leadership of an elected executive modeled on the British cabinet system. It stated that parliamentary and party government were synonymous, and only under such a system as found in Great Britain could the legislature and administration function efficiently together.

The memorial created a furor not only within the ruling hierarchy but also among later scholars of Japanese history in regard to its authorship and source. Ōkuma stated that both Yano Fumio and Ono Azusa wrote the 1881 memorial and that he gave it to Arisugawa with a draft constitution.[22] Kaneko

Kentarō and Inada Masatsugu believe that the memorial was written by Yano alone, using Todd's *Parliamentary Government in England* for reference.[23] Enomoto Morie, who has written several articles on Ono, is of the same opinion.[24] Yano, who had studied at Fukuzawa's Keiō Gijuku and was an employee of the Bureau of Statistics in 1881, wrote:

> At that time, I was studying law and believed I was a first rate scholar on the investigation of the parliamentary system. Therefore, I wrote many opinions about it. This [opinion of Ōkuma's] is one of these writings, but he said nothing about it [s presentation] to me. It is said that Ōkuma reported secretly to the emperor, and attracted people's attention. I think he had no intention of reporting secretly to the emperor. He thought that it was important to have Prime Minister Sanjō, Minister of the Right Iwakura, and Minister of the Left Arisugawa no miya make up their minds in order to carry out [the emperor's request]. Thus, as I remember the incident, this was his intention when he asked me to write this work. I strongly insisted on the point making the prime minister, the minister of the left, and the minister of the right holders of permanent office and putting them outside of the party conflict. Ōkuma agreed to this. Thus, I wrote the chapter on the classification of permanent and party officials.[25]

In 1880 Yano had twice appealed to the cabinet on the need to establish constitutional government. He believed it essential to have several ministers who stood above the cabinet and beyond politics control the police, local officials, and judiciary. In this way, these areas of government would be free from political conflict and interference at the time of election. The exact number of ministers was not so important as the ability of the men themselves, because they were to assure support for the imperial household. Yano insisted on placing similar ideas in the draft constitution produced by the *Yūbin hōchi shimbun* the following April, and he hoped that this would reassure Sanjō, Arisugawa, and Iwakura and gain their support for the establishment of constitutional government.[26] Ono's exact role in the drafting of the memorial is not documented. Watanabe Ikujirō, Ōkuma's biographer, writes: "Ono came to participate in the project after the Marquis presented the petition." He concludes that, because the memorial is not specifically mentioned in Ono's diary, *Ryūkakusai nikki,* which covers the period January 1, 1879, to October 8, 1885, Ono did not participate in writing the memorial and came to know of it at a later date.[27] Enomoto is not certain whether or not Ono had anything to do with the document.[28]

In contrast, Osatake Takeki and Nishimura Shinji have written that Ono was directly involved in writing the 1881 memorial. Osatake has stated that Ono may have made several revisions of the work,[29] while Nishimura has pointed out similarities between *Kinsei jūgi* and the memorial.[30] This view is also given in *Meiji seiken no kakuritsu katei* (*Process of Establishing the Political Power of Meiji*).[31]

Among the sources for Ōkuma's 1881 memorial, the second point—the formation and dissolution of party cabinets—is from Todd's *Parliamentary Government in England,* volume 2, pages 116 to 130. The section on the separation of the permanent and party officials is from volume 1, page 166.[32] However, the second point of the memorial also has close similarities to *Kinsei jūgi,* which Ono presented to Ōkuma on March 18, 1881. Ono stated in his first point that the organization of the cabinet had to be changed to allow the prime minister to select ministers from the same party. As in Europe, this system would enable the prime minister to unify and control the policies of the administration.[33] The same ideas were also advocated in 1881 in *Shigi kempō iken,* which described a system of ministerial responsibility to parliament whereby the cabinet would resign following a loss of confidence.[34] *Shigi kempō iken* was also based upon Todd's work, and both Yano and Ono used *Parliamentary Government in England* to formulate their ideas on responsible ministerial government. Furthermore, because the ideas expressed in the first point in *Kinsei jūgi* are quite similar to those in the second point of the 1881 memorial, it may be concluded that Ono's work influenced Ōkuma's ideas on the cabinet system.

The fifth point of Ōkuma's memorial was that representatives should be elected by the end of 1882 and parliament convoked at the beginning of 1883. In December 1879 Ono wrote to Ōkuma on the need to reform the governmental structure and to unify political power and the right to issue administrative orders in the cabinet. He proposed that the government convene the Diet in 1881 after a two-year preparatory period.[35] At the Atami conference, Ōkuma had called for the opening of parliament in the autumn of 1881.[36] In the fifth point of his memorial, Ōkuma called for the inauguration of parliament within a two-year period. Ono's influence can be seen in this aspect of Ōkuma's memorial. The sixth point of the memorial stated that the principles of administration should be decided upon by the cabinet. The second point of *Kinsei jūgi* states: "The direction of the administration must be decided upon . . . it must follow a single course and eliminate self-contradiction.[37] Ōkuma's document stated that the principles of administration should be decided upon, and that when the principles of a party are supported by the majority of the people, the party should win control of the government. Therefore, both *Kinsei jūgi* and *Bō daijin ni teisuru no sho* served as reference works for Ōkuma. The ideas contained in these letters were united with concepts, particularly that of rule by the majority party in parliament, which would be responsible to the assembly, taken from *Parliamentary Government in England.* Thus, when Ōkuma said that Yano and Ono wrote the 1881 memorial to the throne, he did not mean that Ono directly participated in writing the work; he was, instead, referring to Ono's two essays, which were a primary source for his ideas.[38]

In his diary Ono stated that during January and early February 1881 he wrote *Kokken ronkō* (*Study of the National Constitution*), and that from January 31 until early May he wrote *Genkō kokken shisan* (*A Contemporary Private View on the Constitution*).[39] Both works were written in response to the interest generated by the question of the contents and timing of the constitution and parliament. *Shisan,* as it is called in the diary, began by criticizing the concentration of power in the Dajōkan and the resulting breakdown of the separation of ministerial powers and weakening of the judiciary. It then attacked the method of appointing officials without examination or fixed terms of office. Official responsibility was vague and discipline lax, since the power to punish infractions of the rules lay with the chief of each ministry. Senior officials had no legal responsibility, and only the emperor was responsible to the nation. In discussing the Dajōkan, *Shisan* stated that it was more important in Japan than similar institutions in Europe. The emperor and Dajōkan together were the primary source of policy and decision-making. The Dajōkan held executive, legislative, and judicial power. In Europe, however, the prime minister organized the cabinet with members of his party so that it would follow a unified policy. In Japan neither the senior nor junior councilors followed the same policy. The cabinet was a "secret organization," and only the senior and junior councilors and departmental secretaries were permitted to attend meetings. Following a description of the work of the various departments, Ono concluded by stating that, since the Diet was not yet established, it was an appropriate compromise to have the Dajōkan settle disputes between the prefectural assemblies and governors.[40]

Genkō kokken shisan incorporated many of Ono's previous ideas, including his criticism of "government by the Dajōkan," his call for the establishment of a cabinet responsible to the Diet, the unification of the administration by promoting one set of policy and principles through a party cabinet, clarification of official responsibilities, and the establishment of laws to supervise and discipline officials. These points had been included in his 1879 letter to Ōkuma and in *Kinsei jūgi*. Ono worked on *Shisan* almost daily in February and March 1881. On March 18 he visited Ōkuma to present *Kinsei jūgi*, and two days later he again called on Ōkuma. In his diary Ono wrote: "We wholeheartedly discussed the present political situation. He [Ōkuma] agreed with my point that the government should decide upon its policy."[41] In his writings, specifically *Bō daijin ni teisuru no sho* and *Kinsei jūgi*, and these two meetings, Ono stated his position on responsible ministerial government, early establishment of a parliament, and the need to determine administrative policy, and thereby influenced the 1881 memorial by impressing his views on Ōkuma. That he did not directly participate in drafting the memorial can be seen from his diary, for there is no mention of it whatsoever. *Ryūkakusai nikki* is a daily record of what Ono did, wrote, and with whom he spoke and mentions

Yano's name only twice by 1882: on May 13, 1879, and February 17, 1882.[42] Although Yano had not yet been abroad, he had become familiar with the operation of parliamentary politics through his studies at Keiō Gijuku and his participation in the Kōjunsha. He favored the establishment of a constitutional system within two or three years.[43] His views, therefore, were similar to Ono's on these points, and both took as their model the British system of parliamentary government. Yano's use of Todd's description of the English party cabinet and Ono's ideas, though stated in less detail to Ōkuma, were easily united without conflict or contradiction.

Up to 1881 Ōkuma had never advocated government by political parties. His memorial showed that he regarded imperial decrees as absolute and the emperor as the center of his political thought. On the fundamental issues of imperial power and sovereignty, his views were the same as his fellow councilors.[44] According to Yano, the ideas expressed were known in advance, since Ōkuma had always stated his opinions to the cabinet members and had discussed his ideas at the Atami conference.[45] However, before submitting the memorial, Ōkuma had failed to confer with Itō and Inoue. This was his fatal error;[46] for although Arisugawa had been asked to keep the memorial secret before submitting it to the throne, the prime minister informed Sanjō and Iwakura of its contents. Since it differed from the opinions of the other councilors in regard to time and composition of the cabinet, they regarded it as too radical and informed Itō Hirobumi of the contents. Professor Itō Isao of Sophia University, who has written numerous articles on Meiji and Taishō political history, believes that Iwakura told Itō about the memorial in order to have Ōkuma lose his position in the cabinet. After reading the report, Itō became furious with Ōkuma for violating the promise made at Atami not to present his views suddenly and secretly. On July 2 he wrote to Iwakura stating that Ōkuma's memorial was too radical and his own views were different. After studying the history of European reform, he concluded that Japan could not obtain beneficial results from a system such as Ōkuma described. Since the views of the two were incompatible, he could not serve with Ōkuma and could not help but resign. Ōkuma apologized to Itō, but neither Sanjō nor Iwakura were able to bring about a reconciliation.[47] Councilor Sasaki Takayuki denounced the memorial because the selection of government officials, including both ministers and those serving the emperor, by popular election was the same as the idea of giving sovereign rights to the public en masse. The other councilors also joined in the attack on Ōkuma's proposal.

The memorial provided a long-awaited opportunity for the Satchō group in the bureaucracy to isolate Ōkuma and undermine his position. Ōkuma's views were not unknown to his colleagues, and after the meeting at Atami, they knew he favored promulgating the constitution in 1882 and opening the Diet in 1883. Therefore, the contents of the memorial were not surprising to Itō, who had heard these ideas several months before. Ōkuma himself states that there was no conflict between him and Itō over the date for the opening of the national assembly and that at first Sanjō and Iwakura approved of his opinion. He believes that they might have been persuaded to change their minds by Itō and Inoue. Underlying Itō's anger at Ōkuma's broken promise and the other councilors' objections to his "radical views" was a power struggle among opposing factions in the ruling hierarchy. Following the death of Ōkubo and Kido, Ōkuma had been the head of the cabinet from 1878 to 1881. Itō, Inoue, and the other councilors from Satsuma and Chōshū feared that their power and control of the government were in decline even though they dominated the military.[48] This was their reason for the administrative reform of 1880 that ended Ōkuma's exclusive hold on the Ministry of Finance and for their outcry against his memorial. In order to get Ōkuma out of Tokyo, it was arranged for him to accompany the emperor on his tour of the Northeast, which began on July 29[49] and was to last until October 11.[50] During these three months, the incident involving the sale of government-owned properties in Hokkaido and the Kuriles occurred, thereby completing Ōkuma's isolation and accelerating the movement for popular rights and a national assembly.

THE COLONIZATION COMMISSION INCIDENT

The government's decision to dispose of the properties owned by the Colonization Commission in Hokkaido and the Kuriles to the Kansai Bōeki Shōkai stimulated those calling for a national assembly to increase their attack on the government. The method and terms of the sale demonstrated the dangers of oligarchic rule and thereby accelerated pressure on the administration to announce the opening of parliament. The Colonization Commission had been established in 1869, enlarged in 1871, and given a ten-year mandate to develop the northern islands. Under the leadership of General Kuroda Kiyotaka, who was also a member of the Privy Council, it had been granted a yearly expenditure of one million yen from the national treasury and the special privilege to carry over any surplus from the year's account to the ensuing year. In addition, it was allowed to issue paper money, which was to be used for the development of Hokkaido for a period of ten years. In June and July 1881, as the commission's term came to an end, rumors began to appear in the press of impending reforms and of a possible division of the island into two or three prefectures, which were to be governed similarly to those already established.[51]

On July 21 the chief secretary of the commission, Yasuda Sadanori, and three assistant secretaries petitioned Kuroda to permit them to resign and to establish a private company to take charge of the separate industries and properties of the commission. In addition, the company would act as the agent of the government in the transportation and sale of the merchandise collected as taxes in kind for ten years for a commission of six percent on sales. It would purchase the properties owned by the commission and valued at over ¥14 million for the sum of ¥387,000 in thirty annual, interest-free payments, which would be converted into a loan to be repaid over a fifteen-year period at three percent interest. The secretaries then joined with two Osaka merchants, Godai Tomoatsu and Nakano Goichi, to establish the Kansai Bōeki Shōkai and petitioned Kuroda to accept their proposal. Kuroda then informed the government that, because profits could not be envisioned in the near future due to the size of the commission's undertaking and because similar sales had resulted in the breaking-up of the enterprises for speculative profits, no private company could be found to carry out the projects in their entirety. Those best able to do so were those officials who had endured exile in the North and worked zealously to develop the enterprises for the past ten years. There was no need to fear that they would abandon plans to develop the area. However, as they lacked sufficient working capital, a state loan was required. On August 1 the Dajōkan announced that the petition was accepted, with the exception of the provision on collecting taxes in kind. Once Hokkaido was reorganized into prefectures, taxes would be collected as in other areas.[52]

Both within and without the government, there was unfavorable reaction to the sale. Several Kagoshima *shizoku* denounced their fellow clansman Kuroda for the arbitrary sale of "the common property of our countrymen" to a private company irrespective of regulations. They complained that he had the prime minister follow the emperor north on his trip to seek approval and declared Kuroda to be "partial and unjust." They compared the privileges given to the company as similar to the monopoly exercised by the British East India Company.[53] On September 7 six men representing the urban district of Hakodate wrote to Arisugawa, Ōkuma, and Ōki to refute Kuroda's assertions. They described the condition of the people under the commission "as in a state of slavery," which could end only with the establishment of prefectural government. The inhabitants of Hokkaido had applied to Kuroda to purchase the government steamers and factories, but they had been told that the properties were to be sold to the secretaries by special permission of the throne, and, furthermore, that the lack of private enterprise in Hokkaido was due to lack of neither ability nor capital but to the commission's refusal to allow it. They reported that Kuroda had ordered Yasuda to compile a secret report on the exports, imports, profit, and loss of goods to and from Hokkaido in preparation for the proposed company monopoly. The report, entitled *Ni fu shi ken sairan hōbun* (*Report of Observations Collected in Two Cities and Four Prefectures*), showed that the commission could further its control by dominating all money-lending activities. If the company was to be granted a monopoly on salt and rice purchases, they predicted that people would leave the island. They advised that the commission be abolished and replaced by a new prefectural administration, that freedom of trade be granted, and that the proposed monopoly be rejected.[54] As early as August 25 Fukuchi Gen'ichirō, the proprietor of the *Nichi nichi shimbun* and president of the Tokyo Assembly, spoke in public against the sale. He revealed the price that could be obtained through public bidding and showed that the company would earn a yearly profit of ¥155,000 after payment of the annual installment. Fukuchi declared that public tax money had paid for the development of Hokkaido and that the government was merely the guardian of the people's property. Therefore, the administration could not sell the property of the people. He attacked the evils of despotic power as wielded by a few men and urged the establishment of a constitution to check unsound measures, such as the current sale, and to act as a safeguard against unstable administrative policies.[55] Implications of corruption and the use of commission funds totaling ¥265,000 to improve its property in Tokyo and for agricultural and industrial expansion in the last year of its existence were also raised in the press. The *Japan Weekly Mail* questioned the commission's handling of its revenues and accounting procedures. It claimed that the yearly revenues of Hokkaido alone totaled ¥800,000, a sum sufficient for all the needs of the island.[56] News of the sale was first revealed by the *Nichi nichi shimbun* and *Yūbin hōchi shimbun,* edited by Yano Fumio. As a result, mass meetings were held to protest the government's decision, and the *mintō* (popular parties) gained additional fuel for their charges of clan government and maladministration.[57]

Within the bureaucracy by early September, The Department of Agriculture and Commerce, the Department of Justice, the Genrō-in, and the Board of Audit were said to be considering memoralizing the government on the inexpediency of the sale. Ōkuma, who was responsible for the affairs of three departments, Director of the Treasury Sano Tsunetami, Asano Nagakoto, and Soejima Taneomi opposed the sale. Asano secretly sent Nomura Fumio to Arisugawa to ask him "to adhere to justice." Ōkuma and Nomura reported that Kuroda secretly ordered ten select individuals to come to Tokyo, but these orders were countermanded and only one person was sent. Sanjō strongly opposed the sale in a letter to Iwakura and stated he would resign from office if it was not canceled.[58] Notice of cancellation was given on October 12, but the political repercussions continued to be felt for a long time thereafter. Although the commission was replaced by the prefectural government that received control of the commission's properties, the *Ibaraki nichi nichi shimbun* and *Mainichi shimbun* were suspended. The *Mainichi's* acting editor was imprisoned for a year for comments on the incident. Kuroda, angered by events, resigned from the Privy Council and brought charges of defamation and slander against the *Yūbin hōchi, Chōya, Mainichi, Akebono,* and *Seidan* newspapers before the Board of Public Prosecutors.[59]

Of the ten junior councilors, Ōkuma alone opposed the sale of the commission's properties. Sasaki Takayuki, Kawada Kageoki, and Nakamura Hiroki of the Genrō-in, and Miura Gorō and Tani Tateki of the army also came out against the sale. However, Kuroda was a leader of the Satsuma faction, which still remembered Ōkuma's reforms of the navy and police board, two bases of Satsuma power. Kuroda wanted to expel Ōkuma from the administration and found support not only from the Satchō leaders but also from Sasaki, Kawada, Nakamura, and other members of the Tosa faction, who opposed Ōkuma personally but not his objections to the sale. Sasaki wrote in his diary that Ōkuma was advocating a "fair opinion" but Itō could not act against the sale because of the "complicated situation." Public opinion turned against Kuroda, and Ōkuma became a popular hero for his stand. Mass meetings were held at many places to denounce the sale; Itagaki and Gotō, who regarded Ōkuma as their enemy now called on him, and even Fukuchi Gen'ichirō of the *Tokyo nichi nichi shimbun,* regarded as the "government newspaper," spoke out against the incident.[60]

Ōkuma's views represented a direct challenge to Satsuma control of Hokkaido and to Satchō power and, along with his memorial on constitutional government, solidified opposition to him within the ruling hierarchy.[61] Ōkuma's close ties with the main opponents to the sale, the *Yūbin hōchi shimbun* and *Tokyo-Yokohama mainichi shimbun,* made him suspect of revealing details of the secret sale to the press. The *Mainichi* was edited by Numa Morikazu (Moriichi), a former judge in the Genrō-in and the leader of a political discussion group, the Ōmeisha (Parrot Society).[62] *Yūbin hōchi* was the spokesman for the graduates of Fukuzawa's Keiō Gijuku and, under the leadership of Yano, was the voice of popular rights advocates. The Satchō oligarchs, therefore, believed that Ōkuma was plotting against them in conspiracy with Fukuzawa and his followers and with the financial aid of Iwasaki Yatarō of Mitsubishi, who had received government shipping contracts and financial assistance while Ōkuma was in the Ministry of Finance.[63]

Although Ōkuma's opponents lacked direct evidence for their charges against him,[64] Ono had given Ōkuma and selected newspapers detailed information on the proposed sale and on the accounts of the commission. In April 1880 Ono was appointed to the Board of Audit; in June 1881 he was ordered to investigate the management of government-owned properties; two months later he was promoted to auditor first class and ordered to draft legislation on the control of government property.[65] His diary shows that beginning in late June 1881, and especially in August and September, he was investigating the commission's accounts and working with the traveling inspectors who were sent to Hokkaido. From *Ryūkakusai nikki,* it is evident that following the presentation of *Kinsei jūgi,* he was becoming increasingly close to Ōkuma, who was one of the three councilors responsible for the affairs of the Ministry of Finance to which the Board of Audit was subordinate. Between April 15 and July 29, 1881, he saw Ōkuma six times; at one meeting on April 23 he also spoke with Iwasaki. During these visits he discussed the business of the Board of Audit and his views on the current situation. On July 29, shortly before the emperor's and Ōkuma's departure for the Northeast, Ono and Ōkuma met again to "discuss matters relating to the Dajōkan." At the same time, Ono was in contact with Fukuzawa Yukichi and Shimada Saburō, a member of the Ōmeisha and associate of Numa Morikazu. On April 1 Ono wrote to Fukuzawa; between May 12 and August 27, he either saw or wrote to Shimada six times.[66] Ōkuma, Fukuzawa, and Numa all opposed the sale of the Hokkadio properties; and Ono, as the chief investigator of the commission's records, was the man who informed them of the details of the sale.

On September 29 Ono made the following notation in his diary: "Tōsai [Gishin] is going to start for Ishinomaki and on his way there will meet Councilor Ōkuma. I entrusted him with a letter on recent conditions in Tokyo in which I encouraged him [Ōkuma] to stand firm on the subject we discussed previously [i.e., the sale of government properties]."[67] The main points of the letter, now in the Library of Waseda University, are:

> I am deeply resentful of the recent incident [involving the sale of the commission properties]. I respect your fair attitude. I believe this is a good chance to improve politics. I ask you to maintain an impartial attitude and save our country from the darkness of anarchy on this occasion. I earnestly ask this for the sake of the imperial household and for our country.
>
> Although I suppose you have already heard about the circumstances of the incident, I told Gishin what I have seen and heard in detail so he will let you know.
>
> There is a villain [Kuroda?] who schemes to separate you from Councilor Itō. I hope you will be careful about this. I suppose you are dissatisfied with Councilor Itō's handling of the incident, but please be patient now. I think [patience] is the best way to present your opinion which is correct.
>
> As I have told Gishin about the movements of Councilor Itō and the others, you will hear of this directly from him.
>
> I do not have to remind you to remain calm and firm because I sincerely believe you will win in the end, even if you are defeated in the first round.
>
> As it is a great honor for me to have made your acquaintance, I am firmly determined to make every effort to attain justice for you and to share success, failure, honor, and disgrace with you. I hope you will direct me in regard to everything when you return to Tokyo. I hope you will offer me a chance to return your kindness.

Ono then encouraged Ōkuma to continue his plans as before, despite attacks on his policies when Minister of Finance, since this was "not only my personal hope but also the public viewpoint." He informed Ōkuma of the memorial being written by the auditors, which was to be submitted to the Dajōkan six or seven days before the emperor returned. In addition, he "heard that the Genrō-in and the Ministries of Agriculture, Finance, and Justice are going to discuss it [the sale]." He concluded: "Now, those who appreciate justice both among the government and the people support your administration and place great expectations in you." The letter was signed: "Ono Azusa, a servant of Junior Councilor, Marquis Ōkuma." Appended to it was a note that stated that Ono had finished writing the draft of the law to control government property and was preparing to present it to Ōkuma.[68]

The information that Ono was sending to Ōkuma was too important to be committed to writing and was to be delivered verbally by a most trusted intermediary, Ono's brother-in-law, who was also one of Ōkuma's subordinates. It was directly related to the Colonization Commission incident, which Ono was investigating in his official capacity. Nine days after Ono wrote to Ōkuma, the *Nichi nichi shimbun* reported: "With reference to the Kaitakushi [Colonization Commission] question, we hear that two Departments, those of Agriculture and Commerce and of Justice, together with the Senate and Board of Audit, have now under consideration the expediency of memorializing the government on the inexpediency of the project as announced." By October 1 the *Mainichi* was said to be circulating "a rumor that a certain Privy Councilor [Ōkuma] who is opposed to his colleagues in regard to the Kaitakushi question has forwarded a memorial to the government in favor of a national assembly. This has caused much discussion among members of the cabinet, two or three of whom are even said to have proposed that the petitioner shall be dismissed from the ministry." A week later, the *Mainichi* reported on a rumor that the vice-minister of the Home Ministry and two or three secretaries were insisting on the establishment of a national assembly.[69]

Ono, therefore, was in a key position in the government before, during, and after the Colonization Commission incident. The record of his meetings with Ōkuma and Shimada during the spring and summer of 1881 and his letter of September 29 to Ōkuma show that he was the person responsible for informing Ōkuma, *Mainichi, Nichi nichi,* and *Yūbin hōchi shimbun* of the issues involved in the sale. As seen from the memorial he wrote for the auditors, Ono was personally opposed to the means of disposition as illegal and favored a "fair and impartial" public sale to prevent the *hanbatsu* from taking advantage of the situation.[70] He believed that the incident would result in some change in the political world but advised Ōkuma to bear with Itō, for only these two councilors could save the country from anarchy. Ono, however, did not know that an agreement had been reached among the Satchō leaders to force Ōkuma out of the government.[71]

With change hovering over the political horizon, Ono began to formulate plans which would enable Ōkuma and his followers to take advantage of the situation. *Moshi ware mizukara ataraba* (*If I were to Take It Upon Myself*) was begun on September 24, the day after Ono completed the draft of his September 29 letter to Ōkuma; due to illness, it was not completed until October 7 when Ono sent a copy by a messenger to Ōkuma. Even before Ōkuma received it, he was visited by Gishin at Fukushima, and Gishin wired his brother-in-law that the Councilor's "bravery continues. His stand has not changed. He insists on its justice. You needn't worry about him." [72] The plan sent to Ōkuma begins:

> If I were to take upon myself the responsibility for the current political situation, what methods would I use?. . . .
>
> . . . our party should make use of the bill for the sale of the Colonization Commission [properties] and plan with great care how to save Japan. Our plan should, above all, aim at the improvement of politics. It is most important for our party to win. If [our plan] improves contemporary government effectively, we will be satisfied even if we are defeated. In other words, we should take advantage of the sale of the Colonization Commission's property and take a chance to win in the future.
>
> How can we improve the current administration? There are only two ways: 1) despotism which would improve a bad situation quickly; 2) establishment of a constitution to improve a bad situation gradually. The second way will not be easy;

> but if carried out steadily and orderly, it would save Japan from a miserable situation and from anarchy. We should follow the second way in the most effective manner possible.
>
> To do this, we must present a proposal on the establishment of a constitution before the problem of the sale is resolved and attack the government by asking why it hesitates to promulgate one. . . . The problem of the sale and our arguments are so closely connected that we must be careful to attack the government on both measures. Then we must think about the results in advance.

Ono stated that he did not believe "it possible for us to win completely," due to the opposition of the cabinet and bureaucracy. Sanjō was described as unsure of how to refute arguments against the sale and was ready to resign; Iwakura was avoiding the problem and intended to organize a new leadership group; Yamagata was trying to decide which side was more powerful and therefore worthy of support; Yamada was viewed as "against us." Itō was "quite uncertain" and "dreaming that he could do something in cooperation with Satsuma and Chōshū." With the exception of Kuroda, all former Satsuma clansmen were opposed to Ōkuma "for fear their clan power in government will end." Neither the army nor police could be called on for support due to their Satsuma leadership, and the Home Ministry could also be counted among Ōkuma's opponents. Among the Dajōkan and bureaucracy, those supporting Ōkuma's position on the sale included only Ōki Takatō, Kōno Togama, and a few officials in the Ministries of Finance, Commerce and Agriculture, and Justice, of whom many were uncertain of their views on the constitution. The number of "true supporters and ambitious patriots" was about forty. Ono advised leading them to Ōkuma's side by reasonable arguments in order to gain their support voluntarily. In this way "it is not necessarily impossible for us to win to improve current politics."[73]

By mid-September, Ōkuma's colleagues in the Dajōkan had begun to unite against him. Ōkuma's position on the timing and composition of the national assembly and constitution and his opposition to the sale of the Colonization Commission's properties had become the culminating points in a rift whose origin lay in his growing power within government. Because of his opposition to the sale, he was hailed as a spokesman of the people at a public meeting on August 25 at which Yano, Itagaki Taisuke, Gotō Shōjirō, and Fukuchi Gen'ichirō spoke. Ōkuma's ties with Iwasaki Yatarō, however, made him vulnerable to claims of outside influence on his decision, since Mitsubishi's competitor in Osaka was the Kansai Bōeki Shōkai. Ōkuma was less concerned with Hokkaido per se than with the necessity to oppose a *hanbatsu* victory on the issue that would be a blow to those elements favoring the promulgation of a constitution. The Satchō oligarchs assumed that Ōkuma was leading a plot against the government and were determined to force him out of office. Even neutral members of the bureaucracy believed that Ōkuma should be punished for aligning himself with critics of the government. On September 18 Councilor Yamada asked Iwakura to dismiss Ōkuma; and Kuroda, who favored direct imperial rule on the basis of a Satchō coalition and had supported the sale, followed suit on October 3. Although opposed to Ōkuma's 1881 memorial, Iwakura tried to mediate the dispute, for he feared that a split in the oligarchy would cause the government to fall. On his return to Tokyo on October 7 he met with Itō and agreed to forsake Ōkuma, who had been his close friend. He saw Itō and Kuroda as a means whereby Ōkuma's "radical" views could be checked and therefore agreed to Ōkuma's removal from the government. Two years later, when he was seriously ill, Iwakura apologized to Ōkuma for these actions. Itō, who had been jealous of Ōkuma's rise to power since Ōkubo's death and angered at his views on the constitution, which represented a further threat to Satchō power, joined with Kuroda of Satsuma to get Iwakura to agree to Ōkuma's dismissal.[74] Rumors of Ōkuma's memorial on the necessity to establish a national assembly began to circulate at this time, further infuriating his fellow councilors. As public debate over the issue of the Colonization Commission and assembly became vigorous and as leaders of public opinion such as Fukuchi and Numa held public meetings to denounce the government, pressure increased for Ōkuma's resignation.[75]

When the emperor returned to Tokyo on October 11, Iwakura met him at the station and spoke with him. Then Arisugawa, Sanjō, Iwakura, Itō, Kuroda, Yamagata, Terajima, Inoue, Saigō, and Yamada Akiyoshi discussed the establishment of the Diet with him and asked the emperor to let the people know the exact date of the opening of the Diet and the direction the nation would follow. The seven councilors also presented an opinion calling for Ōkuma's resignation under their joint signature. The next morning Itō and Saigō called on Ōkuma and asked him to submit a letter of resignation. He replied that he would first attend a cabinet meeting and resign after he had been granted an audience by the emperor. Ōkuma then went to the palace, but the guards would not admit him. Neither Prince Arisugawa nor Prince Kitashirakawa would receive him, and he now found himself *persona non grata* to the sovereign and courtiers whom he had accompanied the previous day. Yamada, whom he regarded as one of his friends, brought him the writ of dismissal.[76] Under the circumstances Ōkuma had no choice but to offer his resignation.

The government was now ready to arrest Ōkuma as a rebel, but Arisugawa prevented this. Fukuzawa and his nephew, Nakamigawa Hikojirō, who was first secretary of the Foreign Office, also feared arrest and wrote their wills to their families. In looking at these events in retrospect, Ōkuma later stated that Itō had persuaded Sanjō and Iwakura to have him dismissed. On October 11 Sasaki Takayuki, who was then vice-president of the Genrō-in, noted what he had been told about the incident by Arisugawa. Arisugawa stated that he would speak for Ōkuma in regard to the memorial because originally Ōkuma did not write his opinion in the form of a memorial. He dictated his views to the prince, who wrote them down; thereafter, Iwakura showed the memorial to Itō, and the problem arose.[77] The news of Ōkuma's resignation took Fukuzawa by surprise, and he reacted with indignation. He asked why Ōkuma alone had resigned when he, Itō, and Inoue all had the same opinion on constitutional government. Declaring it immoral that they felt no shame in doing such a thing, he wrote to Itō and Inoue to express his views. Yano himself told Fukuzawa that Ōkuma's and Fukuzawa's followers in the group did not act in harmony from the beginning. Like quarreling children, they acted as two separate groups with different aims and so destroyed themselves.[78] Ōkuma had thus lost both office and power, and on October 29 he was presented with the "sum of ¥7,000 in consideration of his long service rendered to the government." [79]

THE POLITICAL CHANGE OF 1881

The political change of 1881 was heralded by the Imperial Decree of October 12 announcing the establishment of parliament in 1890, the cancellation of the sale of the Colonization Commission properties, and the resignation of Ōkuma.[80] Although Ōkuma had been expelled from the administration for challenging the power of the dominant faction and the government was now completely a *hanbatsu* regime, the "coup d'état of the Satchō coalition" was a turning point in the political history of modern Japan. The political world which had been animated by Western political theories and arguments in favor of popular rights, which implied opposition to the clan oligarchy while calling for a national assembly, now came to focus on the methods and means of preparing for the new government. The by-product of this was the formation of political parties. Thus, October 12, 1881, came to be a distinct dividing point in Japanese political life.[81] The announcement of the date for the opening of the Diet, though a decade in the future, was a victory for the advocates of popular rights, who had become the most articulate segment of public opinion. The Privy Council's withdrawal of permission for disposal of the northern properties similarly represented a victory for Ōkuma and the more liberal elements of the press, which had opposed the sale. In regard to his own activities and future, Ōkuma wrote:

> I have done right in the sight of Heaven and man. . . . When I see the attitude taken by the imperial appointees, namely, Etō Shimpei, Maebara Issei, Saigō Takamori, and Itagaki Taisuke, I think it unwise that they should have resigned from their offices in the Meiji government.[82]

Ōkuma refused to follow the example of Itagaki, who waited until after his resignation to call for representative government, and declared:

Whether I am in office or not, my principles are always the same. I left the government on principle, and now I appeal to the whole nation on the same principle. This attitude will prove to be quite right. I really think that the formation of this political party is necessary. Judging from the conditions in our country, I feel that political talks, dialogues, and speeches must be continued. We shall hear them more frequently day by day.[83]

Ono, who had participated behind the scenes in the events leading to Ōkuma's 1881 memorial and the disclosure of the Colonization Commission incident, called on Ōkuma on October 12 and 13 to discuss the councilor's resignation.[84] He wrote, in an undated paper now in the Ono collection, his personal evaluation of his part in the political change of 1881: "When the problem of the disposal of state developed industries was revealed, you questioned the cabinet on the control of public property and censured its error and made it decide on 1890 as the date to open the Diet." [85] By 1881 Ono had begun to play an increasingly important part In Ōkuma's political life and had declared that he would follow Ōkuma through success and failure. Yano Fumio was also one of Ōkuma's "important brains, but we should also evaluate Ono Azusa more highly on this point, too. That Ono influenced Ōkuma and swayed his opinions is a fact we have to admit. Yano's conjecture that Ono might have looked over Ōkuma's opinions, letters, and other writings is quite an accurate supposition." [86] In this period and thereafter, Ono and Yano were "Ōkuma's internal weapons." [87]

Ōkuma's expulsion from the government was followed by the resignation of those most closely associated with or sympathetic to him. These included: Yano Fumio, who held concurrent posts as secretary to the Bureau of Statistics and Dajōkan; Ushiba Takuzō, Inukai Tsuyoshi, and Ozaki Yukio from the Bureau of Statistics; Nakamigawa Hikojirō and Komatsubara Eitarō from the Foreign Ministry; Kōno Togama, the Minister of Agriculture and Commerce, and his subordinates Mutaguchi Gengaku and Nakano Buei; Shimada Saburō and Tanaka Kōzō from the Ministry of Education; Maejima Hisoka, who held the three offices of the vice-minister of home affairs, inspector-general of the postal service, and cabinet secretary simultaneously; judges Haruki

Yoshiaki and Kitabatake Harufusa; Morishita Iwakusu, the vice-minister of finance; and Ono Azusa.[88] The political change of 1881 therefore resulted in complete Satchō control of the administration and the expulsion of all its opponents from the power structure. Once freed of bureaucratic restraints, the former officials united around Ōkuma and the standard of popular rights to oppose the *hanbatsu* oligarchy. For this purpose, they moved into outright party politics under the leadership of Ōkuma. Thus the 1881 political change accelerated the formation of the Japanese parliament and parties and gave Ōkuma the opportunity to test his statement that "constitutional government is party government." [89]

NOTES

1. Osatake Takeki, *Nihon kensei shi taikō,* 2 vols. (Tokyo: Nihon Hyōronsha, 1938–39), 2:550.

2. Havens, *Nishi Amane,* pp. 62, 63.

3. Osatake, *Nihon kensei shi taikō,* 2:549.

4. Fujii, *Constitution of Japan,* pp. 67, 71, 72. In September 1871 the Dajōkan (Council of State), which had been the central administrative organ since August 1869, was divided into three chambers. The Sei-in (Central Chamber) held final control over the general administration. Presided over by the emperor, who was assisted by senior and junior councilors, it passed final judgment on all matters of state. The U-in (Right Chamber) drafted legislation needed by the executive departments and debated executive policy. The Sa-in (Left Chamber) deliberated on legislation drafted by Sei-in. Cf. Ishii, *Japanese Legislation,* pp. 119–27.

5. Fujii, *Constitution of Japan,* pp. 75–99.

6. Pittau, *Political Thought,* pp. 80, 81, 83, 84.

7. Inada, Masatsugu, *Meiji kempō seiritsu shi,* 20 vols. (Tokyo: Yūhikaku Kabushiki Kaisha, 1960–62), 1: 645.

8. *JWM,* 4, no. 38 (September 18, 1880): 1219. Translated from *Nichi nichi shimbun.*

9. *JWM* 4, no. 3 (January 17, 1880): 77, 78. Translated from *Chōya shimbun.*

10. Ibid. 4, no. 4 (January 24, 1880): 110, 111. Translated from *Akebono shimbun.*

11. Ibid. 4, no. 9 (February 28, 1880): 280–82. Translated from the *Chōya shimbun.*

12. Ibid., pp. 280, 281. Translated from *Mainichi shimbun.*
13. Ibid. 4, no. 23 (June 5, 1880): 734, 753. Translated from the *Akebono shimbun.*
14. Osatake, *Nihon kensei shi taikō,* 2: 545–48; Fujii, *Constitution of Japan,* p. 139.
15. *JWM* 4, no. 36 (September 4, 1880): 1155, 1156. Cf. Havens, *Nishi Amane,* pp. 185–90.
16. Osatake, *Nihon kensei shi taikō,* 2:548.
17. Ōkuma Kō Hachijūgonen Shi Hensan Kai, ed., *Ōkuma kō hachijūgonen shi,* 3 vols. (Tokyo: Nisshin Insatsu Kabushiki Kaisha, 1926), 1: 820–27; Lebra, *Ōkuma Shigenobu,* pp. 70–72.
18. Itō, "Struggle for Power," *JHR,* pp. 60, 62.
19. Ōkuma Hensan Kai, *Ōkuma kō hachijūgonen shi,* 1: 826.
20. Nishimura, *Ono Azusa,* p. 130.
21. George M. Beckmann, *The Making of the Meiji Constitution* (Lawrence, Kan.: University of Kansas Press, 1957), pp. 136–42.
22. Ōkuma Hensan Kai, *Ōkuma kō hachijūgonen shi,* 1: 794.
23. Itō, "Struggle for Power," *JHR,* p. 56; Inada, *Meiji kempō seiritsu shi,* 1: 461.
24. Enomoto, "Ono Azusa no seiji ronri," *NRR,* p. 555.
25. Hiratsuka Atsushi, *Itō Hirobumi hiroku* (Tokyo: Nihon Hyōronsha, 1929), pp. 216–18.
26. Oguri, *Yano Fumio,* pp.165, 174–76.
27. Watanabe, *Monjo yori mitaru Ōkuma,* pp. 447–49.
28. Enomoto, "Ono Azusa no seiji ronri," *NRR,* p. 548.
29. Osatake Takeki, *Nihon kensei shi* in *Gendai seijigaku zenshū,* ed. Nihon Hyōronsha, 13 vols. (Tokyo: Nihon Hyōronsha, 1930), 4: 283. The same idea is repeated in Osatake, *Nihon kensei shi taikō,* 2: 567.
30. Nishimura, *Ono Azusa den,* pp. 129, 131.
31. Meiji Shiryō Kenkyū Renrakukai, *Meiji seiken no kakuritsu katei* (Tokyo: Ochanomizu Shobō, 1956–1957), pp. 117–18.
32. Todd, *Parliamentary Government,* 1: 116; 2: 116–30.
33. Ono Azusa, "Kinsei jūgi," *Ono Azusa zenshū,* 2:265–67.
34. Sashihara, *Seishi hen,* 2; *MBZ,* p. 415.
35. Ono, "Bō daijin ni teisuru no sho," in Nagata, *Ono Azusa,* pp. 100–104.
36. Itō, "Struggle for Power," *JHR,* pp. 60, 62.
37. Ono, "Kinsei jūgi," p. 267.
38. The exact date on which Ōkuma presented the memorial is uncertain. In his diary, *Taruhito shinno nikki,* Arisugawa notes that Ōkuma visited him on March 11 and July 7, 1881, but no mention is made of the memorial. Whether the two met between these dates and exactly when Ōkuma gave Arisugawa his letter is not known; however, the similarities between *Kinsei jūgi* and the memorial are such that I conclude it was after March 18 but before July 2, when

Itō Hirobumi submitted his letter of resignation in opposition to Ōkuma's views.

39. Ono, "Ryūkakusai nikki," pp. 335–43.

40. Ono Azusa, *Genkō kokken shisan, Ono monjo,* Document no. 90, National Diet Library, Tokyo (unpublished, undated manuscript in the handwriting of Ono Azusa, n.p.).

41. Ono, "Ryūkakusai nikki," pp. 335–39.

42. Ibid., pp. 327, 381.

43. Joyce Chapman Lebra, "Yano Fumio: Meiji Intellectual, Party Leader, and Bureaucrat," *Monumenta Nipponica* 20, nos. 1–2 (1965): 5.

44. Pittau, *Political Thought,* p. 86.

45. Ōkuma Hensan Kai, *Ōkuma kō hachijūgonen shi,* 1: 819, 820.

46. Oguri, *Yano Fumio,* p. 176.

47. Itō, "Struggle for Power," *JHR,* pp. 56–62; Ōkuma Hensan Kai, *Ōkuma kō hachijūgonen shi,* 1: 818, 819, 860.

48. Ibid., 1: 827–29.

49. Nishimura, *Ono Azusa den,* p. 131.

50. Iddittie, *Shigenobu Ōkuma,* p. 216.

51. *JWM* 5, no. 25 (June 25, 1881): 718–719; 27 (July 9, 1881:799 Translated from the *Tokyo-Yokohama mainichi shimbun* 36 (September 10, 1881): 1046.

52. *JWM* 5, no. 36 (September 10, 1881): 1046, 1059, 1060; Nishimura, *Ono Azusa den,* p. 121; Hagihara, "Baba Tatsui," *CK* 81, no. 948 (October 1966): 386–88; Ōkuma Hensan Kai, *Ōkuma kō hachijūgonen shi,* 1: 829–32. The usual procedure was for prefectural governments to return any surplus from the prefectural account to the national treasury at the end of the fiscal year.

53. *JWM* 5, no. 37 (September 17, 1881): 1087, 1088.

54. Ibid., no. 38 (September 24, 1881): 1117, 1118; no. 39 (October 1, 1881): 1145, 1146.

55. Ibid., no. 35 (September 3, 1881): 1017.

56. Ibid., no. 41 (October 15, 1881): 1187, 1188.

57. Itō, Struggle for Power," *JHR,* p. 51.

58. Nishimura, *Ono Azusa den,* pp. 124, 125, 127; Ōkuma Hensan Kai, *Ōkuma kō hachijūgonen shi,* 1: 831.

59. *JWM* 5, no. 41 (October 15, 1881): 1212; no. 42 (October 22, 1881): 1238; no. 43 (October 29, 1881): 1252; no. 52 (December 31, 1881): 1523.

60. Ōkuma Hensan Kai, *Ōkuma kō hachijūgonen shi,* 1: 831–33; 2: 5.

61. Itō, "Struggle for Power," *JHR,* pp. 46–51; Nishimura, *Ono Azusa den,* p. 127.

62. Lebra, *Ōkuma Shigenobu,* pp. 105, 106; Itō, "Reform Party," *JHR,* p. 19.

63. Nishimura, *Ono Azusa den,* p. 144; Itō, "Struggle for Power,"

JHR, pp. 46, 47, 50; Ōkuma Hensan Kai, *Ōkuma kō hachijūgonen shi*, 1: 21, 833.

64. Itō, "Struggle for Power," *JHR*, p. 46.
65. Nishimura, *Ono Azusa den*, p. 13.
66. Ono, "Ryūkakusai nikki," pp. 341–47, 349, 351.
67. Ibid., p. 364. Watanabe, *Monjo yori mitaru Ōkuma*, p. 451.
68. Ono Azusa, *Mitsugi ni tsuki shinten o wazurawasu* (September 29, 1881), from the original manuscript in the Library of Waseda University, Tokyo, n. p.; Watanabe, *Monjo yori mitaru Ōkuma*, p. 451–53; Ono Azusa, "Ōkuma Shigenobu ate shokan," *Ono Azusa zenshū*, 2, 105–7.
69. *JWM* 5, no. 39 (October 1, 1881): 1142; no. 40 (October 8, 1881): 1173.
70. Ishizuki, "Meiji no jishikijin," *ZG*, p. 84.
71. Watanabe, *Monjo yori mitaru Ōkuma*, pp. 453, 454; Ono, *Mitsugi ni tsuki shinten o wazurawasu*.
72. Ono, "Ryūkakusai nikki," pp. 363–65.
73. Ono Azusa, "Moshi ware mizukara ataraba," *Ono Azusa zenshū*, 2: 74–78. From the statement on Kuroda, it appears that Kuroda did not fear Ōkuma's threat to Satchō power, as did his fellow clansmen. Kuroda, however, was a leader in the movement to expel Ōkuma due to his opposition to the sale.
74. Lebra, *Ōkuma Shigenobu*, pp. 63, 84–86, 90; Itō, "Struggle for Power," *JHR*, pp. 42, 45, 46–49.
75. Tokyo Hakubunkan, ed., *Seitō shi*, in *Meiji shi*, 13 vols. (Tokyo: Tokyo Hakubunkan, 1907), 6: 176, 177.
76. Ōkuma Hensan Kai, *Ōkuma kō hachijūgonen shi*, 1: 856, 860; Aono Gon'emon, *Nihon seitō hensen shi* (Tokyo: Ankyūsha, 1935), p. 54.
77. Ōkuma Hensan Kai, *Ōkuma kō hachijūgonen shi*, 1: 860, 861.
78. Oguri, *Yano Fumio*, pp. 187–89.
79. *JWM* 5, no. 42 (October 29, 1881): 1252.
80. Ibid., no. 41 (October 15, 1881): 1198, 1199.
81. Itō, "Constitutional Reform Party," *JHR*, p. 1.
82. Watanabe Ikujirō, *Ōkuma Shigenobu kankei monjo*, 6 vols. (Tokyo: Nihon Shiseki Kyōkai, 1927–1929), 5: 14, 15.
83. Watanabe, *Monjo yori mitaru Ōkuma*, p. 129; Osatake Takeki, *Seitō no hattatsu* (Tokyo: Iwanami Shoten, 1933), pp. 76–77.
84. Ono, "Ryūkakusai nikki," p. 366.
85. Ono, *OM*, no. 18.
86. Meiji Shiryō, *Meiji seiken*, p. 115.
87. Fujii, *Teikoku kempō to Kaneko haku*, p. 183.
88. Nishimura, *Ono Azusa den*, pp. 136, 137; Hakubunkan, *Seitō shi*, *MS*, 6: 176, 177; Kohayakawa, *Meiji hōsei shi*, p. 644; Hagihara, "Baba Tatsui," *CK* 81, no. 948 (October, 1966): 388, 389; Lebra, *Ōkuma Shigenobu*, p. 92; Oguri, *Yano Fumio*, p. 186.

89. Portions of this chapter have appeared previously in Sandra T. W. Davis, "Ono Azusa and the Political Change of 1881," *Monumenta Nipponica* 25, nos. 1–2 (1970): 137–54.

6
The Political Years Begin

The political change of 1881 and the imperial edict announcing the establishment of the national assembly in 1890 were the culmination of trends set in motion by the opening of the country and the Restoration of 1868. The power struggle among the clans that led to the fall of the *bakufu* continued in the new bureaucratic structure clothed in the terms of Western philosophy and political institutions, which were seen as the symbols of modern statehood, independence, and power, and as steps leading to treaty revision. The struggle to end the absolutism of the shogunate became in the new era a movement to end *hanbatsu* control and to secure a wider distribution of the reigns of power.

October 12, 1881, inaugurated a decade of intensified political activity known as the "era of freedom and popular rights." The principal figures of this period were by training and experience practical implementors of political theories. As leaders of the movement for freedom and popular rights, their main concern was politics and their primary objectives the overthrow of the *hanbatsu* regime and the achievement of political power.[1] The expulsion of Ōkuma from the bureaucracy and the decision to convene the Diet in nine years served to intensify anti-government activities and resulted in the formation of the first political parties, the Jiyūtō (Liberal Party) and the Rikken Kaishintō (Constitutional Progressive Party). However, these were not parties founded on political principles and subject to strict parliamentary discipline as in Europe. These were loosely united groups of factions continually vying for power within the party structure. Although the aim of the parties was similar, namely, to seize control from the oligarchs, mutual distrust and jealousy prevented them from working together. They sought justification for their activities and ideas in Western theories and democratic principles, but the defects inherent in their clan orientation and composition were such that "the origin of the political parties was like to birth of a deformed child."[2]

THE POPULAR PARTIES BEGIN
THE JIYŪTŌ

The initial split in the ruling oligarchy occurred over the issue of chastising Korea and led to the resignations of Itagaki Taisuke and Gotō Shōjirō of Tosa, Etō Shimpei of Hizen, and Saigō Takamori from the government in 1873. Kido Takayoshi, who opposed both the Korean and Taiwan campaigns, resigned in 1874 over the decision to send an expedition to Taiwan. Kido had been a member of the Iwakura mission and had returned to Japan convinced of the need to concentrate on domestic development and political reform.[3] He urged the immediate enactment of a constitution with direct imperial rule to check the arbitrariness of the ruling clans. This would be preparatory to a second constitution, which would grant suffrage to the people. He maintained that a nation without a constitution was to be pitied, and drafted a sample for the government.[4] Itagaki, in retrospect, believed that he should have joined forces with Kido, who held similar views on constitutional government, in order to hasten the establishment of constitutional government. Differences in personality and over foreign policy prevented confidential discussions, and Itagaki regarded the failure of the "progressive" elments in the oligarchy to join forces as contributing to the postponement of the establishment of the constitution and to the increase in Satchō misrule. The "conquer Korea" argument was the first conflict in the long struggle between the clan leaders and their opponents for domination of the government. Once out of office, Itagaki and his colleagues devoted themselves to the task of regaining power through the use of new political institutions based on the premise that the Diet would be convened in the future.

Before Saigō Takamori left Tokyo for Satsuma, Itagaki told him that he planned to devote his energies to the "great project of establishing a council chamber chosen by the people." Saigō agreed with Itagaki's objective, but said it could not be attained by speech making but by gaining control of the government in their own hands. Saigō, Itagaki wrote, was not merely a supporter of military power but also an advocate of representative government. Itagaki, Soejima Taneomi, Gotō Shōjirō, and Etō Shimpei together evaluated the current situation and concluded that contemporary social "evils" arose from despotic government; it was therefore necessary to establish a system wherein public opinion could be put into effect and national unity and prosperity promoted. Itagaki also consulted with Kataoka Kenkichi and Hayashi Yūzō, who also left the bureaucracy over the Korean issue, about a proposed memorial on constitutional government; but both felt they were not sufficiently known to "lead public opinion." Itagaki then discussed the memorial with Gotō, who introduced him to Komuro Nobuo and Furusawa Urō (Shigeru), who had studied in England and now were ready to apply their knowledge of Western government to Japan. Soejima, who had formerly stood for direct imperial control, now changed his views and came out in favor of an elected national assembly. Etō had advocated constitutional government at the time of the Boshin campaign. The outcome of these discussions was the decision to present a memorial to the Sa-in urging the establishment of a council chamber chosen by the people.

At the same time, Itagaki along with Gotō, Soejima, Etō, Komuro, Furusawa, Yuri Kimimasa, the former governor of Tokyo, and Okamoto Kenzaburō, an official of the Ministry of Finance, planned to establish a political party in order to arouse public opinion The resulting organization was the Kōfuku anzensha (Happiness Security Society), located in Tokyo and, in January 1874, renamed the Aikokukōtō (Patriotic Public Party). Because during the feudal period the organization of a party was regarded as an act of rebellion, the term *kōtō* or "public party" was used to distinguish the Aikokukōtō from a *shitō* or "private party" in the eyes of the public. Itagaki justified the organization of his party by saying that when responsibilities such as conscription, national defense, and taxation of industry and commerce are placed on the people, it is natural for them to insist on suffrage and political rights in return. This inevitable demand of the people led him to organize a party to awaken them politically, to urge the establishment of a national assembly chosen by the people, and to insure suffrage. The major achievement of the Aikokukōtō was the memorial written by Furusawa and presented to the Sa-in on January 12, 1874, under the signatures of Itagaki, Gotō, Etō, Soejima, Yuri, Furusawa, and Komuro.[5]

The memorial began:

> According to our observations, the political power in our country lies neither in the imperial household nor in the people but in the officials. This does not mean that officials do not respect the emperor or care for the people. In the present situation, government ordinances are issued in the morning and revoked in the evening and punishment depends upon private considerations. How can we maintain public peace under such circumstances? Unless we correct this vicious cycle, our country will be ruined. We subjects can not cease to love our country and seek the means to save it. Thus, we conclude that the only way is to listen to public opinion; and the only way to do this is to establish a national assembly chosen by the people. This is the way to restrain the power of the officials and to maintain the people's happiness and security.

Those required to pay taxes had the right to be informed about government, and the best and quickest way to enlighten the people was through the establishment of a national assembly. Here they would be forced to defend their rights; this would increase their self-respect and ability for self-criticism while enabling them to follow social trends. If not allowed to develop in this way, they would remain ignorant and would never try to improve themselves. Those who objected to a Diet, saying it would do nothing but collect the fools of the nation together, were contemptuous of the people and ignored the fact that there were learned and intelligent men outside the government. Man's intellect and ability grew when used as seen in the quality of officials since the Restoration. This was why a council chamber would enlighten and improve the people. It was therefore the duty of the administration to provide leadership and to establish the Diet, which would enable popular participation in government. Only through such means could the nation become strong. As could be seen from the European and American experience, all the present legislative bodies have had a long history of progress and change. If Japan selected and adopted the best institutions of Europe, great progress would be possible. Thus, the happiness and security of the nation depended on the establishment of a national assembly.[6]

The memorial inaugurated a public debate on the issues of representative government and the constitution. Although Itagaki claimed that Aikokukōtō popularity and prosperity increased, lack of public interest and suspicion of Aikokukōtō participation in both Etō's rebellion in Saga and in an attack on Iwakura by a Tosa clansman led to its collapse after two months. Despite Soejima's and Gotō's discouragement and readiness to abandon the movement for representative government, Itagaki decided to take the issues to the people in order to arouse public opinion and political consciousness. He and Furusawa returned to Tosa and organized the Risshisha (Society of Independence) in the hope of developing a model political party on the local level. With this as the foundation of the movement for representative government, he would establish a national party in Tokyo. Komuro followed his example and organized the Jijosha (Self

Help Society) in his native Awa, now Tokushima prefecture. As the local parties prospered, Itagaki and his followers issued a call for a general meeting to be held in Osaka in February 1875. The resulting organization was the Aikokusha (Patriotic Society) which, led by the Tosa Risshisha and located in Tokyo, was of even briefer duration than the Aikokukōtō. In addition to Itagaki, the members included Komuro, Fukuoka Kōtei, Kataoka Kenkichi, Hayashi Yūzō, Okamoto Kenzaburō, and Nishiyama Yukizumi (Shicho) of Tosa. Lack of funds and Itagaki's decision to reenter the government as a result of the Osaka conference of February 1875 brought an end to the Aikokusha.[7] By late October Itagaki, who insisted on the immediate establishment of a national assembly, had resigned from the cabinet and once again resumed the leadership of the *jiyū minken undō.*

Itagaki, once more the leader of the Tosa Risshisha, encouraged Kataoka Kenkichi to memorialize the government for political and social reforms. The memorial and the participation of Hayashi Yūzō and other members of the Risshisha in the Satsuma rebellion, which was led by Saigō Takamori, resulted in government measures to suppress the society. As a result, the Aikokusha was reorganized in 1878 in Osaka by former Risshisha members. In March 1880 it was renamed the Kokkai kisei dōmei (League for the Establishment of a National Assembly), and it also memorialized the cabinet and Genrō-in to establish a parliament promptly. At a general meeting held in Tokyo in November, the name was changed to Dai Nihon kokkai kisei yūshikai (Greater Japan Voluntary Association for the Establishment of a National Assembly). During meetings held on December 12 and 15, Numa Morikazu, Ueki Emori, and others decided to establish a political party.[8] As public opposition to the sale of the Colonization Commission properties increased, Itagaki, in August 1881, called for the leaders of various political factions and groups to cast aside petty differences and form one political party. Ōkuma and his followers did not respond to the appeal,[9] and Itagaki went on a speaking tour of the Northeast[10] and on his return to Tokyo participated in a series of public meetings.[11]

Government efforts to control the developing party movement by the Regulations on Public Meetings were of no avail.

Even within the administration there was a sense of the inevitability of change and debate over the timing and type of constitutional government. The call for parliamentarianism, as George Akita has shown, lent a sense of urgency to official decisions. Combined with the crises caused by Ōkuma's 1881 memorial and the Colonization Commission incident, *jiyū minken* forces forced the government to accelerate the date for convening the assembly. The proclamation announcing the establishment of the Diet was the symbol of success of the movement led by Itagaki and his followers. Since the aim of the Kokkai kisei dōmei had been realized, it was now reorganized as a full-fledged political party at a series of meetings between October 18 and 28.[12]

On October 29, 1881, the Jiyūtō was established at an assembly attended by seventy-eight representatives from all over the counry. Itagaki Taisuke was elected president and Nakajima Nobuyuki vice-president, and the permanent committee members included Gotō Shōjirō, Baba Tatsui, Suehiro Shigeyasu, and Takeuchi Tsuna. The party was composed of four factions: (1) the rural element formerly centered around the Kokkai kisei dōmei; (2) the Tosa faction with Gotō as its leader; (3) the Kokuyūkai (Friends of the Nation Association), led by Baba, Suehiro, and Taguchi Ukichi; and (4) a group centered around Nakae Chōmin, Tanaka Kōzō, and Kawano Sukeyuki. The Jiyūtō charter began with a statement adopted from the French *Declaration of the Rights of Man and the Citizen*: "Liberty is the natural right of man." The first article declared that the party would attempt to expand liberty, promote popular rights and the happiness of the people, and reform society. The second article said it would strive to establish "rightful" constitutional government. The third article stated it would seek to cooperate and unite with those holding similar principles and objectives. In June 1882 the *Jiyū shimbun* was established as the voice of the Jiyūtō.[13]

THE ESTABLISHMENT OF THE ŌTOKAI

As the movement for the establishment of a national assembly and Ōkuma's isolation from his fellow oligarchs moved toward a climax in the summer and autumn of 1881, moderate elements within the bureaucracy began to formulate plans for a political party centered about the councilor from Hizen. The plans were to culminate in the establishment of the second major party, the Rikken Kaishintō; and the key figure in the organization of the party was Ono Azusa. Ono first mentioned these plans in his diary on June 10 when he wrote that he and Ogawa Tamejirō had discussed the establishment of a neutral party. Ogawa was a close friend who was employed in the Bureau of Statistics, and he either visited or wrote to Ono twenty-four times between July 10 and October 11.[14] Ogawa introduced Ono to Takada Sanae, who was instrumental in organizing the Ōtokai (Gull Society), often referred to as the Ono *gumi* (group), one of four factions in the Kaishintō. At that time, Takada was a student in the Department of Literature at Tokyo University and he had often heard Ogawa speak about Ono. In his diary Takada stated that they were introduced by Ogawa in February 1881,[15] but Takada's name first appears in *Ryūkakusai nikki* on August 20, when he, Ogawa, and several others called on Ono to discuss establishing a political party.[16] By then Ono was openly discussing his ideas with Takada who, as a student of politics, was a potential ally and resource person in modern political theory. At a meeting sponsored by Fukuchi Gen'ichirō and Numa Morikazu to denounce the sale of the Colonization Commission properties, Ono told Takada that the incident was due to clan despotism, which was made possible because there was no powerful opposition party.[17] To remedy the situation he proposed:

> The Jiyūtō . . . is a group based on a very abstract and ambiguous concept of political principle which admires and emphasizes Rousseau's *Social Contract*. Thus, there is an urgent need to establish a party which bases its general platform and principles on administrative policy. The Jiyūtō is a party with nothing but principles but has no general plans.

> Thus, it is necessary to establish a party which can plan for the administration [of government] and can accept the responsibility of realizing such plans. There are a few among Ōkuma's group who have progressive ideas and who agree with me on this point. As you are a Tokyo University student who actually is studying politics, I would be delighted to have you and your friends study this plan with me and help me with it.

Takada, then age twenty-one and in his senior year, was impressed by Ono's ideas and selected several classmates to join him in the study of practical politics. These included Okayama Kenkichi, Yamada Ichirō, Sunagawa Taketoshi, Yamada Kinosuke, Ichishima Kenkichi, and Amano Tameyuki.[18] Fearful of detection, the young men would leave the university in secret to escape the watchful eyes of the dormitory supervisor and meet at Ono's home to study political problems and hold debates. Since their trip required crossing the Sumida River, at Yamada Ichirō's suggestion they referred to themselves as a group of gulls crossing the river and took the name of Ōtokai (Gull Society) in February 1882.[19]

From August 20 to January 1882, Ono frequently noted in his diary that he had "taught the students" or "gave the students a lesson."[20] The seven students, fearing government suspicion, met secretly with Ono at least once a week,[21] usually in Gichin's drawing room because of lack of space in Ono's home, a "small and frugal" cottage in his brother-in-law's garden.[22] The meetings became an informal teaching situation in which the seven received their introduction to politics, a field they were to become masters of in both theory and practice. From Ono they received their first exposure to the problems of government and inside information on current issues. Here they also began to practice public speaking subject to their *sensei's* criticism. Ono soon became their "very learned, very kind friend," and Ichishima, who lived near him, frequently carried messages and information between the students and Ono. In long hours of discussion and by his example of sacrifice of career and ultimately health and life for principle, Ono unconsciously left his mark on the students as mentor and model, and the naive and inexperienced undergraduates soon became, with their teacher, a potent force in Meiji political life.[23]

In these discussions Ono expressed his indignation over the unequal treaties and criticized government institutions and the character and ability of the various ministers. When the Hokkaido scandal broke, he disclosed the facts to the group.[24] Yamada Ichirō described in *Godō tsuishiroku* Ono's "deep inclination" toward Bentham's utilitarianism, which he had studied in England, and firm belief that emotional drives and urges were not sufficient to lead the world toward development and advancement. Instead, he stressed the need for careful planning and the selection of the best possible method as the most important elements in bringing about progress.[25] The students also kept Ono informed about their studies, particularly the lectures delivered by Fenollosa. At the time, Fenollosa was discussing Bentham's philosophy of utilitarianism, and in one lecture he stated that the objective of life was to obtain happiness by deliberate means. A copy of this particular lecture was given to Ono. The idea was similar to Bentham's doctrine of the "greatest happiness of the greatest number." This is the reason why Ichishima, in his diary, stated that Fenollosa influenced the Kaishintō declaration.[26] Ono, however, never read Fenollosa's works nor met him personally.

Fenollosa's ideas resulted in a "consensus of principles"[27] among the students, who took as their motto social betterment by gradual and orderly change. This was similar to Ono's viewpoint and was later incorporated into Kaishintō policy. When the Colonization Commission scandal broke, the seven decided to oppose the *hanbatsu* government, to work to establish a national assembly at an early date, and to work for the welfare and happiness of the nation.[28] They therefore began to study specific political problems. The results of their investigations were incorporated into the policy statements of the Kaishintō.[29] The group now became Ono's research staff and advisers and the sounding board for his ideas. In this way, the seven helped prepare for the political party that was to fill the gap between the government and the Jiyūtō.

Initially, the Ono *gumi* was an informal study group; but as plans for the party began to crystallize, it was reorganized as a formal political association. At a ceremony held on February

27, 1882, the group took the name "Ōtokai," based on a suggestion made by Amano. Then at about eight in the evening, after concluding their discussion, the students noticed that dinner had not been served and they were "unbearably hungry." Yamada wrote some congratulatory phrases on the establishment of the Ōtokai and read them aloud before Ono and the others. As he concluded, he announced that since the organization of the Ōtokai was a matter of congratulation for the nation, the members should drink to its establishment with gusto. Ono, who disliked *sake,* finally became aware that his youthful protégés' attention had wandered and requested that wine be served. Food accompanied the *sake,* and the Ōtokai was auspiciously inaugurated by a group of feasting "gulls."[30]

The literary title of the Ono *gumi* did not conceal its political intent, and the administration was not unaware of the students' activities. In a lecture to members of the Department of Literature, Fenollosa said that it was impudent for university students to have ties with political parties that were opposed to the government. Nevertheless, the group remained loyal to their principles and graduated, with the exception of Ichishima, from the university "as if they had been exiled in 1882."[31]

THE ESTABLISHMENT OF THE KAISHINTŌ

As political tension increased during the summer of 1881, Ono, Ogawa, Takada, Ono Yaichi, Ugawa Morisburō, Tachibana Kaijirō, and others began to discuss the establishment of a new political party. Between June 10 and September 23, agreement was reached on plans for the Kaishintō.[32] From September 23 to 25, the party principles were decided upon and "the greatest good of the greatest number" was adopted as the political philosophy of the party. Talks continued on a daily basis, and on September 26 and 29 Ono spoke with Gishin on "current problems." On October 6 Ono discussed *Moshi ware mizukara ataraba* with his colleagues, and the next day, Mr. Kawamoto was sent to Ōkuma with a copy of the work. On

October 8 Gishin met Ōkuma and gave him a letter and message from Ono. Thus, by the time Gishin and Kawamoto were sent to Ōkuma, who was traveling with the emperor's party in the Northeast, Ono and his associates in Tokyo had reached agreement on the formation of a party and on its general principles and purpose. Gishin had been sent to Ōkuma to inform him about the new party that was being organized as well as about the situation in Tokyo. This was the reason why Ono stated his determination to share the future with Ōkuma and asked for directions "in regard to everything" in his letter of September 29. Furthermore, the fact that Ono referred to "our party" in *Moshi ware mizukara ataraba* shows that agreement had been reached on the formation of the party by late September. Beginning on September 23, Ono's diary contains notations about "our party." The "founding fathers" discussed Ono's plan of action before it was sent to Ōkuma and agreed upon the course to follow in regard to the Colonization Commission affair.

If one looks back at the timing of his visits to Ōkuma, Ono's diary shows that he visited the councilor on June 13, three days after he and Ogawa discussed the establishment of a "neutral party" and again on June 25 and July 29.[33] Ono and Ōkuma had the opportunity to discuss the formation of a party before Ōkuma left for the Northeast. During the entire period when plans leading to the formation of the party were being discussed, Ōkuma was not in Tokyo. By late August, when Fukuchi and Numa began to hold public meetings on the Colonization Commission sale,[34] talks had proceeded to the point where at one of these gatherings Ono could tell Takada that "some of Ōkuma's group" felt it necessary to establish a party.[35] By September 23 general agreement had been reached on the party's purpose and principles, and by October 6 agreement had been reached on the means whereby the party could take advantage of the debate on the national assembly and sale of the properties of the Colonization Commission.[36] Thus, by the time Ōkuma returned to Tokyo, agreement had been reached on the establishment of a political party by his followers under the leadership of Ono. In the words of Watanabe Ikujirō, "when we talk about the organization and beginning of the Kaishintō, there is only one person who is indispensable, and that is Ono Azusa."[37] Watanabe, however, does not add the reason why Ono was so essential to the party: Ono, not Ōkuma, was the founder of the Kaishintō. With the aid of Ogawa, Takada, and a few close associates, he prepared the ground for the establishment of the Kaishintō before the political change of 1881.

Immediately following Ōkuma's return to Tokyo on October 12, Ono visited him. That evening three imperial decrees were issued, and Ōkuma was discharged from office. On October 13 Ono wrote in his diary: "At last the matter has been resolved. I should have known that it would affect me. I have made up my mind to give up my public office." Ono visited Ōkuma to inform him of his decision and then notified Gishin and Ogawa. The next day, Ono, Ogawa, Gishin, and Anami Hisashi met to discuss the situation.[38] With the political change of October 12, plans for the party progressed rapidly.[39] According to Amano Tameyuki, as soon as the seven students learned of Ōkuma's resignation, they concluded that there now was no alternative but to establish the party. At the same time, Ono said he was looking for a theoretical base for the party's principles and platform and asked them to do research on the problem.[40] From mid-October until the end of January, Ono was almost continually engaged in discussions on the formation of the party. Those involved included his youthful "brain trust," Ogawa, Miyamoto Yorizō, Anami Hisashi, Okuda Shinnosuke, Matsudaira Nobumasa, Sakamoto Shunkan, Ono Gishin, Nakamura Takeo, Nakamura Shuei, Ono Yaichi, Tachibana Kaijirō, Sawada Shunzō, Suzuki Ryōsuke, Miyoshi Taizō, the auditors Fukai Kurisato and Mizutani Kinsen, and Kōno Togama.

While Ono and his associates were preparing to form a party led by Ōkuma, Itagaki sought to draw Ōkuma and his followers into the Jiyūtō. As early as September 20, 1881, Hayashi Yūzō, one of the leaders of the Tosa Risshisha and Ono's fellow clansman, wrote to Ono and recommended that he meet Itagaki. Ono replied directly, saying: "If he does not mind my common ways and wants to meet me, I do not dare to refuse to meet him." Other letters from Hayashi followed on

September 24, October 9, and November 6; but although the latter contained congratulations on Ono's resignation, the proposed meeting did not take place.[41] Whether Hayashi knew at the time that Ono was engaged in preparing a rival party is uncertain, but he was well aware of Ono's talents and hoped he would join the Tosa-dominated Jiyūtō. Immediately after Ōkuma left the cabinet, Itagaki visited him and assured him of future cooperation from the Jiyūtō. Ōkuma thanked Itagaki for his kindness but ignored the offer. He regarded Itagaki's behavior in the cabinet as too radical, and because the two differed in personality and viewpoint,[42] each politician relied on his personal following to promote his political ideas and search for power.

On October 29 Ono received a letter from Shimada Saburō, a member of Numa Morikazu's Ōmeisha, and on December 2, Numa suggested that he and Ono meet. Ono wrote in his diary that he did not trust Numa's character, but as long as he wanted to meet Ono, he could not refuse to see him. If he refused, he would be shortsighted, so he accepted the proposal.[43] Numa had developed a cohesive group of supporters while in office who were, as Joyce Lebra has shown, a natural nucleus about which to organize a party. In November 1881 Numa had urged Ōkuma to organize a party,[44] and his invitation to Ono was a prelude to the union of his own followers with those of Ōkuma. Other former government officials also began to advise Ōkuma that if he wanted to succeed in the future, he had no alternative but to organize a political party with men of similar viewpoints.[45]

Following their meeting on October 13, Ōkuma left the details of organizing the party in Ono's hands. On November 3 the two met at the councilor's home to discuss the future of "our party" at great length. Ten days later, following a conversation that lasted for several hours, they came to understand each other more closely. During much of November, Ono was bedridden with a painful eye ailment. Despite his illness, he wrote the party declaration,[46] which was based upon reference material prepared by the seven students. Ono had earlier decided to place the party principles on an academic foundation and had asked them to look into the matter. Fearing that the theory espoused by the Jiyūtō was dangerous to national polity and overly radical due to its debt to Rousseau and French revolutionary ideas of liberty, equality, and fraternity, they decided to have the Kaishintō stand for gradual and orderly progress. Ōkuma and Ono agreed with this idea, and the seven combined reading, research, and the results of their studies at the university into a utilitarian concept of deliberate, gradual, and orderly progress. Their theory and research served as reference materials for Ono, who wrote the declaration and platform of the Kaishintō by adapting their ideas to the Japanese scene. Although Ono had been ordered to draft the party principles and platform by Ōkuma, he secretly consulted with the seven; and since the sentences were rewritten more than ten times, he often read them aloud in "an elegant voice" to his youthful followers.[47] On November 27 Ogawa, Takada, Ichishima, Okayama, Tachibana, and Suzuki agreed on the declaration he had produced. Three days later Ono called on Ōkuma and spoke to him for several hours. In early December Ono's activities were again interrupted by illness, but he continued to meet almost daily with the students and others.[48] The reports prepared by the students were now combined with many of his earlier ideas into the draft platform of the Kaishintō, entitled *Nani o motte tō o musuban* (*How to Unite a Party*).

Ono began *Nani o motte tō o musuban* by stating that the party should decide upon its basic principles, proclaim them clearly and explicitly, and point out how they could be applied to fundamental problems. The inability of the Jiyūtō to influence the public and the government was due to its "empty theory which was not applicable to the present situation." It was necessary to develop a well-planned platform and to establish a newspaper to publicize the views of the party. Fashions in the political world should be eschewed, and principle should always be adhered to. The party should lead public opinion and not be led by it. Ono favored careful selection of party members to maintain unity. To develop administrative ability, he suggested the organization of a shadow cabinet. To gain public support, he advised that members conduct themselves with proper decorum. To increase the party's following, members should tour the prefectures, starting with the Northeast and then move south to spread the party's ideas. In particular, "respected persons" in each region should be brought into the party fold. Furthermore, the party should take the view of the "middle class who now control public opinion." Government officials should be attracted to the party subtly, and the police in local areas should be enrolled to keep them from interfering in party activities. To prevent the use of military pressure on the party, disaffected officers should be invited to join and then party philosophy could be disseminated among the troops. Ono concluded by stating the party principles:

> When an imperial rescript is given, it is to be regarded as the law of the land. We Japanese are now in an age of prosperity, and we are going to live in a world governed by constitutional procedures. We should optimistically plan for this and do our duty, so we will not be ashamed to call ourselves "Japanese." We must join together into a political party to cooperate in pointing out the correct direction in politics. . . .
>
> Happiness is what man desires; but if it is the happiness of only a minority of the people, it is useless. . . . What we want is happiness for all the people in this country.

Those who sought to control politics for their own purposes were enemies; those with similar views were invited to join the party. The first step toward the party's goal was "to maintain physical and spiritual independence," to decide on rational methods of action, and to put principles into practice as the situation demanded. Last, Ono declared his opposition to those who ignored the imperial household and strove for immediate equality.[49] The work was presented to Ōkuma on December 17 and then to Takada and Yano Fumio, who made corrections and suggestions. Thereafter, it was rewritten as the declaration of the Kaishintō.[50]

On January 31 Ono, Kōno Togama, and Maejima Hisoka visited Ōkuma at his villa to discuss the party. At this meeting it was decided that Ono should write the regulations for the party, and that evening, Ono began to work on the draft. Between February 1 and 6 Ono wrote the party regulations, policy statements, and declaration. During this period he was in continual contact with Ōkuma, his seven students, and Gishin. On February 7 Ono delivered copies of the documents to Ōkuma; thereafter, they were discussed and corrected by the students, Gishin, Fukai, Matsudaira, Andō Minamoto, Kawamoto, Anami, Ogawa, and Ōkuma. Ono then rewrote the declaration and sent it to Yano Fumio on February 17. On February 23 Ōkuma, Ono, Kōno, and Maejima met and agreed upon the name of the party and the declaration, rules, and covenant that Ono had written. That day, the name "Rikken Kaishintō" appeared for the first time in Ono's diary, along with the comment: "My rules to improve the political party have advanced another step to success." The decisions made at the meeting of the twenty-third became the subject of continuous discussions between Ono and his colleagues, including Yano Fumio, whom he visited on February 25.

Ono's closest associates in planning the party were Ogawa and the students, led by Takada, whom he saw almost daily. As progress accelerated on the organization of the party, the Ono *gumi,* an informal study session, began to take on the character of a political association. On February 27 the members therefore formally established their group under the title of the "Ōtokai." They were now ready to enter the party as a cohesive unit centered around Ono. On March 27 Ono introduced the members of the Ōtokai to Ōkuma for the first time.[51]

By February 25 Ono had completed drafting the basic policy documents, and on March 11 and 12 Ono and Ōkuma decided on how the party would be presented to the public for the first time. On March 14 a meeting was held at the Meiji kaidō, a large lecture hall in Tokyo capable of seating three thousand people, to announce the establishment of the party and the *Rikken Kaishintō no sengen (Declaration of the Rikken Kaishintō).* Written by Ono between February 5 and 25,[52] it represented a basic statement of party policy.

> The establishment of the constitution was decided upon in the Imperial Rescript. We Japanese [now] have a wonderful opportunity; but what plans must we form and what duties must we accept to realize it? As citizens of the Japanese empire, there is only one thing for us to do. We must

organize a party to publicize our opinions. Therefore, you . . . are gathered here to perform your duties as subjects of the emperor.

Happiness is what man desires, but our party does not seek only the happiness of a few. Such happiness is egotistical. It is opposed to our desire for the prosperity of the imperial family and the happiness of the people.[53]

If there are any who belittle the authority and prosperity of the imperial household and the happiness of the people, who seek momentary ease and take no heed of the permanent harm [caused by this viewpoint], this party will consider them as the enemies of the public. We intend to unify this party through our deep desire for the eternal continuity of the authority and prosperity of the imperial household and the permanent happiness of the people. . . . This party wants to see improvement and progress in the political world. However, this party does not desire radical change. Change brought about with haste and without orderly procedures would upset and prevent political development.[54]

Therefore, those who advocate radicalism . . . are not welcome in our party. We hope to improve the government by proper order and methods and to promote steady advancement.

For this purpose, we declare the following two principles:

1. The title of our party shall be the Rikken Kaishintō.
2. Our party shall consist of subjects of the Japanese empire who want the following:

   Prosperity for the imperial family and happiness for the people.

   Administrative improvement which would strengthen the nation.

   Non-interference by the central government [in local matters] and the establishment of local autonomy.

   The right to vote to be extended as society progresses.

   Non-interference in the affairs of foreign countries and and increased commercial relations.

   A monetary system based on specie.[55]

Although the formal inaugural ceremony and election of officers did not take place until a month later, the March 14 meeting represented one of the high points of Ono's organizational activities. It ushered in a period of even more intensified activity as Ono worked to increase the number of Kaishintō supporters.

Ono was the key figure in the establishment of the Kaishintō. He instituted and guided the negotiations that resulted in the decision to organize a party, and then handled all arrangements leading to the formation of the party. He acted as the intermediary between Ōkuma and the members and among the various factions, which he sought to merge into a unified political group. Before any major decision relating to the Kaishintō was taken, Ono first consulted Ōkuma and then Numa, Yano, and the former bureaucrats and elder statesmen of the party, Kōno and Maejima. After agreement had been reached, Ono released statements to the members and general public, sometimes in Ōkuma's name. At the same time, he worked to publicize the party and handled all contacts with the government.

On March 17, following a meeting with Ōkuma, Ono wrote on measures needed to improve the party. The next day he discussed his ideas with Ōkuma, Kōno, and Maejima; thereafter he visited Narishima Ryūhoku, Shimada, Yano, Mutaguchi Gengaku, Hirose Tameoki, and Fukuzawa. After this he wrote two letters to party members, one, under Ōkuma's signature, on the principles needed to improve the Kaishintō and on the party covenant. On March 22 Ōkuma, Kōno, Maejima, and Ono went to the Meiji kaidō to arrange for the formal inauguration of the party. That evening Ono informed the government of the establishment of the Kaishintō. Although the police at first rejected his letter, on March 25 he told Ōkuma that it had finally been accepted.

As the party became known in late March and early April, many people began to call on Ono. Local officials such as a prefectural representative from Miyagi and a councilor from Tochigi came to request changes in the Kaishintō declaration, and the governor of Nagasaki visited Ōkuma. On March 28 Ono wrote the speech Ōkuma was to give when he accepted the party presidency. Three days later Ono began to draft the Kaishintō platform and Ōkuma and thirty others approved it as well as his plan to promote the party on April 1. The group then elected seven representatives, including Ono, to write the party regulations, admission procedures, and financial arrangements. After speaking with Ōkuma, Ono drafted the bylaws, which were then sent to Ōkuma, Maejima, Kōno, Yano, Numa, and Ushiba for correction. On April 8 about one hundred Kaishintō members met at Ōkuma's villa. The next day the *Rikken Kaishintō shuisho (Prospectus of the Rikken Kaishintō)* was sent to the printer. Shortly thereafter, Ono and Ōkuma decided to hold the inaugural ceremony of the Kaishintō on April 16, and Ono informed the members of this.

After almost a year of planning, the Kaishintō was formally established on April 16, 1882. At the ceremony held at the Meiji kaidō, the members first signed the membership list and exchanged name cards. Then Kōno stood up and asked the members to recommend a president according to the rules governing the party. Ono described this moment in his diary. He saw Ōkuma look around, and he volunteered to recommend Ōkuma as president. Maejima seconded the motion, and other members gave their approval. Then Kōno, representing all the members, asked Ōkuma to be the president. Ōkuma accepted and said that, since a political party was the responsibility of all its members, he really hoped they would assist him and tell him when he made any mistakes. Maejima then asked Kōno to thank Ōkuma on behalf of the members. Thereafter the officers of the party, including Mutaguchi and Haruki Yoshiaki, two of the elder statesmen of the Kaishintō, and Ono were selected.[56] Ono, who had stated the need for party government in *Kinsei jūgi* in March 1881, and had conceived the idea of forming the party the following June, now saw the realization of his efforts. From the first mention of a party to the opening ceremony, he had personally guided every aspect of the organization. On April 16, 1882, he recommended Ōkuma for the presidency of Kaishintō and then listened to him deliver an inaugural address, *Waga tōjin ni tsugu (To The Members of Our Party),* which Ono had written on March 28.[57]

In this speech Ono defined the character and objectives of the Kaishintō. Thus Ōkuma began by stating: "My duty is to reform the present policy [of the government]. I want, first of all, to repay the emperor for his kindness and to fulfill the expectations which society places in us; and it is my pleasure to share this purpose with those of you in our party in order to promote reform." He then opposed the concentration of power in the hands of one or two clans and declared that the aim of the Restoration was to end the "private domination of political power." He declared: "I want to achieve eternal prosperity for the emperor and everlasting happiness for the people by consolidating my ideas and, thereby, accomplish the great task of the Restoration and lay the foundation for an empire which will last forever." Those who were satisfied with temporary expedients, with shortsighted solutions to financial and diplomatic problems, or who favored using the national treasury to interfere in private enterprise, sought only "momentary happiness" for the people. They ignored the imperial family and despised the people and were to be regarded as enemies. Progress was the "usual state of the times," and it was essential to allow modern trends to come into the country. The party was to move toward its goal with gradual and orderly means and firm measures in order to promote progress in political life. In regard to the Jiyūtō, Ōkuma stated:

> I will not go along with those who are merely followers of Rousseau. These latter-day Jacobins are quick tempered and aggressively demand change. It is important to distinguish clearly between ourselves and parties which pretend to prefer gradualism in order to hide their conservatism. Our party favors policies which shall promote improvement and progress. We shall try to improve political life by orderly means and firm measures to the greatest extent possible. In looking at European history, I think we can say that English political life improved and progressed by orderly means and effective measures. On the contrary, in France change was instituted rapidly and aggressively. As a result, the social order was destroyed and political development retarded. Now look at the world and see which royal families are most prosperous and which people are most happy. When I think of this, I cannot help but admire England greatly. If we, too, progress by policies based on such orderly means and firm measures, we shall come to be ranked with England or even to surpass it.[58]

The second major policy statement that Ono wrote was the party platform entitled *Shisei no yōgi* (*Essentials of Administration*). This had been drafted on March 31 and was delivered at the April 16 meeting. It began:

> Our party's principles have just been declared. The people want the prosperity of the imperial family and their own happiness. Who in our country, other than a traitor, can forget the prosperity of the imperial family and ignore the happiness of the people? The only difference among the people is in their methods on how to reach these goals effectively. This is the reason why we have different ideas on administration; and interparty conflicts are based on this difference. Therefore, if all [parties] cease to declare their principles, the people would be at a loss over which party to follow. Thus, our party declares its policy on administrative matters so that the people can judge it.

The principles, in brief, were as follows:

1. To await the emperor's decision on the constitution and organization of the national assembly and to work for stable party government. The purpose of constitutionalism is party cabinets according to the will of the Diet.
2. To insure imperial succession, influence, and popularity by placing control over royal property in one organization.
3. To strengthen the army by placing it under the control of the central government and to reduce military expenses by concentrating army installations in selected areas.
4. To reduce the period of military service for conscripts by teaching the use of arms in primary schools.
5. To reduce naval expenditures by maintaining a small permanent navy and having most officers and sailors work for private shipping firms; money saved on salaries should be used to manufacture armaments.
6. To draft the coastal population for service in the navy rather than for the army.
7. To free the national university from state control, promote academic independence, and raise the level of education in the nation.
8. To prevent political interference in religious matters.
9. To establish a ministry of industry to improve and develop roads, harbors, and rivers.
10. To reduce nonessential government spending and use the money saved to reorganize the judicial system; to promote judicial independence.[59]

The third document written by Ono was *Kiyaku* or the *Covenant* of the Kaishintō. The major points of this document were:

1. Our party is named the *Heiwa Kaishinseitō* (Political Party of Peace and Progress) [*sic*].
2. Our main office is in Tokyo where we maintain a list of all members; district branches maintain lists of local members.
3. The business of the main office is divided into six departments; legislation, finance, diplomacy, internal affairs, military affairs, general affairs. Branch offices can organize business according to need and will handle local party matters.
4. We have one president chosen by majority decision and serving an unlimited term.
5. A permanent committee of twelve members, half elected by local party members, will be located at the head office to handle party business.
6. Both the main office and branch offices will appoint a clerk and accountant to handle general affairs.
7. The president is responsible for all party business. Decisions on party matters will be made at an open meeting of representatives from all over the country held once a year. The president has the power to call special meetings when necessary.
8. Candidates for membership must apply to the branch office and ask to be registered as a member. Those desiring to leave the party must notify the main and branch office.
9. Detailed rules to carry out these regulations can be decided upon later.[60]

The party bylaws, which Ono had completed writing in April, were also announced at this time.[61] These stated:

Article 1. Our party has one president who is elected by a majority of the members.

Article 2. Our party has three directors and two secretaries selected and appointed by the president.

Article 3. Prospective members require the recommendation of more than three members; their names should be reported at the monthly meeting.

Article 4. Those desiring to leave the party should inform the directors, who will report this at the monthly meeting.

Article 5. Members who oppose party policy or disgrace our party will be expelled by resolution of the monthly meeting.

Article 6. In order to provide funds, dues for members in Tokyo are one yen per year and for those in other areas fifty sen a year. Dues should be paid by June 30.

Article 7. Members will meet at 3 P.M. on the fifteenth of every month at the Tokyo office. Attendance fee is fifty sen.

Article 8. Revision of the bylaws can be done at the monthly meeting.

Parliamentary procedures for meetings were included in the bylaws, and the party president was designated as the chairman of the meeting.[62]

The inaugural meeting also served to introduce the party leaders to the public. In addition to Ōkuma, Yano, Ono, Numa, Shimada, Fujita Mokichi, Inukai Tsuyoshi, and Takanashi Tetsuhirō spoke. According to Takada, the speeches of the *Yūbin hōchi* and *Mainichi* groups were regarded as exceptionally good; but for some reason, Ono was not so eloquent as usual and Takada was disappointed in his oratory.[63] Kōno, who served as chairman, discussed the reasons why a party was needed to oppose Itagaki's group. The Jiyūtō, he stated, advocated justice and equality and certainly was the friend of the poor; but, as a result, the wealthy were not pleased with it. The Jiyūtō was concerned mainly with practical objectives, and so scholars were not happy with it. The Jiyūtō attracted young and active spirits; thus, the mature did not like it. Therefore, the rich, scholars, and elderly remained outside the Jiyūtō even though they constituted a powerful group whose support political parties must have. The Kaishintō planned to include them in its membership in order to have solid backing in the future. Therefore, it must seek to build a coalition of men of wealth, scholars, and "neutral" men of high reputation.[64]

The Kaishintō declaration, Ōkuma's inaugural address, and the party platform represent a summarization of Ono's views on political reform and party structure and activities. As early as 1876 he had written of the need to develop representative government and to give voting rights to the people.[65] In December 1879 he had told Ōkuma that administrative change was necessary to end "government by the Dajōkan" and had warned of the danger of political radicalism. To prevent "the misery of the Paris revolution," he had advised convening the Diet in 1881.[66] In 1881 he again wrote to Ōkuma on the need for fiscal and judicial reform, party cabinets, the unification of administrative policy, and budget cuts.[67] In another letter to Ōkuma on June 13, 1881, Ono attacked Satchō control of the government and the lack of direction in administrative policy.[68] As his plans began to crystallize during the summer of 1881, Ono discussed his views of the Jiyūtō's "naive political principles" and the need to establish a party with concrete policies with Takada Sanae.[69] In *Nani o motte tō o musuban,* written at the end of 1881, he repeated his criticism of the Jiyūtō's "empty theories" and said that a party had to gain the support of "respectable persons." He stated that imperial rescripts should be regarded as law and that dissident elements should unite into a party capable of instituting political reform, and declared that those entering politics for selfish purposes or who ignored the imperial household were to be regarded as enemies.[70]

In *Moshi ware mizukara ataraba,* Ono advocated the establishment of a constitution as a means whereby change could be instituted gradually.[71] In a conversation with Ichishima Kenkichi, Ono said that Japanese national polity was a guiding principle, one that possessed its own rationale. Thus, things should be done in logical order. Political freedom could be achieved by following a certain pattern; and to attain freedom, it was necessary to choose moderate and gradual means.[72] Ichishima, who was studying British political theory under Fenollosa, reported that Fenollosa lectured on the need to follow moderate, orderly procedures to achieve freedom and happiness. These ideas were taken down and later shown to Ono, who agreed with them.[73] Fenollosa's ideas were written into the first draft of the declaration but gradually became less distinguishable as the document was rewritten.[74] Ono then added the utilitarian doctrine of "the greatest happiness of the greatest number" to his earlier ideas. The members of the Ōtokai, using notes taken from their studies at Tokyo University, including Fenollosa's lectures, drew up the guidelines for the party policy statements. Their views corresponded with those of Ono and Ōkuma. Thus, according to Takada Sanae, Ono drew up the declaration, principles, and platform of the Kaishintō on orders from Ōkuma and in consultation with Ōkuma's most important followers and the members of the Ōtokai.[75] The seven students participated secretly in this process, and the original Ono-Ōtokai draft was adopted by the Kaishintō without any major change.[76]

The principles and platform of the Kaishintō were enumerated in its declaration, Ōkuma's inaugural address, and the party plaftorm. These declared that it was the duty of the party to oppose the "private domination of politics" and to promote the "eternal prosperity of the throne and the everlasting happiness of the people." Those who oppose these aims or "ignored the imperial family" were to be regarded as the enemies of the people and party. Radical political theories and rapid, unsettling change advocated by "the followers of Rousseau," a euphemism for the Jiyūtō, were eschewed in favor of gradual progress by "orderly means" following the British example.[77] In *Shisei no yōgi,* the party publicized its platform "in order to have the people judge it."[78] This was essential, for differences on administrative policy were the causes of interparty conflicts, a statement adopted from Ōkuma's 1881 memorial.[79] However, in emphasizing the "everlasting happiness of the people," the Kaishintō had adopted the utilitarian thesis that pleasure can be used as the basis of morality; thus the proper use of hedonistic guidelines, as enumerated in Bentham's *Introduction to the Principles of Morals and Legislation,* could produce "eternal happiness."[80] *Shisei no yōgi* was therefore a utilitarian document, which took the theme of "the greatest happiness of the greatest number" to oppose the privileges of a specific group.[81] Ono, who had lived and studied in England, and his students were deeply impressed by British political life and theory, by what they regarded as "practical commonsense developments" and the "moderate steadfastness of England."

England, the most advanced nation in Europe, had shown to the world its skill in conducting parliamentary politics, an example from which they believed Japan could learn a great deal.[82]

Thus the major documents and policy statements of the Kaishintō were written by Ono with the advice and assistance of the students in the Ōtokai. These works were first drafted by Ono, who then showed them to Ōkuma and other members of the party who offered suggestions or corrections. Ōkuma was not the originator of the party's principles or platform, but, as seen from Ono's diary, he sanctioned those works which Ono had produced. The declaration and platform of the Kaishintō should not, as Watanabe Ikujirō has written, "be regarded as [the result] of collaboration by Ōkuma and Ono,"[83] but rather as the work of Ono with the assistance of the Ōtokai. Nagata Shinnosuke, a contemporary of Ono's, and Suzuki Yasuzō both regard Ono as the author of both documents as well as the party covenant.[84] One himself was especially proud of the declaration; and shortly after it was completed, he wrote his brother, Shigematsu:

> We—Ōkuma, Kōno, Maejima, and I—are going to form a great political party together with others . . . in order to contribute to [the welfare of] our country to the best of our abilities. I wrote the declaration. It took me a very long time, and I am rather proud of my work for it is almost perfect. I have gradually been getting the trust of the people and I am sure I will succeed in life. It is all the result of our late father's [admonition] though in part it is due to the current political situation. Indeed the current situation is the first step in my success.[85]

He repeated these ideas in an undated note written in the second person after the establishment of the Kaishintō:

> This year, you joined with Ōkuma, Kōno, and Maejima to form the Rikken Kaishintō. People heard that you drafted its prospectus, and many prominent persons added to it.[86]

Ono's importance to the Kaishintō was appreciated by the government, which now tried to get him to return to the bureaucratic fold. On February 4, 1882, Ono recorded in his diary that he had had a visitor who asked if he would like to become minister plenipotentiary to the United States. Ono laughed at the suggestion and replied: "It is a clever trick. The administration wants to exile me to a foreign country. I have many things to do here in regard to domestic problems. I cannot go abroad for amusement. How can I be a diplomat? I won't give up." On March 14, several hours before the Kaishintō held its preliminary meeting, Ono went to Yokohama to say farewell to Itō Hirobumi, who was going abroad. He described the meeting: "He [Itō] was extremely polite to me and shook hands with me when we parted. I still cannot figure out why he treated me that politely." On April 8 Kaneko Kentarō called on Ono, who noted in his diary: "Kaneko Kentarō visited. I still cannot figure out the reason why he came. I have no ideas. He might have come here to betray me or to support me, but it is certain that I must be extremely cautious."[87] Unable to woo Ono from Ōkuma with an enticing ambassadorship, the ruling oligarchs sought to win him over to their ranks by offers of friendship. Ono was aware of their tactics, which revealed both the administration's recognition of his abilities and his personal commitment to the Kaishintō and Ōkuma.

Ono's followers in the Ōtokai were also cognizant of his importance to the Kaishintō. Thus Okayama Kenkichi stated in *Godō genkōroku*: "When Marquis Ōkuma petitioned for the establishment of a national assembly, Ono helped him with great enthusiasm. Ono understood Ōkuma's ideas and [realized] the petition would not result in changes which would bring political reform. Ono consulted with Ogawa Tamejirō on ways to carry out political improvements, and Ogawa told his friend Tachibana Kaijirō. Tachibana discussed the establishment of a political party with Ichishima and Yamada." Thus the nucleus of the Kaishintō was formed. Takada in his memoirs wrote: "After Ōkuma resigned, his faction decided to form a political party. . . . The Ōkuma faction did not agree with the Jiyūtō because its theoretical base was taken from the French revolutionary, Rousseau. These ideas were regarded as dangerous as they were opposed to our national polity and were too radical.

So [the Ōkuma faction] agreed to uphold [the standard] of moderation and orderly progress. This was the opinion of Ōkuma and of Ono."[88]

Watanabe Ikujirō, the biographer of Ōkuma and former curator of the Ōkuma Collection at Waseda University, regarded Ono as a major adviser to Ōkuma but underestimated Ono's actual importance to the Kaishintō. Watanabe wrote that close ties developed between the two after Ono was transferred to the Board of Audit in 1880 because it was Ōkuma's intervention that kept the outspoken young official from losing his position. As a result, Ono "became close to the marquis and cooperated with him in organizing the Kaishintō." He analyzed the relationship between Ono and Ōkuma as follows: "Although human resources around the marquis in the days of the Kaishintō were abundant, no one was as erudite as Ono. His relationship to the marquis was like that of Inoue Kowashi to Itō Hirobumi." In regard to the establishment of the Kaishintō, Watanabe concluded that Ono shared Ōkuma's view that constitutional politics should be founded on political parties and "formed a plan to organize a political party with his colleagues Ogawa Tamejirō and Takada. It seems clear that the marquis heard about the plan and participated in it to a certain degree. However, nothing is further from the truth than [to say] the marquis was plotting to take over power as the Satchō group claimed."[89] Unfortunately, Watanabe did not pursue these ideas further nor did he analyze Ono's diary or daily political activities.

In regard to Ono's importance to Ōkuma, Matsuda Yasuji quoted Ōkuma as saying: "He [Ono] used to tell me that the clan government, which was a military government, would never be able to produce continual prosperity. He said the only way left would be to destroy the clan government, to realize constitutional government like that of Western civilized countries, and to unite the divided powers of the nation under a single authority."[90] Ōtsu Jun'ichirō in *Dai Nihon kensei shi* stated that on March 22, 1881, Ono suggested to Ōkuma: "If you wish to decide upon an administrative policy which would change completely the organization of the cabinet, you ought to adopt constitutional government for that purpose, you ought to form a political party."[91] On March 22 Ono wrote *Sangi Ōkuma kō ni teishi shiji no hōkō o sairon suru no sho,* which he presented to Ōkuma on June 13. Although Ono bitterly attacked the Satchō councilors and advised Ōkuma to "deal with them according to the will of the public and take away their power,"[92] he did not make any statement to the effect that Ōkuma should adopt constitutional government or form a party in this letter. His first written notice to Ōkuma about a party occurs in *Moshi ware mizukara ataraba.*[93] Ōtsu has not given a source for this quotation, and it has no foundation in any of Ono's writings that are still extant. Kohayagawa Kingo has written: "Ono, Yano, Minoura [Katsundo], and Shimada were the best scholars [of the Kaishintō]."[94] However, he did not analyze their contributions to the party nor discuss Ono's role.

A more accurate evaluation of Ono's importance to the Kaishintō is given by his biographer, Nishimura Shinji. Following a brief study of *Ryūkakusai nikki,* Nishimura concluded that Ono was responsible for the establishment of the party.[95] Suzuki Yasuzō in *Kindai Nihon rekishi kōza* quoted Ōkuma as stating: "I hoped to realize the second restoration by establishing a powerful political party. The intellectuals on whom I relied, in addition to Ono, included Yano Fumio, who was Ono's senior, Inukai Tsuyoshi, Ozaki Yukio, and Shimada Saburō."[96] In a similar statement, Ōkuma added that after he left the cabinet and began to organize the Kaishintō, he was concerned over the future of the nation and "attempted to bring about a second restoration by establishing a great political party, having made a secret agreement with Mr. Ono on the matter." After lauding Ono's academic and economic talents, he added: "I was surprised at his skill in dealing with matters. Thanks to Mr. Ono, the Kaishintō was well organized."[97] Ōkuma, while praising Ono's scholarship and assistance, at no time mentions his role in the political change of 1881 nor gives him the credit due as the founder of the Kaishintō. Recognition of Ono's key position in the revelation of the Colonization Commission incident would leave the councilor open to new charges of conspiracy, accusations that he continually refuted. Yet it seems doubtful that he would not be aware of Ono's activities. Acknowledgment of

Ono's position as the man responsible for the establishment of the Kaishintō would detract from Ōkuma's fame and reputation. In a society that held age and social status in great esteem, the young advisers of leading politicians and statesmen remained in the background and saw their superiors introduce and take credit for their ideas and activities. Ono's early death and obscurity allowed Ōkuma to appropriate for himself the honor that belongs to his youthful "brain truster."

More recent studies offer greater insight into Ono's contribution to the Kaishintō. After examining the diaries and memoirs of Ichishima and Takada, Suzuki Yasuzō has concluded that Ono advised Ōkuma, assisted in establishing the party, and played a determining role in it. He acknowledges the main documents and policy statements of the Kaishintō as well as Ōkuma's presidential address as Ono's work and concludes that Ono may have suggested the establishment of the party to Ōkuma.[98]

Of the few Japanese historians who have studied Ono's activities during 1881 and 1882, Itō Isao alone has recognized Ono's importance. In *Jōchi hōgaku ronshū* he asks: "Who advised Ōkuma to form a political party? It is rumored that it was Numa Morikazu. But the need for a political party had already been stressed by Ōkuma's brain truster, Ono Azusa. . . . He [Ono] also retired from public office on the occasion of the change of government in the 14th year of Meiji and endeavored to build the Reform Party [i.e., Kaishintō] in cooperation with Ōkuma . . . the great achievement of rapidly establishing the Reform Party was largely due to Ono's intelligence." Itō further states: "In concert with the Imperial Rescript and in accordance with Ono's opinion, Ōkuma after careful consideration determined at last to form a political party not identical in character with the Liberal Party. Therefore, it is no exaggeration to say that the true founder of the Reform Party was Ono Azusa."[99] Joyce Chapman Lebra, the only other Western scholar to study Ono, similarly regarded him as the "brain" of the Kaishintō, who exerted the greatest influence on the formulation of the party principles and on Ōkuma in the early days of the Kaishintō.[100]

It should also be noted that Yano Fumio, whom George Akita

calls "one of the closest, if not the most intimate, of Ōkuma's supporters,"[101] was at his home in Oita prefecture from July until the end of August 1881, when he returned to Tokyo. His biographer, Oguri Mataichi, discusses Yano's role in regard to the *Yūbin hōchi shimbum* but not in relation to the establishment of the Kaishintō.[102] Although Ono and Ogawa began to discuss the party on June 10, 1881, and the inaugural ceremony of the Kaishintō was held on April 16, 1882, the name *Yano* does not appear in *Ryūkakusai nikki* until after February 17, 1882. Ono saw Yano a total of twelve times in the first four months of 1882: February 17, 21, 25; March 12, 22, 24, 28, 29; April 3, 6, 9, 11. Yano's name usually appeared in conjunction with others with whom Ono discussed party business and policy. Because only the surname is given[103] and because Yano Sadae, the brother of Fumio, was also listed among the original members of the party,[104] it is possible that not all of these references refer to Fumio. Therefore, prior to February 17, 1882, Yano Fumio was not closely involved in the activities leading to the organization of the party. In the period when the party was being organized, the designation of "the most intimate of Ōkuma's supporters" is more aptly applied to Ono. Ono's writings, Kaishintō policy statements, and *Ryūkakusai nikki* show that Ono Azusa was the founder of the Kaishintō, the author of its major policy statements and platform, and the closest associate of Ōkuma during the formative period of the Kaishintō.

As Ōkuma saw in Ono a young scholar who could be useful to him, so Ono saw in Ōkuma a statesman and politician of national reputation, moderate, progressive ideas, and modern outlook, who was opposed to *hanbatsu* domination of the government. Ōkuma's receptivity to change and ideas of parliamentary government, as well as his ability to move beyond the confines of clan relationships,[105] made him an appropriate leader who could promote national unity and modernization. He became, therefore, the man through whom Ono, a young, relatively obscure, and impoverished scholar-bureaucrat could realize his ideas on constitutionalism and poltical reform. The second decade of the Meiji era was a period conducive to rapid change, and the combination of Ōkuma's own ambitions and struggle for power with his fellow oligarchs and Ono's particular position and contacts within the bureaucracy occurred in a climate favorable to the implementation of ideas on political parties and representative institutions adopted from the West. In such a scene, Ono gravitated toward Ōkuma and built for the councilor from Hizen a party through which he could fulfill his political objectives and through which Ono could carry out his duty as a *shishi,* namely, the remodeling of the government structure along the lines of that of Great Britain. In this way, he would live up to his father's expectations and to his duty to the imperial family. In the founding of the Kaishintō, Ono and Ōkuma served each others' needs and jointly contributed to the modernization and democratization of Japan.

NOTES

1. Kōsaka, *Japanese Thought,* p. 134.
2. Itō Isao, "Nihon seitō no kigen," *Hōgaku shimpō* 67, no. 6 (1960): 21, 24, 32.
3. George Akita, *Foundations of Constitutional Government in Modern Japan, 1868–1910* (Cambridge, Mass.: Harvard University Press, 1967), pp. 16–22.
4. Fujii, *Constitution of Japan,* pp. 75–77.
5. Itagaki Taisuke, "Waga kuni kensei no yurai," *Meiji kensei keizai shi ron,* comp. Takano Iwazaburō (Tokyo: Yūhikaku Shobō 1919), pp. 14–18.
6. Itagaki Taisuke, ed. *Jiyūtō shi,* 3 vols. (Tokyo: Iwanami Bunko, 1957–1958), 1: 87–90.
7. Nishimura, *Ono Azusa den,* pp. 142, 143; Osatake Takeki, *Nihon kensei shi taikō,* 2: 449–56, 526; Itō Isao, "Itagaki Taisuke no jiyūshugi undō-shisō to kōdō," *Hōgaku shimpō* 71, no. 9 (1964: 61–66; Itagaki Taisuke, *Jiyūtō shi,* 1: 137–46; Itagaki, "Waga kuni kensei no yurai," pp. 18–20.
8. Nishimura, *Ono Azusa den,* p. 143; Itagaki, *Jiyūtō shi,* 1: 272; Ōtsu Jun'ichirō, *Dai Nihon kensei shi,* 10 vols. (Tokyo: Hōbunkan, 1927–1928), 2: 287; Osatake, *Nihon kensei shi,* 2: 526.
9. Shimomura, *Nihon zenshi,* 9: 113.
10. Itō, "Nihon seitō," *HS,* p. 21.
11. Nishimura, *Ono Azusa den,* p. 143.
12. Itō, "Nihon seitō," *HS,* pp. 21–24; George Akita, *Foundations,* pp. 26–28.

13. Hagihara, "Baba Tatsui," *CK* 81, no. 948 (October 1966): 389, 391, 406; Itō, "Nihon seitō," *HS*, pp. 25, 26.

14. Ono, "Ryūkakusai nikki," pp. 346–66.

15. Nishimura, *Ono Azusa den*, p. 111; Takada Sanae, *Hanhō mukashi banashi* (Tokyo: Waseda Daigaku Shuppanbu, 1927), p. 64; Kyōguchi Motokichi, *Takada Sanae den* (Tokyo: Waseda Daigaku, 1962), p. 60.

16. Ono, "Ryūkakusai nikki," p. 351. There are conflicting views on the date of the organization of the Ōtokai. Takada Sanae in *Hanhō mukashi banashi*, p. 68, has stated he first met Ono in February 1881. Shirayanagi Shūko in *Kensei juritsu hen* in *Meiji Taishō kokumin shi*, 3: 60, has stated that the Ōtokai was organized in February 1881. Kyōguchi Motokichi in *Takada Sanae den*, pp. 72–73, has written that the Ōtokai participated in the formation of the Kaishintō "a half month after the political change of 1881." Beginning on August 20, there are frequent notations in Ono's "Ryūkakusai nikki" about meeting or teaching the students, namely, Takada and his six associates; but they did not organize themselves into a formal political association under the name "Ōtokai" until February 27, 1882. Therefore, both Shirayanagi and Kyōguchi were mistaken when they took the date of Takada's first meeting with Ono as the date of the establishment of the Ōtokai. The informal study group, the Ono *gumi*, began to participate in discussions leading to the establishment of the party from August 20, or possibly even earlier that month; but it was not organized as the Ōtokai until six months later (Ono, "Ryūkakusai nikki," pp. 350–51).

17. Hakubunkan, *Seitō shi*, *MS*, 6: 177–78; Suzuki Yasuzō, *Kindai Nihon rekishi kōza*, 8 vols. (Tokyo: Hakuyōsha, 1939), 3: 185–87.

18. Hakubunkan, *Seitō shi*, *MS* 6: 177, 178.

19. Suzuki, *Kindai Nihon*, 3: 186, 187; Ōkuma, *Hachijūgonen shi*, 2: 22.

20. Ono, "Ryūkakusai nikki," pp. 350, 351, 367–79.

21. Enomoto Morie, "Ono Azusa no hanbatsu seitōron," p. 78.

22. Nishimura, *Ono Azusa den*, p. 215.

23. Takada, *Hanhō mukashi banashi*, pp. 73, 74. Shimomura Fujio in *Nihon zenshi*, 9: 114, erroneously states that the Ōtokai was not too influential as a political force.

24. Kyōguchi, *Takada Sanae*, p. 67.

25. Nishimura, *Ono Azusa den*, p. 117.

26. Takano Zen'ichi, ed., *Takada, Ichishima seitan hyakunen kinen no tame ni* (a copy of Ichishima's unpublished diary in the library of Waseda University, Tokyo), pp. 17–22. Ichishima Kenkichi was a native of Niigata prefecture and his name is pronounced "Ichishima" in Niigata dialect. This form rather than "Ichijima," which is the pronunication in Tokyo dialect, will be used throughout the book.

27. Enomoto, "Hanbatsu seitōron," *HGDK,* p. 78.
28. Nishimura, *Ono Azusa den,* p. 117; Kyōguchi, *Takada Sanae,* pp. 68–70.
29. Suzuki, *Kindai Nihon,* 3: 187.
30. Usuda Zan'un, *Tenka no kishā—Yamada Ichirō kun genkōroku* (Tokyo: Jitsugyo no Nihon Sha, 1906), p. 65.
31. Uyabe Shuntei, *Meiji jinbutsu shōkan* (Tokyo: Hakubunkan, 1902), pp. 125, 126.
32. Ono, "Ryūkakusai nikki," pp. 346, 350, 351, 359–65.
33. Although Ono merely states the name Tachibana in his diary, the name refers to Tachibana Kaijirō, a close friend of Takada Sanae (Kyōguchi, *Takada Sanae,* p. 68). Watanabe Ikujirō states that Ono and Ōkuma discussed organizing a political party about August or September 1881; discussions did not progress greatly until after the political change of October 12, 1881. Cf. Watanabe Ikujirō, *Ōkuma Shigenobu* (Tokyo: Ōkuma Shigenobu Kankokai, 1936), p. 157. It is the author's contention that Ōkuma discussed the formation of the party with Ono in June prior to his departure for the Northeast and that Ono through messengers and letters kept him informed of the progress of negotiations leading to the organization of the party while he was on tour with the imperial party.
34. *JWM* (Yokohama), 5, no. 35 (September 3, 1881): 1017.
35. Hakubunkan, *Seitō shi, MS* 6: 177, 178.
36. Ono, "Ryūkakusai nikki," pp. 362, 363. From notations in "Ryūkakusai nikki," Nishimura Shinji concluded that the general plans for the party had been thoroughly discussed by September 23, 1881 (Nishimura, *Ono Azusa den,* p. 119).
37. Watanabe, *Ōkuma Shigenobu,* p. 156.
38. Ono, "Ryūkakusai nikki," p. 366.
39. Watanabe, *Ōkuma Shigenobu,* p. 456.
40. Suzuki, *Kindai Nihon,* 3: 185.
41. Ono, "Ryūkakusai nikki," pp. 362–72.
42. Oguri, *Yano Fumio,* p. 196.
43. Ono, "Ryūkakusai nikki," pp. 369, 373.
44. Lebra, *Ōkuma Shigenobu,* p. 97.
45. Nagata, *Ono Azusa,* pp. 161–62.
46. Ono, "Ryūkakusai nikki," pp. 366–73.
47. Takada, *Hanhō mukashi banashi,* pp. 17–22, 73, 76, 77.
48. Ono, "Ryūkakusai nikki," pp. 373–75.
49. Ono Azusa, "Nani o motte tō o musuban," *Ono Azusa zenshū,* 2: 287–92.
50. Ono, "Ryūkakusai nikki," p. 375; Nishimura, *Ono Azusa den,* p. 150.
51. Ono, "Ryūkakusai nikki," pp. 378–85.
52. For contemporary accounts of the meeting see Ishida Bunshirō, ed., *Shimbun zasshi ni arawareta Meiji jidai bunka kiroku shūsei,*

2 vols. (Tokyo: Jidai Bunka Kenkyū Kai, 1934), 1: 311. From *Yūbin hōchi shimbun,* March 14, 1882. *Shōhei yomon-Tokyo shinshi,* 6, no. 291 (1882): 1, 2; Ono, "Ryūkakusai nikki," pp. 380–83; Asakura Haruhiko and Inamura Tetsugen, eds. *Meiji sesō hennen jiten* (Tokyo: Tokyodō, 1965), p. 194.

53. Aono, *Nihon seitō,* p. 55.

54. Itō, "Constitutional Reform Party," *JHR,* pp. 8–10.

55. Aono, *Nihon seitō,* pp. 56–57.

56. Ono, "Ryūkakusai nikki," pp. 383–89; Ōkuma Hensan Kai, *Ōkuma kō hachijūgonen shi,* 2: 29.

57. Ibid., pp. 337–39, 346, 383, 388–89; Meiji Shiryō, *Meiji seiken,* p. 118.

58. Ono Azusa, "Waga tōjin ni tsugu," *Ono Azusa zenshū,* 2: 293–97; cf. Itō, "Reform Party," *JHR,* pp. 23–24.

59. Ono Azusa, "Shisei no yōgi," *Ono Azusa zenshū,* 2: 299–302; cf. Ōkuma Hensan Kai, *Ōkuma kō hachijūgonen shi,* 2: 30–33.

60. Ono Azusa, "Kiyaku," *Ono Azusa zenshū,* 2: 303–4. This is the only document referring to the Rikken Kaishintō by another title and may be an earlier draft or a misprint.

61. Ono, "Ryūkakusai nikki," pp. 386–88.

62. Nakamura Gizō, ed. *Naigai seitō jijo* (July 30, 1882), pp. 134–36.

63. Takada, *Hanhō mukashi banashi,* pp. 81, 82.

64. Shimomura, *Nihon zenshi,* 9: 114, 115.

65. Ōno Azusa, "Dare ka kokkai no kaisetsu wa shōsō nari to iu ya," *Ono Azusa zenshū,* 2: 61–64.

66. Ono Azusa, "Bō daijin ni teisuru no sho," pp. 101–4.

67. Ono Azusa, "Kinsei jūgi," pp. 264–75.

68. Ono Azusa, "Ōkuma kō," pp. 276–79.

69. Hakubunkan, *Seitō shi, MS* 6: 177, 178.

70. Ono, "Nani o motte tō o musuban," pp. 287–90.

71. Ono Azusa, "Moshi ware mizukara ataraba," pp. 74–78.

72. Matsuo Shōichi, *Jiyū minken shisō no kenkyū* (Tokyo: Kashiwa Shobō, 1965), p. 175.

73. Enomoto, "Meiji shonen," *SC,* pp. 175, 176.

74. Takano, *Takada, Ichishima seitan,* p. 21.

75. Takada, *Hanhō mukashi banashi,* pp. 76, 77; Suzuki *Kindai Nihon,* 3: 185, 188.

76. Uyabe, *Meiji jinbutsu,* pp. 125, 126.

77. Ono, "Waga tōjin ni tsugu," pp. 293–97.

78. Ono, "Shisei no yōgi," pp. 299–302.

79. Beckmann, *Meiji Constitution,* pp. 141, 142.

80. Satō Kiyokatsu, *Dai Nihon seiji shisō shi,* 6 vols. (Tokyo: Tōa Jikyoku Kenkyū Kai Hakkō, 1934), 6: 730.

81. Enomoto, "Ono Azusa no seiji ronri," *NRR,* p. 1; Torii Hiroo, *Meiji shisō shi* (Tokyo: Mikasa Shobō, 1947), p. 32.

82. Ōkuma, *Hachijūgonen shi,* 2: 19–20.
83. Watanabe, *Ōkuma Shigenobu,* p. 157; idem., *Monjo yori mitaru Ōkuma,* p. 456.
84. Nagata, *Ono Azusa den,* p. 175; Suzuki, *Kindai Nihon,* 3: 184.
85. Ono Azusa, "Ono Shigematsu ate shokan," *Ono Azusa zenshū,* 2: 110, 111.
86. Ono, *OM,* no. 18. ...
87. Ono, "Ryūkakusai nikki," pp. 379, 383, 387; Nishimura, *Ono Azusa den,* pp. 155, 156.
88. Suzuki, *Kindai Nihon,* 3: 187.
89. Watanabe, *Monjo yori mitaru Ōkuma,* pp. 445, 449–50, 455. Watanabe also compares the relationship between Ono and Ōkuma and between Inoue Kaoru and Itō Hirobumi in a similar quotation in his *Ōkuma Shigenobu,* p. 156.
90. Matsueda Yasuji, *Ōkuma kō sekijitsu tan* (Tokyo: Hōchi Shimbunsha, 1922), p. 276, 277.
91. Ōtsu Jun'ichirō, *Dai Nihon kensei shi,* 2:531. This passage was translated by Itō Isao and also appears in his "Constitutional Reform Party," *JHR,* p. 4, and "Nihon seitō no kigen," p. 29.
92. Ono, "Ōkuma kō," pp. 276–79.
93. Ono, "Moshi ware mizukara ataraba," pp. 74–78.
94. Kohayagawa Kingo, *Meiji hōsei shi,* 2: 646, 647.
95. Nishimura, *Ono Azusa den,* p. 153.
96. Suzuki, *Kindai Nihon,* 3:185.
97. Ōkuma, "Junkyōsha to shite no Ono Azusa kun," p. 14.
98. Suzuki, *Kindai Nihon,* 3: 184.
99. Itō, "Reform Party," *JHR,* pp. 4–6.
100. Joyce [Chapman] Lebra, "Kaishintō no sōritsusha oyobi rironka Ono Azusa," *Nihon rekishi,* no. 148 (October 1960), pp. 61–67.
101. Akita, *Foundations,* p. 48.
102. Oguri Mataichi, *Ryūkei Yano Fumio kun den* (Tokyo: Shunyodō, 1936), p. 178.
103. Ono, "Ryūkakusai nikki," pp. 381, 383, 386–88.
104. Nakamura, *Naigai seitō jijō,* pp. 147, 150.
105. Cf. Lebra, "Ōkuma Shigenobu."

7
The New Politician

Ono saw a moderate liberal party as the best means to control *hanbatsu* absolutism and Jiyūtō "radicalism" while promoting the cause of parliamentary government. Despite the similarity of objectives and activities, the popular parties regarded one another as enemies[1] in the struggle for supporters and ultimate power. Inability to effect a working compromise irreparably damaged the *mintō* and led to acrimonious relationships among men who had been close associates and friends before the organization of the Kaishintō. Ono and Hayashi Yūzō had grown up together in Sukumo, and Ono and Baba Tatsui had worked together in the Nihon gakusei kai and Kyōzon dōshū.[2] In 1880 Baba organized a political discussion society for Keiō graduates; and the members included Inukai Tsuyoshi, Minoura Katsundo, Fujita Mokichi, and Hatano Denzaburō, all of whom later joined the Kaishintō. After several months, they left the association, and in April 1881 Baba reorganized it as the Kokuyūkai (Friend of the People Association). Composed primarily of Tosa clansmen and offering greater freedom of discussion than the Kyōzon dōshū, it was led by Baba into the Jiyūtō. Baba alone of the Mita faction joined Itagaki. Following the suppression of political speeches, Baba came to believe that the only way to maintain sound politics was to strengthen public resistance in direct proportion to the increase in official repression. He later came to favor an all-inclusive political union to further the *mintō* position and to prepare for the day when the parties would oppose the oligarchs in the national assembly.[3] Three days before the Jiyūtō inaugural ceremony, he asked Ono to join his party. Although Ono discussed the issue with him and promised to give an answer at a later date, he told Baba it was wrong to have a party comprised mainly of Tosa men. On November 19 the two met at Ono's home, and Baba repeated his request. Ono offered to reconsider but wrote in his diary that he refused to join the Jiyūtō.[4] Baba also was close to Iwasaki Yatarō, a native of Tosa, through the marriage of their relatives.[5] Iwasaki maintained ties with the Kokuyūkai because of its clan orientation.[6] Taguchi Ukichi and Suehiro Shigeyasu of the Kokuyūkai were former members of the Ōmeisha and had contacts with the Numa faction, which the Jiyūtō originally regarded as a "partner" even though it belonged to the Ōkuma group.[7] Gotō Shōjirō was in the Kōjunsha,[8] and therefore there were personal ties between Baba and Gotō and the followers of Numa and Fukuzawa.

Following the announcement of the Imperial Rescript of October 12, 1881, Itagaki and Fukuzawa both decided to organize political parties. Fukuzawa intended to establish a party on the British model but was not successful.[9] Itagaki suggested to Ōkuma that they cast aside petty differences and form one party, but the Ōkuma faction rejected his offer and advised concentrating on concrete issues such as the alienation of public land and changing the composition of the cabinet. Ideological and personal differences, fear of Jiyūtō radicalism, and the struggle for power prevented union among the opposing forces in the *mintō* and weakened the parties in the face of united government opposition.

Itagaki then went on a tour of the Northeast.[10] In the latter half of October, seventy-eight representatives of the Kokkai kisei dōmei and other political groups from all over Japan assembled in Tokyo according to an agreement made the previous year. Following eleven days of meetings chaired by Baba Tatsui,[11] the Jiyūtō was established and its pact and rules announced to the public on October 29. Despite Ōkuma's lack of receptivity to Itagaki's request for joint action, several former bureaucrats who belonged to his and Fukuzawa's factions attended the meeting as private individuals. Members of the Ōmeisha caused confusion during the election of the party president by nominating Gotō instead of Itagaki. The nomination was opposed by the Kyushu delegates, Kōno Hironaka of the Tōhoku Yūshikai, and the Tosa Risshisha led by Ueki Emori. They forced a new election, which saw Itagaki named as party leader, Nakajima Nobuyuki of Tosa as vice-president, and Gotō relegated to the party staff. Faced with the prospect of a Tosa-dominated leadership, Ōkuma's and Fukuzawa's followers left while the election was in progress. Itagaki returned to Tokyo in November and was installed as party president, and the division between the *mintō* was complete.

Although the Tosa faction had taken the lead in the formation of the party, the Jiyūtō was a national organization that included former samurai, landowners, shopkeepers, and farmers who were dissatisfied with existing conditions. Nakae Chōmin, who wrote for the *Jiyū shimbun,* Ueki of the Risshisha, and Baba of the Kokuyūkai were the leading theorists of the party. They advocated concepts based on Rousseau's *Social Contract* and declared the objectives of the Jiyūtō to be the development of freedom, protection of rights, promotion of happiness, reform of society, and consolidation of constitutional government. Shortly after the party was established, Nakajima Nobuyuki founded a branch called the Rikken Seitō (Constitutional Political Party) in Osaka, and in March an office was established in Kumamoto. Other branches were established in the Northeast, Niigata, Fukui, Nagano, Shizuoka, Hamamatsu, Mikawa, Aichi, Ōtsu, Awaji, Kōchi, Matsui, Ishimi-Shimane, Hiroshima, Hagi, Hyōgo, Gifu, Toyama, and Kōfu.[12] The widespread popularity of the liberal movement alarmed the government, which even sent three spies from the Metropolitan Police Board to Kōchi in June 1882. This did not go unobserved and a notice board capped with a dog's head soon appeared outside their lodging house with the threat:

> You human beasts, will you venture to try the hearts of southern men such as we? Indeed you would be as much pitied for your folly as you are obnoxious in intention. You would do well to keep watch over your own heads and strive to preserve your lives. Otherwise punishment by the sword will sooner or later fall on you.[13]

Government pressure did not curb party enthusiasm, and Itagaki left for a speaking tour of the Tōkaidō in March 1882, followed by a trip to Shizuoka, Gifu, Okazaki, and Nagoya. On April 6, following a speech on the need for constitutional government at a shrine in Gifu, an attempt was made on his life by Aihara Naomi. The would-be assassin regarded him as a rebel and feared that the advocates of popular rights might go so far as to condemn the imperial household. Aihara believed the Jiyūtō would collapse if its leader was no longer on the scene. Itagaki, whose life was saved by his followers, is said to have cried out when attacked: "Liberty will not die even if Itagaki dies." As a result of the incident, Itagaki's reputation grew and his speeches and party canvassing and publications increased political opposition to the oligarchy.

While Itagaki represented the liberal wing of the *jiyū minken undō*, minor radical offshoots of the movement developed that added to public and official fears of the dangers presented by the advocates of popular rights. For example, the short-lived Tōyō Shakaitō (Oriental Socialist Party) organized by Tōkichi Tarui in Shimabara, Nagasaki prefecture, in May 1882 was an anarchic group that was neither socialist nor a party in the contemporary sense. The contemporary press reported that most members of political societies in Nagasaki were said to be associated with the Shakkintō, which took as its main tenents: "When people have educated themselves to esteeming morality and the principles of equality and freedom above everything, then all politics and laws will be unnecessary. It is our objective to bring about such a favorable time. The government, being the legatees of evil, we must remove. . . ." It also called for common ownership of property and revision of the Charter Oath to state that "long existing abuses shall be abolished in conformity with public principles," and for the amendment of the conscription law to include "the rights of the higher and lower classes shall be equalized, and every individual shall enjoy equal liberty." The party was banned by the government in July 1882. Okumiya Takeyuki, a radical member of the Jiyūtō who was later executed for the lese-majesty affair, and Ueki Emori, one of the principal Liberal theorists, organized rickshaw men in Tokyo into the Shakaitō (Association of Drivers) to oppose the expansion of the railroad between Shimbashi and Nihonbashi in June 1882. When ordered by the government to dissolve, the association broke up in confusion at its meeting in November.[14] Without respected and nationally known leaders and concrete policies, these anarchic and obstructive societies were swiftly banned by the government.

To meet the threat of the parties, the administration urged the owners of three pro-government newspapers, Fukuchi Gen'ichirō of *Tokyo nichi nichi shimbun,* Mizuno Torajirō of *Tōyō shimpō,* and Maruyama Saraku of *Meiji nippō,* to form a party. The Rikken Teiseitō (Constitutional Imperial Party) was established on March 18, 1882, with Prime Minister Itō Hirobumi as chairman. With principles based on the *Kojiki* and *Nihon shoki* and on the concept of an "eternal empire," it advocated modernization by "keeping pace with the times."[15] The Teiseitō stated that the emperor alone had the power to promulgate the constitution and that a bicameral national assembly should be established, with members of at least one house elected. The assembly should exercise legislative power subject to the consent of the throne. This platform represented the ideas of Itō, Yamagata, Inoue Kaoru, and Kuroda Kiyotaka, and alone of the party platforms referred to the need to protect freedom of speech, association, and publication. It favored, as did the Kaishintō, restricted suffrage, hard currency, a bicameral legislature, and the "emperor-in-parliament"; and both parties stood in opposition to the Jiyūtō call for popular sovereignty and a unicameral Diet.[16] The Teiseitō was formed by Fukuchi through an understanding with the government and, though regarded as the weakest of the three parties, gained prominence as the spokesman of the government. The members included discontented former samurai, Shintō priests, and young urban bureaucrats. Its platform followed official policy and was approved by the prime minister. As such, it could not be regarded as a popular party and, because of its influential press support, was often referred to as the *Sanmintō* or "Three-Man Party." Branches were established in Kumamoto, Kyoto, Okayama, Yamanashi, and Kōchi;[17] and in the first half of 1882, when the parties were at the height of popularity, it held a series of public lectures to augment its following.[18]

Among the former officials, only Ōkuma had sufficient prestige and financial ties to lead a second major party.[19] The Kaishintō justified its existence by denouncing government absolutism and calling for the realization of the Diet as announced in the Imperial Rescript of October 12, 1881. It attacked the Jiyūtō as destructive to society and national polity.[20] Only the establishment of parliamentary government and party cabinets responsive to the will of the people could prevent revolution. The Kaishintō alone could fill the vacuum between the extreme conservatism of the oligarchy and the extreme radicalism of the Jiyūtō to protect the throne and social order. The Kaishintō saw itself as a British-style party and advocated a bicameral legislature and restrictive electorate that would be expanded as "society progressed." It emphasized reforming domestic political life first before concentrating on treaty revision.[21] On the advice of Ono, it sought to appeal to the middle class, and Kōno Togama repeated this in his speech at the party's inaugural ceremony. Following the precedent set by Ōkuma's 1881 memorial, it called for the establishment of party cabinets responsible to both houses of the national assembly. The Kaishintō saw itself as the party of moderation and reform, and its principles as the means whereby "eternal prosperity" could be achieved for the imperial household and people. These principles were found in the initial policy statements of the party and later explanatory documents. They were primarily the work of Ono Azusa and represented the ideas that he had developed in his writings from 1874 to 1882.

As a moderate progressive party, the Kaishintō was able to attract men of knowledge, wealth, and reputation, including a number of leading intellectuals of the time, from all over the country. At the inaugural ceremony, Ōkuma of Hizen was elected as president, Kōno Togama of Tosa as vice-president, and Ono Azusa of Tosa, Mutaguchi Gengaku of Nagasaki, and Haruki Yoshiaki of Tokyo as secretaries.[22] Ōkuma, Kōno, and Mutaguchi were listed as *shizoku* (former samurai), and Ono and Haruki as *heimin* (commoners) in the party's membership list. All five were from areas of southwest Japan other than those of Satsuma and Chōshū. Of the original one hundred sixteen members, fifty-nine were *shizoku,* fifty-five were *heimin,* and two members did not give their status. Sixty of the members were listed as from Tokyo, and the rest came from twenty different prefectures and one metropolitan prefecture (*fu*), as shown below:

Prefecture (unless otherwise listed)	Members (numbers)	Percentage of Membership
Niigata	7	6.0
Fukushima	3	2.5
Tochigi	1	0.8
Saitama	4	3.4
Ibaraki	1	0.8
Chiba	2	1.7
Tokyo	60	51.7
Kanagawa	2	1.7
Shizuoka	4	3.4
Nagano	4	3.4
Gifu	1	0.8
Fukui	1	0.8
Mie	2	1.7
Wakayama	1	0.8
Osaka	1	0.8
Hyōgo	4	3.4
Hiroshima	3	2.5
Shimane	1	0.8
Yamaguchi	2	1.7

Fukuoka	1	0.8
Ōita	4	3.4
Nagasaki	7	6.0

Kōchi was not represented on the list; but many of the members, such as Ono and Kōno, gave Tokyo as their residence and not their home prefecture.[23] The regional distribution of the membership shows the national character of the party, and the importance of those residing in the capital in party affairs. Unlike the Jiyūtō leadership, which Joyce Lebra has described as a "Tosa-*batsu*" or "Tosa clique," the Kaishintō represented, from the standpoint of geographical diversity and importance of Tokyo, a national party. By transcending prefectural and clan boundaries, the Kaishintō moved toward the ideal of national unity that Ono had called for in *Kokumin nanzo kore o omowazaru* and toward national leadership. Among the initial members, sixteen had been members of the bureaucracy before 1881, twelve were journalists, six had teaching experience, and five had been trained in law. The members were well educated in either Chinese studies or Western languages and several, including Ono, had studied abroad. Yano and his colleagues in the Tōyō gisei kai were graduates of Keiō Gijuku, and all but one of the Ōtokai group held degrees from Tokyo University. One party member had received his doctorate in law from Yale University, and six others had special military training and experience. In June 1883 the Kaishintō had 163 representatives in local and prefectural assemblies, nine alone in the Tokyo assembly.[24] The party therefore represented a largely urban, intellectual elite that would, due to its membership, take the "views of the middle class" as Ono had advocated. Ono, a Western-educated *shizoku* from Tosa and self-styled commoner from Tokyo, was one of the outstanding examples of the new, urban intellectual to whom a modern party like the Progressives would be attractive.

The members of the Kaishintō were united not by clan ties but by similarity of views and opposition to the government.[25] They were divided into four main factions, each of which was centered about a major figure. The factions were united by bureaucratic experience, education, ideas, and even age. Each group existed prior to the establishment of the party and entered the Kaishintō as an integral whole as the result of negotiations with Ono, who was also a faction leader. Three of the four published their own newspaper. They operated as individual units with interlinking relationships within the party structure and in their contacts with Ōkuma, the party president. The groups were the Ōtokai, which under Ono had been responsible for drafting the party principles, platform, and bylaws; the Tōyō gisei kai (Oriental Parliamentary Discussion Society); the Ōmeisha (Parrot Society); and the Kanriha (Government Officials Faction).

The Ōtokai was composed of seven undergraduates from Tokyo University under the leadership of Ono Azusa. Takada Sanae (1860–1938), a native of Tokyo, was instrumental in organizing the group and became a close associate of Ōkuma and Ono, from whom he received his political apprenticeship and philosophical orientation.[26] In his first published work, *Kokka gaku genri (Principles of Statecraft),* he wrote that there was both a philosophical and a historical approach to political science and the latter was justified by the concept of utility envisioned by Bentham and Mill. Takada defined utility as the means used to reach a given objective. According to the utilitarian school, happiness and prosperity were the purpose of life; however, self-satisfaction did not provide a sufficient foundation for political theory, and moral philosophy and ethics were disciplines that justified concern with individual gratification. Politics is a science related to society as a whole, and the goal of a nation is to develop its potential and to perfect its way of life.[27] In the Kaishintō, Takada had his first opportunity to contribute toward these objectives. His classmate Amano Tameyuki (1859–1938) was from Saga prefecture and had learned English as a child. In 1877 he entered the national university and majored in political economy. His specialization soon led him to the works of John Stuart Mill, and Amano became an advocate of economic liberalism. Ichishima Kenkichi (1860–1944) was the son of a wealthy landowner in Niigata and attended the Niigata and Tokyo English Schools before entering Tokyo University. Unlike his colleagues, he left the university in 1881, one year before his graduation, when Ōkuma resigned from the cabinet, and soon established himself as a writer on political theory and newspaper editor. Okayama Kenkichi (1854–1894), the oldest member of the group, was the son of a high-ranking official of the Yokosuka *han* of Shizuoka. Enrolled in the clan school at age eight, he later studied in Tokyo and at the Niigata English school before being admitted to the Law Department of Tokyo University. Sunagawa Taketoshi (1860–1933) was born at Himeji in Hyōgo prefecture. As a child, he was taught Chinese and Japanese literature. In 1872 he came to Tokyo to continue his education, first at the Tokyo Foreign Language School and then at the Tokyo English School. He majored in English and French law at Tokyo University, where he became friends with Takada and Amano. Yamada Ichirō (1860–1905) studied English in his native Hiroshima and then in the Literature Department at Tokyo University. Yamada Kinosuke (1859–1913) was the son of an Osaka sugar merchant and had been taught Chinese classics from childhood. He too came to Tokyo to continue his education at the leading school in the nation.[28] The seven students, though representing diverse backgrounds and birthplaces, were scheduled to graduate together in 1882 and were known as both the "University faction"[29] and the Ono *gumi.*

The Ōtokai was composed of representatives of three student factions at Tokyo University. These included the Kyōwa kai, a political discussion society with twenty members, including Sunagawa, Okayama, Yamada Kinosuke, and Ichishima. A quarrel over Okayama's heavy smoking resulted in the secession of several members, including Sunagawa and Yamada, and the formation of a new group, the Boinsha. The third element was the Banseikai, led by Takada and Amano. Nicknamed the "Shirotabitō" ("White Socks Party") because of the footwear of the members, it was the official faction among the university dormitory residents and included Tsubouchi Shōyō.[30] The three factions were in constant competition,[31] and Ogawa, who had been in the Banseikai when an undergraduate, selected seven members from among the different groups to meet Ono.[32]

The Ōtokai had played a major role in the formation of the Kaishintō, and despite the antipathy between the Ono *gumi* and Tōyō giseikai, it tried to act as a neutral party to mitigate intrafactional rivalry. A limited following of eight formal members and four or five additional undergraduates from Tokyo University restricted its influence, as did lack of public confidence and political organization. It therefore decided to establish a newspaper to increase its influence within the party and to exert pressure on the government. Ono decided to use the *Chōya shimbun,* published by Narishima Ryūhoku and Suehiro Shigeyasu, as the voice of the Ōtokai. This would be achieved by having Yamada Ichirō and Ichishima Kenkichi join the staff of the paper. Although the *Chōya shimbun* supported the Kaishintō independently of factional ties, these plans did not materialize. When the Mita faction's *Yūbin hōchi shimbun* and Numa's *Mainichi shimbun,* both of which were regarded as the voices of the Kaishintō, expressed different opinions on the Korean incident of July 23, 1882, and other matters, the Ōtokai felt it necessary to establish a publication to state its own views. While conferring with the other factions in order to define party policy, Ono began to look for a publication that could become the spokesman for the Ōtokai.

At that time, Hattori Seiichi, one of the members of the Kaishintō, decided to expand the *Kōkō shimbun,* which he owned, into a large newspaper, and asked Ono to recommend reporters. Although the publication was a small magazine containing reviews of current events and was popular among young people for its radical articles, it had a long history and several wealthy supporters. These included Iwasaki Yatarō and two others from whom 700 yen had been borrowed to purchase type and printing equipment. Ono saw the *Kōkō shimbun* as the means whereby his faction could become known to the public and began to correspond frequently with Hattori. His followers investigated the history, property, and debt of the paper, and Ōkuma and other important members of the Kaishintō initially agreed to purchase shares of its stocks. This financial support was withdrawn because of uncertainty over the exact amount and disposal of the debt. Hattori hoped to increase circulation by naming Ono as president and placing four members of the Ōtokai who held degrees from the national university on the staff. Although Ono and his group consented, Ōkuma opposed the plans because the Ōtokai members were serving as instructors at Tokyo Senmon Gakkō, a college he had recently founded and the predecessor of Waseda University. It was finally agreed that Yamada Ichirō would be appointed editor, but this angered the other faction members. To overcome this, Ichishima was named manager of the paper. In order to alleviate Yamada's and Ichishima's concern at bearing all responsibility, they were to take charge of editing while all members of the Ōtokai were to write for the editorial page. Ono and Hattori, after numerous discussions over the debt and payments, decided to issue the publication and settle financial problems later. Actual control of publication was placed in the hands of Yamada and Ichishima, but they were not to handle business arrangements. They believed that Hattori would soon give up the paper because of financial difficulties and concentrated on hiring good reporters. Since the two were in a dangerous position due to the Press Law and lack of funds, Ono promised to purchase the paper and to take responsibility in case problems arose. Yamada and Ichishima worked incessantly to prepare the first edition of the new *Naigai seitō jijō*, but due to printing delays, it did not appear until October 8, 1882.

In December the editors were charged with violating the Press Law, and the *Naigai seitō jijō* was suspended for a month. This increased financial difficulties, since the payroll still had to be met in order to keep employees. Hattori was unable to solve the problem, and Suzuki Renta was asked by Okayama to take over the paper. Suzuki had come to Tokyo to establish a publishing company which, with Okayama's support, was to print texts for Tokyo Senmon Gakkō. He agreed to the request. To made ends meet until the end of the year, Yamada and Ichijima attempted to borrow money from Ōkuma and Maejima. When they refused, Yamada and Ichishima obtained a loan of 200 yen from a Mr. Komatsu. They argued with Ōkuma and asked him to allow Ono to take over the paper, for it was indispensable to the Kaishintō. Furthermore, the cessation of publication would blacken the name of the party and the Ono *gumi* by announcing its failure to the public. When Maejima and Ono both supported them, Ōkuma dropped his opposition and donated 1200 yen. Because this would permit the company to operate only for three months, Maejima and Ono became discouraged. Yamada then tried to persuade Hattori to cease publication temporarily in order to gain total control of the *Naigai seitō jijō,* but Hattori refused. Yamada at last persuaded Ono to have the Kaishintō purchase the paper and name Ono as president. Although Hattori agreed, two or three party leaders prevented this. Yamada and Ichishima were angered and blamed Ōkuma for not pressuring those in opposition to change their stand and for not appointing Ono to head the paper. Ono tried to mediate the dispute and promised to enter the business, but Yamada and Ichishima now refused to work without a definite plan for the future of the company. Ono's pleas to Maejima were ignored and, according to Ichishima, his explanation to Ōkuma was not adequate. Ōkuma ordered Ono to cease publication, and the last issue appeared in February 1883.

Ichishima and Yamada accused Ono of not keeping his word, and Ichishima left for Niigata, where he established a newspaper to support the local branch of the Kaishintō. This publication was soon suppressed by the government, and Ichishima, as editor-in-chief and president, was imprisoned for eight months.

The Tōyō gisei kai consisted of graduates of Fukuzawa's Keiō Gijuku and was the successor to the Mita kyōgi kai (Mita Discussion Society). The group was led by Yano Fumio[33] (Ryūkei, 1850–1931), a native of Ōita prefecture and the son of the former governor of Oda, now Okayama prefecture. As a youth he studied the Chinese classics at the *han* school, and in 1872 he entered Fukuzawa's Keiō Gijuku. Within one year he was appointed to teach English at the school, and three years later he was sent to lead the Osaka and then Tokushima branches of Keiō. Yano returned to Tokyo in 1876 and became assistant editor of *Yūbin hōchi shimbun.* In 1878, after Ōkuma, as Minister of Finance, asked Fukuzawa to recommend suitable persons as his subordinates, Yano was named to the Ministry of Finance, where he served under Ōkuma and simultaneously as secretary to the Dajōkan. At Fukuzawa's suggestion, he and several other Keiō graduates, including Inukai Tsuyoshi and Ozaki Yukio, were transferred to the Bureau of Statistics. Yano soon gained Ōkuma's confidence and was the author of his memorial on constitutional government in 1881. He resigned from the government with Ōkuma and, along with several of Fukuzawa's followers, entered the Kaishintō as a separate faction known as the Tōyō gisei kai or Mita *ha* (faction), after the district of Tokyo in which Keiō was located. During 1882 and 1883 he toured the country, canvassing for the party while editing *Hōchi*. The effect proved too great a strain on his health, and in the spring of 1883 Yano fell ill. While recovering, he wrote a political novel entitled *Keikoku bidan (Laudable Tales of Statecraft)*, which stressed the need for the extension of political rights and the establishment of constitutional government. Using a theme from Greek history, Yano created an allegory on the repressive effects of tyrannical government when in collusion with the military. These ideas were not lost on his readers and the book found a ready reception among youth and political activists. It sold so well that Yano was able to tour Europe and America for two years, 1884 to 1886, on the royalties. Yano advocated a synthesis of Eastern and Western political concepts, argued for a constitutional monarchy, and warned against the danger of excessive egalitarianism. He believed that the Kaishintō should not seek a base in the farming community, for this group was too far from the center of political power. Although regarded as a "radical" within the Kaishintō, Yano opposed the Jiyūtō for its extremism. After his return to Japan he took over *Hōchi*,[34] but gradually became disillusioned with politics and refused to join the Ōkuma cabinet in 1898. In 1897 he retired from politics to take the position of master of ceremonies of the Imperial Household Agency.[35]

In addition to Yano, the Tōyō gisei kai included Fujita Mokichi, Inukai Tsuyoshi, Ozaki Yukio, Minoura Katsundo, Taguchi Ukichi, Morita Shiken, and Katō Masanosuke. Ozaki and Inukai had been appointed to government office by Ōkuma and had served in the Bureau of Statistics under Yano's supervision. They resigned following the political change of 1881, and Fujita, a fellow clansman of Yano's who had gotten through

Keiō by sharing Yano's allowance, also joined the staff of *Hōchi.* Fujita's cousin, Yamaguchi Masakuni, had been a supporter of Yano's father and knew Inukai. He introduced Inukai to Fujita, who allowed Inukai to live and work in his home while he attended Keiō. Inukai was a skillful writer and became a reporter for *Yūbin hōchi shimbun.*

As assistant editor for *Hōchi,* Yano was in contact with many people outside his faction, including Inoue Kowashi, Inoue Ryoichi, Kikuchi Dairoku, then a young university professor, Ono Azusa, and Iwasaki Yatarō. Despite his opposition to the Jiyūtō, he occasionally published Itagaki's opinions in *Hōchi.*[36] As one of the founders of the Kōjunsha,[37] he knew both Baba Tatsui and Ono; he also met Ono at the Kyōzon shūkan in 1879. Since both worked in the same ministry, they must have had other contacts before joining the Kaishintō. Within the party, he and Ono had infrequent meetings and their factions represented rival groups among the younger members. The Mita *ha* welcomed former samurai who had survived the Satsuma rebellion after their release from prison[38] and representated the means whereby Fukuzawa's ideological influence was exerted on the party. It drafted *Shigi kempō (Personal View of the Constitution),*[39] which explained the Kaishintō position on party cabinets,[40] and used *Hōchi,* which Yano purchased with Ōkuma after their resignation from office, as its mouthpiece as well as the voice of the Kaishintō. Through the paper Yano propagated his ideas on constitutional government, and its offices functioned as the headquarters of the Tōyō gisei kai[41] and gave the impression of serving as a lodging house for young statesmen.

The "Old Shogunal Retainer" element of the Kaishintō was represented by the Ōmeisha led by Numa Morikazu. The son of a Tokugawa adherent who had been trained in Chinese, English, and military tactics, Numa had served with Tokugawa forces at Aizu. He had attracted the attention of Itagaki Taisuke, who appointed him as inspector of the Kōchi clan forces in 1869. Numa traveled abroad with Kōno Togama, the senior representative from Tosa in the government, and studied law in England for one year. On his return to Japan in 1873, he was appointed secretary and judge in the Genrō-in. He and

Kōno organized a course in legal studies in the Hōritsu kōshū kai (Institute of Jurisprudence). Numa was an advocate of popular rights, was opposed to the evils resulting from bureaucratic absolutism, and had a reputation for unbiased legal decisions. Following the prohibition on public speeches by officials in 1879, Numa and his followers resigned from the government. With the aid of Shimada Saburō, grand chancellor to the Genrō-in and chief secretary to the Ministry of Education, Numa organized a political discussion group called the Ōmeisha, one of the pioneers of the movement for parliamentary government. Other members included Ōoka Ikuzō, Koezuka Ryū, Tsunoda Shinpei, and Kawazu Sukeyuki. Numa, Shimada, and Kawazu were former retainers of the *bakufu,* and the group represented the graduates of Kyōritsu Gaku, a school that was the rival of Keiō Gijuku. The Ōmeisha published its political speeches in its *Ōmei zasshi (Ōmei Magazine).* In 1879 Numa became vice-chairman of the Tokyo metropolitan legislature and president of the *Tokyo-Yokohama mainichi shimbun,* which he organized to promote the establishment of parliamentary government. At first he used his influence in support of Itagaki, but after a quarrel with Baba Tatsui and Suehiro Shigeyasu (pen name, Techō) of the Jiyūtō, Numa began to move toward Ōkuma's faction. Kōno Togama, a close friend of Ōkuma, introduced the two.[42] The Ōmeisha entered the party as a cohesive unit with a well-established news organ and laid much of the basis for Kaishintō influence in the Tokyo-Yokohama area. The Ōmeisha continued to function as such even after it was ordered to dissolve by the police in June 1882.[43] The faction was in conflict with Yano's Tōyō gisei kai,[44] and this friction ultimately contributed to the dissolution of the party.

The Kanriha (Bureaucratic Faction) was a group of powerful, middle-aged, former officials whose years and experience increased public trust in the Kaishintō. Led by Kōno Togama of Tosa, its members included Maejima Hisoka, the founder of the modern postal system in Japan, Kitabatake Harufusa, Mutaguchi Gengaku, and Haruki Yoshiaki.[45] The faction was important in the discussions leading to the establishment of the Kaishintō, and Kōno and Maejima were present at the conferences of January 31 and February 23, 1882, when major decisions were made to form the party and to approve Ono's draft-policy statements.[46] Kōno was vice-president and Haruki and Mutaguchi were secretaries of the Kaishintō.[47] Although important in policy-making decisions, the Kanriha was neutral in intraparty disputes[48] and left the actual work in the party to the younger members of the Ono, Yano, and Numa groups.[49]

As a party led primarily by former bureaucrats, intellectuals of whom several were recent college graduates, and journalists and appealing to "the middle class," the Kaishintō lacked firm financial support. In addition to membership fees and dues, Ōkuma and other members donated money, but these funds were limited and temporary. Ōkuma is said to have received help from Iwasaki Yatarō of Mitsubishi,[50] but the amount and type of aid are unknown. Iwasaki's complaints against government assistance to the Kyōdō Un'yu Kaisha (Union Shipping Company), his state-supported competitor, received the backing of both *Hōchi* and *Mainichi*.[51] However, in a period of inflation and government retrenchment,[52] these contributions were also restricted. Ono, therefore, saw the establishment of enterprises such as banks, newspapers, publishing companies, and mines as a means to provide a stable source of funds for the party and, at the same time, promote modernization. However, due to his own poverty, these ventures were begun with borrowed capital, generally from Ōkuma and Ono Gishin.[53] On Ono's recommendation in late 1882, Ōkuma established a bank, the Jingo Ginkō. Ono borrowed five thousand yen from his brother-in-law to purchase its stock and in return received loans for Kaishintō needs and to start his own publishing company. The bank, unfortunately, soon failed. Ono then advised Ōkuma to go into mining, for it was profitable and essential for the progress of civilization. This enterprise, too, was a failure, as were the *Naigai seitō jijō* and a bookshop and publishing house that Ono established. Financial difficulties continued to plague the Kaishintō and its members and were ultimately a factor in the break-up of the party. The Kaishintō was not self-supporting; since membership meant ineligibility for official position, its followers were often in financial difficulties.[54]

From the day he resigned from office in October 1881 until he left the party in December 1884, the Kaishintō was Ono's foremost concern and its members his closest companions. Because of his position as secretary, Ono was in constant contact with Ōkuma and the members of all four factions. Ono's diary is a daily record of Kaishintō activities and problems and of his own key role in party affairs. During the period from April 17, 1882, to December 1, 1883, Ono saw or wrote to Ōkuma approximately 343 times and contacted the members of the Ōtokai, both individually and as a group, 190 times. In contrast, he met or sent letters to the party elders, Kōno, Maejima, and Mutaguchi, only 125 times. Yano, Fujita, Inukai, and Ozaki of the Tōyō gisei kai are mentioned in "Ryūkakusai nikki" only 56 times in this period and Numa and Shimada of the Ōmeisha only 43, which reveals a continuation of Ono's earlier distrust. In the first twenty months the party was in operation, with the exception of Ōkuma, Ono's most frequent contacts were with Yamada Ichirō and Kinosuke (mentioned 66 times), Kōno (51 times), Takada (48 times), Mutaguchi, Maejima, Ono Gishin (each 34 times), Yano (28 times), Shimada (26 times), Narishima Ryūhoku of the *Kōkō shimbun* (19 times), Anami Hisashi of Ōita (17 times), and Ichishima, who was in prison for eight months beginning May 19, 1881 (14 times). Kōno and Maejima were present at Ōkuma's villa for the conferences that decided on the establishment of the party on January 31, 1882, and on the party platform, principles, and bylaws on February 20. They acted as the *genrō* of the Kaishintō and had a determining voice in major policy decisions. Ono had entered the bureaucracy on Kōno's recommendation, and Kōno, a fellow clansman, was a personal friend of Ōkuma. Ono's ties with the elder statesmen of the party indicate his preference for their moderating influence as opposed to the "radical element" in the Tōyō gisei kai and the Ōmeisha.[55] His diary indicates that the Tōyō gisei kai and Ōmeisha were less important than the Kanriha and Ōtokai in formulating party policy and that the eldest and youngest members of the Kaishintō worked together without apparent friction to develop and maintain a consistent theme of moderate liberalism in the Kaishintō.

KAISHINTŌ ACTIVITIES 1882–1884

As founder, chief organizer, and secretary of the Kaishintō, Ono was directly involved in all party activities. Much of his work consisted of holding meetings to inform people of the party's platform and criticism of the government and Jiyūtō. Such meetings began shortly after the organization of the party, and the first was held on May 13, 1882, at Meiji kaidō with Ono as chairman. Over two thousand people heard Numa, Fujita Mokichi, and Inukai Tsuyoshi discuss the party's principles. The next day Inoue Kan'ichi, Shimada Saburō, Masuda Katsunori, Koezuka Ryū, and Ono spoke to an audience of equal size. The purpose of both meetings was to publicize the party's platform and gain public confidence, and Ono found that the attentiveness of the audience and the fluency of the speakers at these meetings were exceptional.[56]

These meetings introduced the Kaishintō leadership and platform to the public and presented the party's views on the major issues of the time, namely, the economic situation, foreign policy, and treaty revision. The unstable economic situation of the late 1870s and early 1880s was the result of economic problems inherited from the Tokugawa shogunate and problems stemming from the establishment of the new regime. Excessive note issues released by the national banks and government to meet the costs of the pension bond issue for the former warrior class and suppression of the Satsuma rebellion led to inflation, violent fluctuations in the value of currency, and an outflow of specie. Bank notes in circulation rose from 95 million yen in 1876 to 150 million yen in 1878, while the national debt rose from 55 million yen to 254 million yen in the same period. Government expenditures rose from about 50 million yen in 1877 to approximately 87 million yen in 1880. The cost of living increased and the price of rice doubled; with the currency subject to fluctuations of up to ten percent a day, unstable exchange rates made foreign trade difficult. Ōkuma as Minister of Finance had been responsible for the policy of pension commutation and financing the campaign against Satsuma and now was accused of initiating irresponsible fiscal policies while in office. In October 1881, Matsukata Masayoshi, Ōkuma's successor, announced a plan designed to redeem the inconvertible paper currency, accumulate a specie reserve that would back a new issue of convertible notes, and develop a central bank based on European models.[57] With Ōkuma under attack, Ono found himself defending the party president's former policies while justifying the Kaishintō's position on hard money.

At the meeting of May 14, Ono compared the contemporary financial situation to that of France during the revolution, when over-issuance of unbacked paper money resulted in inflation. Although Ōkuma had authorized the release of 100 million yen, which had declined forty percent in value, he was a firm advocate of metallic currency. When Minister of Finance, Ōkuma had been forced to issue paper money by the necessity of financing the Southwest campaign, but he had planned to retire the bills in twenty-eight years. He had begun to enforce this policy before his dismissal; but since his departure from the government, who now would institute financial reforms? It was therefore necessary for the government to institute a stable fiscal system based on a limited currency issue backed by a constant reserve of gold and silver and convertible into specie, as called for by the Kaishintō.[58]

Since inflation and economic policy were areas in which the administration was vulnerable to attack, Ono, Numa, Shimada, and Fujita carefully noted and analyzed the public reaction to the speeches. On June 26 the party prospectus entitled *Rikken Kaishintō shuisho* was released to further publicize its views.[59]

On November 12 Ono spoke to over one thousand merchants at the Yokohama Port Theater on the causes of the decrease in imports. The speech, written between November 6 and 11 and shown to Ōkuma before delivery, was, according to Ono, the first public discussion of the subject[60] and was prompted by a nine to twenty percent decline in imports. Ono stated that this was not due to increased domestic production but to reduced purchasing power. This was the result of inefficient use of Japanese resources because of the monetary system and government interference in business. To remedy the situation, the government had to change the present system of inconvertible paper money into specie and speed up the withdrawal of paper notes. Moreover, the government, which had lent Mitsubishi a large sum of money to buy the fleet used in the Taiwan expedition, was now going to establish a competitor. This was interference in private enterprise, and the administration should desist from such activities. Ono concluded that the country was well endowed with resources and would be prosperous if government policies were improved.[61]

Ono recognized that Ōkuma was vulnerable because his party stood for repeal of the inflationary notes issued during his tenure as finance minister. Attacks on the inconsistency between Ōkuma's policies while in office and on the platform espoused by the Kaishintō often ignored the plan he had formulated to reduce the notes in circulation and national debt. For example, on February 8, 1880, the *Japan Weekly Mail* noted:

> It is pleasing to observe that the plan sometime since formulated by the Finance Minister for the gradual extinction of the national debt of Japan is being steadily carried out. In the introduction to the estimates for 1879–80 Mr. Ōkuma mentioned that 7,499,217 yen of the paper currency would be withdrawn during the financial year. This, we learn, has already been accomplished.[62]

But, two and a half years later, the same paper attacked Ōkuma because he "sacrificed expediency to sentiment and set greater store by the name of independence than by the ability to be independent. The policy of his successor [Matsukata] appears to be more wholesome. . . ."[63] In November 1882 the *Nichi nichi shimbun* accused Ōkuma of "marked inconsistency between the principles he professes at present and those to which he conformed while in office." Ōkuma was criticized for his responsibility in allowing the "excessive issue of paper money" and for giving official protection to Mitsubishi when minister of finance. Yet, in the role of party president, he now "became a staunch advocate of a return to specie payments," while *Hōchi* and *Mainichi,* the "organs of the Progressists," opposed the government program to establish a shipping company to compete with Mitsubishi. Ōkuma had yielded to ambition; even though isolated as the only remaining representative from Hizen, his opinions were "not avowedly different from those of his confrères." His sudden advocacy of a national assembly, a measure he was never known to propose prior to his memorial, came because "he believed it possible to take his place at the head of a successful revolution."[64] The debate over Ōkuma's financial policies continued, as did the effects of the excessive note issue, and in July 1884 *Nichi nichi* declared that Ōkuma's policies had not reduced the volume of currency but added 22 million yen to circulation as a "special reserve." This was contradicted by the *Japan Gazette*.[65] At the same time, the *Jiji shimpō* declared that inconvertible paper currency with its fluctuating value made legitimate trade impossible and urged the immediate use of specie to reduce the amount of paper in circulation.[66]

The Korean attack on the Japanese legation in Seoul on July 23, 1882, gave Ono an opportunity to criticize the government on foreign policy and to define the Kaishintō position on the incident and on treaty revision. His views were stated in a speech written on October 1 and 2 and presented to Ōkuma on October 13. It was delivered the next day at the Meiji kaidō before an audience of two thousand and began with a discussion of the situation in Turkey. The Ottoman Empire, Ono stated, had lost its independence of action because of inadequate diplomacy. The collective treaty concluded by the *bakufu* with the Western powers was similar to the Middle Eastern case. If it was not revised, Japanese government policies would soon cease to be respected by foreign nations, which would intervene in domestic affairs. It was imperative to conclude separate treaties with each of the powers, attain tariff autonomy, and prohibit foreign residence within the interior of the country. The abolition of extraterritoriality was essential from the point of national honor. Nonetheless, extraterritoriality was not so harmful as the lack of tariff autonomy, which was indispensable for economic development. This was the area where diplomatic efforts should first be concentrated. Since India was a British colony and Indochina a French colony, the only independent Asian countries were Japan and China. Japan was the leader of the Far East and was important. Chinese distrust of and Korean enmity toward Japan had to be ended. The Western powers were expanding in the Far East and the situation was tense. Japan, as the leader of the Far East, had to overcome these difficulties, and determination was necessary. Sino-Japanese relations were not close. Korea concluded a treaty with the United States of America. Rioters in Korea attacked the Japanese legation, and the minister, who was rescued by an English fleet, managed to return to Japan. Korean animosity continued, and the Chinese tried to interfere in the negotiations between Japan and Korea. Chinese suspicions of Japan had not ended. Ono hoped that the government would not make errors in this situation. Fortunately, Japan was able to end the conflict with Korea through the virtue of the emperor and the power of the people, but the situation was not advantageous for the Far East. It was the responsibility of Japan to improve this situation. A half million yen in compensation was not a satisfactory amount, but this could not be helped; Ono hoped that the government would use this money to end Chinese and Korean distrust. The half million yen should be used to enlighten Korea by promoting progress in the form of post offices, telegraph lines, and other means. Then Korean enmity would end, and China's groundless suspicion would be resolved. This would promote progress in the Far East. If the issue of reparations was pursued, the conflict would never end. Whether or not Korea was an independent country or a possession of China was a major issue. There were those who would ask Western countries to normalize relations with Korea. England was going to interfere in this situation, and this was not to the advantage of the Far East. If the powers should intervene, China and Japan would be in the same position as Turkey. The powers were trying to interfere in Oriental problems. Japan, China, and Korea had to normalize relations. Whether or not Korea should be independent or semi-independent should be decided from the viewpoint of the Far Eastern situation. The prosperity of the Far East was not only advantageous for the Far East but also for Western nations. The powers would agree with his opinion. Diplomacy is the heart of a country. Once mistakes are made, the injury lasts for a long time. Diplomatic problems should be handled with broad vision.[67]

In addition to the meetings held in Tokyo, the Kaishintō tried to expand its following by establishing local offices throughout the country and by sending speakers into rural areas. Shortly after the party was founded, branches were established in Aichi, Hyōgo, Shizuoka, Mito, Wakaetsu (Fukui prefecture), Etchū (Toyama prefecture), Akita, Niigata, Ōita, and Yanagawa (Fukuoka prefecture).[68] The groups were in continual contact with the Tokyo headquarters, particularly with Ono, who was one of the party's three secretaries. Ono handled daily matters and correspondence for the Kaishintō and traveled extensively on speaking tours. On October 25 Ono, Yano Fumio and his brother Yano Sadao, Kitabatake Harufusa, Koezuka Ryū, Inoue Kan'ichi, and six others spoke to a group of nearly one thousand in Hoshūbana village, Ibaraki prefecture. The audience was composed primarily of wealthy merchants and farmers who "were quite accustomed to political discussions." Ono spoke on the Meiji Restoration, and during the evening Ono, Yano, and Minoura Katsundo gave speeches to a group of about eighty, which included a representative of the Saitama prefectural assembly. The next day, several members left to speak in various areas, and Ono, Yano, and others returned to Tokyo by ship. In the spring of 1883 Yano and Ozaki Yukio went on a speaking tour of the Tōkaidō. In Nagoya they attended a party with a group of Kaishintō followers who were planning to form a local branch office to which the Jiyūtō district leader and several members had been invited. Although they spoke frankly on this occasion, several days later the Jiyūtō members called on them to complain that *Hōchi* did not discuss Mitsubishi openly.

On November 5 Ono discussed the postal system at the Meiji kaidō. The speech, written between October 28 and November 5,[69] was ostensibly a protest against increased postal rates. In actuality it was a call for freedom of communication and the right to secrecy in private correspondence. Ono began it by stating that man possessed freedom even before government existed. Freedom of communication is a basic demand of mankind, and government is established to protect this freedom. Freedom of communication is necessary if men are to organize society, exchange knowledge, help others, and live together. If this freedom is violated, happiness cannot be obtained. It is the responsibility of the members of society to maintain and protect freedom. Francis Lieber said: "The basic freedoms of man are indispensable. We must now elect good government to permit freedom and protect freedom by some means." This view was radical, but Lieber's opinion was correct. There are several kinds of freedom of communication—freedom of speech, assembly, and exchange of opinion, among others. Freedom of correspondence is also indispensable and important. Since freedom of communication is essential, it is entrusted to the government as a state monopoly. This trust, however, does not give the government the right to open or inspect private correspondence. The press reported that in Ōita prefecture all letters of members of a certain political party were inspected by the police before they were mailed, and this was a violation of a basic right.[70]

Ono's discussion on diplomacy of October 14 and speech on the causes for the decrease of imports of November 5 received a vitriolic review from the *Japan Weekly Mail,* which referred to him as "a certain Mr. Ono, one of the Radical leaders." While agreeing with his basic ideas, the paper asked why he failed to show how a return to specie payment could be effected and failed to substantiate his charges against the government, since his only example of assistance was to a company supported by the Kaishintō. Ono's opposition to the removal of restrictions on foreign trade and travel was bitterly attacked and he was described as a "political agitator." Furthermore:

> All the comfort he gave his audience was contained in a vague intimation that "his party is struggling to ameliorate the administration, and will never hesitate to undertake whatever is necessary for the political improvement of the people." So by a prettily rounded curve we come back to the old position, that government interference being fatal to healthy progress, the thing to substitute for it is—government interference in the guise of another party.[71]

Ono's views on treaty revision and government policy were not taken well by the foreign community, which regarded him as more radical than did his own government.

Each member of the Kaishintō was assigned an area in which he was to deliver political speeches, and Ono's particular domain was Tokyo and the Kantō region. When on tour Ono often gave two or three speeches daily in addition to talking to interested persons. Since he was a skilled calligrapher, he was often asked to give samples of his writing, and he would stay up to past midnight working to meet requests. His colleagues on these trips, as described by Minoura Katsundo, "were always astonished by his systemic, studious, hardworking attitude."[72] On November 20 Ono began a five-day tour of Chiba prefecture and the Bōsō peninsula to publicize the Kaishintō and to assess the political situation in the area. He spoke at seven different villages to a total of over one thousand enthusiastic listeners, who included members of the prefectural assembly and village headmen. Some of the audience had traveled several miles to hear his speeches, and each meeting was followed by the customary reception at which Ono again delivered a brief talk. The topics included politics, "academic" matters, the regulations on public meetings, and the Restoration. Ono declared that the Restoration was the result of the wisdom of the emperor, who sought to avoid the evils of clan government. It was not due to the power of Satsuma, Chōshū, or Tosa. Ono wrote in his diary that the speeches were neither anti-government nor detrimental to public peace and order. Nonetheless, the police interrupted three meetings and attended three social events, one of which was told to disband. When this occurred the guests became angry and, at times, demanded explanations. Ono and the chairman were forced to intervene between the audience and officers and to request their supporters to observe the law and, on one occasion, to leave.[73]

After reporting to Ōkuma on his tour and hearing an account of events in Tokyo, Ono left for a tour of Ibaraki prefecture on November 27. In a period of three days he made three speeches, one to an audience of 1,500. On December 5 Ono went to Utsunomiya in Tochigi prefecture to speak at the invitation of local party members. However, not until the ninth did he receive permission from the police, and the audience that assembled to hear him numbered over six hundred. Ono returned to Tokyo with Ozaki Yukio; and on December 19, he, Shimada Saburō, and Ōoka Ikuzo went to Iwatsuki in Saitama prefecture at the request of the local Kaishintō. Here they spoke to a group of about six hundred; the next day, Shimada and Ōoka continued their tour while Ono returned to Tokyo.

As 1882 drew to a close, Ono wrote of his experiences in his diary:

> The happiest events of my life are those of 1882. After my inability to reach agreement with government officials last year and my resignation from office, I was indeed fortunate to gather together friends with similar views into a party and to spend my time giving speeches. Many have supported our party. The Kaishintō is known throughout all fifty prefectures. These [speeches and political activities] are my happiest experiences. However, the laws enforced at the end of this year restrict the movements of our party. Since the future of our party is surely a long and prosperous one, I cannot be satisfied with the present situation.[74]

The winter of 1883 saw Ono busy with party affairs in Tokyo, and not until April did he take to the public rostrum. On April 7 he again went to the Yokohama Port Theater, where he addressed an audience of seven hundred on current business conditions. The speech was the sequel to his November 5 discussion on the causes of the decrease of imports. Ono began by describing the current situation in which several large foreign trading houses had failed, the problem of low wages, and the decline in foreign trade. These were recent examples of current economic problems. Silk exports alone had increased, and this was due to decreased purchasing power within Japan. Merchants, fearing to buy goods because of falling prices, and businessmen fearing to invest in industry and commerce because of low interest rates, purchased government bonds and did not contribute to increased productivity. Business conditions had deteriorated because of fluctuations in the value of paper money. There was, Ono declared, no alternative but to institute a monetary system based on specie, as advocated by the Kaishintō, or else to back paper notes sufficiently with gold and silver. Ōkuma as Minister of Finance had tried to recall coins to establish a base for the note issue, but this plan was not successful because of public ignorance of financial problems. Ono concluded with a call for the cabinet to improve the monetary system and for the public to concentrate on economic problems.[75] He wanted to pursue the topic further at meetings held on April 10 and 11, but although his ideas were not new, he was prohibited from speaking by the police.

On April 16 a small group of forty party members met at Ōkuma's villa to celebrate the first anniversary of the Kaishintō. Within one year the membership list had risen to two thousand, and to counter the rising popularity of the parties, the government announced new restrictions on the press on April 16. However, neither press nor police regulations dampened Ono's determination, and on June 8 he and Minoura Katsundo left for a brief speaking tour in Gumma prefecture.

In September Ono spoke to the followers of Ozaki Yukio in Urawa, north of Tokyo, and gave several speeches in Saitama prefecture. On November 4 he left for a three-week tour of the Tōhoku region. There he held political discussions and gave speeches on the causes of Japanese underdevelopment and on the need to revise the land tax. In some areas the crowd numbered seven hundred; at other times the group was as small as seventy "gentlemen and merchants" or "some scholars." In Niigata city Ono had many visitors, including members of the governor's cabinet. In Kashiwazaki, Niigata prefecture, he invited sixty members of the local Jiyūtō to attend a meeting.[76] Ono described their reaction and the results of the trip in a letter to Ōkuma on November 12:

> When I left Tokyo, I wanted to use this trip to sow seeds to bear fruit in the future; but when I arrived at Takada [in Niigata prefecture], I found several unexpected developments. . . . At first I thought that in Echigo [i.e., Niigata], most of the people had become supporters of the Jiyūtō after Itagaki campaigned in the area. However, we had large audiences of about one thousand at Takada and Kashiwazaki, and many people had come from a distance of several miles. At Kashiwazaki in particular, the [Jiyūtō] party men tried to break up the gathering. In spite of these efforts, our meeting was very successful. It seemed that people there respect us more after comparing our speeches with those of the dis-

> orderly Jiyūtō followers. This district was originally one of the Jiyūtō strongholds. I heard the [Jiyūtō] party men appeal to those in the neighborhood and saw them gather about sixty followers. They intended to use them to disrupt our meeting. However, our speeches were sufficiently strong and moderate to disappoint them. At first when we stood up on the platform, some of them cried out: "No!" Later, when they listened to us, they called out in surprise: "Hear! Hear!" All this occurred on the tenth. That night a Jiyūtō follower visited me and asked what was the difference between our party and the Jiyūtō. After that, he left immediately. Thus, we broke down what they had built up for their party; and I am sure it was a most effective way to unite our men together and to indirectly enlighten those who support our party. Perhaps, for that reason, members of the Kashiwazaki Society of Commerce asked me to lecture on economics on my return trip. I promised to do so.

He then mentioned that a former member of the Jiyūtō from Shibata asked him to speak there and he agreed. Ono did not expect the local Jōetsu Rikken Kaishintō in Takada to disband immediately in order to join the main party organization, but he concluded "we can say the prefecture is for our party."[77]

Ono analyzed the results of his trip and compared the success of the Kaishintō with the results attained by Itagaki Taisuke during his recent visit to the Tōhoku region. He wrote in his diary on November 23:

> On my visits, I cannot extend the influence of my party far enough. The only thing to do is to wait for [a trip at] a later date. After going to Takada, I heard that Itagaki did not do too well and people were disappointed. Furthermore, because of the unfortunate experiences of the Jiyūtō, some followers left the party. Let's concentrate on the future and plan for it! In Takada and Kashiwazaki, upper-class people are very willing to join our party. People around Niigata do not care about politics. Because Itagaki mentioned some revolutionary ideas, they were frightened and avoided him. As what I said was very clear and firm and unlike Itagaki's words, people began to respect our party. A certain member of the prefectural cabinet was the first to join the Kaishintō. Many came and joined after that. While I was in Niigata, a meeting of the [prefectural] cabinet was held and all cabinet members were there. I thought this was our chance

> and called Iizuka [Ginya], Yamada, Nakamata, and Seki [Seiuemon] together. They came and discussed the situation in the nation. I encouraged them to work for the party. They all agreed and promised to do their best before they left. This trip took less than three weeks, and during this time plans were made for the future. This spring I will come here again. The seeds sown this time will have borne fruit by then.[78]

As a result of this tour, Ono became well-known in the area and had the honor of being invited to join the prefectural governor in a ceremony opening a new road. The party structure in Niigata had been strengthened, and Ono returned to Tokyo on November 23 and reviewed the results of the trip with Ōkuma. He later reported on the situation in Niigata at the December meeting of the Kaishintō.

During 1884 Ono concentrated on party affairs in the capital and only made two brief speaking tours to Shizuoka prefecture and in the suburbs of Tokyo. His efforts to develop a viable party and to arouse public interest in politics were rewarded on August 1 when the *Kaishin shimbun*, a newspaper not affiliated with Kaishintō, unveiled a stone bust of him. Ono wrote of the occasion: "I do not feel proud. It was others who did this for me. I could not refuse it. I am writing this to clarify my intentions." Ono continued to maintain contact with local branches during the rest of the year, but he ceased making extensive political tours and began to concentrate on educational activities. By December, however, the party began to experience internal difficulties, and Ono noted in his diary the need for improvements.[79]

In addition to political canvassing, the Kaishintō relied on faction-affiliated newspapers to get its messages across to the public. *Yūbin hōchi shimbun*, the voice of the Tōyō gisei kai, was the party's most influential spokesman and reflected the Kaishintō stand on major issues of the time. Yano, the chief editor of the paper, believed that the unfavorable balance of trade and excessive import of goods were due to the premodern state of Japanese industry. He discussed this problem with Inoue Kowashi, Ono, and Miyoshi Taizō and they decided to organize a movement to "Buy Japanese." After Iwakura received complaints from one foreign ambassador, he advised Inoue that it would not be possible to develop such a movement and the plan was dropped.[80] Through *Hōchi,* Yano concentrated on arousing public opinion on the key issue of treaty revision. Shortly before the political change of 1881, *Hōchi* published an article entitled "Should We Not Now Check The Arbitrary Conduct of Foreigners, Our Commercial Rights Will Never Be Restored." Foreign interference in Japanese commercial affairs was seen in the opposition of the Western merchant community to the organization of a new Japanese company designed to handle silk exports and to replace foreign dealers. The foreign community tried to get the American minister to intervene with the Japanese government and now threatened to refuse to ship goods directly exported by Japanese firms. The issue was but one example of the need for treaty revision:

> Who can refrain from anger at the extraordinary harshness and arbitrariness of the foreign traders? Indeed, these are not matters born in a single morning. Reflection shows us that, when the ports were first opened, our merchants, then being ignorant of the modes of foreign trade, were void of even enough knowledge to discover the deception and ridicule of foreigners, from which they always suffered, and consequently all their dealings were subject to the management of the strangers, while our merchants had, it seemed, no control of any kind of the transactions [*sic*]. As the result, our commercial rights are still usurped by them; and the losses sustained by us are not small. But our merchants have by degrees become familiar with the methods of foreign trade, and are now in condition to complete fairly well with foreigners. They are no longer childlike Japanese merchants of bygone times. Notwithstanding this, foreign traders, being accustomed to a monopoly of benefit, attempt, whenever our business men purpose to restore our commercial rights, to stifle their efforts by menaces, acting just as a despotic monarch does towards his subjects. How obnoxious they are![81]

Yūbin hōchi's reply to an "address" circulated by the foreign merchants in Yokohama was even more vitriolic:

> Thus, the barefaced foreign merchants assiduously endeavor

to dissociate our brethren from us with specious words, without acknowledging the fact that they, having themselves acted arbitrarily during more than twenty years, have molested the native merchants and gone so far that our brethren must be well aware of their highhandedness, even though we should not cite any particular instance. Will there be any of those who have a trifle of patriotic spirit, who will believe the words of foreigners, and injure our brethren? . . .

Is it indeed not an exorbitant demand that the sellers should hand over their goods to the buyers before fixing upon prices and weight, and leave them to the latter's willful arrangement? But still the foreign merchants obstinately desire to maintain the old customs on account of deception practised by the Japanese. We therefore venture to ask, while foreigners blame the guile of Japanese, do they not reflect upon their own violence in detaining goods purposely and using compulsory measures for settling price and weight? If they say that fraud is practised on the part of the Japanese, then we, on our side proclaim that there is violence on the part of the foreigners. Both fraud and violence are equally wrong, and therefore we and the strangers should mutually endeavor to check them. Nevertheless, can not the Japanese reform their own abuses in order to prevent the violence of foreign merchants, while the latter still continue their arbitrary method of taking delivery into their own godowns, in order to check the deception of the Japanese? Even supposing that there are wrongs on both sides, the reform contemplated by the Japanese does not interfere with the rights of the foreigners, but simply straightens our deflected rights. In other words, our desire is to conduct our commerce according to the methods which are usual in all parts of the world. Yet the foreigner, under some pretext or other, desires to preserve the original customs, etc.[82]

In February 1882 *Hōchi* tied the issue of treaty revision to Japanese policy toward Korea and to the need for a national assembly. Beginning with the thesis that those who oppose revision "are unjust and iniquitous" and are concerned only with their own selfish interests, the writer explained that such attitudes were the result of foreign disdain for Japan due to the state of the nation. Yet, while "exasperated with the disdain and rudeness of foreigners," Japanese merchants acted in a similar fashion toward Koreans and scorned "them as bitterly as the Westerners despise us." If Japanese acted this way toward Koreans, was it unreasonable for foreigners to act in the same fashion toward Japanese? "To accomplish revision, we must let them know the actual conditions of our country, thus averting their scorn; and on our side we must abolish the abuses which arise from despising any inferior nation." Great Britain, the major opponent of revision, had a government subject to public opinion.[83] Yet, the British public opposed revision out of ignorance of Japan and despised Japan without just cause merely because there was no national assembly, the mark of an advanced nation. *Yūbin hōchi* continued:

> Hence, it seems that, in order to show . . . that our political organization, laws and social conditions, are not seriously inferior to theirs, we must establish a national assembly in order to allow people to participate in the government of the country; we must make speech and public meetings free, and organize a jury system. Our Emperor has already promised that a national assembly would be established in 1890; but when shall we be free to obtain the latter two institutions? Indeed, their non-existence is the prime proof of our inferiority, and therefore, so long as present conditions prevail in this country, aliens will continue to regard us as beneath themselves, no matter how earnestly we may insist upon the contrary. On the other hand, should we clear the track and demonstrate our real perfection in these matters, they will soon admit our pleas, and treaty revision will be accomplished with ease. Hence we say that the required change is not difficult, and that, should we adopt sensible measures today, revision can be effected tomorrow.[84]

While the relationship of the movement for parliamentary government and treaty revision had yet to be proved, *Hōchi*'s assumption that a national assembly automatically would be followed by treaty revision was the product of its orientation, A letter printed in *Hōchi* on February 24 opposing the introduction of foreign capital into Japanese business and freedom of travel for foreigners for commercial purposes led one "Foreign Capitalist" to denounce the paper as "distinguishing itself by the amazing supply of *canards* and false news." While recognizing *Hōchi* as "a serious organ of the 'liberal party' " and a "formidable thorn in the side of the government," the writer declared that the paper was "clamouring for Korea," where Japan had extraterritorial rights. Furthermore, the real object of the "so-called liberal party" in regard to the abolition of extraterritoriality was to bring foreigners under Japanese law and to keep them from doing profitable business in Japan.[85]

The Sino-French War and Chinese military weakness led *Hōchi* to compare the paths taken by China and Japan in an article entitled "A Contrast." While noting that the *bakufu* had fallen due to its failure to keep abreast of the times, "the state of affairs in the Middle Kingdom" directly affected other nations in Asia. Knowledge of British activities in China and the resulting threat to Japan awoke the patriotic spirit of the Japanese people. The irresistible power of English arms stimulated the Meiji government to adopt Western armaments and discipline in order to promote national strength. For thirty years China and Japan had followed opposite policies. Japan had learned from the Chinese example, both in 1840 and in the Sino-French engagements, that foreign weapons can not be used without understanding and assimilating the true spirit of Western civilization. Weapons and discipline alone could not assure future prosperity. Japan had to study the spirit and thought that produced such developments. Wealth was the greatest factor in national strength, and improvements were expensive and required increased taxes. The government had to devise "judicious schemes to increase natural wealth . . . to so administer the affairs of the nation, that the spirit of patriotism which so often has protected the weaker states may be maintained."[86] Inherent in this article was the idea that the true spirit of Western civilization was parliamentary government, which would promote the prosperity and love of country needed for national survival. Yet, the admiration of Western weapons and discipline as signs of national and moral strength was contradictory to earlier *Hōchi* attacks on the merchant and diplomatic community which, backed by modern weapons and the Chinese precedent, supported the unequal treaties. The Western attributes *Hōchi* admired in 1884 were those that produced arrogant foreign businessmen, extraterritoriality, lack of tariff autonomy, and the disadvantageous commercial conditions attacked in 1881 and 1882. These had not changed in the brief space of two years, and *Hōchi* failed to justify the contradictory stand taken in the 1884 article. Expediency and the popular theme of nationalism took precedence over earlier complaints.

Although the Kaishintō spokesmen publicly stated their views on many topics, neither they nor their opponents in the Jiyūtō or Teiseitō presented a draft constitution as a party policy statement. Prior to the emergence of the parties and before the announcement of the establishment of the Diet, there was controversy over the date when the national assembly would commence, over whether the constitution would be promulgated before or after the assembly opened, and on the position and rights of the sovereign. The various private constitutions, termed *shigi kempō,* dealt with these matters and indicated the views of the parties on the constitution. It was realized that if the Diet was to be opened after the establishment of the constitution, the position of those advocating a constitution granted by the emperor would be strengthened. On the other hand, if the Diet opened before the constitution was promulgated, the parties would have the opportunity to write the constitution. The issue resulted in the confrontation between the liberal parties and the government. The question of whether sovereignty rested in the emperor or the people became controversial in 1882, when the debate over the type of assembly was taken up by the parties and press. Fukuchi Gen'ichirō advocated imperial sovereignty in *Nichi nichi.* Numa came out against him in *Mainichi* and called for the sovereignty of both emperor and people as exemplified in the British parliamentary system. He gave his views in greater detail in *Kokuyaku kempō ron (Discussion on the Promised National Constitution)* in the *Kōchi shimbun.* In the same paper Ueki Emori wrote an essay entitled *Kokka shuken ron (Discussion on State Sovereignty),* which he described as not a genuine theory of popular sovereignty but a theory inclined toward the sovereignty of the people. The private constitutions were not draft constitutions presented by the parties but rather individual works written for publication largely between 1881 and 1889.[87] As drafts written by private persons, groups, or the press, they did not represent official party policy. On the key issues of sovereignty and the date of the promulgation of the constitution, the parties were mute. The imperial edict of October 12 had removed these questions from their sphere of action. The Kaishintō acknowledged this in *Shisei no yōgi*, the party platform, when it declared it would await the emperor's decision on the constitution. Until the constitution was promulgated, the parties would not know the role of representational institutions or their place in the future political structure.

Yet, while cognizant that the government would decide by itself the institutional framework of Japanese political life, the Kaishintō worked to publicize the importance of political parties and to promote a climate favorable to change. On December 17, 1882, the members established an intellectual society called Meiji kyōkai (Meiji Association) dedicated to the improvement of politics, the economy, and industry. The association published the *Meiji kyōkai zasshi* starting in January 1883 and built a meeting hall capable of accommodating over three thousand people. The society had four hundred members, including some who were not followers of the Kaishintō. The officers and governing board included Maejima Hisoka, the chairman, the writer Narishima Ryūhoku, and the journalist and politician Fujita Mokichi,[88] all members of the Kaishintō, and the economist and historian Taguchi Ukichi of the Jiyūtō. The initial members included Hatoyama Kazuo, Haruki Yoshiaki, Hattori Seiichi, Numa Morikazu, Ōkuma Shigenobu, Ono Azusa, Kōno Togama, Mutaguchi Gengaku, Nomura Fumio, Yano Fumio, Maeda Kenjirō, Masuda Katsunori, Fujita Takayuki, Koezuka Ryū, Kitabatake Harufusa, Minoura Katsundo, Shimada Saburō, and Sudō Tokiichirō.[89] With the exception of Hattori and Sudō, all were in the Kaishintō. Ono was one of the major organizers of the association and mentioned handling matters concerning the Meiji kyōkai while at the Kaishintō office and attending meetings until May 3, 1884, in his diary. He spoke at the opening ceremony, but although elected secretary, he refused the position "in order to avoid suspicion of seeking power."

A second Kaishintō affiliated group, the Jingo kyōkai was organized on September 26, 1882, by Ono, Maejima, Okayama, and Ichishima to study and debate politics, economics, and law.

Shimada, Katō Hyōkō, Ōkuma, and others soon joined its meetings. The members belonged to the Kaishintō and first met at Maejima's home and then at Ōkuma's villa for heated discussions. Ono, who had discussed the organization of the group as early as May 31, 1881, drafted its regulations and frequently attended meetings, which on November 20, 1882, grew to twenty participants.[90] The Meiji kyōkai represented a continuation of the work and aims of the Kyōzon dōshū; and Jingo kyōkai, a political study and debating society, may have been envisioned by Ono, its founder, as a more sophisticated version of that early study group, the Ōtokai.

DENOUEMENT AND DECLINE

The first half of 1882 saw the parties at the height of their popularity. *Nichi nichi,* in an article on the brief history of the party movement, noted that everywhere people "had become imbued with the idea of forming political societies. . . . The organization of these societies became a common topic of conversation, while discussions on the subject were enthusiastically carried on by lecturers and in the newspapers. Those people who entertained political ideas, but hesitated to join a political party, were stigmatized as the dregs of society, destitute of spirit." The Teiseitō and Kaishintō held public meetings in Tokyo to increase their followings. On October 12, 1882, the first anniversary of the political change of 1881, the Imperial Party held a meeting in Osaka to discuss the best means of expanding its influence. To increase Jiyūtō support, Itagaki personally undertook an inspection tour of northern Honshu and the Tōkaidō. Yet, at the height of their popularity, the parties discredited themselves and began to decline.[91]

In the early 1880s, the parties functioned within an environment which, with the exception of an educated and vocal minority of the population, was mainly indifferent and often hostile to their development. In a period when they could not hope to attain power through control of a national assembly, they were forced to justify their raison d'être by slogans of progress and reform and opposition to the ruling clan oligarchs. Despite their different character, both parties were anti-government and had a common goal, party cabinets and the attainment of political power.[92] Ōkuma had refused Itagaki's offer to form one large political group, and Ono similarly rejected requests to join the Jiyūtō. The very organization of a second party implied disagreement with the first. Yano recognized that the Liberal leaders included the militants of the Restoration, such as Itagaki and Kataoka Kenkichi; but he acknowledged that any attempt to merge the two groups would be "just like mixing oil and water. It is impossible and also undesirable." Since both had the same objectives in regard to reforming the national administration, they at least could work together for the political rights of the people and could associate as relatives or cooperate as friends. As each group worked to extend its influence and recruit new members, Yano's views were ignored and the gap between the popular parties widened while the government worked to divide and weaken them.[93]

Party leadership and composition prevented unity of action. Itagaki's liberalism was superficial and impractical. His followers were primarily from rural areas, often unemployed, fired with the ideals of the French revolution, and prone to quick and direct action. Ōkuma was less idealistic, had turned his back on the samurai spirit and life,[94] and even while in the government had favored neutral and moderate ideas. His early studies of English political thought led him to favor political moderation and practical ideas, and to distrust the Jiyūtō for its words and violent attitudes.[95] His followers were intellectuals, wealthy city dwellers, and well-to-do landowners, and Ōkuma's personal finances were aided by Iwasaki Yatarō of Mitsubishi. Itagaki and Ōkuma's contrasting personalities were characterized in a contemporary saying: "If Itagaki is the dragon which wanders the heavens, then Ōkuma is the tiger which roams the earth." At the inaugural ceremony of the Kaishintō, Kōno Togama, the vice-president and a close friend of Ōkuma, stated: "The object of our group is to form a party which will parallel the Jiyūtō." He later added: "We do not consider the Jiyūtō as our enemy but rather as our brother." Itagaki replied to this: "The Kaishintō regards the Jiyūtō as its hunting dog and intends to steal all the spoils from our hands. It is, indeed, an extremely crafty party." Neither party desired an accommodation with the other, and their mutual rivalry and vituperations discredited the entire party movement and contributed to its ultimate failure.[96]

The intense antagonism between the popular parties was publicized openly in the autumn of 1882 when the Jiyūtō and Kaishintō affiliated press began a program of mutual disparagement. At the end of August, Itagaki and Gotō Shōjirō began to discuss the need for a trip to Europe to study Western systems of government and to meet foreign statesmen and political theorists. The oligarchs approved of the trip and through Gotō encouraged the Jiyūtō leaders to go abroad. Itagaki took Gotō's advice, and the two left Japan on November 11, 1882, without disclosing the source of their funds. The trip was financed by the administration, and both the timing and funding antagonized Baba Tatsui and other Liberals who began to doubt Itagaki's ability to lead the party. Baba, Ōishi Masami, and Suehiro Shigeyasu asked Itagaki to postpone the journey until after the opening of the national assembly. They sent a resolution on the issue to all members of the party and declared that they would purge Itagaki from the presidency. Baba believed that Itagaki was corrupting the movement for popular rights from within by accepting government money. Itagaki, furious at Baba's actions, had him expelled from the *Jiyū shimbun,* the Liberal newspaper, before he could use its columns to appeal to Liberal followers throughout the nation.[97] The Jiyūtō erroneously suspected the Kaishintō of manipulating Baba, whose actions were precipitated by his independent and idealistic outlook. After Itagaki and Gotō's departure, Baba, Ōishi, and Suehiro left the party. Rumors on the source of funds for the trip were intimated by *Mainichi* and *Yūbin hōchi.* This infuriated Itagaki's supporters, especially Furusawa Shigeru, chief editor of the *Jiyū shimbun.* He denounced the Kaishintō[98] and counterattacked by pointing to the relationship between Ōkuma and Iwasaki Yatarō, whom he called the financial patron of the Kaishintō. *Mainichi* and *Yūbin hōchi* rose to Ōkuma's defense, and the battle was on. Watanabe Ikujirō blamed the government for leaking information on the source of Itagaki's funds and on Ōkuma's ties with Mitsubishi in order to further divide and weaken its major opponents.[99]

The administration suspected Mitsubishi of supplying large donations to the Kaishintō and tried to destroy the company in order to defeat the party. In February 1882 the government reinforced controls on Mitsubishi and in July established the semi-governmental Kyōdō Un'yu Kaisha. It decided to end Mitsubishi's 103 million yen subsidy for marine transportation and transfer the funds to the new company. Shinagawa Yajirō, the Minister of Agriculture and Commerce, under the direction of Inoue Kaoru, took direct charge of the campaign against Mitsubishi. As *hanbatsu* pressure on Iwasaki's firm increased, the Jiyūtō joined in the attack. It pointed out that as Minister of Finance, Ōkuma had lent Iwasaki ships owned by the government, allowed him to monopolize coastal navigation rights, and given him a state subsidy. Ōkuma had enriched Mitsubishi at public expense, and the Kaishintō now campaigned with the financial support of the company. It declared the Progressives to be "a vicious party which joins hands with Mitsubishi and deprives the nation of benefits and the people of happiness," and took up the slogans of "exterminate the sea monster, exterminate the false party." Having fallen into the *hanbatsu* trap, the Jiyūtō and Kaishintō fought one another and ignored their real enemies, the administration and Teiseitō. Despite the popular belief that the Kaishintō depended on funds from Mitsubishi, Yano wrote that the party had not accepted money from the company either at the time it was established or afterwards. The capital used to purchase *Yūbin hōchi* came from another, unidentified source;[100] Ono never discussed the origin of the party's financial resources.

In November the *Japan Weekly Mail* reported that the *Jiyū shimbun* had published a copy of a memorial presented to the government by the leading members of the Kaishintō in conjunction with Iwasaki Yatarō. The documents condemned the policy of state aid to shipping, meaning aid to Mitsubishi's new rival; and since the public "ascribe[d] the privileges enjoyed by Mitsubishi" to Ōkuma's patronage, it was regarded as practical for his support to continue even when out of office. Iwasaki, the *Mail* wrote, was inconsistent in petitioning the administration not to grant to others the same privileges he now enjoyed. The *Jiyū shimbun* said that Iwasaki and Gotō tried to persuade the editors not to publish the memorial but their advice was disregarded; the document and the government's reply were returned to the compilers.

The memorial noted that earlier competition between Mitsubishi, Yūbin Jōkisen Kaisha (Pacific Mail Steamship Company), and other lines had led to cutthroat freight rates, the ruination of many companies, and government intervention. Such rivalry meant that when ships were needed for the Taiwan expedition, few were available in good condition and the administration was forced to purchase new ones. Because of poor organization, Yūbin Jōkisen Kaisha soon went out of business, and the administration turned over the new ships to Mitsubishi, which also received official protection, a state subsidy, and public business. Mitsubishi then took over the Pacific Mail Line fleet and other bankrupt companies and received a charter from the government in 1875. It performed an "important service" by transporting troops and supplies for the imperial army during the Satsuma rebellion. "Experience has taught the authorities that competition is not the way to develop maritime enterprise." In comparison with foreign shipping firms, the ten-year-old Mitsubishi was a "pigmy." The company had prospered with official support and had been in business for only half the period stipulated in the charter. Why then was a new company needed? Renewed competition would lead to a repetition of events; and when another national crisis arose, no trustworthy vessels would be available. The door would again be opened for foreigners to dominate the coastal trade unopposed. In conclusion, the petitioners wrote: "We, therefore, denounce as pernicious the policy of giving state aid to a new company." Mitsubishi, the petition continued, does not have a monopoly on shipping between Osaka and Kyushu or among Yokohama, Kobe, Nagasaki, and Hongkong, and faces foreign competition on the route to China. Freight rates are not excessive, and the charter gives the government the right to alter them if overly high. High rates are due to conditions and costs in Japan, and the charter requires company ships to be held at the disposition of the state without reference to business. Freight charges for such service are "accurately defined." Coastal shipping is seasonal. Only during the July–December period is there a shortage of ships. During the rest of the year, there is an excess of carriers.[101]

The memorial was drawn up by Iwasaki Yanosuke, the brother of Yatarō. It did not receive Yatarō's approval and was shown privately to Iwakura by a mutual friend but never presented formally. Yatarō disavowed the memorial, but the *Japan Weekly Mail,* which received a copy of the document and official reply from the *Jiyū shimbun,* claimed that it was submitted by the chief manager of Mitsubishi to the postmaster general, who forwarded it to the cabinet where it "could not fail to receive official notice." The paper further noted that Iwasaki had been under a serious misapprehension in regard to his relations with the government. He had assumed that the steamers transferred to his company for the payment of 12 thousand yen in fifty annual installments and the special privileges granted it were intended to enable Mitsubishi "to stamp out all opposition." Such easy terms of payment were due to Ōkuma's intervention. In addition to mail subsidies, Iwasaki had received 3 million yen from the government within a seven-year period. Profits from his shipping operations were invested in mines and banks with Ōkuma's full consent. "In condemning Mr. Iwasaki's proceedings, the Minister of Agriculture and Commerce virtually prefers an indictment against the late Minister of Finance, and in defending himself, Mr. Iwasaki proves nothing but that Mr. Ōkuma was his accomplice." In replying to Iwasaki's memorial, the government counterattacked by declaring Iwasaki's opposition to the new company to be motivated by fear "of detriment to his own private interests" and without concern for the public welfare. The new company was justified by the fact that most of Mitsubishi's vessels belong to the government by purchase or loan; since Mitsubishi had to charter ships to transport coal to China, it did not have surplus vessels as claimed. Its freight rates were double those of foreign shippers and its profits forty to fifty percent, whereas other concerns realized only ten to fifteen percent. Was Iwasaki "so benighted as to be unable to see that his fleet of some thirty vessels, with an aggregate capacity of 20,000 tons is inadequate to meet all the requirements of our trade? . . . the demand for shipping increases *pari passu* with the march of civilization. . . ." The "paper controversy" continued for several weeks until ended in late December by Prince Arisugawa, who ruled in favor of maintaining Mitsubishi's monopoly.[102]

Acrimonious charges and countercharges also cooled personal ties between former friends and colleagues and widened the gap between the parties. After the March 1882 assassination attempt on Itagaki, Ōkuma suggested that the Kaishintō should express its regrets over the attempted assassination. He personally drafted the party's letter of sympathy, but neither the letter, condolence money,[103] nor messengers sent to check on the wounded politician led to any improvement in relations. On April 19 Ono visited Ōkuma and said that the Kaishintō should stop sending Mutaguchi to check on Itagaki's health. The same day, he wrote to Baba and four other Jiyūtō leaders and told them to speak more respectfully of the Kaishintō. Ono and Baba were no longer friends and drinking companions. While they had not, as suggested by Inukai Tsuyochi, become enemies, they had gone different ways and were never again close. Ono's trip to Niigata was partially to offset gains made by Itagaki on a previous tour. Ono was subject to continual harassment by Jiyūtō followers in the area, and he discussed the problem of the "left-wing party members," that is, the Jiyūtō, with Ōkuma on January 31, 1883.[104] On August 11 he wrote to Okuma about the problems local branches were having with the Jiyūtō and of Kaishintō countermeasures:

> The other day I met some of our party followers who came to Tokyo from Saitama, Ibaraki, and Tochigi. They told me that our rivals tried to destroy our party, which they spoke of as a false party. However, they lost popular support due to their efforts. As you know, we sent the *Jiyū mainichi tairon shū (Daily Free Discussion Series)* and the *Kaishintō wa (Story of the Kaishintō)* to each area. Perhaps they had

some effect, for [the local branches] sent us letters of appreciation saying the efforts of our rivals had no effect.[105]

Kaishintō-Jiyūtō rivalry discredited the parties in the eyes of the public and prevented them from forming a united front against the government. A series of incidents between 1882 and 1885 saw Jiyūtō members involved in attempts to assassinate officials, foment rebellion among the garrison at Nagoya, and take over local governments. When these failed, they tried armed uprisings, attacks on police stations, arson, bombings, and robberies to obtain funds for domestic uprisings and aid to the Independence Party in Korea.[106] These further reduced popular support and lent credence to administration claims that the parties disturbed public peace and incited the people against the government.[107]

The administration further limited the permissible sphere of political activities by tightening the legal limits within which they could operate. The revised Regulations for Public Meetings of June 1882 were the most effective measure taken by the government against its opponents. Political associations, no matter how named, were required to furnish the police with the names of members, rules, and headquarters address prior to organization, and to answer all inquiries made by the authorities. The police were not to sanction meetings or associations "deemed injurious to public peace." Following the dissolution of any assembly, the governor, the chief of the metropolitan police in Tokyo, or the home minister could prohibit the speakers from lecturing in public for one year. Political associations could not advertise summaries of lectures, send out "commissioners" or circulars, correspond with one another, or merge. The police could attend scientific or any other public meetings, and those introducing political subjects into scientific meetings were liable to punishment. Violators of the rulings were subject to fines and/or imprisonment. The Newspaper Press Law of 1875 was amended in April 1883 to place increased responsibility on the owners and publishers of newspapers and to discourage evasion of the law. Newspapers were required to post security money, amounting to one thousand yen in Tokyo, which was returned if the publication was discontinued or suspended. All newspapers belonging to an individual or publisher automatically were suspended if any one publication owned by the person was suppressed. The home minister could prohibit and suspend any publication prejudicial to public peace, order, or morals; in serious cases he could seize the publication or its equipment. Certain categories of official and prefectural proceedings, military affairs, criminal investigations, and official documents not announced to the public were banned from publication.[108]

With the laws written for the purpose of harassing the parties and rendering their activities illegal, political activities were restricted. When Ono tried to submit a copy of the Kaishintō declaration to the police in March 1882, they at first refused to accept the document. On May 2 he reported his intention to deliver a political speech to the police and waited three days before receiving approval. To circumvent the laws, the parties declared that they were organized only for social purposes. As a result, on June 13 Ono reported the establishment of the Kokken hanron kai (Society to Introduce the National Constitution) to the Kyōbashi police station, and a month later the society received official approval. Since it is mentioned only twice in Ono's diary, it appears to have been a pseudonym for one of the political groups associated with the Kaishintō.

The police, however, insisted that the Kaishintō was a political organization, which required official sanction.[109] Haruki Yoshiaki, the party secretary, was summoned to the Kyōbashi police station on May 14, 1882, and asked five questions. After hasty discussions with Ono and other members, he submitted his answers to the police the next day. The dialogue went as follows:

QUESTION: The purpose of organizing the Kaishintō was to discuss politics, wasn't it?

ANSWER: This is a social gathering of those with similar aspirations. The purpose is not to discuss politics.

QUESTION: Why is it necessary to keep a list of members?

ANSWER: We keep a list to know those who are members and those who have left.

QUESTION: How are the fees spent?

ANSWER: The fee is one yen for those who live in Tokyo and fifty sen for those who live outside Tokyo. It is used for correspondence and so forth.

QUESTION: What is the purpose of the monthly meeting?

ANSWER: It is a social gathering of members.

QUESTION: Was the speech meeting held on May 13 at the Meiji kaidō a meeting of the Kaishintō?

ANSWER: Our party had nothing to do with the speech meeting.[110]

In June Fujita Mokichi, then editor of the *Yūbin hōchi shimbun*, was summoned to the Kyōbashi police station and questioned on the party's aims. On June 23 the party was ordered to present its membership list to the police and to request permission to meet as a political association.[111] In June the police ordered the Ōmeisha to dissolve.[112] One was deeply concerned about the police inquiry and had earlier conferred with Haruki on his encounter with the police. Ōkuma also visited the police but was unable to change their view of the Kaishintō as a political party. As a result, Ono, Ōkuma, Kōno, and others met at Ōkuma's villa on June 23 and 24 to discuss the problem. They concluded that it was necessary to compromise and act according to the provisions of the Regulations for Public Meetings. After deciding on the corrections this would require in the party's regulations, they called an emergency meeting of the Kaishintō at the Meiji kaidō on June 24.

Ōkuma opened the meeting by stating that the police had decided to apply the laws on public meetings to the Kaishintō; if the party did not conform to the regulations, it would be prohibited. As a result, it was necessary to find some solution to the problem. Kōno, who was acting as chairman, gave an account of his experience with the police. He suggested that it would be best to obey the laws, since the party could not ignore them. The members discussed this and finally accepted Kōno's suggestion. Thereafter, Ono, after consulting with Ōkuma, prepared the party's report to the government. This was delivered on June 27, and two days later he distributed copies of the report to party members.[113]

On June 5 the Ōmeisha and Tōyō gisei kai were formally dissolved in accordance with police instructions.[114] This, however, did not keep the members from participating in the Kaishintō. Police harassment of the party continued. On May 12, 1883, One was called to the police station in regard to the activities of party members in Etchū (Toyama). In May, Ichishima Kenkichi, who was serving as chief editor of the *Niigata shimbun,* was imprisoned for violation of the Press Law.[115] As the government began to apply pressure on the Kaishintō, the political activities of the party and freedom of action of its members were increasingly restricted. As the scope of political action became limited, the Kaishintō moved toward dissolution.

THE DISSOLUTION OF THE KAISHINTŌ

By 1884 the political environment was no longer conducive to the growth of the party movement, which still had six years to wait before it could justify its raison d'être in the parliamentary arena. Economic conditions were also unfavorable to the cause of the *mintō*. A series of bad harvests between 1881 and 1885 caused widespread agricultural distress. The deflationary program instituted by Finance Minister Matsukata Masayoshi in 1881 froze government expenditures for four years, reduced the amount of notes in circulation in favor of foreign-purchased specie, and increased land taxes. As a result prices fell, business expansion ended, and mortgage foreclosures increased in rural areas.[116] The *Jiyū shimbun* reported that in Sagami (Kanagawa) "the poverty and consequent misery of the agricultural classes are beyond description . . . in general landlords and tenants are alike sufferers." Among the coastal population of Kaga and neighboring provinces, the continuing depression in trade forced many artisans to turn to fishing. As a result, the price of fish and marine products fell; but even this occupation temporarily halted during winter. The condition of the people was one of "general distress" and they "are at the lowest depth of poverty."[117] Unable to meet their own expenses, landlords and cultivators had no additional funds for political contributions.

Faced with dispossession and falling prices, especially those for silk, tenants and small farmers rose in revolt, often with the support and leadership of radical elements in the Jiyūtō. The year 1884 saw outbreaks in Iida (Nagano prefecture), Gumma, Shizuoka, Chichibu (Saitama prefecture), Niigata, Nagoya, and Osaka. The government, fearing that economic depression would lead to a general uprising under party leadership, revised the public assembly and press laws in order to make it impossible for the parties to function effectively.[118]

The Rikken Teiseitō set the stage for the decline of the *mintō*. Its leaders were the first to recognize that events had created public antipathy to political parties. Popular attitudes had changed and the parties were now seen as detrimental to society, as hampering the work of the administration, and as harboring men of dangerous character.[119] At the request of Itō Hirobumi, who returned from Germany hostile to parties, the Teiseitō disbanded on September 24, 1883.[120]

On October 29, 1884, the Jiyūtō held its yearly meeting in Osaka and, to the surprise of the public, dissolved. Tarnished by its association with "agitators," and with its major supporters in financial difficulty, the party found its popularity waning and treasury empty. Unable to control activist members who resorted to violence and collisions with the law, Itagaki chose to end the party. The "Manifesto by the Liberal Party on Its Dissolution" justified the act as the only possible response to the Regulations on Public Meetings and the Press Law. The former prohibited the establishment of local branches of political parties and, thereby, left local members free to act at their own discretion. Such actions were "characterized by impetuosity rather than prudence. Large political bodies require management and control as does an army," and the law now prohibited such control. This caused confusion that defied restraint. The regulations infringed on the liberty of association and led to individual actions resulting in radicalism and its attendant dangers. Both regulations restricted liberty and freedom of speech and led individual members to resort to violence and rash actions while their leaders were unable to exert any guidance. Under such conditions, there was no choice but to "dissolve the organization of the Liberal Party and wait for our opportunity, when society shall be prepared for its reconstitution."[121]

According to Ozaki Yukio, the *hanbatsu* feared not Itagaki and the Jiyūtō but Ōkuma and the Kaishintō and tried to obstruct the Progressives by every means. Ōkuma, while one of the most influential members of the government, had gathered about himself some of the great men of the time and used them to form an opposition party. To the Satchō leaders, Ōkuma's insistence upon party cabinets was equivalent to disloyalty and to some he was a traitor who had to be subjugated by any means. Contemporary politicians regarded political strife as though it were warfare, and Inoue Kaoru worked to destroy the *mintō* by cutting off funds. Because of Mitsubishi's dominant position in Japanese shipping, the government feared that Ōkuma could gain control of maritime power in an emergency and so it established a rival company. Ōkuma's financial supporters were regarded as traitors and were cut off from public funds and supplies. Under attack from all sides, the party was helpless, and some members began to make their peace with the oligarchy in order to find positions in the bureaucracy. With his backers pressured not to lend him money, Ōkuma was able to meet only part of Kaishintō financial needs with money supplied by the former *daimyō* of Hizen, Nabeshima Naohiro. Ōkuma personally was in financial difficulties in 1884; the situation was even worse for his followers, who were shut out from official positions. In an attempt to improve their condition, Ōkuma had tried to establish banking, publishing, and newspaper enterprises, but these all fell into bankruptcy. Even the salaries for the teachers at Tokyo Senmon Gakkō, the school he had founded, were often delayed. Popular interest in politics declined in 1883 and 1884. Government oppression, financial difficulties, and "great weariness together with discord" among the members forecast a bleak future for the parties.

Under these circumstances, the Kaishintō had to choose

between two courses of action: to take advantage of the fact that the Jiyūtō was discredited and on the verge of collapse and expand, or to leave the political arena. Okayama and Yamada favored expansion; but Kōno Togama, who had been in Osaka and had seen signs of a coming depression, advocated dissolution of the party as early as February 1884. He felt that unfavorable economic conditions would inhibit Kaishintō growth and that it would be better for the party movement if the members dispersed and worked as individuals. Mutaguchi, Haruki, and Fujita Mokichi supported his decision. They were motivated to a degree by Ōkuma's financial difficulties, which had forced him to sell his mansion in Tokyo in March 1884 and to move to his villa at Waseda. Ōkuma could no longer offer financial support to elderly party members such as Maejima, Kōno, Kitabatake, and Haruki because of lack of economic and political power. Since the Kaishintō membership list was equivalent to a political blacklist, he thought that it would be best to release his followers so that they could resume their former careers. He thus came to look favorably on the idea of dissolving the Kaishintō in order to enable more members to retire from the party and seek employment elsewhere. Kitabatake Harufusa, however, opposed dissolution, and a group led by Maejima Hisoka remained neutral. At the same time, internal dissension within the party had increased, particularly the division between the Tōyō gisei kai and Ōmeisha. Although Takada Sanae of the Ōtokai attempted to reconcile the feuding factions,[122] the breaking point came in late November when the Numa faction decided to petition the Genrō-in to reduce the land tax.[123]

On November 29, 1884, Kōno, Shimada, Minoura, Ozaki, and Yamada Ichirō called on Ono, who was ill at home, to discuss the petition. Ono opposed the idea because it was "not the policy of our party"[124] and immediately wrote to Ōkuma:

> I have heard that our party members are going to present a proposal on tax reduction to the Genrō-in under their joint signature. Though I do not know much about the details, I think there are only two reasons for us to propose a reduction in taxes. First, we can save the people from impoverishment by reducing taxes. Second, we can attract people to our party

even if we are not successful in obtaining tax reduction. In my opinion, this proposal will not achieve either purpose. If we want to attain the first purpose, we should show how to reduce various expenditures and should present our estimates, based on decreased yearly revenues, to the home minister or prime minister. We should also appeal to the government by explaining the condition of the people. This is very important. But [the party members], on the contrary, want to present the proposal to the Genrō-in. This is childish, not patriotic. To make matters worse, the Genrō-in will do nothing with the proposal except keep it for future reference. The second point [i.e., the petition], also is not good. It would require careful, astute preparation to get the signatures of a few hundred thousand people. If we appeal in this way to the home minister, finance minister, or prime minister, then it would be possible to gain public support. Thus, I think it is regrettable that this important issue is now brought to the attention of our country and party.

Although this [petition] is not official party policy, it will be regarded as such because it bears the joint signatures of important members of our party. Our party will be regarded with contempt by the intellectuals of the country.

Appended to the letter was a notice that he would not add his signature to the proposal.[125] The land tax in the period between 1880 and 1897 accounted for fifty-eight percent of government revenue,[126] and the Kaishintō had not advocated reduction in any of its policy statements. Ono and Ōkuma realized that the tax could not be lowered without a corresponding cut in expenditures. The petition did not deal with this problem and was designed to win over to the Kaishintō former Jiyūtō followers. Ono had never got along well with Numa, and now he and Ōkuma both came out against the Ōmeisha sponsored plan.

Since September Ono had been spitting up blood, and he was bedridden and unable to attend party meetings.[127] On December 1 he wrote in his diary that the party was in great confusion and wondered whether it was possible to improve the situation. He decided to resign as secretary in order to work for the gradual improvement of the party. On December 4 he noted:

I wrote my letter of resignation from the party. Itō

> [Senzō] came and said Kōno and Maejima want to hold a meeting of the active members of the party tomorrow. I am quite worried about it. Yamada [Ichirō] also came and told me that Kōno and Maejima will dissolve our party and have sent out invitations for the meeting tomorrow. I was quite surprised to hear this. We believe that the existence of this party is advantageous to our nation, and I see no point in dissolving it. If we dissolve our party now, we would be mocked by the people as well as by history. I asked Yamada about the opinion of the party chairman [Ōkuma], and his answer was: "I do not know." I wrote a letter and asked Yamada to take it to Waseda [Ōkuma] for me. I explained why it was not good to dissolve the party and asked for his decision. I also asked Yamada to find out Maejima's real purpose.[128]

News about the dissolution came as a shock to Ono, who strongly opposed it. On December 5 Ozaki Yukio informed Ono about plans to end the party. Ono said he believed that Ōkuma had agreed to Kōno's idea without deep consideration and that this could not be his real intention. Ono remarked: "I shall be the only one left to support the Kaishintō." Ozaki agreed with Ono and promised to visit Ōkuma. Mutaguchi Gengaku then called to state that he favored dissolving the party. Ono told him:

> The formation of our party was for the [welfare of the] country, and it should not be dissolved unless there is a good reason. If dissolution occurs, Councilor Ōkuma will have to retreat from politics. If our president is really tired of political life, then, perhaps, it is excusable for him to dissolve our party; but if he still wants to be in political life, he should not do this. As his friend, I do not agree with his decision or with his desire to commit [political] suicide.[129]

Mutaguchi said he would convey Ono's views to Ōkuma, but since Ōkuma had already agreed to Kōno's proposal, he could not retract his statement without appearing disrespectful. Ono replied that even if he was disrespectful to one individual, namely Kōno, they should do what was proper and respectful for the public and for the state. Yamada later stated that Maejima had been pressured to accept the proposal. Then

Minoura and Kōno came to discuss the problem and Ōkuma's decision.

The next day one of the party members brought Ono the report written by Mutaguchi on the proceedings of the meeting held on December 5. The report described how Kōno first suggested the dissolution of the party and how Numa and Ozaki rose and denounced him. The members then became angry and left, and Kōno and his followers declared that they would leave the party. Ono told Yamada that nothing could be done to prevent news of the meeting from leaking to the public, but that all concerned had acted disgracefully. However, if the members just gave up, the situation would worsen. He told Yamada to ask Ōkuma to arrange some solution to the problem. Ōkuma then agreed to talk with Kōno and Maejima in order to devise some remedial measure. On December 7, Ono wrote in his diary:

> I wanted to do my best for the Kaishintō. I wanted to do my best for the president of the Kaishintō. Thus, I wanted to fulfill my responsibility to Japan.[130]

With his principal advisers divided, Ōkuma hesitated. When the party members gathered to hear his decision, the confusion was compounded. According to Ozaki, who attended the meeting, Kōno said that Ōkuma decided to dissolve the party. Mutaguchi stated that Ōkuma decided not to dissolve the party, and Maejima admitted that he did not know what Ōkuma had said. The divergence in views shocked the younger party men, who recognized that, despite their age and influence, the party elder statesmen were being treated as children by Ōkuma.

On December 12 Ōkuma called on Ono, and after two hours Ono agreed to plans to dissolve the party. Ono had organized the Kaishintō around Ōkuma, and once Ōkuma decided to resign, the party had lost its leader and its raison d'être. Therefore Ono and the other party secretaries, Mutaguchi and Haruki, advised Ōkuma and Kōno Togama to submit their letters of resignation to them.[131] Ōkuma's letter, which was delivered on December 17, went as follows:

> When I explained the membership list was no longer necessary but rather harmful for our activities under the current situation in Japan, some members in the Tokyo area expressed strong opposition. I think it is not necessary to vote on the treatment of those opposed to my proposal. Therefore, I now wish to be permitted to leave the party.[132]

Mutaguchi, Kitabatake Harufusa, Haruki Yoshiaki, and Maejima Hisoka also left the party at the same time.

Ono discussed the break-up of the party with Numa and others on December 21, and at a meeting held the same day, the party regulations were revised and the office of president abolished. Seven commissioners were appointed to handle party business, including Fujita Mokichi, Ozaki Yukio, and Minoura Katsundo of the Tōyō gisei kai, and Shimada Saburō, Hizuka Ryū, Nakano Buei, and Numa Morikazu of the Ōmeisha. Okayama Kenkichi and Ōtsu Jun'ichirō also remained with the party. Thus, the party did not dissolve but was reconstructed with a limited membership composed primarily of Ōmeisha followers and some elements from the *Yūbin hōchi shimbun*. Following the decision to alter the structure of the Kaishintō, Ono believed that he could no longer serve as secretary and resigned on grounds of ill health. His resignation was accepted on December 27. Once again he followed Ōkuma into retirement. Although his diary for 1885 was to mention continual contacts with his former comrades in the Kaishintō, his political years had come to an end.[133] In the last notation for 1884 in *Ryūkakusai nikki,* he even failed to mention the Kaishintō and wrote:

> 1884 has come to an end. This year the population increased rapidly, and the people do not look very good. In addition, feudal attitudes are becoming popular again. The clans act so badly that they do not seem to care for Japan as a whole. In regard to foreign affairs, treaty revision has not yet been accomplished; and the affair in Korea has not been settled. Prices for gold and silver increase rapidly while the value of paper money declines. It is an unlucky year. I have also been ill. Yet the rise and fall of one's career is natural. When there is failure, there will be success. I will not worry about the failure and will hope for success in later years.[134]

Neither the political climate, economic conditions, nor party structure was conducive to the survival and growth of parties in the period before the establishment of the Diet. Lacking a public forum in which to contest their ideas and seek public support and wherein the members could be gainfully employed as representatives of the people, the parties faded away. As popular interest declined, government pressure increased, and funds disappeared, the parties either dissolved or modified their structures to meet the hostile environment. Following the dissolution of the Teiseitō in September 1883, several former members led by Sasa Tomofusa established a party, called the Kokkentō, to maintain the party's principles in Shizuoka and Yamanashi prefectures. Thirteen months later the Jiyūtō disbanded. The Kaishintō did not dissolve, and a small group led by seven members of the Ōmeisha and a few followers of the Tōyō gisei kai continued to hold meetings. Without the unifying force of Ōkuma and sufficient funds, and subject to increased government control, their influence declined and newspaper circulation decreased. In the absence of neutral intermediaries, such as the party president, Ono, and the Ōtokai, factional rivalries were given full vent. For all practical purposes, however, the Kaishintō ceased to function as a party on the political scene after December 1884.

Although factionalism was inherent in the very structure of the parties, the failure of the Kaishintō to overcome factional rivalries and to continue to promote the cause of parliamentary government was Ono's bitterest disappointment. Ono did not live to see the Diet for which he had campaigned nor to see his party participate in the era of constitutional government. After a period of physical suffering and financial difficulties, he died on January 11, 1886, a month before his thirty-fourth birthday.[135] Ōkuma, whose reputation as a champion of popular rights and party government was the product of Ono's ideas and organizational skills, grieved over his death and mourned that it was a worse blow than losing both his arms.[136] Okayama, on hearing of Ono's death, wrote to his companions in the Ōtokai a letter that was his epitaph to their friend and political mentor:

> Who was our benefactor who guided us in the unknown and dangerous world of politics? Who was the righteous and honest politician that did not fear any difficulties. Who . . . helped you obtain the position, fame, and confidence you enjoy?
>
> We should plan the future of our party to carry out his will, that is, the principles of our party. We made a mistake, and we have lost confidence and fame. . . . but more regrettable is that we have lost enthusiasm. When our party was organized, the people expected much of us, and we were full of energy. Since we once failed, the public no longer listens to us and there is chaos within our party. Why were we prosperous in the beginning?
>
> You may justify your actions by saying that the people are just sleeping, and it is not an appropriate time for us to do anything important or that we now have no leaders. I do not think you are right. When we observe the political situation, we see that the imperial court has initiated a major reform. The time is ripe for action.

Okayama called on his friends to continue their work, to ask the cabinet to define its principles of administration, to call for freedom of speech and assembly. What was most important was to participate in the establishment of the constitution. The Kaishintō had been organized to teach the people about the establishment of parties and, despite the changed structure, was still in a position of power. If One had anticipated his death and had left a will, he would have told them to concentrate on politics, to train men of ability, and to plan for the future of their party. To carry out his will, they had to achieve academic independence for the school he had founded for Ōkuma, Tokyo Senmon Gakkō, and to unify the party. The Kaishintō alone among political groups had men of outstanding ability able to concentrate on long-term goals. It was therefore necessary to reorganize the party, to end personal feuds and division, and to focus the attention of all members on the problems that lay ahead.[137]

Ono's name was removed from the party roll, but his activities had established a precedent for a modern party system, and the concepts of party organization and structure that he founded were carried on by the Kaishintō, by its successors in the prewar period, and by its contemporary heir, the Jiyūminshutō (Liberal Democratic Party), which has dominated Japanese political life since 1955.

In his concern for fulfilling his duty as a *shishi* and for promoting the greatest good of the greatest number, Ono created the Ōtokai as a group to aid in the formation of policies leading toward the establishment of a new, modern, popular party. As founder, theorist, and organizer of the Kaishintō, Ono Azusa laid the basis for the continuing tradition and institutions of party politics, which came to dominate the political life of Japan and thereby contributed to the democratization of political institutions in modern Japan.

NOTES

1. Gorai Kinzō, *Ningen Ōkuma Shigenobu* (Tokyo: Waseda Daigaku Shuppanbu, 1938), p. 327.
2. Ono, "Ryūkakusai nikki," pp. 318, 324–26, 368–69. Baba called at Ono's home on February 1, 1881, but Ono was not in. The two planned to meet on March 12 but were unable to get together, and Ono wrote to Baba on October 26. On November 1, Baba asked Ono to join the Jiyūtō, and on November 13, Baba invited Ono to go drinking with him. Ono refused because of the late hour. On November 19 Baba asked Ono to join the Jiyūtō; but Ono refused.
3. Hagihara, "Baba Tatsui," *CK* 947 (August 1966): 403–4; 949 (September 1966): 326–27.
4. Ono, "Ryūkakusai nikki," pp. 368–69, 371–72; Enomoto, "Ono Azusa no seiji ronri," *NRR*, p. 547.
5. Hagihara, "Baba Tatsui," *CK* 947 (September 1966): 405. Baba in 1880 wrote an outline of commercial law entitled *Shōritsu gairon* for the journal *Tōkai keizai shimpō (Oriental Economic News),* published by Toyokawa Ryōhei, the former manager of the Mitsubishi Shōgyō Gakkō (Mitsubishi Commercial School). Toyokawa, a native of Tosa and a cousin of Iwasaki Yatarō, married Baba's niece Yasuko in 1880. Because of Toyokawa, Baba developed a close relationship with Iwasaki.
6. Shimomura, *Nihon zenshi,* 9: 114.
7. Fujii, *Constitution of Japan,* pp. 100, 146; Gorai, *Ningen Ōkuma,* p. 327.
8. Shimomura, *Nihon zenshi,* 9: 113.
9. Itō, "Reform Party," *JHR,* pp. 11–12.

10. Shimomura, *Nihon zenshi,* 9: 113.

11. Hagihara, "Baba Tatsui," *CK* 948 (October 1966): 391–93.

12. Shimomura, *Nihon zenshi,* 9: 113–14, 117. The branch offices were known specifically as the Kyushu, Tōhoku, Hokutatsu, Keijyo, Nanetsu, Shinyō, Gakunan, Enyō, Sanyō, Aichi, Ōtsu, Awaji, Kainan, Matsue, Sekiyō, Geiyō, Chobō, Tajima, Nobitō, and Etchū Jiyūtō, the Osaka Rikken Seitō, and the Kyōchū Rikkentō.

13. *JWM* 6, no. 23 (June 10, 1882): 708.

14. Ibid., 6, no. 27 (July 8, 1882): 821, 837. Aihara Naomi, a native of Aichi prefecture, was sentenced to life imprisonment with penal servitude. Shimomura, *Nihon zenshi,* 9: 117, 118; Itō Isao, "Meiji jidai ni okeru shakaishugi seitō undō," *Jōchi hōgaku ronshū (Sophia Law Review)* 3, no. 1 (1959): 89–107.

15. Nishimura, *Ono Azusa den,* p. 150; Itō, "Nihon seitō," *HS,* pp. 29, 30.

16. R. H. P. Mason, *Japan's First General Election, 1890* (Cambridge: Cambridge University Press, 1969), pp. 14–15.

17. Itō, "Nihon seitō," *HS,* pp. 29, 30; Shimomura, *Nihon zenshi,* 9: 115, 117. The local branches were the Shien Kai (Kumamoto), Miyazu Zenshintō (Kyoto), Chūsei Kai (Okayama), Kyōchū Rikkentō (Yamanashi) and Kōyō Rikken Teiseitō (Kōchi).

18. *JWM* 9, no. 11 (November 22, 1884): 501.

19. Suzuki Yasuzō, *Nihon kensei seiritsu shi* (Tokyo: Gakugeisha, 1933), p. 230.

20. Enomoto, "Hanbatsu seitōron," *HGDK,* p. 74; Watanabe Ikujirō, *Ōkuma kankei monjo,* 5: 5–12.

21. Ōkuma Shigenobu, "Nihon no seitō," *Meiji kensei keizai shi ron,* comp. Takano Iwazaburō (Tokyo: Yūhikaku Shobō, 1919), pp. 134, 135, Itō, "Reform Party," *JHR,* p. 10.

22. Itō, "Reform Party," *JHR,* pp. 2, 26–28; Nishimura, *Ono Azusa den,* p. 151; Itō, "Nihon seitō," *HS,* p. 27.

23. Nakamura, *Naigai seitō jijō,* pp. 147–50.

24. Joyce [Chapman] Lebra, "The Kaishintō as a Political Elite," *Modern Japanese Leadership,* ed. Bernard S. Silberman and H. D. Harootunian (Tucson: University of Arizona Press, 1966), pp. 373–75. Lebra lists fifty-eight or a total of fifty percent of the Kaishintō members as coming from Tokyo. My figure of 51.7 percent is based upon the list of party mmbers given in the *Naigai seito jijō* (July 30, 1882), pp. 147–50.

25. Lebra, *Ōkuma Shigenobu,* p. 265.

26. Nakanishi Keijirō, *Waseda Daigaku hachijūnen shi* (Tokyo: Waseda Daigaku Kan, 1962), pp. 39–40.

27. Kyōguchi, *Takada Sanae den,* p. 276.

28. Rengo Press, ed. *Japan Biographical Encyclopedia and Who's Who,* 3d. ed. (Tokyo: Rengo Press, 1964–1965), p. 34; Nakanishi,

Waseda Daigaku hachijūnen shi, pp. 40–41; Waseda Daigaku Toshokan, ed. *Shunjō hachijūnen no oboegaki* (Tokyo: Waseda Daigaku Toshokan, 1960), p. 73.

29. Ōkuma Hensan Kai, *Ōkuma kō hachijūgonen shi,* 2: 145.

30. Nishimura, *Ono Azusa den,* pp. 114, 115; Takano, *Takada, Ichishima seitan,* pp. 13–15.

31. Itō, "Reform Party," *JHR,* p. 19.

32. Nishimura, *Ono Azusa den,* 113, 144.

33. Waseda, *Shunjō hachijūnen,* pp. 56–60; Takano, *Takada, Ichishima seitan,* pp. 30, 157, 271.

34. Oguri, *Yano Fumio,* pp. 117, 120, 135, 205, 212–15; Joyce [Chapman] Lebra, "Yano Fumio," *MN,* pp. 2–14; Itō, "Reform Party," *JHR,* p. 12.

35. Lebra, "Ōkuma Shigenobu," p. 105.

36. Oguri, *Yano Fumio,* pp. 106, 120, 135, 192; Ōkuma Hensan Kai, *Ōkuma kō hachijūgonen shi,* 2: 21–22.

37. Lebra, "Yano Fumio," *MN,* p. 3.

38. Ono, "Ryūkakusai nikki," pp. 326, 381, 383, 386–88; Oguri, *Yano Fumio,* pp. 199–201. Oguri mentions Ono's name only six times in his biography of Yano, and each time it is merely included among a list of Kaishintō members (pp. 170, 186, 197, 198, 200).

39. Lebra, *Ōkuma Shigenobu,* p. 164.

40. Itō, "Reform Party," *JHR,* p. 28.

41. Oguri, *Yano Fumio,* p. 192; Nishimura, *Ono Azusa den,* p. 144.

42. Ōkuma Hensan Kai, *Ōkuma kō hachijūgonen shi,* 2: 21; Itō, "Reform Party," pp. 19–20; Enomoto, "Ono Azusa," *HGDK,* p. 20; Lebra, *Ōkuma Shigenobu,* pp. 105, 106; Mason, *Japan's First General Election,* p. 100; Oguri, *Yano Fumio,* p. 199.

43. Kawade Takao, *Nihon rekishi daijiten,* 20 vols. (Tokyo: Kawade Shobō, 1956), 3: 83; Itō, "Reform Party," *JHR,* pp. 19–20.

44. Suzuki, *Kindai Nihon,* 3: 184.

45. Ōkuma Hensan Kai, *Ōkuma kō hachijūgonen shi,* 2: 22; Itō, "Reform Party, *JHR,* p. 21.

46. Ono, "Ryūkakusai nikki," pp. 379, 381.

47. Nakamura, *Naigai seitō jijō,* p. 134.

48. Ōkuma Hensan Kai, *Ōkuma kō hachijūgonen shi,* 2:22.

49. Oguri, *Yano Fumio,* p. 199.

50. Yanagida Izumi, *Meiji bunmeishi ni okeru Ōkuma Shigenobu* (Tokyo: Waseda Daigaku Shuppanbu, 1962), pp. 220, 221.

51. *JWM* 6, no. 47 (December 2, 1882): 1209.

52. Thomas C. Smith, *Political Change and Industrial Development in Japan: Government Enterprise, 1868–1880* (Stanford, Calif.: Standard University Press, 1955), pp. 86—100.

53. Yanagida, *Meiji Bunmeishi,* pp. 220, 221.

54. Nishimura, *Ono Azusa den,* pp. 171–72, 239–41.

55. Ono, "Ryūkakusai nikki," pp. 368, 389–516. The percentage of

contact of Ono and Ōkuma and the four factions in the Kaishintō between April 17, 1882, and December 1, 1883, was as follows:

Name	Contacts with Ono	Percentage of Contacts
Ōkuma	343	47.2
Kanriha	125	17.2
Ōtokai	157	21.6
Tōyō gisei kai	56	7.7
Ōmeisha	46	6.3
Totals	727	100.0

56. Ibid., p. 393.

57. Allen, *Short Economic History,* pp. 44–46, 50; Emi Koichi, *Government Fiscal Activity and Economic Growth in Japan 1868–1960* (Tokyo: Kinokuniya Bookstore Co., Ltd., 1963), pp. 15 (Chart I), 16 (Table I).

58. Ono, "Kahei no seido o ronzu," *Ono Azusa zenshū,* 1:459–68; Aono, *Nihon seitō,* pp. 56, 57.

59. Ono, "Ryūkakusai nikki," pp. 346, 394, 399.

60. Ibid., pp. 415, 416.

61. Ono, "Yunyū genshō no gen'in o ronzu, "*Ono Azusa zenshu,* 1: 491–500.

62. *JWM* 4, no. 6 (February 7, 1880): 163.

63. *JWM* 6, no. 22 (June 10, 1882): 700, 701.

64. *JWM* 4, no. 27 (December 2, 1881): 1208–10. From the *Nichi nichi shimbun* of November 17, 1881.

65. *JWM* 9, no. 3 (July 9, 1884): 64. From *Nichi nichi shimbun.*

66. *JWM* 9, no. 26 (December 27, 1884): 623. From *Jiji shimpō.*

67. Ono, "Gaikō o ronzu," *Ono Azusa zenshū,* 1:469–81; idem, "Ryūkakusai nikki," pp. 410–12.

68. Aono, *Nihon seitō,* pp. 56, 57; Shimomura, *Nihon zenshi,* 9: 117.

69. Ono, "Ryūkakusai nikki," pp. 395, 397, 402, 403, 410–16; Oguri, *Yano Fumio,* pp. 205–6.

70. Cf. Francis Lieber, *On Civil Liberty and Self-Government* (Philadelphia: J. P. Lippincott and Co., 1899), pp. 89–95; Ono, "Yubin o ronzu," *Ono Azusa zenshū,* 1: 482–90.

71. *JWM* 6, no. 47 (December 2, 1882): 1202.

72. Nishimura, *Ono Azusa den,* pp. 154, 155.

73. Ono, "Ryūkakusai nikki," pp. 417–20; Ono, "Yūbō kikō," *Ono Azusa zenshū,* 2: 79, 80, 84.

74. Ono, "Ryūkakusai nikki," pp. 420–26.

The laws referred to included the Regulations for Public Meetings of April 1880 and the amended regulations of 1882, which provided for heavy fines and imprisonment for speakers, audience, lecturers, organization leaders, and owners of meeting halls that violated the regulations. In addition, the governor of Tokyo could prohibit orators at offending meetings from publicly lecturing for up to one year and could dissolve the offending association. The home minister could prohibit offending speakers from lecturing in public for one year. Cf. Ishii, *Japanese Legislation*, pp. 262, 263 for the 1880 regulations and *Japan Weekly Mail*, 6, no. 23 (June 10, 1882): 713, for the 1882 regulations.

75. Ono, "Ryūkakusai nikki," pp. 425–37, 439; idem, "Shōkyō ron," *Ono Azusa zenshū*, 2: 307–14.

76. Ono, "Ryūkakusai nikki," pp. 440, 441, 450, 451, 462–71.

77. Ono, "Ōkuma Shigenobu ate shokan," *Ono Azusa zenshū*, 2: 112–14.

78. Ono, "Ryūkakusai nikki," pp. 473, 474. The name Nakamata does not appear in the list of party members or elsewhere in the diary.

79. Ibid., pp. 473–75, 479, 480, 488, 491, 503, 504, 516.

80. Oguri, *Yano Fumio*, p. 120.

81. *JWM* 5, no. 40 (October 8, 1881): 1176. Trans. from *Yūbin hōchi shimbun.*

82. *JWM* 5, no. 44 (November 5, 1881): 1293–94. Trans. from *Yūbin hōchi shimbun.*

83. *JWM* 6, no. 7 (February 18, 1882): 207. Trans. from *Yūbin hōchi shimbun.*

84. *JWM* 6, no. 8 (February 25, 1882): 234–35. Trans. from *Yūbin hōchi shimbun.*

85. *JWM* 6, no. 11 (March 18, 1882): 323.

86. *JWM* 11, no. 22 (November 29, 1884): 526–27. Trans. from *Yūbin hōchi shimbun.*

87. Shimomura, *Nihon zenshi,* 9: 115.

88. Asakura Haruhiko and Inamura Tetsugen, eds., *Meiji sesō hennen jiten* (Tokyo: Tokyodō, 1965), pp. 212, 213.

89. Nishimura, *Ono Azusa den,* pp. 346, 347, 349.

90. Ono, "Ryūkakusai nikki," pp. 395, 410, 411, 415, 416, 423, 424.

91. *JWM* 11, no. 21 (November 22, 1884): 501–2. Trans. from *Nichi nichi shimbun.*

92. Shimomura, *Nihon zenshi,* 9: 114.

93. Oguri, *Yano Fumio,* pp. 202–3.

94. Itō, "Nihon seitō," *HS*, p. 28; Lebra, *Ōkuma Shigenobu,* p. 44.

95. Ōkuma, *Hachijūgonen shi,* 2: 18, 19.

96. Itō, "Nihon seitō," *HS,* p. 28; idem, "Reform Party," *JHR,* pp. 15, 26, 31.

97. Hagihara, "Baba Tatsui," *CK* 948 (October 1966): 410–16;

949 (November 1966): 430; Gorai, *Ningen Ōkuma,* p. 325.

98. Oguri, *Yano Fumio,* pp. 205–6.

99. Hagihara, "Baba Tatsui," *CK* 950 (December 1966): 317–18; Watanabe, *Monjo yori mitaru Ōkuma,* p. 458.

100. Oguri, *Yano Fumio,* pp. 210–12.

101. *JWM* 6, no. 44 (October 11, 1882): 1155, 1156.

102. *JWM* 6, no. 45 (November 11, 1882): 1171; 6, no. 47 (December 2, 1882): 1210–16; 6, no. 49 (December 16, 1882), 1248–52; 6, no. 50 (December 23, 1882): 1258.

103. Nishimura, *Ono Azusa den,* p. 167.

104. Ono, "Ryūkakusai nikki," pp. 387, 431; Hirao Michio, "Tosa hyakunen shi o kazaru kōtekishu, Ueki Emori to Ono Azusa," *Kōchi kenjin* 16, no. 8 (August 1967): 9.

105. Ono, "Ōkuma Shigenobu ate shoken," *Ono Azusa zenshū,* 2: 116–18.

106. Hayashida Kametarō, *Nihon seitō shi,* 2 vols. (Tokyo: Dai Nihon Yūben Kai, 1927), 1: 199–205, 211–23; Sugiyama Heisuke, et al. eds., *Gendai Nihon shi kenkyū* (Tokyo: Mikasa Shobō, 1955), p. 131; *JWM* 11, no. 26 (October 18, 1884): 385; 11, no. 24 (December 13, 1884), 577–78.

107. Aono, *Nihon seitō,* p. 58.

108. *Transactions of the Asiatic Society of Japan,* pt. 1 (1914), pp. 499–501; *JWM* 6, no. 23 (June 10, 1882): 712–13; Ishii, *Japanese Legislation,* pp. 465–68; *Asahi Shimbunsha,* ed., *Meiji Taishō shi,* 6 vols: (Tokyo: Asahi Shimbunsha, 1930–1931), 1: 13.

109. Nishimura, *Ono Azusa den,* pp. 153, 158; Ono, "Ryūkakusai nikki," pp. 391, 392, 395, 397; Lebra, *Ōkuma Shigenobu,* p. 132.

110. Nagata, *Ono Azusa,* p. 182.

111. Lebra, *Ōkuma Shigenobu,* p. 132.

112. Kawade, *Nihon rekishi daijiten,* 3: 83.

113. Ono, "Ryūkakusai nikki," pp. 397, 398.

114. Nakamura Yasumasa, ed., *Shimbun shūsei Meiji hennen shi,* 15 vols. (Tokyo: Meiji Hennen Shi Sankai, 1956), 5: 106. From the *Tokyo nichi nichi shimbun* (July 6, 1882).

115. Ono, "Ryūkakusai nikki," pp. 446, 447; Kawade, *Nihon rekishi daijiten,* 1: 342; Takano, *Takada, Ichishima seitan,* p. 33.

116. Mason, *Japan's First General Election,* p. 16; Borton, *Japan's Modern Century,* p. 135.

117. *JWM* 11, no. 24 (December 13, 1884): 578. Trans. from the *Jiyū shimbun.*

118. Nishimura, *Ono Azusa den,* p. 162; Hayashida, *Nihon seitō shi,* 1: 215, 223; Borton, *Japan's Modern Century,* p. 135.

119. *JWM* 11, no. 11 (November 22, 1884): 502.

120. Mason, *Japan's First General Election,* p. 16.

121. *JWM* 11, no. 21 (November 22, 1884): 496, 501–2. Trans. from *Nichi nichi shimbun*; no. 22 (November 29, 1884): 525.

122. Gorai, *Ningen Ōkuma,* pp. 324–27; Watanabe, *Monjo yori mitaru Ōkuma,* p. 458; Nishimura, *Ono Azusa den,* pp. 163, 164, 171, 172; Aono, *Nihon seitō,* p. 58.

123. Lebra, *Ōkuma Shigenobu,* p. 34.

124. Ono, "Ryūkakusai nikki," p. 514.

125. Ono Azusa, "Ōkuma Shigenobu ate shokan," *Ono Azusa zenshū,* 2: 119–21; Nishimura, *Ono Azusa den,* pp. 165–67.

126. Smith, *Political Change,* pp. 33, 75.

127. Nishimura, *Ono Azusa den,* pp. 167, 172, 173; Yamada, *Ono Azusa kun den,* 2: 18.

128. Ono, "Ryūkakusai nikki," p. 516.

129. Ibid., p. 517

130. Nishimura, *Ono Azusa den,* pp. 169, 170; Ono, "Ryūkakusai nikki," p. 518.

131. Gorai, *Ningen Ōkuma,* pp. 170–171, 325, 328; Ono, "Ryūkakusai nikki," pp. 518, 519.

132. Nishimura, *Ono Azusa den,* p. 163.

133. Aono, *Nihon seitō,* p. 58; Ono, "Ryūkakusai nikki," pp. 520–48; Nishimura, *Ono Azusa den,* pp. 164, 165, 170–73.

134. Ibid., p. 521.

135. Nishimura, *Ono Azusa den,* pp. 14, 163–67.

136. Watanabe, *Monjo yori mitaru Ōkuma,* p. 462.

137. Waseda, *Shunjō hachijūnen,* pp. 67–70.

8
In Search of a New Order

Ono Azusa was deeply involved in the major political controversies and movements of Japan's early modern period, and his principal influence was to hasten the trend toward the establishment of constitutional government and on party organization. As a Meiji intellectual trained in both the Chinese classics and Western studies, Ono worked within a philosophic structure that encompassed theories on human relations and history and concrete proposals on political development and institutional structures. As a result of this world outlook, he had to provide a theoretical base for the new political institutions he advocated, a philosophy that would allow for party politics and, at the same time, justify the existence of the Kaishintō and parliamentary rule. Such a theory had to be grounded on historic precedents and justified by the words of internationally recognized savants if it was to be an acceptable foundation for a new system of legal and political relationships.

In a time when public attention was focused on the issue of the future structure of the Japanese state and when private draft constitutions frequently appeared in the press, Ono sought to underwrite the movement for a national assembly with a major study on constitutional government based on leading Western scholarship but geared to the special needs of his country. The result was *Kokken hanron (Outline of the National Constitution),* the most detailed work on modern politics written in Japan prior to the promulgation of the constitution in 1889 and the most systematic work on political science published during the early Meiji era.[1]

As early as April 1875[2] Ono had expressed approval of the imperial edict establishing the Genrō-in or Senate, Supreme Court, and local assemblies.[3] In 1874 or 1875 he decided to write a sample constitution but did not begin work on the draft until February 1877. Two years later, after a lengthy interruption due to cholera, *Kokken ronkō (Study of the National Constitution)* was finished[4] and was serialized in the *Kyōzon zasshi.*[5] Ono was not satisfied with this work and began to rewrite it in early 1881 for publication as a three-volume work.[6] His purpose in writing it was,

> At this time, the government officials are tired of things and have lost patience. The Satsuma men go to extremes of self-indulgence and self-interest, and the Chōshū men follow the example of Satsuma. The administration is executed mainly for private consideration. It lacks justice. The trend of public opinion has gradually strengthened, and [the administration] does not tell the truth. The officials are two-faced. They make excuses in the name of people's rights. The government is losing the confidence of the people. The world is full of corruption, but only the emperor and his subjects can remedy these evils. At this time, a patriot cannot but arouse himself for [the sake of] his country. Therefore, I will revise *Kokken ronkō* and offer it to the emperor in order to make the administration issue an order to establish the constitution.[7]

Ono regarded *Kokken hanron* as his major legacy to his descendants and the means whereby his name would "become known to the world—better than a carving in iron, stone, or a golden monument." He lectured on the work at Tokyo Senmon Gakkō, the predecessor of Waseda University, and even discussed it at the Jingo kyōkai several times in 1883;[8] and by it, he established himself as a major pioneer in the field of modern political science in Japan.[9]

KOKKEN HANRON

Kokken hanron begins with a definition of the term *kokken* or "national constitution" and with the reason why it is necessary to establish a constitution for Japan:

> *Kokken,* that is, the constitution, is the most important law [of the land]. . . . It defines the power of the ruler, defends us from the tyranny of his power, and relieves our worries. Its purpose is to explain the relationship between ruler and subject, to show the limitations [on the power] of each, and to designate the power of the officials and the rights of the people.
>
> This is the reason why Europeans consider the constitution as important and the foundation of law. . . . This is because the relationship between the ruler and the subject is more serious than that among the people. If we had no such laws as civil or criminal law, it would be difficult to maintain our rights. Without a constitution, some men may lose their rights because of the tyranny of a few men or the ruler. The governed would be happy with an honest ruler; but if a bad ruler wields power, the navy, army, and even the courts of justice which should protect the people will change and side with the ruler. . . . Laws become good or bad according to the ruler. Therefore, the constitution, which defines every [power of the state], is very important. When we establish the constitution to clarify the rights and duties of the ruler and the subject, we can redress not only the relationships between the ruler and subject but among the subjects themselves. . . . From the viewpoint of the special circumstances of Japan, we need the constitution to maintain the succession and dignity of the imperial family. Though, at present, people do not disregard the greatest law of Japan which states that the imperial family will rule forever, we cannot be sure that men unfaithful [to the throne] will not appear as times change. Everyone now respects the dignity of the emperor,

> but some might desire independence so earnestly that they will ignore imperial dignity. We must prevent this.[10]

Ono then went into a brief summary of the history of European constitutions, which were wrested from rulers who abused their power by angry subjects and which have "the reek of blood" on them. He exhorted his countrymen not to follow "the foul ways of the Europeans," but because the emperor had summoned the Diet for 1890, they should prepare for the event not with blood or force but with the intellect. The Japanese constitution, he wrote, "will be born from the joint efforts of ruler and subjects over the past twelve years." It had its origin in the following imperial decrees: the proclamation of the Meiji Restoration and the Imperial Oath of 1868, which stated that public opinion would be heard in the decision-making process; the decrees of April 14 and June 14, 1875, which said that public opinion would be listened to more closely upon the abolition of the clans and establishment of the prefectures; and the decision to establish the Council of State. Thus the constitution grew rapidly, while the dissolution of the feudal system released the people from the state of slavery and gave them some liberty.[11]

Having shown the historic necessity for a constitution and official statements favoring the gradual development of deliberative and advisory bodies, Ono then proceeded to point out the mythical, religious, and historic precedents for such organs and for the constitution. In the legendary meeting of the gods on the river bank of Amayasukawa no Kawara and in the discussions and considerations of Omoikane no Kami, the Thinking God, he found that "the political form in which everything was decided by the many in free discussion" had already been initiated.[12] Moving then to the realm of history, he found in statements attributed to the legendary rulers Jimmu, Sujin, Nintoku, and Suiko the precedent for the concern of the throne for the welfare of the people. In the instructions of the Empress Suiko not to decide important matters without reference to the people, in the orders of the Emperor Richū to write down his political decisions and the Emperor Kōtoku to listen to the people's opinions, he saw the gradual development of ideas on a constitution. The establishment of *shō* (administrative departments) and *kan* (government posts) by Kōtoku and the promulgation of rules for the *shō* and *kan* by the Emperor Mommu was proof that the Japanese, early in their history, had had the conception of a constitution and had established fundamental laws for the government. However, since the feudal period, monarchial government had waned because the military despised these laws. These imperial decisions were not forgotten, and the purpose of the Restoration was to resurrect and further develop these laws. As a result of the Imperial Oath, a constitution was now in the process of development. Although governmental reorganization was not yet complete, the three powers of government, namely, the executive, legislative, and judicial, have been separated; and the Genrō-in, the legislative organ, was the dominant body. As a result, the political structure was moving toward democracy.[13]

Ono believed that the imperial decrees of May 1874 expressed the emperor's desire to govern the nation together with the people. Thus he established the Senate and the Supreme Court (Taishin-in), and summoned prefectural governors to Tokyo to plan for the welfare of the people and gradually establish a government according to a national constitution. After the suppression of the Satsuma Rebellion, an imperial decree again summoned the governors to Tokyo to discuss prefectural laws and also created elected prefectural councils to establish methods of taxation and draw up prefectural budgets. This was the first time in the history of Japan that voting rights were given to the people. In 1880 the cabinet was separated from the other branches of the government and the roles of each department were clarified. Two years later the emperor announced the convening of the Diet in 1890 and declared: "In this, government by the emperor and people will first take shape. . . ." The Imperial Proclamation of 1882 was, therefore, the culmination of developments that had historic precedents and reflected the wishes of the emperors of Japan, past and present. Ono concluded the introduction by stating: "The constitution is established according to imperial decree.

We Japanese live under constitutional government. . . . The emperor deeply desires to reform the government, and it is necessary for Japan to study forms of government."

Having justified his purpose, Ono then undertook a study of the three forms of government: republic, oligarchy, and autocracy. He defined a republic as a country governed by the people themselves and an oligarchy as a government by one or a few persons. The republic, he found, functioned only when all the people participated in political life. This was possible only in a small state where the people were free to concern themselves wholly with politics owing to the existence of a large group of slaves and menials. Such a situation existed in ancient Athens, but was neither probable nor desirable in the modern world. In an oligarchy the government was composed of members of a distinguished family or of the aristocracy, but there was no guarantee that the oligarchs would rule wisely. On the contrary, when they hold full power, they are less likely to restrain their desires and more likely to enrich themselves at the expense of the state and society. Autocracy is close to monarchy; and if the autocrat is wise, he will govern for the good of the public. If he is a tyrant, he will injure the people. A wise monarch is born only once in a thousand years, and a man cannot expect to met him in his lifetime. Therefore, autocracy is not always good. A government that is a composite of monarchy, oligarchy, and republicanism will not work, because each estate, throne, peers, or people will look after its own interests, and any two may unite to defeat the others. A union of any two of the forms of government will similarly fail, because of mutual jealousy and greed and lack of some means to maintain the balance of power. A nation such as England, the major world power of the time, achieved strength not by a union of classes but by the union of monarch and parliament following a series of reforms, which occurred after the reign of William III. In England the throne has been united with the different clases represented in Parliament, and this is the reason why the emperor proclaimed that constitutional government will be established in 1890. Parliamentary or representative government is possible and desirable when united with monarchy. For three thousand years Japan has been under the leadership of the imperial family, which has held power in its hands; representative government will not make any change in its status. Once suffrage is granted, "high and low will be happy," and events such as the Paris Commune will be prevented. "If we adopt representative government, we may maintain the imperial family forever."[14]

By presenting historic precedents and the necessity for representative government, Ono sought to justify a constitution from the viewpoint of national history and need. His definition of a constitution as the fundamental law that adjusts the powers of the ruler and subject appears to be based on ideas from Theodore D. Woolsey's *Political Science or The State* (1877),[15] while his survey of the forms of government and of the British political system is taken from the second and third chapters, "Forms of Government" and "British Constitution," of Jeremy Bentham's *A Fragment on Government,* originally published in 1776. The third chapter of *Kokken hanron* is entitled "Forms of Government" and is based on the arguments Bentham used against Blackstone's interpretation of the three forms of government, here referred to as democracy, oligarchy, and monarchy, and of the British constitution as a union of the three. Bentham's description of the weaknesses of each system of government and against a system composed of the three forms in an equal and balanced combination is also adopted. However, Ono has substituted "republic" for the term *democracy,* for democracy would be detrimental to the concept of imperial sovereignty. In his definition of the three forms of government, he uses the very wording presented in Bentham's chart entitled the "British Government is all-perfect" but again replaces *democracy* with *republic.*[16] Ono concluded the chapter by showing, as did Bentham, that the contemporary British system was the culmination of historic developments, which ultimately led to the union of the throne with the different classes in society as represented in Parliament.

The fourth chapter of *Kokken hanron,* entitled "The Grand Axioms of the Constitution," is concerned with the theoretical reasons for the establishment of the state. Ono opened this chapter with a discussion of the changes in the primary duties of a state, which vary according to time and circumstances. In the period of the Taika Reform, the people thought the main duty of the state was to maintain the system of equal distribution of farmland (*kinden* and *handen*), to lessen the distinction between rich and poor, and to establish regulations on etiquette and ritual. However, in time these functions came to be regarded as beyond the province of the government. People now believed that the state should establish laws on education, sanitation, food control, commerce, and public welfare, and should encourage industry. Ono, however, questioned whether the state should be concerned with such functions. Men, he claimed, organize government because of fear and insecurity. In primitive times societies were organized because individuals were not strong enough to survive invasion or conflicts. Therefore men expect the state to provide security, subsistence, abundance, and equality. Security is the main duty of a country, and the purpose of the constitution is to establish order in society and the state.

Subsistence, abundance, and equality are closely related. Abundance, or the accumulation of property and wealth, is indispensable to life, for man earns his livelihood by his labor. Equality means that the state should not discriminate between people because of their social status. Real equality is the ability to be independent. When this is no longer possible, equality of opportunity will also disappear. When men lose the hope of equality of opportunity, they lose the will to work, which is the vital force of life. Therefore the constitution must provide security and alleviate man's fear of disasters. Natural disasters are sometimes inescapable, but some catastrophes can be prevented. For example, smallpox epidemics can be controlled by vaccination. Man-made disasters fall into two categories: foreign invasion and internal problems. Defense is one of the main duties of the state. Incidents such as murder can be caused either by the common people or by officials. Crimes involving commoners can be prevented by punishing criminals according to law. Problems involving officials are the result of power struggles, and the constitution can control such conflicts.

The purpose of the constitution is to insure that qualified persons hold government positions. These ideas on the relationship between law and morality and the constitution as an instrument to guarantee national security, Ono wrote, came from the works of the "famous English social philosopher, Bentham."

Ono then asked: "What are the qualifications for official position?" His answer was morality, intelligence, and diligence. Morality, the concern for the welfare of society as a whole and not for private benefit, was the foremost qualification. Intelligence, the ability to make prompt decisions to benefit people and the knowledge to see where truth lies, was the second prerequisite. Diligence, the ability to apply oneself to an assigned task, was third. In addition, officials should be appointed according to public opinion, official power should be limited so that it does not exceed given authority, public funds should be supervised closely, and officials should be held personally responsible for the consequences of their actions. The tasks, responsibilities, and limits of power of each office should be clearly defined and positions should be assigned according to ability.[17]

Professor Takano Zen'ichi of Waseda University has shown that chapter 4 of *Kokken hanron* is based on the sections entitled "Ends Aimed At" and "Principal Means Employed for the Attainment of the Above Ends" in Bentham's *Leading Principles of a Constitutional Code for Any State,* written in 1823. He has also pointed out that the title "Rikken no Daikishi" means "Ends Aimed At." Much of this chapter is a close translation of Bentham's work, which has as its theme: "[The] ends of this constitution are subsistence, abundance, security, and equality." Ono translated these terms as *seizon, fushu, hogo,* and *byōdō,* but he gave priority to security. He adopted Bentham's views on abundance and security almost verbatim. He said that his discussion of the prerequisites needed to insure the correct attitude in civil servants was taken from "Principle Means Employed for the Attainment of the Above Ends."[18] Ono's reasons for the organization of the state was from the chapter "Formation of Government" in the *Fragment on Government.*

In this Bentham attacked the theories of the state of nature and original contract, and wrote: "It is the sense of their weakness and imperfection that keeps mankind together; that demonstrates the necessity of this union; and that therefore is the solid and natural foundation, as well as the cement of society."[19]

Chapter 5 of *Kokken hanron* is concerned with the political subdivisions of the state. Ono suggested dividing the country into administrative units based on size and called, in descending order, *kuni* or counties, *gun* or districts, *ken* or prefectures, *machi* or towns, and *mura* or villages. This was similar in ideas though not in terminology to that used in contemporary France and would enable administrative and judicial institutions to be reorganized along identical lines.

In chapter 6, Ono is concerned with the question of sovereignty, which he defined as "the entire power of a state." Ono then gave several definitions of sovereignty, quoting John Austin's view that sovereignty should be laid on one or very few persons. He also introduced the ideas of Theodore Dwight Woolsey, who opposed Austin's definition and said that sovereignty is the power to maintain the independence and security of the state. Sovereignty, Ono stated, was the source of all political power, and there are five concepts about the locus of sovereignty. Grotius, Hobbes, and Spinoza believed that it should rest in one person. Rousseau and Bentham both favored placing sovereignty in the hands of all the people, who appoint their own officials. Austin and Anchilles wrote that one or a few persons should hold sovereign power. The fourth view was that sovereignty resides in "truth." For example, Guizot believed that sovereignty could not lie in elected representatives, who hold office temporarily, or in the impermanent laws they pass. Ono found that Guizot's views were similar to the Confucian ideal that truth, virtue, and benevolence are necessary attributes of the ruler. However, Ono concluded that sovereignty was too important to be held by one or a few persons, and the time was not suited to pure democracy. Truth, or virtue, was too abstract a concept to be the locus of supreme political power. Therefore sovereignty had to rest in the state, which must have the power to protect its independence and security. Ono believed that his opinion was the same as that of Woolsey, who wrote that the government must do good for the state and the people.[20] Woolsey in *Political Science or The State wrote*: "This power of independent action in external and internal relations constitutes complete sovereignty." Woolsey then asked if the sovereignty of a state emanated from the ruler or whether the ruler was sovereign only when representing the state, and offered the following answer:

> The state stands for an untold amount of good to be secured to present and future generations by a just and wise government, at the head of which the ruler is placed. He is a means for a great permanent end; he dies and someone else succeeds to him . . . by law of the state. All this shows that the ultimate power in theory rests with the state or the people constituting it, and that the prince is a delegated or disputed sovereign.[21]

Ono adopted Woolsey's view, and from this he concluded that, since the emperor was in the position to rule the land and the people, sovereignty should reside in the state as symbolized by the throne.

The issue of sovereignty led to the question of the position held by the imperial family. Ono believed that while "rule of pure blood lineage" was the major law relating to the imperial family, the constitution had to clarify the details of imperial succession. Decisions on imperial succession and finances should be made by the national assembly. Ono regarded the emperor as holy, exalted, and inviolate, not because of an antiquated belief in imperial divinity but because, as the sovereign, he possessed the highest status, represented the people, and was a descendant of the imperial line. He was beyond the interference of the law; but if, unfortunately, a vicious emperor did appear in the future, the law should punish those men who led him astray. In this way, Ono avoided the issue of dealing with the sovereign when his conduct was detrimental to his office or to the state. The empress dowager, empress, and crown prince are also exalted and inviolate; the constitution should state that their dignity is next to that of the emperor. Ono agreed with the law that limited the imperial family to two generations of descendants of an emperor, not the traditional five, and extended the peerage to other princes. This law reduced state expenditures and, thereby, prevented popular disaffection, which might arise if too many members of the imperial household lived a life of luxury. Imperial household expenses should be decided upon and met from the national treasury, and parliament should provide sufficient funds to maintain imperial dignity. Ono then discussed various laws relating to the status, succession, and finances of the royal families of England, Belgium, and fourteen other European countries. He concluded that England and Belgium provided the examples most useful for Japan.

Having defined sovereignty and the position of the throne, Ono turned to the rights, duties, and powers of the people. In relation to these, he believed that the concepts of independence and liberty were most important. He defied independence as freedom of association. This, Ono admitted, was not an adequate definition. He also quoted Leibnitz as saying that self-government meant resistance to unreasonable interference in the affairs of the individual. Ono regarded independence as a basic right with which there can be no interference. Personal freedom is the most basic freedom, and independence means physical security. If one's person is not secure, the pleasures of life cannot be enjoyed nor suffering avoided. Therefore, independence is the main element of liberty; and in the discussion of liberty and its practical applications, it is necessary to examine various rights and how to guarantee them against outside interference.

Ono believed that security against unreasonable arrest was the most important element of liberty and the most difficult to obtain. He regarded protection against illegal search and seizure as the most important legal theory of civilized countries. *Habeas corpus* was essential to protect accused persons and to inform them of the reasons for their arrest. Bail was important because it was inhuman to detain persons not yet proven guilty. Prisoners, especially political prisoners, should not be subject to torture. Ono completed his discussion of security with comparisons of British, American, and European constitutional guarantees of security of person.

Ono wrote that freedom of communication was one of the major aspects of liberty, and he included freedom of discussion, public assembly, publication, and correspondence in this category. These freedoms are easily destroyed by sovereigns who fear the free exchange of ideas, as in the Tokugawa period; but they are necessary if civilization is to progress and knowledge is to be transmitted. Freedom of movement for residential and business purposes as well as for pleasure is a very important right. In a country as densely populated as Japan, emigration should be encouraged. Freedom of religion is another fundamental right. A government should not interfere beyond material matters into the abstract areas of the mind. Politics and religion have different origins, and when a government compels the people to accept a state religion, it squanders the national treasury and destroys the people's dignity. As Bentham has shown, people can be coerced into accepting a state religion only by reward. This depletes the treasury and forces the people to deceive themselves and to lose confidence in the government. In Europe many people were killed, exiled, or deprived of their rights because they did not follow the same faith as the sovereign, but now the British, Prussian, French, and American constitutions guarantee freedom of religion.

Ono also regarded the right to hold, own, and accumulate property, and freedom of production, exchange, and competition as important aspects of independence. In the past the ownership of property and commerce were subject to government interference; but this is contrary to basic economic principles. The riches of a state consist of the wealth of the people, and any increase in their wealth thereby increases the wealth of the nation. Therefore it is necessary to encourage people to accumulate more property and wealth. Both England and France guarantee the security of personal property, and their laws state that the government must provide compensation if private property is used for the benefit of the public. Freedom of petition must be guaranteed in the constitution; and the English constitution gives the people the right to present petitions without fear of imprisonment. Freedom of public assembly is essential; but because thoughtless people sometimes abuse this right and injure society, some precautions are necessary. Freedom to know government policies in regard to parliamentary and court proceedings, administrative reports, and treaties is necessary if the people are to be well informed and to have confidence in the government. An informed public is the best way to secure internal peace and unity; in England and the United States, this right is taken for granted. However, in European states, it is guaranteed by the constitution.

Ono believed that supremacy of law was of paramount importance in maintaining liberty and independence. The supremacy of law meant rule by laws that have been proclaimed according to established procedures. The law can not be changed because of temporary expedients, and neither the people nor the officials need obey laws issued without due process or obey imperial decrees that have not been enacted according to established procedures. The duty of the legislature is not only to legislate but also to make people observe the laws, but first the people must be informed of the laws they are to obey. The English constitution states that people cannot be imprisoned unless tried according to law. The English king cannot interfere with the laws without the aproval of Parliament, nor can he impose taxes without its approval. Therefore taxes can be laid upon the people only with their consent. If they recognize the necessity of taxation, they will be willing to pay. If they do not believe taxes are necessary, they will be discouraged from working hard and the national income will decline. For this reason, England and the United States place the power of taxation in the Lower House. Ono then quoted passages by Lord Acton and Adam Smith to show that taxation should be based upon the financial ability of the taxpayer. He warned that taxes should be as low as possible while still providing security of life and property. National security required a standing army, and some system of conscription was necessary to provide recruits. However, since people object to military service, Ono suggested instituting military training in primary schools in order to reduce the length of service. This was similar to the ideas advocated in *Shisei no yōgi,* but Ono did not realize that his suggestion carried the danger of widespread militarism.

Ono regarded these ten freedoms as fundamental rights. He wrote that since men organized society in order to protect these rights, they should be guaranteed by the constitution. Men so desire freedom that they become enraged when deprived of it, but thoughtless politicians misunderstand this and so destroy society. Liberty is just and sound. Great rulers and governments are prosperous because they grant freedom, as is seen in Belgium and England. "Now our great emperor wisely realizes this fact and is going to secure freedom for the people, and no subject should interfere with his intention." Although there may be no need to clarify the people's rights in the British constitution, it is necessary to guarantee them in Japan. Ono thought that clarification was needed in the constitution to point out the people's rights, to make the officials know the limits of their authority, and to make the people know their rights. Although the officials are appointed for the benefit of the people, they are apt to forget this and abuse their authority. The constitution alone has the strength and authority to limit the power of the officials. Therefore it must clarify the rights of both the people and the government, especially in a state where the people have been accustomed to official oppression and have not known what rights they should enjoy.[22]

Ono's discussion of liberty and popular or civil rights represents a summary of the ideas expressed by Francis Lieber (1798–1872) in *On Civil Liberty and Self-Government* (1853). Lieber, after defining civil liberty and emphasizing that "all men desire freedom of action," states that it is essential for the government to guarantee liberty. He then discusses bail, penal trials, treason, communication, "locomation," emigration, liberty of conscience, property, the supremacy of law, the army, petition, association, publicity of government action, and taxation, all mentioned briefly in *Kokken hanron*. However, Ono omitted several important aspects that Lieber mentioned. For example, in the chapter entitled "National Independence. Personal Liberty," Lieber pointed out that personal or civil liberty depended on national independence or autonomy. "This implies that the country must have the right, and, of course, the power, of establishing that government which it considers best, unexposed to interference from without or pressure from above. No foreigner must dictate . . . ; no claim superior to that of the people's, that is, superior to national sovereignty, must be allowed."[23] Here was a clear call to the champions of treaty revision and popular rights; yet Ono, who had long advocated both, ignored these ideas. As a member of the "loyal opposition" demanding protection of civil rights that would permit opposition parties to function, it is also surprising to find that Ono excluded from his major work both Lieber's defense of the need for a loyal opposition to protect minority interests as represented in Parliament from absolutism by the majority and Lieber's discussion of the role of party government. He also ignored Lieber's view on representative government as the main aspect of civil liberty. Lieber, like Bentham, stressed the need for "liberty of conscience" or the "liberty of worship" and declared that "conscience lies beyond the reach of government" and "thoughts are free."[24] Ono adopted Lieber's strongly anti-French bias and agreed with him that radicalism led to revolution, which disturbed social stability and interfered with progress. His admiration for British political institutions as the best example of moderate and progressive parliamentary rule was shared by the Prussian-born, naturalized-American scholar.[25] Lieber's ideas of sovereignty were easily reconciled with his own loyalty to the imperial family. At the same time, while advocating government by both emperor and people, Ono identified both ruler and subject with the concept of polity. *Civil Liberty and Self-Government* served as a convenient reference work for the discussion of liberty and popular rights in *Kokken hanron*; to Ono, such rights meant freedom from government control and civil liberties.[26]

After presenting a discussion of fundamental human rights as seen in the constitutions of Western nations and by Western scholars, Ono moved on to a discussion of civil liberty and political rights in Japan. The *Nihon shoki (Chronicles of Japan)* reveals that the men of antiquity were free to discuss politics openly. Although they had no right to participate in political life, they had an attitude of self-respect and independence in regard to political matters. The *Engi-shiki,* a collection of laws and ordinances compiled during 905–27, gave the people some civil rights, such as the right to accuse officials of illegal actions; but they had never had rights such as freedom of association and of religion. The people possessed some civil rights in the early feudal era, but the warrior government neglected almost all of the people's rights. It acknowledged only one fundamental concept: the people are the basis of the state and there are officials because there are people. "This alone maintained the fragrance of civil rights throughout the dark ages." Civil rights, which had been suppressed under the military government, were set free by the Restoration and now flourished under the rule of the emperor and foreign influence.

Ono regarded the Imperial Proclamation of 1874, which announced the emperor's intention to call representatives from all over the country to establish laws by public opinion, and the establishment of the Genrō-in and Supreme Court, as a promise that suffrage would be extended to the people. He stated that freedom of speech and publication were not only fundamental rights but basic civil rights. However, when these rights were carried to excess and unjustly injured the reputation of others, the state had to intervene and establish laws to control libel, the press, and publication. These laws need not be detrimental to freedom of speech and publication if properly understood and applied by officials.

Civil rights were extended with the establishment of local assemblies empowered to make decisions on local budgets and taxes. To handle disputes between the various local assemblies, the Shinri kyoku or Deliberative Bureau was established in the Dajōkan. In 1880 three important proclamations were issued. These were the Law for Public Assemblies, the Law Establishing Standing Committees, and the Legal Procedure for Petitioning. The first law prohibited soldiers, policemen, teachers, students, apprentices, and members of the standing army and first and second reserves from attending political meetings. Despite criticism that it limited freedom of assembly, this law did establish legal procedures for political meetings and did not prohibit them. It is therefore hasty to conclude that there was no freedom of assembly. Rule Number 53 of 1881 established the procedure to present petitions relating to public welfare and legislative matters and the means to appeal petitions rejected by the Genrō-in or Dajōkan. It opened the way for the right to petition. The new code of criminal procedure secured most civil rights and declared the supremacy of law, while prohibiting officials from arbitrarily disposing of cases. This and the laws of 1875 and 1879, which prohibited torture, protected the rights of the accused. Thus, people's rights in Japan have undergone a gradual improvement since the Meiji Restoration. The process has been uneven and these rights are not yet fully enjoyed, but they should be developed with moderation and patience. If the people act violently, in order to attain basic civil rights all at once, they are sure to lose all rights.

In his discussion of fundamental human rights and basic civil rights, Ono Azusa emphasized several points. First and foremost were those basic human rights which men ought to have in order to maintain their security, livelihood, and happiness. These rights may be regarded as divinely granted or as essential correlates of life in human society, and they are recognized by all modern states. When guaranteed by the constitution of a state they become civil rights or civil liberties, and the constitutions of most Western nations guarantee them. It is the duty of the state by its legal and other institutions to protect these rights from interference. When security exists and men can fully exercise these rights, they are content with the political situation and are psychologically motivated to strive to increase their wealth and property, and, thereby, the wealth of the state. However, irresponsible men will carry one or all of these rights to excess; therefore, the state must act to protect itself and its citizens by establishing norms of political conduct and setting the limits for the responsible exercise of civil rights. In a society where fundamental rights have been neither traditional nor expected, both a written constitution and laws establishing reasonable limits for the exercise of these rights are necessary. Civil rights must be granted gradually and practiced with moderation in order to lay a firm foundation for such rights and freedoms.

The last section of the first volume and the first chapter of the second volume of *Kokken hanron* are concerned with the distribution of political power. Ono began the discussion by stating that the powers of government are generally divided into the legislative, administrative or executive, and judicial branches. The legislature has the power to issue legislation. The administration is empowered to execute these laws; grant patents and amnesty; allocate official positions; coin money; control the armed forces, treasury, police, arms, and government property; make war and peace; and conclude treaties. The judiciary is independent and handles problems that are sent to it on appeal. The legislature, administration, and judiciary, however, are not political powers in themselves but merely offices that share political power. They are concerned with seven areas, which directly affect the fate of a nation. These are:

1. Rights directly concerned with the lives of the people.
2. Rights directly concerned with private property.
3. Rights directly concerned with government property.
4. The right to issue orders to individuals.
5. The right to issue orders to groups.
6. The right to establish classifications, that is, to decide upon names and terms, court ranks, national holidays, ceremonial dress, and denominations of money.
7. The right to appoint officials.

Ono wrote that this idea originated in the works of Bentham, but he "made use of it and developed it because Bentham had not explained it in detail."

Having defined and discussed the components of political power, Ono then sought to locate the source of this power. After studying and comparing the ideas of Rousseau, Locke, Lieber, and Montesquieu, he concluded that political power is easily misused by those who control it and that there is no freedom or security in countries where legislative, administrative, and judicial authority are placed in the hands of one person or group. Ono regarded the synthesis of political power as extremely dangerous and advocated the distribution of political power among the several divisions or branches of government. However, he opposed the theory that allocated power among the legislative, executive, and judicial branches and instead looked to Bentham's theory of the four powers of government. The fourth power was the right to elect and dissolve the national assembly. Bentham regarded this right or power as so important that he stated it should belong to a separate branch of the government, which he entitled the "supreme constitutive." Ono translated this as *seihon no shoku,* the power which was the source of all official position and policies.

Although the object of the theory of the three main branches of government is to avoid concentrating political power in any one division, Ono found that in practice power resided in the legislative branch. In the Constitution of the United States, the legislature was given power to override a presidential veto, to impeach the executive, and to control national finances. He therefore misinterpreted the American system as actually one of congressional superiority. Rousseau wrote in the *Social Contract* that the people entrust omnipotent power to their representatives in the legislature. Lieber, however, stated that legislative domination is the beginning of autocracy, for if unsupervised, the national assembly will augment its power for its own benefit. Ono agreed with Leiber and concluded that this theory actually placed control in the hands of the legislature.[27]

Ono envisoned a fourfold division of political power within a state. The source of this power lay in the people, who had the right to appoint, dismiss, and supervise the national assembly. The people were, in Bentham's words, the supreme constitutive, from whom all power flowed. The legislature was empowered by the supreme constitutive to debate state policy, promulgate laws, and supervise the administration and judiciary. The administration was to enforce legislative directives, and the judiciary was to maintain the standards set by the assembly. The relationship of the four separate but unequal divisions of the government can be seen in the following chart:

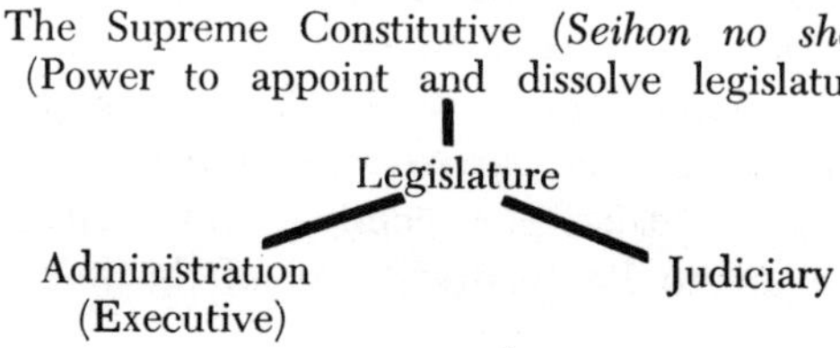

These ideas were borrowed from Jeremy Bentham, but Ono found that in actual practice all Western constitutions provided for the fourth power, the right to select and prorogue the legislature.

What then, Ono asked, was the situation in Japan, where the government structure was still being revised? He answered this question by stating that the dominant element in the political structure was the Dajōkan, which made all legislative and administrative decisions. Cabinet decisions, once approved by the emperor, became state policy, and therefore the Dajōkan was the dominant power in the government. The Genrō-in was established to act as an independent legislative body; but when its powers are examined, it is seen that it can only debate laws submitted to it by the Dajōkan. It has no right to institute new laws. The Dajōkan was also the main administrative organ, and by the government reforms of February and December 1880, the secretaries of every ministry were included in the cabinet. They held administrative power in each ministry and sometimes exercised legislative power. The Dajōkan was also the main judicial power, because judges could not sentence offenders without its permission. Judges were subject to appointment and dismissal by the Secretary of the Ministry of Justice. Hence there was no threefold division of state power among the Dajōkan, Genrō-in, and judiciary. Power was actually concentrated in the Dajōkan, and no means were provided for the people to present their views to the government.[28]

In his discussion of political power, Ono was deeply indebted to Jeremy Bentham. Many of his fundamental ideas are drawn directly from Bentham's *A Fragment on Government, Leading Principles of a Constitutional Code for Any State,* and the *Constitutional Code.* For example, chapter 4 of *Kokken hanron* is based not only on the *Leading Principles,* as shown by Takano Zen'ichi,[29] but also on the *Constitutional Code.* In the section entitled "Civil or Distributive Law," Bentham defined subsistence, abundance, and equality, and declared security to be the foremost concern of the state. In the same chapter he emphasized the need for protection against maladministration.

In chapter 9, "Good Rule and Bad Rule," he analyzed the relationship between law and morality, stated that officials should be appointed according to public opinion, and gave a series of rules to check corruption in public office. Bentham also preferred the French system of local government and translated the various units as districts, subdistricts, bi-districts, and tri-districts. Ono used traditional Japanese terms to translate these divisions in the fifth chapter of *Kokken hanron.*

According to Bentham, sovereignty rested in the people, who were the supreme constitutive. The people alone had the power to elect and dismiss the legislature and "other authorities in the state." This is the essence of Bentham's political liberalism; thus: "a pure representative democracy is instituted: and this form of government, and this alone, as has been already shown, can have the greatest happiness of the greatest number for its effect."[30] Bentham and John Stuart Mill, two of Ono's major sources of ideas, were both hostile to monarchy as detrimental to representative institutions and as restricting popular participation in government.[31] Lieber was an admirer of "England a royal republic" and felt that the king was a necessary "element of conservatism apparently high above the contending elements of progress and popular liberty."[32] This view was more acceptable to Ono, who carefully avoided carrying the idea of the supreme constitutive to its logical conclusion of popular sovereignty. To do so would be to refute imperial sovereignty. By divorcing the theory of the four branches of power from that of popular sovereignty, he avoided the onus of democracy and republicanism while showing the need for a national assembly. He therefore placed sovereignty in the state as symbolized by the throne and presented the state as an abstract concept separate from the people of whom it was composed. He was, in effect, advocating the supremacy of the throne in which sovereignty resided indirectly. In stating that the position of the emperor was due to the "sovereignty whereby he possesses the highest status, [and] represents the people,"[33] Ono was presenting Todd's argument on the supremacy of the British monarch, which was that "the supreme executive authority of the state in all matters . . . belongs to the sovereign of the

British Empire by virtue of his kingly office."[34] In similar fashion, Woolsey wrote: "The king or queen of England, although having in matter of fact an exceedingly limited power, is called sovereign to denote the dignity of the office as above all others in the kingdom. . . ."[35] Such ideas enabled Ono to merge his personal loyalty to the imperial household with the Meiji ideal that the Restoration was a return to imperial rule and with his espousal of parliamentary government into one coherent political system. Popular sovereignty, as defined by Bentham, refuted imperial sovereignty and rule and was too radical a concept for Ono to accept. As a result, the political work that Ono produced contained many inconsistencies, which were the product of the merger of discordant elements into an imperial-parliamentary system. Such logical inconsistencies were a characteristic of Ono's writings and also of the Kaishintō policy statements that he wrote, but were the outgrowth of the viewpoint and experience of the Meiji intellectual.

The first volume of *Kokken hanron* was a theoretical explanation of the necessity of constitutional government and was intended to serve as a basic text in political science that would be useful to the framers of the proposed constitution. As a result, it contained careful explanations of constitutional government, of those civil rights which Ono regarded as essential for the citizen of the modern state, and of the basic divisions of power among the branches of government. While advocating representative institutions, Ono so worded his ideas as to declare that supreme power lay in the people, who alone had the right to elect and dismiss the legislature; yet at no time did he advocate democracy or imply that the locus of sovereignty was in any place other than the throne. While modeling the structure of the book on Lieber's *Civil Liberty and Self-Government*, he merged major sections of Bentham's and Lieber's works with elements of ideas from other Western writers and Japanese history to present a composite introduction to the subject of modern government and civil liberties and to justify the need for political reform.

Most of the second volume of *Kokken hanron* is a detailed text on the structure, organization, and duties of the legislature.

Ono advocated the formation of a bicameral legislature in which the emperor, administration, and upper and lower houses would harmonize and balance one another. He wanted the members of the upper house to be men of experience and achievement who could supplement the disabilities of an elected lower house; but the exact means whereby they attained their positions is unclear, for Ono opposed both direct and indirect election and imperial appointment. The upper house was to have the power neither to ratify treaties nor to try civil servants. Treaties were of such importance that ratification should be a function of the Diet as a whole, and the power to try impeachment cases belonged to the judiciary. Members of the lower house should be elected by limited suffrage granted to male citizens over twenty-one years of age who met specific financial, occupational, and educational requirements. Each house was to select its own chairman and administrative staff.[36]

In *Kokken hanron* Ono went into a detailed description of the various systems used to elect members of the lower house, and the section on direct and indirect election is adopted from the chapter entitled "Modes of Voting" in John Stuart Mill's *On Representative Government*.[37] Of the various systems mentioned, Ono preferred that developed by Hare, in which successful candidates had to receive a given percentage of the number of available votes. The only qualification he required of a member of the lower house was to be elected by the will of the people whom he represented. Ono favored a three-year term of office, with all members standing for election at one time and a total of one to two hundred seats in the lower house. Members were to represent the entire country and not merely their constituents, and were to base their decisions on their own opinion. They were to receive a modest salary in order that men of ability and members of the middle class might be able to serve as legislators.[38]

Ono then described the duties of the lower house. In Europe and England they included preparation of the state budget and finance bills, for these were the means whereby the people's rights were maintained and public funds spent wisely. The lower house should have the right to impeach public officials, and all members of the Diet should have the right to draft and debate bills. They must have immunity for speeches made or published and from arrest while the Diet was in session or while on their way to attend sessions. To secure legislative independence and to facilitate business, the Diet should have the right to examine the election and qualifications of its members and decide its own rules of procedure. Because the political scene was continually changing, there should be no time limit on Diet sessions. Diet proceedings should be made public according to circumstances. However, in time of war or domestic rebellion, or when debating questions related to the honor of an individual or not beneficial to the public, proceedings should be recorded but not disclosed. Over one-half of the Diet members would constitute a quorum.

Following a detailed discussion of procedural rules, Ono moved to the relationship between the sovereign and the Diet. As a check on the legislature, he favored having the emperor sign all bills into law; and if the throne regarded a decision of the Diet as unjust, it could exercise special prerogatives to prevent its enactment. It was the duty of the sovereign to refuse to sign unreasonable acts, but this power must not be abused. When the sovereign and the people governed together, if the emperor did not agree with the legislature on important matters, he could dissolve the Diet and order new elections. If the emperor should not approve of cabinet rulings, the cabinet must resign and be replaced by members of the opposition party. This was the advantage of party cabinets and the spirit of governing with the people as found in England. The right to grant amnesty belongs to the legislature and should be exercised by a special committee, which should include several judges, with royal permission. The power to conclude treaties is the power to create duties and impose them on the nation. Therefore it must belong to the Diet, but, for convenience, it is left in the hands of the sovereign acting on the advice of the Diet. The power to declare war is important because it determines the "glory and fortune of the nation" and is costly in human life and treasure. Hence it should be discussed and enforced by both the sovereign and the legislature. In general, the power to decide national policy lies in the lower house, not the throne.[39]

The second volume of *Kokken hanron* contains numerous ideas derived from Bentham, Lieber, and J. S. Mill. Ono modeled his ideas of representative government as a major aspect of modern liberty and as the means for allowing public opinion to pass into law on Lieber's *Civil Liberty and Self-Government.* Lieber regarded representative government as the principle means of preventing absolutism by both the executive and "the masses" and as the main guarantee of liberty. Ono did not go along with Mill's idea of the actual supremacy of the legislature or with Bentham's concept of "legislative omnicompetent," but agreed with Lieber on the need for a division of power as a bar to dominance by any one sector of the government. Although he had earlier adopted Bentham's views on a unicameral legislature and his opposition to an upper house composed of hereditary peers, Ono's views changed. In *Kokken hanron* he moved toward the position held by Mill and Lieber on a bicameral assembly and, like Mill, favored an upper house composed of men noted for their experience and wisdom in order to counter despotism by the elected lower house. The recognition that an elected legislature also contained the seeds of absolutism led Ono to follow Bentham's ideas on a limited term for members of the national assembly, subject to reelection, and Lieber on the right of each house to veto legislation passed by the other. Ono did not take up Bentham's views on recall or the right of voters to sue the legislature. Ono opposed placing time limits on sessions of the Diet in order to enable it to transact all necessary business and described in detail British parliamentary procedures, which he took from both Todd's *Parliamentary Government in England* and Bentham's *Political Tactics.* From Lieber he borrowed several concepts: the right of either house to propose any measure or resolution, and the immunity of legislators from arrest during the assembly session. Lieber regarded legislative control of public funds as essential to public liberty, and stated that the power of making war should reside with the people, not the executive. He was a strong advocate of "publicity of public business," including that of the legislature and courts as a means to inform, educate, and unify the public. However, he did concede that in a limited number of cases certain governmental transactions needed to be kept secret. These ideas were also written into *Kokken hanron*.

Lieber, J. S. Mill, and Bentham all conceded that in theory democracy implied universal suffrage. However, to ensure responsible representatives and legislation, they stressed the need for limited suffrage based on qualifications of age, sex, education, property, or taxation. Ono had a similar fear of universal suffrage as leading to control of the lower house by irresponsible elements in society and wanted suffrage restricted to males over twenty-one years of age, as in the American constitution. Although his argument for a limited electorate that would be expanded as "society progressed" was adopted largely from Mill, he ignored Mill's advocacy of women's suffrage. From Lieber he took the idea that the legislator should not be responsible solely to his immediate constituency but to the nation at large. In *Gian hihyō*, Ono had written that election should be by secret ballot to prevent pressure on the voter. Although Bentham advocated secrecy in voting, Ono in *Kokken hanron* changed and adopted Mill's ideas on open ballots. Mill had taken over Hare's idea on signed or open ballots and wrote that suffrage was a matter of public trust and secret ballots would degrade the voter's sense of responsibility.[40] Ono accepted this premise but did not say how the voter could be protected from undue pressure or from retaliation if his decision was unpopular. Although an advocate of representative institutions, Ono did not espouse democracy. He feared that the majority of his countrymen were not yet ready for political responsibility and the extension of suffrage to those without sufficient education, experience, or an economic stake in the established order would lead to social instability and harm the position of the imperial family. The relationship of the emperor and Diet, the operation of party cabinets, and the division of responsibility between monarch and assembly in foreign policy and war were based on the British example as described by Todd in *Parliamentary Government in England*.[41] The method of granting amnesty was adopted from an essay entitled "A Paper On The Abuse Of The Pardoning Power" by Lieber.[42] What emerged in the second volume of *Kokken hanron,* therefore, was a picture of representative government similar to that of Great Britain, with power residing in an elected house of representatives subject to check by a more conservative and wiser house of statesmen.

In the third volume of *Kokken hanron,* Ono dealt with the organization and duty of the administrative and judicial branches of the government. He defined the administration as that branch of the government responsible for carrying out legislation passed by the Diet but without the responsibility to interfere in legislative or judicial activities. It should be led by one person. Although there are advantages to both hereditary and elected leaders, the Japanese are accustomed to the role of the emperor, who succeeds to his position because of the virtue of his reign. To assist him, the offices of prime minister and cabinet should be established. To place the emperor in actual charge of the administration is harmful for the prosperity of the imperial family and the nation because it can result in popular disaffection with the throne. If the prime minister is responsible for the actions of the government, the onus for improper administration will fall on him and not on the imperial family.

Ono then explained the purpose of the cabinet which, along with the prime minister, led the administration and handled all affairs of state. Both party and nonparty cabinets functioned in the same way and would serve the emperor. Those who said that party politics would exclude the throne did not understand political conditions in Europe. Party cabinets enabled the ruler to listen to the views of the people and to avoid "obstinate" administrations. In the organization of the cabinet, the leader of the majority party in the legislature is chosen prime minister. If the cabinet does not comply with the requests of the legislature, it must resign and a new cabinet is organized. The sovereign has to fulfill the people's expectations; if the administration has the confidence of the public, it is easier to govern. The emperor is above party politics, but in order to form a good cabinet, he should choose a person from the party supported by the people. Thus, administrative officials fulfill their function effectively, and political stagnation does not occur. Ono concluded this discussion with a description of the British system of party cabinets.

Ono wrote that the specific organization of the government depended on the situation in a country. He did not believe that any national office was needed for public sanitation or poor relief, but some measures were necessary to assist the poor in order to prevent disturbances and to provide for public health. To insure security, the navy had to be strengthened. Strong European states had powerful navies to protect their colonies, and the army should be used only for defensive purposes. Within the country, the police should maintain security. According to Ono, it was the duty of the government to encourage industry, hygiene, and public works, and to make improvements in society that the individual could not make himself. Though favoring a *laissez-faire* policy toward industry except for those manufacturing armaments, he advocated that the government establish standard coinage, weights, and measures. It should establish the Ministries of Home Affairs, Finance, Foreign Affairs, Agriculture and Commerce, Transportation, Education, Army and Navy, and Accounting. Each minister was to be held responsible for his department, and the prime minster was to be responsible for the entire administration. Therefore it was necessary to clarify official responsibility, to appoint responsible officials, and to establish, according to the Benthamite concept of utility, rewards, punishments, and disciplinary proceedings. Administrative officials should have the opportunity to present their opinions and proposals to the legislature. They should be appointed according to the results of civil service examinations and should hold office on good behavior. Only ministers and vice-ministers should be party appointees.

In chapters 37 to 40, Ono was concerned with the judiciary. He began this section by stating that laws are established to protect human rights, and the term *kōgi* or "right" can be defined broadly as the greatest happiness of the greatest number. It literally means *kenri* or "human rights." The purpose of government is to eliminate pain and give pleasure, and this is the basis of moral training and statecraft. Therefore judicial officials must act in accordance with the law to protect the rights of the people. Their duties are to follow and maintain the standards established by the legislature. To achieve this, an independent, unbiased, and perceptive judiciary is needed. Judges should receive life tenure and renumeration, and their official responsibilities should be clarified. To protect human freedom, the jury system should be instituted with potential jurors elected by the people from among those of a given age and property qualification. When a case arises, jurors should be chosen by officials from among those previously selected. Trials should be public. Ono concluded this section with a discussion of the history of the judiciary in Japan.[43]

As a former auditor, Ono was particularly concerned with accounting procedure. Therefore chapter 31 is on the need for independent auditing and accounting organs. These would prevent financial errors, establish standards for budget preparation, and publish an annual statement on the settlement of accounts. They should be under the control of the finance minister, who should establish legislation for auditing. In chapter 42, Ono discussed the budget, which he wanted prepared by the Diet. He also favored issuing domestic loans in order to permit rapid industrial growth. Thereafter he gave a brief history of accounting and taxation in Japan. In chapter 43, Ono again focused attention on the military. Although he declared that he was opposed to war, he regarded, as did Lieber, the army as a necessity, since the "present is not a golden age." However, unlike Lieber, who felt that the military emphasized the trait of obedience to the detriment of the spirit of inquiry, he believed that universal military conscription would "promote freedom for the individual" and wanted marksmanship introduced in to the gymnastic curriculum of the elementary school in order to shorten the period of service.[44] This form of universal military training would, therefore, offset feudal ideas of the exclusiveness of the military.

Thereafter Ono concentrated on the issue of local autonomy. He wanted local governments to take care of public health, poor relief, education, and local public services according to principles established by the central government. Matters such as law enforcement, the judiciary, taxation, foreign affairs, the military, and police were to be handled by Tokyo. Prefectural assemblies should be organized like the Diet, and local governments should have the right to levy taxes. Following a discussion of the history of local government organization and administration in Japan, with emphasis on the Meiji period, Ono criticized the prefectural assemblies as "assemblies of landlords." Although he admitted that this group was more knowledgeable, he regarded elections for the local assemblies as unfair because the general public lacked information on assembly practices. Since the assemblies could discuss only minor matters, the people did not participate in political affairs. Therefore the prefectural assemblies needed to be revised so that local autonomy would be possible. The government should promote local government as the foundation of national prosperity.

Ono then turned to the issue of how the constitution was to be drafted and the qualities needed by people living under constitutional government. Although the Imperial Edict of 1881 declared the constitution would be granted by the emperor, he believed a constitutional drafting bureau should be established under the immediate supervision of the throne. It should be composed of able and intelligent members appointed by the throne. The constitution should be drafted on the basis of traditional regulations with reference to the constitutions of Europe. The draft should be published and free criticism allowed. Officials should hold meetings and listen to the opinions of the intellectuals and general public and then amend the draft accordingly. One then gave examples of European and American constitutional development and warned that failure to realize a royal promise for a constitution had led to revolt in Prussia. He opposed frequent changes of the entire constitution but amendment of certain articles would be necessary in time. This should be done with great prudence. The methods used to amend the English, Prussian, Belgium, Swiss, and American constitutions were cited as examples of cautious amendment.

Having completed his discussion of constitutional theory, Ono turned to the people who would live in a state governed according to a constitution. They needed to develop the capacity for self-government, independence, self-reliance, and public participation in politics. They had to be patriotic, to unite under the national government, and to work for the welfare of the country. Only then could Japan become strong and clan sectionalism be ended. The purpose of the constitution was to provide unity, equality, and to provide for the national welfare; and since it would contribute to national prosperity, it would benefit the people. In order to attain the greatest happiness of the greatest number and maintain order in society, the will of the majority had to prevail. Political improvement was necessary, and progress was a natural phenomenon. The destiny of the nation depended on how well the people could solve problems, and therefore it was necessary to handle the affairs of society properly and steadily. Radicalism would only upset the social order and prevent progress. Therefore both monarch and subjects had to obey the constitution. The constitution would provide the standard by which the people could judge the ruler and it would prevent arbitrary rule.[45] Thus Ono ended his outline of the national constitution.

The third volume of *Kokken hanron* leans strongly on Mill's *Considerations on Representative Government* and Bentham's *Constitutional Code.* Mill rejected the right of parliament to intervene in the work of the administrative branch but stressed the need for the entire government to be subject to the control and authority of one individual. He opposed direct election of the executive and emphasized that the crown alone should appoint the head of the administration in conformity with the wish of the legislature and the members of the cabinet as designated by the prime minister. Mill valued parliament as a committee to dispose of complaints from the public and as a means of expression of public opinion, but he wanted legislation proposed by a special committee of professional legislators to prevent autocracy by the majority. Ono adopted Mill's views on the division of power and on the role of the executive, but not on the negative quality of the assembly. He saw representation as a means of preventing absolutism, not of creating it. Ono purposely ignored Bentham's criticism of hereditary monarchy, while adopting his views on the function of the executive. He combined Mill's description of the British cabinet system and a summary of Bentham's ideas on the functions of the various cabinet departments to support his position on party cabinets responsible to the Diet. Such a ministry was justified by the utilitarian criterion of the greatest good for the greatest number, and Ono left no doubt that in his mind the ideal form of government was the contemporary English system of party cabinets in a constitutional monarchy wherein the monarch reigned but did not rule. He criticized placing supreme power in the hands of the crown, as found in imperial Germany, as detrimental to the political stability of the ruling house.[46] A limited constitutional monarchy combined with representative institutions was most suited to the outlook of the Meiji loyalist and to the Japanese scene.

Ono followed Mill's view that the form and proper function of government vary according to society, but he emphasized, as did Mill and Bentham, the need to maintain order and security of life and property. Thus the army was to be used for defensive purposes only; but, like Lieber, he did not fear the navy as an instrument of executive absolutism and justified naval development by the European threat. He concurred with Mill on the need to appoint professional civil servants on the basis of competitive examinations and subject to removal only for improper activities. His sections on ministerial responsibility and on the function of the cabinet, judiciary, and accounting departments represent a summation of chapters 9, 11, and 12 of the *Constitutional Code,* Book 2. Where Bentham had advised thirteen ministries, Ono recognized the need for only eight and ignored those concerned with poor relief, public health, and specific legislative duties that could be delegated to the Diet or other ministers of state. Although he agreed with Bentham on the need to pinpoint ministerial responsibility, he did not go along with Bentham's advocacy of increased government control. Ono favored a reduction of the areas of state control and a *laissez-faire* policy that would limit the government to essential functions. As a former student of economics, he agreed with Bentham on the need for strict accounting controls and he wanted the government to establish uniform standards of measurement, an idea he may have borrowed from the American constitution. Neither Ono nor his mentors favored the popular election of judges but all called for a judiciary appointed for life. Ono accepted Bentham's idea that the justice minister should appoint judges; but along with Mill and Lieber, he rejected Bentham's belief in popular recall of the judiciary and favored recall by the legislature. Ono lacked Bentham's distrust of juries and wanted the British system of trial by jury to be used in Japan.

Ono's views on local government were based on the chapter in *Representative Government* entitled "Local Representative Bodies." According to Mill, the central government was limited in its knowledge of local needs and should confine its activities to matters concerning security of person and property, equal justice between individuals, prisons, the judiciary, war, and treaties. It should establish and supervise "principles of government" and let local authorities handle the management of details on the practical application of these principles subject to supervision. The administration of poor laws, public charities, sanitation, local taxes, and specific local interests should be left to local authorities. Freedom and a high level of culture required responsibility in politics and not passivity, and local government offered a widely democratic base for popular participation and a means of educating the public.[47] Ono adopted Mill's argument in detail on the division of responsibility between the central and local government but stressed more than Mill local control of tax revenues and expenditures. He added a discussion on the difference between modern local self-government and feudal authority. The former brought together numerous independent areas under one imperial system and no one area could institute policies detrimental to the nation as a whole. Feudal rulers were concerned only with what was good for the clan and ignored the national welfare. Ono believed that local assemblies should be organized in accordance with the same rules as the Diet but felt that a unicameral assembly was sufficient for local needs. Although he went extensively into the suffrage requirements for local government in Europe and into contemporary

Japanese law, he did not state his own views on the requirements for the local electorate. From Mill he took the idea of having the local assembly nominate the prefectural governor and local officials. Ono, in concluding this section, was extremely critical of the lack of power of the local assembly, of its inability to discuss major political matters, of the lack of local autonomy, of its subjugation to the governor and Home Ministry. Local autonomy was the basis of national prosperity and should therefore be promoted.

In *Representative Government,* Mill had pointed out that the end of self-government was the development of the virtue and intelligence of the members of the community, the creation of the "active type of personality which struggles against evil" and works for the public welfare. Self-government promoted education, effort, and "intellectual superiority." Thus "The only government which can fully satisfy—all the exigencies of the social state—is one in which the people participates; . . . it follows that the ideal type of perfect government must be a republic."[48] Ono reversed the argument and declared it was the character of the people that makes self-government work and, as Fukuzawa had done before him, called for the creation of the active, independent spirit needed to promote constitutional government. Only such a personality type could look beyond self-interest to national unity and would, therefore, be fit for self-government.

In his approach to the drafting of the constitution, Ono favored caution in the form of imperial supervision but wanted open discussion of documents with consideration given to public opinion. In this way, the fundamental law of the nation would reflect the will of both sovereign and people and would provide a firm basis for government. Recognizing that he could not discuss the advantages or disadvantages of a constitution granted by the emperor, he stated that was important was not whether sovereign or subjects granted the document, but the means whereby it was prepared. This implied but did not openly state that if the draft could be modified to reflect the public viewpoint, then the *mintō* would have some chance of influencing the drafters of the constitution and securing their role in the future political process. A constitution prepared in concert with the wishes of the people would require few changes for many years and, as a result, changes could be introduced in the future with great caution.

Ono Azusa's search for a new order for the modern Japanese state culminated in *Kokken hanron,* which he regarded as his major work and most enduring monument. He believed that the key to political stability lay in a written constitution that would serve as the fundamental law of the land, define the political relationship between the sovereign and subjects, and set the limits within which the branches of the government would operate. A constitution incorporating essential guarantees would insure the prosperity of the imperial family and provide more effective government responsive and responsible to the people. Thus, monarch, government, and people would be united and the state would be strengthened and prosperous. The Japanese state rather than the individual was the ultimate frame of reference; and while Ono advocated greater individual freedom, he saw this freedom as conducive to strengthening the state by promoting the greatest happiness of the greatest number. Herein lay a basic contradiction between his emphasis on limited democracy and civil liberties and his concern for the state. If the utilitarian goal of the greatest good of the greatest number meant the welfare of the state as a whole, at what point could the state or the greatest number infringe on the rights or welfare of the minority or the individual? Ono never answered this question and wrote that the minority must wait until it could make its will prevail through parliamentary processes.[49] As an ardent believer in constitutional government and representative institutions, he failed to see the weaknesses inherent in the systems he advocated and interpreted them in a way that could be injurious to the growth of civil liberty. Yet, as a Meiji intellectual deeply concerned with the survival of the nation and national unity, he justified greater political liberalism on the grounds of national security and strength. This was a fundamental problem that the Meiji liberal faced and never resolved or, perhaps, never realized.

Ono misinterpreted various aspects of Western history and political theory in *Kokken hanron.* He failed to show how aspects of foreign political systems could be adapted to fit Japan and how to meet the problems and incongruities that would arise from the merger of institutions that developed in highly divergent cultures. His ideas are often contradictory. For example, he is opposed to large military expenditures but proposed extending military training to the elementary school level, which would promote the militarization of society. He stated that the army was needed solely for defense but the navy was necessary because of the naval power of the Western colonial powers. He did not explain terms such as the *stagnation* of Prussian and American politics and the *independence of the spirit.* In the concluding chapter he said that the constitution should be based upon traditional regulations with reference to the constitutions of Europe, but he did not elaborate upon this statement nor enumerate the specific traditions sufficiently.

Ono often wrote of the necessity for independent study and research and opposed uncritical acceptance of Western concepts. In "Kyōiku ron," he stressed the need for a "spirit of independence" that would create the type of personality needed to face new situations and succeed in the modern era.[50] In *Kokken hanron* he attempted to meet his own criticism by a process of selective adoption and adaptation of foreign political theories to the Japanese scene. In his studies abroad he had become acquainted with the works of Bentham, J. S. Mill, and Lieber and, following his return to Japan, he appears to have acquired a copy of Woolsey's *Political Science or The State,* published in 1877. Although he does not refer to these works in the diary, Ono apparently studied them intensively and carefully selected passages for use in *Kokken hanron.* His quotations from Bentham at some points represent full translations and at others summaries, but all are quite accurate with regard to the original work. However, he did not blindly adhere to the borrowed ideas but chose selectively. His essay *Rigaku nyūmon* and the first volume of *Kokken hanron* appeared in print one year before Mutsu Munemitsu's translation of Bentham's *Introduction to the Principles of Morals and Legislation.* Ono's trilogy reveals that he was well versed in English and in Anglo-American political theory, which he modified for use in a Japanese draft constitution. *Kokken hanron* is a case study in the adoption of Western political theory in the early Meiji era and the most detailed work on political science written in Japan prior to the promulgation of the constitution in 1889. It introduced the ideas, though not the terminology, of the "emperor as an organ of government" theory and represented the crystallization of Ono's efforts at independent study and selective adaptation.[51]

Although *Kokken hanron* represented a careful study of constitutional government and was written as a reference work for the framers of the constitution, there is no evidence that it had any influence on the Meiji constitution or on contemporary political life. Kaneko Kentarō, who was secretary to Itō Hirobumi and a member of the committee drafting the constitution, stated that both he and Itō read *Kokken hanron*. Although Ono did send a copy of the work to Itō, nothing exists to show that the work was referred to by the committee.[52] Ono's gift to Itō accounts for Nishimura Shinji's statement that Itō learned about the book when he returned from Europe.[53] Although there are some similarities between Ono's work and the constitution, these appear superficial. Ono regarded the emperor as sacred and inviolate, with the right to convene and dissolve the Diet, but only after the prime minister had lost the confidence of the Diet. There are some similarities in the rights granted to the people, but Ono did not condition civil liberties by placing them "within the limits of the law." The organization of the legislature in both documents followed the pattern set by Western parliamentary institutions; both provided for an independent judiciary, and the Board of Audit provided for in the 1889 constitution was based on one established in 1880 to prepare the annual budget and to supervise government revenues and expenditures,[54] a policy based on Ono's suggestion. Ono's idea that the emperor was only the "operator of sovereignty" for the state had elements of the later *kikansetsu* or organic theory, but there is no evidence that his ideas had any influence on later writers, including Minobe Tatsukichi.[55] *Kokken hanron* was neither "one of the main works in the field of democratic law" nor was it important in Japanese political history as claimed by some writers.[56] Because it was modeled upon the British system of parliamentary government, it was neglected; and as late as 1936, Nishimura Shinji did not risk official displeasure by reprinting it when he compiled the *Ono Azusa zenshū.*

When *Kokken hanron* is analyzed in historical perspective, it emerges as one of the principal, though little-known, works of constitutional theory of the early modern period. Viewed from the standpoint of the early Meiji intellectual raised in a tradition of political absolutism and loyalty to the imperial family and newly trained in Western languages, history, political theory, and institutions, it is a monument to selective adaptation and the use of tradition, and to the merger of past and present as it sought to present an answer to the problem of the future structure of the Japanese state and the relationship between state and people and throne and state. In its treatment of the role of the emperor in a parliamentary system, *Kokken hanron* represents the *mintō* attempt to merge parliamentarianism and the throne into a viable political institution geared to Japanese tradition and modern representative institutions. In its emphasis on political and civil rights and even greater concern for national unity and security, *Kokken hanron* posits the dilemma faced by post-feudal Japan in an age of unequal treaties and Western imperialism. In the problems raised and solutions advocated, *Kokken hanron* represents Ono's blueprint for the new political order in which he envisioned the Kaishintō as the dominant political party in the Diet, the culmination of his political theories, and a major insight into the mind of the Meiji intellectual.

NOTES

1. Yamashita Shigekazu, "Ono Azusa to Bensamu," *Kokugakuin hōgaku* 6, no. 3 (February 1969): 222, 236.
2. Nishimura, *Ono Azusa den,* p. 298.
3. Nagata, *Ono Azusa,* p. 89.
4. Nishimura, *Ono Azusa den,* p. 267.
5. Enomoto, "Ono Azusa no seiji ronri," *NRR,* p. 541. *Kokken ronkō* was finished January 6, 1879, and was published in the *Kyōzon zasshi* from March 1879 to April 1880.
6. Ono, "Ryūkakusai nikki," pp. 333, 335–37, 341–43, 356, 359,

360, 373–83, 397–98, 400–16, 421–49, 452–60, 540–41, 544–49, Ono completed *Kokken hanron* on September 21, 1885. He originally intended to publish *Kokken hanron* as a three-volume work entitled *Kokken shisan (A Private Constitution), Kokken ronkō,* and *Bankoku kempō (Constitutions of Other Nations)*. However, these titles were later dropped. The manuscript of the first volume, named *Genkō kokken shisan (A Contemporary Private Constitution)* and now in the Ono *monjo* of the National Diet Library, was written between January 30 and June 27, 1881, with the intention of combining it with *Kokken ronkō*. It was later rewritten as the first volume of *Kokken hanron,* which was published by Maruzen on December 30, 1882. The second volume was published by the same company on April 18, 1883, while the last volume was issued by Tōyōkan on October 3, 1885. Cf. Ono Azusa, *Genkō kokken shisan* (April 1–21, 1881), n. p., an unpublished manuscript in the Ono *monjo,* Document, Nos. 39 and 90, Constitutional Documents Room, National Diet Library, Tokyo.

7. Ono, "Ryūkakusai nikki," p. 360.

8. Ibid., pp. 334, 427, 431–38, 441, 443, 456, 459–60, 547–48.

9. Yamashita, "Ono Azusa to Bensamu," p. 236.

10. Ono Azusa, *Kokken hanron,* 3 vols. (Tokyo: Maruzen Shoten and Tōyōkan, 1882–1885), 1:5–7.

11. Ibid., pp. 7–11. The proclamation of April 14, 1875, expanded upon the Imperial Oath of 1868 by stating: "Now we expand the Covenant, establish the Senate (Genrō-in) to take charge of legislation, and the Supreme Court (Taishin-in) to clarify jurisdiction, summon local officials to discuss public opinion and take measures for social welfare, and gradually establish a constitutional state so that we may share its benefits with the people." The proclamation of June 14, 1875, stated: ". . . we will summon the representatives of the people, establish laws based on public opinion, harmonize high and low, make the people at ease so that they will understand their duty and participate in national affairs. First, we will summon the chairmen of the prefectural assemblies, who represent the people. Then we will deliver the Diet procedure for them to observe." The proclamation to establish the Council of State stated that some men were so emotional that their opinions were not impartial. However, such opinions were useful in promoting the establishment of a constitution, along with those of local officials (*Kokken hanron,* 1: 9–11).

12. Ono, *Kokken hanron,* 1:13. For a description of the meeting of the gods on the river bank, see Basil Hall Chamberlain, trans., "Ko-ji-ki or Records of Ancient Matters," *Transactions of the Asiatic Society of Japan* (Yokohama: n.d.), Supplement 10: 93–94.

13. Ono, *Kokken hanron,* 1: 14–22. The political structure was organized under the *Seitai sho* (Institute of Government), often

referred to as the first constitution of Japan and promulgated in 1868.

14. Ono, *Kokken hanron,* 1: 25–41. *Genrō-in* can be translated as "Senate" because it served as a legislative body until 1890. Thereafter, the translation "Elder Statesmen's Council" is more descriptive of its functions and status.

15. Theodore D. Woolsey, *Political Science or The State, Theoretically and Practically Considered,* 2 vols. (New York: Charles Scribner's Sons, 1877), 1: 283–84.

16. Bentham, *Fragment,* pp. 57–82. The parts of Bentham's *A Fragment on Government* used in Ono's arguments are from "Forms of Government," pp. 64–67; "British Constitution," pp. 69–70, 80. The chart entitled the "British Government is all perfect" is on p. 80.

17. Ono, *Kokken hanron,* 1: 44–54.

18. Takano Zen'ichi, "Bensamu to Ono Azusa," *Waseda Daigaku shi kiyō,* 1, no. 2 (1966): 1–18. Takano stated that the edition of the *Leading Principles of a Constitutional Code for any State* used is from *The Works of J. Bentham, published Under the Superintendence of His Executor, John Bowring,* 11 vols. (Edinburgh: William Tait, 1843), 2: 269–74. This edition, now in the possession of Waseda University Library, has Ono's signature on it. *The Leading Principles of a Constitutional Code, for any State* was translated and published in October 1882 by Shimada Saburō and Sato Tōshirō under the title *Kempō ronkō.* By that date, the first volume of *Kokken hanron* had been completed; since Ono and Shimada translated terms differently, *Kempō ronkō* could not have been used by Ono in preparing the first part of *Kokken hanron* (Yamashita, "Ono Azusa to Bensamu," p. 277).

19. Bentham, *Fragment,* pp. 34, 35.

20. Ono, *Kokken hanron,* 1: 55–80. *Kuni* implied a large geographic and administrative area similar to the pre-Meiji use of the term.

21. Woolsey, *Political Science,* 1: 204–5.

22. Ono, *Kokken hanron,* 1: 80–171.

23. Francis Lieber, *On Civil Liberty and Self-Government,* enl. ed. (Philadelphia: J. P. Lippincott and Co., 1899), pp. 24–26, 34–37, 40–43, 46–48, 58, 61, 66, 69–76, 81–82, 86–87, 89–90, 94–105, 124–33, 138, 148.

24. Ibid., pp. 99, 152–62, 168–71.

25. Frank Friedel, *Francis Lieber, Nineteenth Century Liberal* (Baton Rouge: Louisana State University Press, 1947), pp. 266–76.

26. Nakamura Kichisaburō, "Ono Azusa sensei kempōron no ippan," *Waseda Daigaku shi kiyō,* I, 2 (March 20, 1966) 76–78.

27. Ono, *Kokken hanron,* I, 171–241.

28. Ono, *Kokken hanron,* I, 241–258. The chart does not appear in *Kokken hanron.* It is an attempt by the author to clarify Ono's views.

29. Takano, "Bensamu to Ono Azusa," *WDSK,* pp. 1–17.

30. Jeremy Bentham, *The Constitutional Code* in *Works of Jeremy Bentham,* 9: 11, 13, 14, 34, 46–64, 96, 98, 149. Cf. Ono, *Kokken hanron,* 1: 57.

31. Bentham, *Constitutional Code,* p. 97; John Stuart Mill, "Considerations on Representative Government," *On Liberty, Representative Government, The Subjugation of Women* (London: Oxford University Press, 1969), pp. 179–86, 198; Yamashita Shigekazu, "Ono Azusa to Miru fushi," *Kokugakuin Daigaku Tochigi Tanki Daigaku kiyō* 3 (January 20, 1969): 30. Yamashita, in an article entitled "Ono Azusa to Bensamu" [Ono Azusa and Bentham], appears to have reached the same conclusions as this author did previously in her article "Ono Azusa—Meiji no chishikijin," *Meiji bunka zenshū,* 31 vols. (Tokyo: Nihon Hyōronsha, 1967–1970), 28: 413–34, and her *Ono Azusa, A Meiji Intellectual* (Ph.D. diss., University of Pennsylvania, December, 1968).

32. Lieber, *On Civil Liberty,* p. 361.

33. Ono, *Kokken hanron,* 1: 92.

34. Todd, *Parliamentary Government in England,* 1: 77.

35. Woolsey, *Political Science,* 1: 203.

36. Ono, *Kokken hanron,* 2: 299, 317–45, 372.

37. Ibid., pp. 381–89, 401–17; John Stuart Mill, "Representative Government," ed. Robert Maynard Hutchins, *Great Books of the Western World,* 54 vols. (London: Encyclopaedia Britannica, Inc., 1952), 43: 392–400.

38. Ono, *Kokken hanron,* II, 393–96, 422, 430–31, 435, 451, 461–66, 471, 472, 478, 480, 483, 484, 486. Cf. Mill, "Representative Government" (Oxford Edition), pp. 312–19, for Mill's description of Hare's ideas.

39. Ono, *Kokken hanron,* 2: 457–557.

40. Bentham, *Constitutional Code,* pp. 117, 119–22, 160, 172; J. S. Mill, "Representative Government" (Oxford ed.), pp. 213, 272–94, 312, 320–22, 335–43; Lieber, *Civil Liberty and Self-Government,* pp. 102, 130–35, 148–51, 160–63, 170–71, 175–77, 185–89, 195, 203–5; Yamashita, "Ono Azusa to Bensamu," pp. 234–42; Yamashita, "Ono Azusa to Miru fushi," pp. 36–40.

41. Todd, *Parliamentary Government in England,* 1: 76–78, 80, 107–9, 112–17, 133, 140, 210; 2: 138–40, 149, 150, 210.

42. Francis Lieber, "A Paper On The Abuse Of The Pardoning Power," in *On Civil Liberty and Self-Government,* p. 453.

43. Ono, *Kokken hanron,* 3: 539–756.

44. Ibid., pp. 759–818. Cf. Lieber, *On Civil Liberty and Self-Government,* p. 121.

45. Ono, *Kokken hanron,* 3: 828–914.

46. Mill, "Representative Government" (Oxford ed.), pp. 119–228, 320, 344–45, 349–51; Bentham, *Constitutional Code,* pp. 128–45,

204–5, 213–26, 428–53; Yamashita, "Ono Azusa to Miru fushi," pp. 38–39; Yamashita, "Ono Azusa to Bensamu," pp. 242, 244–47; Ono, "Kinnō ron," pp. 266–67.

47. Lieber, *On Liberty and Self-Government,* pp. 117–19, 167, 206–8, 221–23, 230–32, 235; Mill, "Representative Government" (Oxford ed.), pp. 167, 190–98, 278, 286–91, 354–58, 363–81, 407; Bentham, *Constitutional Code,* pp. 213–26, 428–554, 568; Yamashita, "Ono Azusa to Miru fushi," pp. 43–45; Yamashita, "Ono Azusa to Bensamu," pp. 245–48; Robert K. Carr, et al., *American Democracy in Theory and Practice* (New York: Rinehart and Co., Inc., 1955), p. 924. Cf. The Constitution of the United States, Art. 1, Sec. 8.

48. Mill, "Representative Government" (Oxford ed.), p. 198.

49. On the role of the prime minister and party cabinets, cf. Ono, *Kokken hanron,* 3:559–64. On the role of the minority, cf. idem 2: 381–84.

50. Ono Azusa, "Kingaku no nikyū," *Ono Azusa zenshū,* 2: 88–91. In this essay, published in the *Meiji kyōkai zasshi* (no. 24), September 10, 1883, Ono called for independent study and research and for higher education through the medium of the Japanese language. He opposed the uncritical acceptance of foreign theories by those intoxicated with Western studies. In "Kinnō ron," *Ono Azusa zenshū,* 1: 273, he said education must enhance academic freedom and the "spirit of independence." Ono Azusa, "Kyōiku ron," *Ono Azusa zenshū,* 2: 92–97. "Kyōiku ron" was delivered as a lecture in Saitama prefecture in April 1884 and was published in *Chūō gakujutsu* (no. 5), May 5, 1885. In it Ono said that modern education must teach men to think and act independently in order to meet new situations and to develop competitive skills.

51. Yamashita, "Ono Azusa to Bensamu," pp. 222–23, 252–53.

52. Tabata Shinobu, *Kempōgaku genron,* 2 vols. (Tokyo: Yuhikaku, 1951), 1: 30–31.

53. A letter from Itō Hirobumi to Ono Azusa, dated May 30 (no year) and thanking Ono for the copy he received, is in the possession of Mr. Kira Shinpei of Tokyo. Nishimura Shinji, *Waseda no hanseki* (Tokyo: Waseda Daigaku Shuppanbu, 1932), p. 104.

54. Nishimura, *Ono Azusa den,* p. 272. See Borton, *Japan's Modern Century,* pp. 490–507, for a translation of the Meiji Constitution. *JWM* 5, no. 18 (May 7, 1881): 512.

55. Ienaga Saburō, *Nihon no minshushugi* in *Gendai Nihon shisō taikei,* 35 vols. (Tokyo: Tsukuma Shobō, 1963–1966), 3:21, 22.

56. Nomura Heiji, "Ono Azusa jiyū minken hōgaku no daihyōsha," *Kindai Nihon no shakaikagaku to Waseda Daigaku,* ed. Waseda Daigaku Shichijūgonen Kinen Shuppan (Tokyo: Waseda Daigaku Shuppanbu, 1957), pp. 314, 315.

9

The Journey Ends

The world of the Meiji intellectual was a world in flux, subject to constant change, an environment in which traditional values and established institutions were subject to condemnation and rejection, reevaluation and modification, and inconsistent mergers with foreign ideas and systems adapted in varying degrees to fit the Japanese scene. The material aspects of Western life were those which most appealed to the Japanese public and often led to uncritical cultural adoption. In this period of rapid change and modernization, pragmatic ideas were welcomed; and Fukuzawa Yukichi was the outstanding spokesman of utilitarianism, of *jitsugaku,* or learning for practical life. Fukuzawa stressed the relativity of ethics and law, which had to be changed according to time and situation. Good and evil were no longer absolute principles but rather criteria that could be measured by the real benefit produced by any action. Fukuzawa's belief in the independence of the spirit and self-respect helped pave the way for weakening the hold of tradition on the Meiji mind and prepared the ground for the practical reformers of the party movement of the 1870s and 1880s and for the individualism and romantic movement of late Meiji. Fukuzawa's call for the independent spirit and for self-respect combined with his stress on the practical and material aspects of life and set the tone for the mainstream of early Meiji thought.

Pragmatism and utilitarianism dominated Meiji politics and political life. Political works emphasizing the concepts of freedom and popular rights were geared to the issues of *hanbatsu* domination of politics, the debate over the constitution and national assembly, national unity and the weakness inherent in clan divisiveness—to the basic questions of political structure and power in the state. Philosophic orientation was tempered by necessity. In Japan the thought of freedom was not radical and gradually developed as a moderate political movement. The national ethic of loyalty to the throne, the threat of Western imperialism and the resulting requirement of unity, the lack of a native philosophy of freedom, and government pressure on the *mintō* kept much of the movement for popular rights on a gradual and moderate level that was limited to political developments and did not call for social equality or change.[1] As the movement increased in intensity, the government channeled it into lines it could direct through official plans for a constitution and for the Diet.

It is within this context that Ono Azusa must be evaluated as a Meiji intellectual, whose writings present a summary of most of the major thought patterns of the early modern era. As a member of the new intelligentsia, he represents the fusion of tradition and change that characterizes the Meiji mind. In his thought pattern, social relationships, and life style, he symbolizes the continuity of tradition. Trained to view the world in terms of encompassing universal principles, a loyalist, and, in his own words, a *shishi*,[2] he found in the works of the English utilitarians a new universal whereby duty, nationalism, and reform could be justified. Young, ambitious, well educated, he had the versatility to adjust to a new era, the ambition to want to help direct the future course of national events, a belief in his own ability and the wisdom of his ideas, and, until his health failed in late 1885, a sense of optimism regarding his future and that of Japan.

Between 1874 and 1885, the eleven-year period that constitutes Ono's mature and active life, his writing reveals a consistent pattern of continuous and simultaneous critical selection, adoption, and adaption of Western political ideals and methods to met the Meiji scene. The utilitarian doctrine of the greatest good of the greatest number and Bentham's practical concerns with livelihood, wealth, security, and equality offered pragmatic and rational principles that could be merged with selected aspects of Japanese tradition and institutions to develop a viable philosophy espousing reform and modernization while retaining the best of the Japanese heritage. Utilitarianism allowed for loyalism, that dominant cornerstone of Meiji thought. Loyalism was an expression of nationalism, for the emperor was to the Meiji mind the living symbol of the cultural continuity of the Japanese people and state. Nationalism implied unity, an end to clan rivalries and localism, and a truly national leadership. National unity was essential in an age of imperialism to preserve national independence and to end the insult of the unequal treaties. Indeed, Ono's break with both his clan and the Satchō-dominated bureaucracy as well as his association with Ōkuma was the product of his fear of the effects of divisive policies. Unity and a sense of nationhood were essential prerequisites for progress and national survival.

Although the word *democracy* was not part of the political lexicon of the Meiji politician, Ono's espousal of the supreme constitutive, the electorate, the people, as the locus of all political power was an indirect acceptance of the basic concept of democracy. The author of *Kokken hanron* placed sovereignty in the state as symbolized by the throne;[3] nonetheless, who but the people constituted the state and were the source of power, the electorate, in a representative system? *Democracy* as a form of political terminology was not a part of the Meiji mind; democracy as a functioning political system in Japanese garb was a basic tenet of Ono's political philosophy.

Popular and civil rights were part of the legal and constitutional framework of Meiji liberal thought. Ono had a sincere commitment to the concept of basic rights, which were deemed essential for the greatest good of the greatest number, for the achievement of the happiness and security of the people. In *Kokken hanron* and in a related text on civil law entitled *Minpō no hone (Essence of Civil Law,* 1883),[4] he sought to explain and to establish a rational justification for basic rights and liberties that were new concepts in Japanese politics and law. By planning for popular participation in politics, by defining and limiting official powers, he sought to lay a foundation for political rights under law and for law in politics. Yet his concept of democracy and of rights was tempered by realism in regard to the level of political sophistication among the general public and the dangers inherent in the international scene for a weak and divided state.

Ono can be described as a parliamentary nationalist whose primary frame of reference was the Japanese nation. Parliamentary government with the gradual expansion of suffrage and basic rights protected by the constitution alone could provide the unity essential for progress, security, and the revision of the unequal treaties. *Kokken hanron* was to be the blueprint for the new political order. The Rikken Kaishintō was to be the means of implementing political reform. Utilitarianism was the principle, Bentham and J. S. Mill the philosophic and political mentors, and Great Britain the model for modern and gradual process.

To Ono Azusa, the political theorist and activist, the key to modernization lay in the psychological outlook of the people, in he caused was always the result of his deep and precise estimate intellectual and national independence. Such a spirit would enable the individual and the state to survive in a world of intense rivalries. Education was the means to develop both the intellect and the independent, competitive, and critical spirit. Independent research and study were essential for this development;[5] a new leadership had to be trained for participation in modern constitutional and parliamentary government. Shortly after the establishment of the Kaishintō, Ōkuma told Ono of his plans to establish a school of higher learning to train young men to meet the future needs of the nation and asked Ono for his assistance. That institution was Tokyo Senmon Gakkō, the predecessor of Waseda University, and Ono was the guiding force, organizer, and spirit behind the school in its first four years. He personally selected the faculty, which included the members of the Ōtokai. The close ties between the Kaishintō leadership and Tokyo Senmon Gakkō founders led critics to ask Ono "if the Kaishintō was establishing its plan for a hundred years." His reply was "it is a 10,000 year plan."[6] The world view now encompassed political theory and action and the education of the next generation, a theme set in Ono's speech at the opening ceremony.

> National independence is based on the intellectual independence of the people, and this is founded upon academic freedom. Thus, academic freedom must be established if there is to be intellectual independence.[7]

This independence was to be promoted further by encouraging young writers and translators of works on modern political and social theory through the establishment of a company to import and publish books called "Tōyōkan Shoten" in 1883,[8] which Ono personally directed during the last years of his life.

Ono the politician and civil servant was regarded by his contemporaries as a man of integrity and diligence, as an intellectual, and as a man of principle, whether in government, politics, or private life. To his friends he was a combination of enthusiasm and scholarship, rare even among the officials of the Meiji era.[9] To Ichishima, one of the students he led into politics, he was "open-hearted, . . . a politician who was pure-hearted and had clean hands, an upright heart." He was a "benevolent man who stood aloof from public criticism, concerned over the welfare of others first and his own enjoyment last." He was a "rare friend," and the Ōtokai were his closest associates.[10] Nagata respected him for his judgment most of all, for opinions based on definite principles and on his own viewpoints. He saw Ono's friend and fellow clansman Baba Tatsui as "heroic, poetic, and argumentative. His life was like a rugged path." Ono, however, was "practical, businesslike, and constructive. The excitement he caused was always the result of his deep and precise estimate of a situation. He did not want to be a romantic hero."[11] Yamada found Ono a "brave character" who exercised extreme self-control to the extent of avoiding alcohol and eating only twice daily. Even when ill he continued to lecture to the students in the Ōtokai and to observe a set schedule of work. Despite his obsession with politics and his scholarship, he was a devoted father who managed to find time to be with his children. Their illnesses worried him greatly;[12] the deaths of three of his five children left him bereft of expression.[13] His published thoughts and diary were of politics, of diplomacy, of public problems; his emotions were a private world unrevealed even to his biographers. If he was, as Ōkuma wrote, a "most pathetic and unhappy person,"[14] it was because he died young, at the height of his ability and before the new era of parliamentary politics he had worked to bring forth was established.

Ono saw himself as a key figure in the drama of Meiji politics and as an initiator of change and reform. He was optimistic on the possibility of change within Japan and on his own future. Ambitious, energetic, and well-known to those in government and in the party movement, his reputation as a new intellectual, a man of principle, and as a politician and organizer attracted both young idealists and older, influential politicians. His importance to the Kaishintō was recognized by his contemporaries, although Ōkuma took public credit for Ono's ideas and actions, and by the *hanbatsu* he opposed. Nonetheless, duty and intellectuality were subject to physical frailty. Despite his own denials,[15] Ono was mortally ill by the autumn of 1884. On September 30, while working at Tōyōkan, he began to spit blood and was bedridden for six weeks. In July 1885 he became severely ill, often bringing up blood and complaining of stomach and intestinal troubles. While in bed he corrected *Kokken hanron,* but by early October he could no longer keep up his diary. On January 2, 1886, Amano Tameyuki called on Ono. Too ill to speak well, he communicated in writing. Although he recognized the gravity of his illness, he did not think of death. On January 11 his condition suddenly worsened and he died.[16] The *Tokyo nichi nichi shimbun* wrote of Ono:

> Mr. Ono Azusa who had been ill in bed for days died on January 11, the day before yesterday, despite all the care received. His ability was highly regarded during the time he was in office, especially when he was an auditor. After his resignation, he contributed greatly to the organization of the Kaishintō as Mr. Ōkuma's right-hand man. He also opened a bookstore called "Tōyōkan" to rival "Maruzen," and he published books at the same time. It is deeply regretted that he died without enjoying the results of his labors. His death indeed is a loss to his country.[17]

Over a thousand people attended his funeral.[18]

Ono Azusa was a new intellectual psychologically moored between late feudal and early modern Japan and between East and West. Living in a society undergoing rapid change, his patterns of thought and action reveal a flexibility and continual adjustment to an ever-changing environment. His brief career as writer, bureaucrat, and political theorist and politician shows a consistency of philosophic outlook and method of operation due, perhaps, to the brevity of years when he was influential on the Meiji political scene but even more to the constancy of his philosophic orientation. Although an advocate of civil liberties and greater political rights for the people, Ono tried to achieve a cautious balance between the ideas of *jiyū minken* and the need for national unity and security in an age of imperialism. In his political writings and draft constitutions, he emphasized that greater political freedom would produce unity and strength; but in foreign policy, the criterion for action was Japanese security and independence. Alienated by *hanbatsu* domination and its divisive effects on the nation, he turned opposition into constructive alienation designed to promote modernization and progress. Caught up in the political battles of his time and in the search for a new order, Ono was the practical reformer and realist concerned with remaking those institutions most receptive to change and believing that he could change his world for the better. Comfortable in the family life and social relationships of the past yet committed by youth and training to a still uncertain future, Ono Azusa represents a case study in intellectual change and political development in early modern Japan.

NOTES

1. Honma Hisao, *Meiji shisō kōwa* (Tokyo: Nihon Bunshō Gakuin, n.d.), pp. 1–23.

2. For example, cf. Ono, "Ryūkakusai nikki," p. 372.

3. Cf. Ono, *Kokken hanron,* 1: 77–80; 2: 261–68.

4. Ono Azusa, "Minpō no hone," *Ono Azusa zenshū,* 1: 5–127.

5. Ono, "Tsūjō no kyōyō o ronzu," *Ono Azusa zenshū,* 2: 5–7; idem, "Kingaku no nikyū," ibid., pp. 89–91; idem, "Kyōhaku kyōiku," ibid., pp. 43–44; idem, "Kyōiku ron," ibid., pp. 92–95.

6. Ono, "Ryūkakusai nikki," pp. 400–2, 406–9; Nishimura, *Ono Azusa den,* pp. 175–79.

7 Ono Azusa, "Tokyo Senmon Gakkō no kaikō o gasu," *Ono Azusa zenshū,* 1: 501–3.

8. Ono, "Ryūkakusai nikki," p. 444; Nishimura, *Ono Azusa den,* pp. 231–33.

9. Yamada, *Ono Azusa kun den,* 2: 24.

10. Waseda, *Shunjō hachijūnen,* p. 68.

11. Nagata, *Ono Azusa,* pp. 275, 350.

12. Yamada, *Ono Azusa kun den,* 2: 22, 25.

13. Ono, "Ryūkakusai nikki," p. 395. Ono's first son and first daughter both died soon after birth and his second son died on June 0, 1882. He noted this in his diary, stating: "My son died today." On March 10 of the same year, he wrote that he went to Tennoji to visit the tomb of his dead children ("Ryūkakusai nikki," p. 383).

14. Ōkuma in the preface to "Tōyō ikō jō" in Nishimura, *Ono Azusa zenshū,* 1: 131.

15. Cf. Ono, "Ryūkakusai nikki," pp. 534, 538.

16. Yamada, *Ono Azusa kun den,* 2: 17, 20–21.

17. Nakamura, *Shimbun shūsei Meiji hennen shi,* 6: 226. From *Tokyo nichi nichi shimbun,* January 13, 1886.
shimbun, January 13, 1886.

18. Yamada, *Ono Azusa kun den,* 2: 22.

Bibliography

Works of Ono Azusa

Jicho Kokken hanron o tatematsuru no hyō (Memorial to the Emperor on the Presentation of the First Volume of *Kokken hanron*). A scroll dated January 7, 1883, and now in the possession of Gotō Norio, Sukumo city, Kōchi prefecture, Japan.

Kokken hanron (Outline of the National Constitution). 3 vols. Tokyo: Vols. 1 and 2: Maruzen Shoten, 1882–1883; Vol. 3: Tōyōkan Shoten, 1885.

Works in the Ono Documents Collection (Ono *monjo*), Constitutional Documents Collection, National Diet Library, Tokyo. This collection contains many of Ono's letters, documents, and manuscripts, some not yet published. Not all the materials are numbered and those that are numbered are not in consecutive order. These works have not been translated previously.

Document No. 18. Unpublished manuscript.

Document No. 20. Unpublished manuscript.

Genkō kokken shisan (Contemporary Private View on the Constitution), Documents Nos. 39 and 90. Unpublished manuscripts.

Minshin ron (On Popular Feelings). Unpublished manuscript dated November 1875.

Works in the Waseda University Library, Tokyo.

"Kyōzon Bunko teisoku" (Regulations for the Kyōzon Library).

"Kyōzon dōshū jōrei" (Regulations for the Kyōzon dōshū).

"Zanshoritsu o oku no gi" (Opinion on the Establishment of the Libel Law).

These works have been compiled and edited by Takano Zen'ichi into an unpublished manuscript entitled *Ono Azusa zenshū hoi* (Supplement to the Complete Works of Ono Azusa) for the Room for Research on University History.

"Mitsugi ni tsuki shinten o wazurawasu" (A Secret Message on A Growing Problem). From a manuscript dated September 29, 1881.

Nagata Shinnosuke. *Ono Azusa.* Tokyo: Fuzanbō, 1897.

Nishimura Shinji. *Ono Azusa zenshū.* 2 vols. Tokyo: Fuzanbō, 1936.

Unpublished Letters in Private Collections

Hayashi Yūzō to Ono Azusa. Dated October (year not given). In the possession of Mr. Hayashi Sunao, Sukumo city, Kōchi prefecture.

Itō Hirobumi to Ono Azusa. Dated May 30 (year not given). Letter in the possession of Mr. Kira Shinpei, Tokyo.

Ono Azusa to Iwamura Michitoshi. Dated January 13 (year not given).

Ono Azusa to Iwamura Michitoshi. Dated May 15 (year not given).

Ono Azusa to Iwamura Michitoshi. Dated December 24 (possible year, 1884). Three letters in the possession of Mr. Iwamura Hitoki, Ogikubo, Tokyo.

Ono Jugurō (Son of Ono Gishin, the brother-in-law of Ono Azusa) to Sandra T. W. Davis, May 19, 1967.

Interviews

Iwamura Hitoki (Youngest son of Iwamura Michitoshi, former guardian of Ono Azusa). Tokyo, July 13, 1967.

Kitamura Kiku, Urata Masano, Yamagata Miyuki, Takahashi Sue (The four nieces of Ono Azusa and the daughters of his sister, Ren, who cared for him during the last ten years of his life). Sukumo city, Kōchi prefecture, March 24–25, 1967. Kitamura Kiku and Takahashi Sue acted as spokesmen for the Ono family.

Ono Fukashi and Ono Tetsuo (Great-nephews of Ono Azusa). Sukumo city, Kōchi prefecture, March 24–25, 1967. Ono Tetsuo, who was a student at Waseda University in 1936, helped Nichimura Shinji collect materials for the *Ono Azusa den* and *Ono Azusa zenshū.*

Ono Fumiko (Granddaughter of Ono Gishin). Tokyo, February 29, 1968.

Takano Zen'ichi (Professor of History, Waseda University, Tokyo). Waseda University, Tokyo, August 30, 1966, and May 12, 1967.

Takemura Teruma and Matsuzawa Takurō (Local historians). Sukumo city, Kōchi prefecture, March 24–25, 1967.

Tsunemitsu Kōnen (Chief editor, the *Bukkyō taimusu,* Tokyo). Tokyo, March 28, 1967.

Japanese Sources

Aono Gon'emon. *Nihon seitō hensen shi* (History of Japanese Political Party Development). Tokyo: Ankyūsha, 1935.

Asahi Shimbunsha, ed. *Meiji Taishō shi* (Meiji Taishō History). 6 vols. Tokyo: Asahi Shimbunsha, 1930–1931.

Asakawa Eijirō, and Nishida Chōju. *Amano Tameyuki.* Tokyo: Jitsugyō no Nihonsha, 1950.

Asakura Haruhiko, and Inamura Tetsugen, eds. *Meiji sesō hennen jiten* (Chronological Dictionary of Aspects of Life in the Meiji Era). Tokyo: Tokyodō, 1965.

Davis, Sandra T. W. "Ono Azusa—Meiji no chishikijin," Vol. 28 of *Meiji bunka zenshū.* Edited by Meiji Bunka Kenkyū Kai. 3d ed. 31 vols. Tokyo: Nihon Hyōronsha, 1967–1970.

Enomoto Morie. "Meiji shonen no kōrishugi—Ono Azusa 'Rigaku nyūmon' no kōsatsu" (Utilitarianism in the Opening years of the Meiji Era—A Study of Ono Azusa's 'Introduction to Utilitarianism'). *Shichō* 8, no. 1, separate issue (1962): 1–16.

———. "Ono Azusa no hanbatsu seitōron" (On the Theories for the Clique of Feudal Clans and the Political Party of Ono Azusa). *Hokkaidō Gakugei Daigaku kiyō* 4, no. 1 (July 1953): 74–80.

———. "Ono Azusa no seiji ronri—*Kokken hanron* seiritsu o chūshin ni" (The Political Logic of Ono Azusa—General Remarks on *Kokken hanron*). *Nihon rekishi ronkyū* (1963), pp. 541–56.

Fujii Shin'ichi. *Teikoku kempō to Kaneko haku* (Imperial Constitution and Count Kaneko). Tokyo: Dai Nihon Yūbenkai Kōdansha, 1942.

Gorai Kinzō. *Ningen Ōkuma Shigenobu* (Ōkuma Shigenobu—The Man). Tokyo: Waseda Daigaku Shuppanbu, 1938.

Hagihara Nobutoshi. "Baba Tatsui." *Chūō kōron* 81, nos. 944–50 (June–December 1966).

Hayashida Kametarō. *Nihon seitō shi* (History of Japanese Political Parties). 2 vols. Tokyo: Dai Nihon Yūben Kai, 1927.

Hiratsuka Atsushi, ed. *Itō Hirobumi hiroku* (Confidential Papers of Itō Hirobumi). Tokyo: Nihon Hyōronsha, 1929.

Hirao Michio. "Tosa hyakunen shi o kazaru kōtekishu, Ueki Emori to Ono Azusa." *Kōchi kenjin* (Worthy Opponents to Honor in Tosa's Hundred Year History, Ono Azusa and Ueki Emori, *Native Sons of Kōchi* 16, no. 8 (August 1967): 8–11.

Honma Hisao. *Meiji shisō kōwa* (Lectures on Meiji Thought). Tokyo: Nihon Bunshō Gakuin, n.d.

Hoshino Tōru. *Meiji minpō hensan shi kenkyū* (Research on the History of the Compilation of Meiji Civil Law). Tokyo: Daiyamondosha, 1943.

Ienaga Saburō. *Nihon no minshushugi* (Japanese Democracy). Vol. 3 of *Gendai Nihon shisō taikei* (Outline of Modern Japanese Thought). 35 vols. Tokyo: Tsukuma Shobō, 1963–1966).

Ikeda Yoshimasa. *Sakamoto Ryōma*. Tokyo: Chūō Kōronsha, 1968.

Inada Masatsugu. *Meiji kempō seiritsu shi* (History of the Framing of the Meiji Constitution). 2 vols. Tokyo: Yūhikaku Kabushiki Kaisha, 1960–1962.

Ishida Bunshirō, ed. *Shimbun zasshi ni arawareta Meiji jidai bunka kiroku shūsei* (Collection of Documents on the Culture of the Meiji Period from Magazines and Newspapers). 2 vols. Tokyo: Jidai Bunka Kenkyū Kai, 1934.

Ishizuki Minoru. "Meiji no jishikijin—'Kyōzon dōshū' to Ono Azusa" (The Meiji Intellectuals—Ono Azusa and the "Kyōzon dōshū"). *Zinbun gakuhō* 24 (March 1967): 64–97.

Itagaki Taisuke, ed. *Jiyūtō shi.* (History of the Liberal Party). 3 vols. Reprt ed. Tokyo: Iwanami Bunko, 1957–1958.

———. "Waga kuni kensei no yurai" (The Origin of Our Constitution). *Meiji kensei keizai shi ron* (Essays on the History of the Meiji Constitution and Economy). Compiled by Takano Iwazaburō. Tokyo: Yūhikaku Shobō, 1919.

Itō Isao. "Itagaki Taisuke no jiyūshugi undō—shisū to kōdō (Itagaki Taisuke's Liberal Movement—Thought and Actions). *Hōgaku shimpō* 71, no. 9 (1964): 61–66.

———. "Meiji jidai ni okeru shakaishugi seitō undō" (Pt. I) (The Meiji Era Socialist Political Party Movement). *Jōchi hōgaku ronshū* 3, no. 1 (1959): 89–107.

———. "Nihon seitō no kigen" (The Origin of Japanese Political

Parties). *Hōgaku shimpō* 67, no. 6 (1960): 13–32.

Kada Tetsuji. *Shisōka toshite no Fukuzawa Yukichi* (Fukuzawa Yukichi as a Thinker). Tokyo: Keiō Tsūshin, 1958.

Kan'in meikan (Directory of the Names of Officials). Rev. ed. Tokyo: Kudō Kenkatsu Han, 1877. Pamphlet in the Constitutional Documents Room, National Diet Library, Tokyo.

Katakozawa Chiyomatsu. "Shimada Saburō." In Vol. 4 of *Sandai genron jinshū* (Discussion on the Men of Three Generations). Edited by Jijitsūshinsha. 8 vols. Tokyo: Jijitsūshinsha, 1963.

Kawade Takao. *Nihon rekishi daijiten* (Dictionary of Japanese History). 20 vols. Tokyo: Kawade Shobō, 1956–1960.

Kazamaki Gen'ichi. *Sakamoto Ryōma—sono hito to shōgai* Sakamoto Ryōma—the Man and Career). Tokyo: Ken'en Sha, 1970.

Keiō Gijuku, ed. *Fukuzawa Yukichi zenshū.* 21 vols. Tokyo: Iwanami Shoten, 1958.

Kodama Yukita and Kitajima Masamoto, eds. *Monogatari han shi* (Tales of Clan History). 8 vols. Tokyo: Jinbutsu Ōraisha, 1964–1965.

Kohayagawa Kingo. *Meiji hōsei shi ron* (On the History of the Meiji Legal System). 2 vols. Tokyo: Ganshōdō Shoten, 1944.

Kōsaka Masaaki. *Shisō genron hen* (Volume of Thought and Speech). Vol. 4 of *Meiji bunka shi* (History of Meiji Culture). Edited by Kaikoku Hyakunen Kinen Bunka Jigyō Kai. 14 vols. Tokyo: Yōyōsha, 1957.

Kyōguchi Motokichi. *Takada Sanae den* (Biography of Takada Sanae). Tokyo: Waseda Daigaku, 1962.

Kyoto Daigaku Bungaku Kokushi Kenkyūshitsu, ed. *Nihon shi jiten* (Dictionary of Japanese History). Tokyo: Sōgensha, 1961.

Lebra, Joyce [Chapman]. "Kaishintō no sōritsusha oyobi rironka Ono Azusa" (Ono Azusa, the Theorist and Founder of the Kaishintō). *Nihon rekishi* 148 (1960): 61–67.

Matsueda Yasuji. Ōkuma kō sekijutsu tan (Talks of Old Times with Marquis Ōkuma). Tokyo: Hōchi Shimbunsha, 1922.

Matsuo Shōichi. *Jiyū minken shisō no kenkyū* (Studies on the Idea of Freedom and Popular Rights). Tokyo: Kashiwa Shobō, 1965.

Meiji Bunka Kenkyū Kai, ed. *Jiyū minken hen* (Volume on Freedom and Popular Rights). Vol. 14 of *Meiji bunka zenshū* (Collected Works on Meiji Culture). Rev. ed. 16 vols. Tokyo: Nihon Hyōronshinsha, 1955–1959.

Meiji Shiryō Kenkyū Renrakukai. *Meiji seiken no kakuritsu katei* (The Process of Establishing the Political Power of Meiji). Vol. 1 in *Meiji shi kenkyū sōsho* (Library of Research on

Meiji History). 5 vols. Tokyo: Ochanomizu Shobō, 1956–1957.

Mutsu Munemitsu. *Rigaku shōshu.* 2 vols. Tokyo: Bararōshi, 1883.

Nagata Shinnosuke. *Ono Azusa.* Tokyo: Fuzanbō, 1897.

Nakamura Gizō. *Naigai seitō jijō* (Domestic and Foreign Political Party Conditions) (July 30, 1882).

Nakamura Kichisaburō. "Ono Azusa sensei kempōron no ippan" (A Glimpse of Professor Ono Azusa's Constitutional Theories). *Waseda Daigaku shi kiyō* 1, no. 2 (1966): 73–81.

Nakamura Yasumasa, ed. *Shimbun shūsei Meiji hennen shi* (Meiji Chronicles Compiled from Newspapers). 15 vols. Tokyo: Meijin Hennen Shi Sankai, 1956.

Nakanishi Keijirō. *Waseda daigaku hachijūnen shi* (Eighty-Year History of Waseda University). Tokyo: Waseda Daigaku Shuppanbu, 1962.

Nishimura Shinji. *Ono Azusa den* (Biography of Ono Azusa). Tokyo: Fuzanbō, 1935.

———. "Takeuchi Tsuna kaikyūden (Takeuchi Tsuna's Reminiscences). *Waseda gakuhō,* no. 157 (March 1908).

———. *Waseda no hanseiki* (A Half Century of Waseda [University]). Tokyo: Waseda Daigaku Shuppanbu, 1932.

Nomura Heiji. "Ono Azusa jiyū minken hōgaku no daihyōsha." *Kindai Nihon no shakaikagaku to Waseda Daigaku* (Ono Azusa, A Representative of Democratic Law. Modern Japanese Social Science and Waseda University). Edited by Waseda Daigaku Shichijūgonen Kinen Shuppan. Tokyo: Waseda Daigaku Shuppanbu, 1957.

Oguri Mataichi. *Ryūkei Yano Fumio kun den* (Biography of Mr. Ryūkei Yano Fumio). Tokyo: Shunyōdō, 1936.

Ōkuma Kō Hachijūgonen Shi Hensankai. *Ōkuma kō hachijūgonen shi* (History of Marquis Ōkuma's Eighty-five years). 3 vols. Tokyo: Nisshin Insatsu Kabushiki Kaisha, 1926.

Osatake Takeki. *Nihon kensei shi* (History of Constitutional Government in Japan). Vol. 6 of *Gendai seijigaku zenshū* (Collected Works on Modern Political Science). 13 vols. Tokyo: Nihon Hyōronsha, 1930.

———. *Nihon kensei shi taikō* (Outline of Japanese Constitutional Government and Politics). 2 vols. Tokyo: Nihon Hyōronsha, 1938–1939.

———. *Seitō no hattatsu* (Development of Political Parties). Tokyo: Iwanami Shoten, 1933.

Ōtsu Jun'ichirō. *Dai Nihon kensei shi* (History of Japanese Constitutionalism). 10 vols. Tokyo: Hōbunkan, 1927--1928.

Rōyama Masamichi. *Nihon ni okeru kindai seijigaku no hattatsu* (Development of Modern Political Science in Japan). Tokyo: Jitsugyō no Nihonsha, 1949.

Satō Kiyokatsu. *Dai Nihon seiji shisō shi* (History of Japanese Political Thought). 6 vols. Tokyo: Tōa Jikyoku Kenkyū Kai Hakkō, 1934.

Shimomura Fujio. *Nihon zenshi* (Complete History of Japan). 10 vols. Tokyo: Tokyo Daigaku Shuppan Kai, 1958–1968.

Shirayanagi Shūko. *Kensei juritsu hen* (Volume on the Establishment of the Constitutional System). Vol. 3 of *Meiji Taishō kokumin shi* (History of the Nation in Meiji and Taishō). Rev. ed. 5 vols. Tokyo: Chigura Shobō, 1940.

Shōhei Yomon—Tokyo Shinshi 6, no. 291 (1882): 1–2.

Sugiyama Heisuke et al., eds. *Gendai Nihon shi kenkyū* (Studies in Modern Japanese History). Tokyo: Mikasa Shobō, 1955.

Suzuki Yasuzō. *Kindai Nihon rekishi kōza* (Lectures on Modern Japanese History). 8 vols. Tokyo: Hakuyōsha, 1939.

———. *Nihon kensei seiritsu shi* (History of the Formation of Japanese Constitutional Government). Tokyo: Gakugeisha, 1933.

Tabata Shinobu. *Kempōgaku genron* (Principles of Constitutional Law). 2 vols. Tokyo: Yūhikaku, 1951.

Takada Sanae. *Hanhō mukashi banashi* (Hanhō's [Takada Sanae] Memoirs of Old Times). Tokyo: Waseda Daigaku Shuppanbu, 1927.

Takano Zen'ichi. "Bensamu to Ono Azusa" (Bentham and Ono Azusa). *Waseda Daigaku shi kiyō* 1, no. 2 (1969): 1–18 (supplement).

———, comp. and ed. *Takada, Ichishima seitan hyakunen kinen no tame ni. Nōto no atarashii kuni o egaita wakamono no ichidan. Meiji shoki no ichigakusei no kiroku* (For the Centenary of Takada's and Ichishima's Birth. A group of youths describe a nation in their notes. From the records of one student in the early days of Meiji). Unpublished materials from the diary of Ichishima Kenkichi, compiled for the Room for Research on University History, Waseda University Library, Tokyo.

Takemura Teruma. *Sukumo shi shi no gairyaku* (Outline of Sukumo City History). Unpublished manuscript dated April 9, 1967, and written in Sukumo city, Kōchi prefecture, Japan. In the author's possession.

Tokoyama Tsunesaburō. "Ono Azusa no 'Udaigasshū seifu ron'" (Ono Azusa's "Theory of United World Government"). *Asahi shimbun* (Tokyo) 12, no. 29297 (July 21, 1967).

Tokyo Hakubunkan. *Seitō shi* (Political Party History). Vol. 6 of *Meiji shi* (Meiji History). 13 vols. Tokyo: Tokyo Hakubunkan, 1907.

Torii Hiroo. *Meiji shisō shi* (History of Meiji Thought). Tokyo: Mikasa Shobō, 1947.

Ukai Nobushige, ed. *Nihon kindai hō hattatsu shi* (History of the Development of Modern Japanese Law). Vol. 2 of *Kōza Nihon kindai hō hattatsu shi* (Lectures on the History of the Development of Modern Japanese Law). 14 vols. and supplement. Tokyo: Keisō Shobō, 1958–1962.

Usuda Zan'un. *Tenka no kisha—Yamada Ichirō kun genkōroku* (The Greatest Journalist—Mr. Yamada Ichirō's Memoirs). Tokyo: Jitsugyō no Nihon Sha, 1906.

Uyabe Shuntei. *Meiji jinbutsu shōkan* (A Brief Look at the Men of Meiji). Tokyo: Tokyo Hakubunkan, 1902.

Waseda Daigaku Bukkyō Seinen Kai, ed. *Ono Azusa.* Tokyo: Fuzanbō, 1926.

Waseda Daigaku Toshokan. *Shunjō hachijūnen no oboegaki* (In Memorandum of Shunjō's [Ichishima Kenkichi] Eighty Years). Tokyo: Waseda Daigaku Toshokan, 1960.

Watanabe Ikujirō. *Monjo yori mitaru Ōkuma Shigenobu kō* (Marquis Ōkuma Shigenobu as seen from His Letters). Tokyo: Nisshin Insatsu Kabushiki Kaisha, 1932.

———. *Ōkuma Shigenobu.* Tokyo: Ōkuma Shigenobu Kanko Kai, 1936 and 1955.

———. *Ōkuma Shigenobu kankei monjo* (Documents relating to Ōkuma Shigenobu). 6 vols. Tokyo: Nihon Shiseki Kyōkai, 1927–1929.

Yamada Ichirō. *Toyo Ono Azusa kun den* (Biography of Toyo Ono Azusa). 2 vols. Tokyo: Dōkōkai, 1886. Document No. 48, Ono Documents Collection (Ono *monjo*), Constitutional Documents Room, National Diet Library, Tokyo. This work has the titles *Tōyō Ono Azusa kun den* on the title page and *Tōyō Ono Azusa sensei den* on interior pages and the publisher's notice.

Yamashita Shigekazu. "Ono Azusa to Bensamu" (Ono Azusa and Bentham). *Kokugakuin hōgaku* 6, no. 3 (February 1969): 221–56.

———. "Ono Azusa to Miru fushi" (Ono Azusa and Mill, Father and Son). *Kokugakuin Daigaku Tochigi Tanki Daigaku kiyō* 3 (January 20, 1969): 35–46.

Yanagida Izumi. *Meiji bunmeishi ni okeru Ōkuma Shigenobu* (Ōkuma Shigenobu in Meiji Cultural History). Tokyo: Waseda Daigaku Shuppanbu, 1962.

Yoshino Sakuzō, ed. *Seishi hen* (Volume of Original History). Vol. 3 of *Meiji bunka zenshū.* 24 vols. Tokyo: Nihon Hyōronsha, 1927–1930.

Western Sources

Akita, George. *Foundations of Constitutional Government in Modern Japan, 1868–1910.* Cambridge, Mass.: Harvard University Press, 1967.

Beckmann, George E. *The Making of the Meiji Constitution.* Lawrence: University of Kansas Press, 1957.

Bentham, Jeremy: *A Fragment on Government and an Introduction to the Principles of Morals and Legislation.* Edited by Wilfrid Harrison. Oxford: Basil Blackwell and Mott, Ltd., 1960.

———. *The Theory of Legislation.* Edited by C. K. Ogden. 2 ed. London: Routledge and Kegan Paul, 1950.

———. *The Works of Jeremy Bentham, published under the superintendence of his executor, John Bowring.* Vol. I: "A Fragment on Government." "An Introduction to the Principles of Morals and Legislation." Vol. II: "Leading Principles of a Constitutional Code for Any State." Vol. IX: *Constitutional Code.* 11 vols. Edinburg: William Tait, 1843.

Blacker, Carmen. *The Japanese Enlightenment, A Study of the Writings of Fukuzawa Yukichi.* Cambridge: Cambridge University Press, 1964.

Borton, Hugh. *Japan's Modern Century.* New York: Ronald Press, 1955.

Carr, Robert K., et al. *American Democracy in Theory and Practice.* New York: Rinehart and Co., Inc., 1955.

Cary, Otis. *A History of Christianity in Japan: Protestant Missions.* New York: Fleming H. Revell Co., 1909.

Chamberlain, Basil Hall, trans. "Ko-ji-ki or Records of Ancient Matters." *Transactions of the Asiatic Society of Japan,* Supplement to Vol. 10 (n.d.).

Crawcour, E. S. "Changes in Japanese Commerce in the Tokugawa Period." *Studies in the Institutional History of Early Modern Japan.* Edited by John W. Hall and Marius B. Jansen. Princeton, N.J.: Princeton University Press, 1970.

Cubberly, Ellwood P. "History of Education." *Encyclopaedia Britannica.* 1955 ed., vol. 7.

Davidson, W. L. *Political Thought in England.* London: Oxford University Press, 1957.

Davis, Sandra T. W. "Ono Azusa, A Meiji Intellectual." Ph.D. dissertation, University of Pennsylvania, 1968.

De Bary, Wm. Theodore; Chan, Wing-tsit; and Watson, Burton, comps. *Sources of Chinese Tradition.* New York: Columbia University Press, 1960.

Dore, E. P. *Education in Tokugawa Japan.* London: Kegan Paul, 1965.

Emi Koichi. *Government Fiscal Activity and Economic Growth in Japan 1868–1960.* Tokyo: Kinokuniya Bookstore Co., Ltd., 1963.

Epp, Robert. "The Challenge from Tradition: Attempts to

Compile a Civil Code in Japan, 1966–78." *Monumenta Nipponica* 22, nos. 1–2 (1967): 15–48.

Friedel, Frank. *Francis Lieber, Nineteenth-Century Liberal.* Baton Rouge: Louisana State University Press, 1947.

Fujii Jintarō, ed. *Outline of Japanese History in the Meiji Era.* Translated by Hattie K. Colton and Kenneth E. Colton. Vol. 10 of *Japanese Culture in the Meiji Era.* 10 vols. Tokyo: The Tōyō Bunko, 1969.

Fujii Shin'ichi. *The Constitution of Japan. A Historical Survey.* Tokyo: Hokuseido Press, 1965.

Fujita Shōzō. "The Spirit of the Meiji Revolution." *The Japan Interpreter,* 6, no. 1 (Spring 1970): 70–97. Translated by Robert Epp from *Ishin no seishin* (Spirit of the Restoration). Tokyo, 1967.

Havens, Thomas R. H. *Nishi Amane and Modern Japanese Thought.* Princeton, N.J.: Princeton University Press, 1970.

Iddittie Junesay. *The Life of Marquis Shigenobu Ōkuma.* Tokyo: Hokuseido Press, 1956.

Ishii Ryosuke, ed. *Japanese Legislation in the Meiji Era.* Translated by William J. Chambliss. Vol. 10 of Centenary Culture Council Series, *Japanese Culture in the Meiji Era.* 10 vols. Tokyo: Pan-Pacific Press, 1958.

Itō Isao. "The Constitutional Reform Party and Ōkuma Shigenobu." *Jōchi hōgaku ronshū (Sophia Law Review)* 7, nos. 1–2 (1963): 1–37.

———. "Fukuzawa Yukichi's Idea of Natural Rights." *Jōchi hōgaku ronshū* 8, no. 1 (1964): 153–78.

———. "The Struggle for Power in the Meiji Oligarchy." *Jōchi hōgaku ronshū* 6, no. 2 (1962): 42–64.

Jansen, Marius B. *Sakamoto Ryōma and the Meiji Restoration.* Princeton, N.J.: Princeton University Press, 1961.

———. "Tosa During the Last Century of Tokugawa Rule." *Studies in the Institutional History of Early Modern Japan.* Edited by John W. Hall and Marius B. Jansen. Princeton, N.J.: Princeton University Press, 1970.

Japan Weekly Mail. 3, no. 51 (December 20, 1879)–11, no. 26 (December 27, 1884).

Kōsaka Masaaki, ed. *Japanese Thought in the Meiji Era.* Translated by David Abosch. Vol. 9 of Centenary Culture Council Series, *Japanese Culture in the Meiji Era.* 10 vols. Tokyo: Pan-Pacific Press, 1958.

Lebra, Joyce Chapman. "Japan's First Modern Popular Statesman, A Study of the Political Career of Ōkuma Shigenobu (1838–1922)." Ph.D. dissertation, Radcliffe College, 1958.

———. "The Kaishintō as a Political Elite." *Modern Japanese*

Leadership. Edited by Bernard S. Silberman and H. D. Harootunian. Tucson: University of Arizona Press, 1966.

———. "Yano Fumio: Meiji Intellectual, Party Leader, and Bureaucrat." *Monumenta Nipponica* 20, nos. 1–2 (1965): 1–14.

Lieber, Francis. *On Civil Liberty and Self-Government*. Enlarged ed. Philadelphia: J. P. Lippincott and Company, 1899.

Mason, R. H. P. *Japan's First General Election 1890*. Cambridge: Cambridge University Press, 1969.

Mill, John Stuart. *On Liberty, Representative Government, The Subjugation of Women*. London: Oxford University Press, 1969.

———. "Representative Government." Vol. 43: *Great Books of the Western World*. Edited by Maynard Hutchins. 54 vols. London: Encyclopaedia Britannica, Inc. 1952.

Mukai Ken, and Toshitani Nobuyoshi. "The Progress and Problems of Compiling the Civil Code in the Early Meiji Era." *Law In Japan* 1 (1967): 25–59. Translated by Dan Fenno Henderson from *Hōsei shi kenkyū, bessatsu* (Studies in Legal History, Separate vol.) (1964), pp. 214–45.

Ōkuma Shigenobu. "A General View of Financial Policy During Thirteen Years." *Japan Weekly Mail* 5, no. 13 (April 12, 1881): 367–368.

———, comp. *Fifty Years of New Japan*. 2 vols. London: Smith, Elder, and Co., 1909.

Pittau, Joseph. *Political Thought in Early Meiji Japan, 1868–1889*. Cambridge, Mass.: Harvard University Press, 1967.

Rengo Press. *Japan Biographical Encyclopedia and Who's Who*. 2d ed., 3d ed. Tokyo: Rengo Press, 1961, and 1964–1965.

Scalapino, Robert A. *Democracy and the Party Movement in Prewar Japan*. Berkeley: University of California Press, 1962.

Smith, Thomas C. *Political Change and Industrial Development in Japan: Government Enterprise, 1868–1880*. Stanford, Calif.: Stanford University Press, 1955.

Todd, Alpheus. *Parliamentary Government in England*. Rev. ed. Revised and edited by Spencer Walpole. 2 vols. London: Sampson Low, Marston and Co., 1892.

Tokio Times 5, no. 4 (January 25, 1879)–6, no. 14 (October 4, 1879).

Transactions of the Asiatic Society of Japan. Pt. I (1914).

Waley, Arthur, trans. and ed. *The Analects of Confucius*. London: George Allen and Unwin, 1956.

Woolsey, Theodore. *Political Science or The State, Theoretically and Practically Considered*, 2 vols. New York: Charles Scribner's Sons, 1877.

Index